REASONING, RATIONALITY, AND PROBABILITY

CSLI Lecture Notes Number 183

REASONING, RATIONALITY, AND PROBABILITY

edited by
Maria Carla Galavotti
Roberto Scazzieri
Patrick Suppes

PUBLICATIONS
Center for the Study of
Language and Information
Stanford, California

Copyright © 2008
CSLI Publications
Center for the Study of Language and Information
Leland Stanford Junior University
Printed in the United States
12 11 10 09 08   1 2 3 4 5

Library of Congress Cataloging-in-Publication Data

Reasoning, rationality, and probability / edited by
Maria Carla Galavotti, Roberto Scazzieri, and Patrick Suppes.

p. cm. – (CSLI lecture notes ; no. 183) (CSLI publications)

Proceedings of a workshop held Nov. 13–16, 2004
at the University of Bologna.

Includes bibliographical references and indexes.
ISBN-13: 978-1-57586-558-4 (pbk. : alk. paper)
ISBN-10:   1-57586-558-0 (pbk. : alk. paper)
ISBN-13: 978-1-57586-557-7 (cloth : alk. paper)
ISBN-10:   1-57586-557-2 (cloth : alk. paper)
1. Practical reason. 2. Reasoning. I. Galavotti, Maria Carla.
II. Scazzieri, Roberto. III. Suppes, Patrick, 1922–

BC177.R3443 2007
128'.33–dc22   2007036937
CIP

Partial support for this
publication came from the
European Science Foundation.

The cover of the paperback edition was designed by Alberto Pratelli.

∞ The acid-free paper used in this book meets the minimum requirements
of the American National Standard for Information Sciences—Permanence
of Paper for Printed Library Materials, ANSI Z39.48-1984.

CSLI was founded in 1983 by researchers from Stanford University, SRI
International, and Xerox PARC to further the research and development of
integrated theories of language, information, and computation. CSLI headquarters
and CSLI Publications are located on the campus of Stanford University.

CSLI Publications reports new developments in the study of language,
information, and computation. Please visit our web site at
http://cslipublications.stanford.edu/
for comments on this and other titles, as well as for changes
and corrections by the authors, editors, and publisher.

Contents

Contributors vii

Foreword xi

Introduction: Reasoning and Patterns of Rationality 1
MARIA CARLA GALAVOTTI, ROBERTO SCAZZIERI AND PATRICK SUPPES

I   Practical Reason

1   **The Good and the Bad, the True and the False** 13
    AIMÉE DROLET AND PATRICK SUPPES

2   **Three Types of Decision Theory** 37
    NILS-ERIC SAHLIN AND NIKLAS VAREMAN

3   **Welfare, Voting and the Constitution of a Federal Assembly** 61
    LUC BOVENS AND STEPHAN HARTMANN

4   **Acting Rationally with Irrational Strategies** 77
    DAVID ATKINSON AND JEANNE PEIJNENBURG

5   **In- and Ex-probabilities: Keynes and Econophysics** 87
    DOMENICO COSTANTINI AND UBALDO GARIBALDI

II Mental Frames and Cognitive Abilities

6 **Reasoning to be Rational**   119
   JOHN BROOME

7 **Pragmatic Arguments for Rationality Constraints**   139
   WLODEK RABINOWICZ

8 **Rationality and Prediction in the Sciences of the Artificial: Economics as a Design Science**   165
   WENCESLAO J. GONZALEZ

9 **Context, Congruence and Co-ordination**   187
   ROBERTO SCAZZIERI

III Situations and Reasoning

10 **Rationality and its Bounds: Re-Framing Social Framing**   211
    MATTHIAS KLAES

11 **Causal Pluralism and Context**   233
    MARIA CARLA GALAVOTTI

12 **Causal Medical Reasoning and Pre-Emption**   253
    RAFFAELLA CAMPANER

13 **Abduction in the Context of a Reasoning Process: the SCIFF Framework**   271
    MARCO ALBERTI, FEDERICO CHESANI, MARCO GAVANELLI, EVELINA LAMMA AND PAOLA MELLO

Name Index   289

Subject Index   297

Contributors

MARCO ALBERTI: Department of Engineering Science, University of Ferrara, Italy.
marco.alberti@unife.it

DAVID ATKINSON: Department of Philosophy, University of Groningen, The Netherlands.
d.atkinson@rug.nl

LUC BOVENS: London School of Economics and Political Science, London, United Kingdom.
L.Bovens@lse.ac.uk

JOHN BROOME: Department of Philosophy, University of Oxford, and Corpus Christi College, Oxford, United Kingdom.
john.broome@philosophy.ox.ac.uk

RAFFAELLA CAMPANER: Department of Philosophy, University of Bologna, Italy.
campanerr@hotmail.com

FEDERICO CHESANI: Department of Computer Science, University of Bologna, Italy.
fchesani@deis.unibo.it

DOMENICO COSTANTINI: Department of Statistics, University of Bologna, Italy.
costantinistudio@libero.it

AIMÉE DROLET: John E. Anderson Graduate School of Management, University of California Los Angeles, USA.
aimee.drolet@anderson.ucla.edu

MARIA CARLA GALAVOTTI: Department of Philosophy, University of Bologna, Italy, and Clare Hall, Cambridge, United Kingdom.
mariacarla.galavotti@unibo.it

UBALDO GARIBALDI: CFSBT-CNR c/o Department of Physics, University of Genova, Italy.
garibaldi@fisica.unige.it

MARCO GAVANELLI: Department of Engineering Science, University of Ferrara, Italy.
marco.gavanelli@unife.it

WENCESLAO J. GONZALEZ: Faculty of Humanities, University of A Coruña, Spain.
wencglez@udc.es

STEPHAN HARTMANN: Centre for Logic and Philosophy of Science, Tilburg University, The Netherlands
S.Hartmann@lse.ac.uk

MATTHIAS KLAES: Department of Economics, University of Keele, Keele, United Kingdom.
economics@keele.ac.uk

EVELINA LAMMA: Department of Computer Science, University of Bologna, Italy.
elamma@deis.unibo.it

PAOLA MELLO: Department of Computer Science, University of Bologna, Italy.
pmello@deis.unibo.it

JEANNE PEIJNENBURG: Department of Philosophy, University of Groningen, The Netherlands
a.j.peijnenburg@rug.nl

WLODEK RABINOWICZ: Department of Philosophy, University of Lund, Sweden.
wlodek.rabinowicz@fil.lu.se

NILS-ERIC SAHLIN: Department of Philosophy, University of Lund, Sweden.
nils-eric.sahlin@fil.lu.se

ROBERTO SCAZZIERI: Department of Economics, University of Bologna, Italy; Gonville and Caius College and Clare Hall, Cambridge, United Kingdom.
Roberto.scazzieri@unibo.it and rs292@cam.ac.uk

PATRICK SUPPES: Centre for the Study of Language and Information, Stanford University, USA.
suppes@csli.stanford.edu

NIKLAS VAREMAN: Department of Philosophy, University of Lund, Sweden.
niklas.vareman@fil.lu.se

Foreword

This volume originated from an 'Exploratory workshop' funded by the European Science Foundation, which took place at the Bertinoro Conference Centre of the University of Bologna on November 13-16, 2004. The workshop, devoted to 'Rationality and patters of reasoning: a European perspective', was meant to bring together researchers from various fields, including philosophy, economics, psychology, statistics, artificial intelligence, and physics, for the purpose of examining the relationship between reasoning and rationality in a genuinely cross-disciplinary framework. Starting with a deep discussion of contemporary research into the pragmatic dimensions of rationality, the workshop moved to consider the many-sided implications of 'rationality at work' in a variety of disciplines. As a result of the talks that were given and the wide discussion they raised, a new perspective took shape, which distances itself from the received conceptions of deductive and inductive inference, being instead related with a situational conception of reasoning.

The editors wish to thank the European Science Foundation for supporting the workshop and this publication. Additional support was given by CIRESS (Interdisciplinary Centre for Epistemology and History of Science 'Federigo Enriques') and ISA (Institute of Advanced Study) of the University of Bologna. Finally, the editors warmly thank the participants in the Bertinoro workshop and the contributors to the present volume.

Introduction

MARIA CARLA GALAVOTTI, ROBERTO SCAZZIERI
AND PATRICK SUPPES

Interest in rational practices has a long tradition in philosophical and scientific thought. To give a few examples, rationality according to Aristotle is primarily a way of *acting* according to good reasons; rational arguments in modern science are associated with conformity to accepted standards of experimental conduct; rational choice in utilitarian philosophy (and economics) is deliberation of the consequential type (such as maximization of subjective expected utility). This intellectual tradition has been reinforced by recent work in cognitive science, decision theory and epistemology.

Research on practical rationality has emphasized the open-ended structure of rational arguments, and the active role of the human mind in developing conceptual tools suitable for problem solving under *contingent* sets of constraints. This pragmatic view of rationality is nonetheless conducive to a rigorous (formal) investigation of reasoning and deliberation. This is done by 'moving backwards' the good reasons for rational decisions to the structure of cognitive frames, and by associating the latter to the case-dependent utilization of cognitive abilities. In short, reasoning comes to be seen as a cognitive state in which a prior set of abilities (that we may take as relatively unstructured with respect to the problem situation at hand) takes a definite shape as shifts in context activate one cluster of cognitive procedures after another. In this way, rationality appears to be closely intertwined with a connectionist model of justified procedures. The identification of good reasons is situation-dependent, and latent connections are made operative by contingent states of the world.

The above view of practical rationality suggests a description of good reasons in terms of local abilities and procedures rather than in terms of universal rules for inference and deliberation. In particular, a rational agent is primarily considered to be an agent who is able to effectively reconfigure herself (himself) after a change of local conditions (a cognitive shock). Not all existing abilities are operative at any given time, and new abilities become available as contexts are varied. This point of view presupposes that rational agents are able to make sense of their own cognitive structure, modes of inference, and practical deliberations. Rationality is thus inherently reflexive, multi-layered, and dynamic. A rational agent is endowed with the ability to distance herself from inherited cognitive states, to evaluate those states from the point of view of local conditions, and to reconfigure through feedback processes.

The Structure of the Volume

It is the purpose of this volume to evaluate concurrent lines of investigation into human thinking as a practical activity, and to investigate the scope and possible limitations of the consilience between the different approaches.

Part One of the volume ('Practical Reason') examines the operational characteristics of rationality in a variety of fields and argues that practical rationality is often associated with reasoning patterns quite different from those encountered in classical theories of rational deliberation (that is, in the standard theories adopted by economists, statisticians and philosophers).

In the first chapter: 'The Good and the Bad, the True and the False', Aimée Drolet and Patrick Suppes argue that a satisfactory empirical analysis of rationality should be based on 'a deeper model of the psychological phenomena of choice'. In their view, such a model should go beyond psychological measurement and address important issues associated with the configuration and working of the human mind. Habit formation and associations are shown to be central to the building of rationality. In particular, a theory of habits is presupposed by normative judgments (what is good and what is bad), whereas a theory of associations is presupposed by descriptive judgments (what is true and what is false). This paper argues that practical rationality should be analyzed by taking advantage of the research traditions concerning the concept of association (as in Hobbes, Hume, and now in psychology and neuroscience) and the concept of habit (as in Aristotle). In particular, the authors argue for the primacy of habits relative to preferences in the analysis of human behavior. A discussion of the connection between practical rationality and Aristotle's theory of 'good reasons' concludes the paper.

In their paper 'Three Types of Decision Theory' Nils-Eric Sahlin and Niklas Vareman distinguish three types of decision theory, namely normative, descriptive and prescriptive theories. Normative decision theory requires that the beliefs of the decision-maker are expressed by a unique probability measure, his (her) preferences are represented by a utility function that reflects the costs and benefits of possible outcomes, and his (her) behaviour is ruled by the principle of maximising expected utility. After research conducted by psychologists, including David Kahneman and Amos Tversky, cast doubt upon the ability of normative decision theory to represent the actual behaviour of decision-makers, various authors developed the so-called narrative methods, devised to account for the values, beliefs and expectations of decision-makers. A promising alternative is represented by prescriptive theories, meant to embody elements of both normative and descriptive theories within a flexible framework, which is sensitive to the context.

The contribution by Luc Bovens and Stephan Hartmann: 'Welfare, Voting and the Constitution of a Federal Assembly' explores collective choice and social welfare under alternative voting systems. Equal and proportional representations are considered as polar cases in a continuum of models. The paper discusses the repercussions on welfare distribution associated with different models of representation, and examines which model would be favored if one starts with a Rawlsian or a utilitarian measure of social welfare respectively. Models of representation are placed on a continuum ranging from equal representation (in which all nations in the federal assembly have the same number of representatives) to a model of proportional representation (in which the number of representatives is proportional to that of inhabitants of each nation). Intermediate models follow the criterion of 'degressive proportionality', in which a larger nation has more representatives than a smaller nation, but less than it would be required by strict proportionality. This contribution shows that degressive proportionality is associated with a social choice function that uses both the Rawlsian maximin and utilitarian criteria. The contribution also shows that, under certain conditions, degressive proportionality may be justified on purely utilitarian grounds.

Good reasons are sometimes associated with patterns of conduct that appear to be sub-optimal or altogether irrational. An extreme case is considered by David Atkinson and Jeanne Peijnenburg in their paper on the Parrondo Paradox: 'Acting Rationally with Irrational Strategies'. Their argument starts with the paradox (originally formulated in 1999) that, under certain conditions, two losing strategies can be combined to yield a successful outcome (see Harmer and Abbott 1999, quoted by Atkinson and Peijnenburg). The authors argue that the paradox calls attention to a 'strange and obscure feature' of the maximizing choices associated with perfect rationality. They also maintain that the success of seemingly irrational strategies may be due to the existence of scale or threshold effects, such that the combination of choices that appear irrational if considered in isolation, might in fact lead to an outcome that is superior, relative to each of the corresponding 'rational' strategies.

Practical reasoning is essentially probabilistic in character. Games of chance and insurance decisions are often considered prototype situations in which probability concepts are central. This has interesting implications for the description and explanation of interdependence among decision-makers. Domenico Costantini and Ubaldo Garibaldi investigate this issue in their paper 'In- and Ex-Probabilities. Keynes and Econophysics'. The starting point of their analysis is the distinction between two different conceptions of probability. One is probability 'external to theory' (ex-probability), resulting from 'ignorance of the real way in which the external world, usually intended as governed by deterministic laws, works'. The other is probability 'internal to theory' (in-probability), that is, a conception in which the essentially non-deterministic character of the external world is acknowledged. The authors take John Maynard Keynes's work on probability and economic theory as a vantage point from which to examine the interplay of probability concepts in economic analysis. In particular, they discuss Keynes's criticism of the principle of indifference, his consideration of the central role of hypothetical expectations and his definitions of aggregate demand and supply functions as stochastic concepts. It is argued that 'the economic theory Keynes developed is an informal probabilistic theory', and it is maintained that the probabilistic character of the economic equilibrium associated with the mutual influence of economic decisions is best described in terms of concepts derived from statistical physics, in which interacting particles 'may give rise to a collective behavior different from that of individuals'. Practical decisions strategies are different from one individual to another, and it is possible to cluster decision-makers into a variety of agent types (such that each type is associated with a particular strategy). Individual agents may switch from one strategy type to another, and multiple sets of different individual decisions may be compatible with any given macroeconomic state of the economy.

Part Two of the volume: 'Mental Frames and Cognitive Abilities', is concerned with a distinct but complementary issue. Once attention is focused upon good reasons and practical choices, we may discover that certain rational devices may be useful in circumscribing the range of possible choices.

John Broome, in his paper 'Reasoning to be Rational' addresses the issue of reasoning as a mental habit leading individuals to satisfy specific rationality conditions. In particular, Broome maintains that 'rationality requires you to do what you believe you ought to do' and argues that reasoning 'is a mental activity of ours that can bring us to satisfy some of the requirements of rationality'. Reasoning is described as 'an operation on contents', such that an individual holding certain beliefs (attitudes) works out their implications computationally. In Broome's view, 'that word "so" indicates your working through the rule-governed process'. The paper distinguishes between theoretical reasoning and practical reasoning. The former 'sets out from some initial beliefs and concludes with a new belief'. The latter 'is reasoning that concludes in an intention'. Theoretical reasoning is not always linear, as in certain cases reasoning may lead rational agents to drop previously held beliefs (this is what Broome calls 'theoretical reasoning in reverse'). It is found that the direction of theoretical reasoning critically depends upon the 'relative robustness' of different beliefs. Instrumental (end-means) reasoning presents a similar pattern of linear and reverse structures. For example, belief in the effectiveness of a means relative to the achievement of a given end seldom entails that the end cannot be achieved if that particular means is not adopted. In this case too, backward reasoning leads the rational agent to drop previously held beliefs. The stability of the means-end relationship (both in the forward and backward looking sense) is found to depend upon the intensity of the initial beliefs. This leads Broome to identify a different type of reasoning *(krasia),* which he describes as reasoning requiring 'if you believe you ought to do something, to intend to do it'.

The following paper by Wlodek Rabinowicz: 'Pragmatic Arguments for Rationality Constraints', addresses the issue originally raised by Frank Ramsey that an individual violating a given rationality constraint (the laws of probability in Ramsey's case) can be made to act to his (her) disadvantage. Rabinowicz maintains that a common feature of the exploitation set-ups is that individuals adopt a disunified frame. In other words, they take decisions on various issues separately and in a piecemeal way rather than confronting the complete set of alternatives with a single act of choice (what Rabinowicz calls the 'unified approach'). The paper examines the conditions for unified decision both when the agent is presented with a number of alternatives at any given time (the synchronic case) and when alternatives are offered sequentially over time (the diachronic case). It is argued that there may be good pragmatic reasons for rationality constraints leveling the ground for disunification, but that the cost of unified decision-making may be stronger in diachronic cases relative to synchronic ones.

Rationality constraints provide a bridge between decision theory and the sciences of the artificial (the domain of 'human-made' products). Wenceslao Gonzalez, in his paper 'Rationality and Prediction in the Sciences of the Artificial: Economics as a Design Science', discusses the role of those rational frames that are relevant to human activity when accuracy and precision are important goals. According to Gonzalez, the sciences of the artificial appeal to rationality constraints at two different levels: the rational reconstruction of professional practices (as in pharmacology, librarianship, management), and the scientific analysis of the artifacts made within natural or social sciences (as in technology sciences or economics). Independently of their different origin, the sciences of the artificial presuppose an intentional structure associated with the concept of 'design', that is, with an activity 'concerned with how things ought to be, with devising artifacts to attain goals' (Simon 1996: 114, as quoted by Gonzalez). Any such activity presupposes a special relationship between prediction and prescription: 'in order to design something [...] the common path is to consider in advance whether the project is possible (i.e. prediction), before we give the indications about how to resolve the problem that is foreseen (i.e. prediction)'. A complex (hierarchical) structure of rationality constraints (especially of the means-ends type common in economics) is thus an essential component of the scientific approach to human-made products.

The chapter by Roberto Scazzieri: 'Context, Congruence and Co-ordination', examines the role of rationality constraints (devices) as tools for co-ordination in a non-parametric environment. This paper starts with the consideration that the identification of good reasons (in a social set-up) is associated with the ability to adopt suitable distancing devices. This amounts to give salience to certain characteristics of the social environment relative to others. Following Aristotle's view that the practice of reason presupposes the ability to detach oneself from the immediate material structure of living (Aristotle, *Metaphysics*, I 982 b), the paper argues that co-ordination arises from specific circumstances and is associated with the identification of a hierarchical structure of contexts (that is, a set of contexts of different order). In particular, different types of contexts give rise to different types of congruence, which may in turn be associated with different patterns of coordination. The analysis of congruence calls attention to reasoning as a cognitive ability by which frames may be fixed and congruence structures 'discovered'. The paper examines alternative criteria for resemblance (congruence) and their implications for the coordination among rational agents. It is suggested that coordination presupposes agents' ability to identify a suitable prototype of mutually compatible choices (actions), and that the ability to switch from one such prototype to another plays a central role in allowing individuals to adjust their mode of interaction to changes of context. It is also argued that identification of context is not a trivial matter, although it is essential in assessing whether coordination is possible under specific circumstances.

Part Three: 'Situations and Reasoning', is meant to assess the role of context-dependent reasoning in shaping rationality constraints in a variety of situations (such as economics, clinical trials, artificial intelligence).

The chapter by Matthias Klaes: 'Rationality and its Bounds: Re-Framing Social Framing' considers the control factors behind the framing of choice problems. His starting point is a discussion of the 'prospect theory' formulated by Daniel Kahneman and Amos Tversky. Klaes argues that prospect theory does not claim to be a complete theory of framing, especially because such a theory is concerned with control factors at the individual level and does not explicitly deal with the issue of social framing. In particular, the paper examines framing effects in transactions (transactional framing) and calls attention to the important role of institutional context. At this point, Klaes notes that framing is closely intertwined with agents' beliefs and desires, and that it may be useful to address framing effects as intentional phenomena. Following John Searle's view that rationality is primarily a faculty allowing human beings to reason about their own actions, Klaes argues for an 'internal' account of rationality, that is, for a view that considers rationality as an attribute of intentional states. This point of view suggests that standards of rationality may vary significantly across the social continuum, and calls attention to the 'fundamentally social nature' of human intentionality and reason.

In 'Causal Pluralism and Context' Maria Carla Galavotti addresses the debate on probabilistic causality, heralding a pluralistic approach. It is held that instead of trying to give a univocal definition of causality one should start from a careful consideration of the context surrounding causal analysis, and proceed from there to a characterization of causal relations within a given context. A main thesis of the paper is that the two fundamental intuitions underlying causal attributions, namely the mechanical view that relates causation to the notion of mechanism and the manipulative view are both useful and should be seen as complementing each other, rather than in opposition. With respect to the mechanical and manipulative concepts of causation, notions like 'regularity' and 'counterfactual' are transversal, and so is the distinction between 'type' and 'token' causality, (namely causality referred respectively to populations and to particular events). Within different contexts, various combinations of such notions enter into causal attributions. It is also argued that in order to characterize context a variety of elements should be taken into account. These include in the first place the assumptions underlying causal attributions, which usually include invariance assumptions of some sort. In addition, the aims to which causal discourse is put, especially in connection with explanation, prediction and manipulation are important. Also relevant is the nature of the information available; in particular one should distinguish between data obtained through direct or indirect observation and data obtained through experimentation. A careful examination of these and other elements characterizing context is an essential step towards the clarification of causal analysis.

The following chapter by Raffaella Campaner: 'Causal Medical Reasoning and Pre-Emption', deals with the structure of reasoning (and, in particular, of causal reasoning) in clinical situations, in which the identification of 'good reasons' is shaped by the need to propose a diagnosis and to identify a treatment. This paper argues that, in medical reasoning, diagnosis and treatment presuppose the adoption of a particular type of causal structure, in which 'C causes E, but E would have occurred even if C had not'. This causal structure, which is based on the concept of 'pre-emption' (certain causes pre-empt other causes to bring about their effect), is considered to be 'the deepest structure of therapeutic reasoning'. The paper examines the working of pre-emptive reasoning in the two cases of HIV and anti-AIDS therapies, and of chemotherapy. In both cases, clinical reasoning deals with situations in which causal factors (viruses, cancer cells) get modified over the course of the illness, so that different therapeutic interventions are implemented at the same time. It is thought that causes pre-empted at a certain stage of the illness may bring about their effect at a different stage, so that combinations of different drugs (drug cocktails) are prescribed. The paper argues that probabilistic pre-emption is the distinctive characteristic of clinical reasoning, especially when diagnosis and treatment are marred by lack of information and uncertainty.

The final contribution by Marco Alberti, Federico Chesani, Marco Gavanelli, Evelina Lamma and Paola Mello: 'Abduction in the Context of a Reasoning Process: the SCIFF Framework', examines patterns of reasoning in artificial intelligence. The paper argues that concepts such as 'surprising fact', 'explanation' and 'confirmation' can be mapped in logical programming. In particular, it is maintained that Charles Peirce's notion of 'abduction' finds a useful counterpart in artificial intelligence. Drawing upon recent contribution to abductive logic programming, this contribution shows that abduction goes beyond purely logical formulations and suggests a context-dependent account of synthetic reasoning. On this basis, the paper outlines a 'sound and complete abductive proof procedure' (SCIFF), and examines its applications in a variety of situations. First, a planning application using abductive event calculus is considered. Second, the authors discuss the application of the SCIFF framework to explore a particular multiagent system (*open society model*), which is characterized by freedom of entry (or exit), and the non-observability of agents' internal architecture. Third, an application to the logic of obligations, prohibitions and permissions (deontic logic) is examined. The paper calls special attention to the property of the

SCIFF language as a useful exploratory tool for the analysis of reasoning patterns associated with the recognition and processing of surprising events.

On the whole, the papers collected in this volume testify to the need, widely felt within recent literature, that patterns of reasoning become increasingly pluralistic, dynamical and sensitive to the context. A similar tendency characterizes the ongoing debate on rationality and the nature of probability. The search for strong theories, to be applied everywhere in science and everyday life, has been superseded by the construction of context sensitive conceptual tools, in the awareness that both science and everyday life are too complex and multifaceted to be forced into ready-made schemata.

I Practical Reason

1

The Good and the Bad, the True and the False

AIMÉE DROLET AND PATRICK SUPPES[*]

In this paper, we argue for a different approach to rationality, one based on a deeper model of the psychological phenomena of choice. We adopt an Aristotelian view which covers a wider range of human behavior compared to classical theories espoused by economists, statisticians, and philosophers. These theories are based on the concept of preferences. Our view is grounded in the concepts of association and habit. We conducted a large empirical study of good and bad habits. Its results strongly demonstrate how much agreement there is on judgments of what is good and what is bad, which is contrary to the mere relativity of preferences commonly assumed. We conclude with a discussion of the implications for rationality of the ideas and empirical data we have introduced, and connect our ideas of rationality to the classical Aristotelian view of the importance of habits. We propose to replace maximizing expected utility by having habits constitute constraints on choices, and the decision-maker lets his associations determine his selection from the constrained choice set, whether consciously or unconsciously.

1 Introduction

In this article, we focus on rationality, but from a perspective that is more empirical than is usual. There are, of course, many empirical studies that have as their purpose the demonstration that a given concept or axiom of rationality, often of the kind found in the theory of preference, is empirically

---

[*] The authors would like to thank Claudia Arrighi and Genevieve Hochwarter for help with data collection and coding. The authors gratefully acknowledge the financial support from the Anderson School Class of 2000 Behavioral Laboratory and the Marketing Science Institute.

false. Our objective is different. We want to argue for a different approach to rationality, based on a deeper model of the psychological phenomena of choice. By 'deeper' we mean the development of a framework of theoretical ideas that, in principle, cover a wide range of human, and even animal, behavior. In spite of their many merits, including that of clarity and precision, the classical theories of preferences of economists, statisticians, and philosophers are notable for the narrow psychological range of the concepts they use. It is not far from the mark to say that the classical theory, and even most modern variants, has concentrated on essentially what are conceptual problems of psychological measurement, especially the measurement of desires or utilities, and the measurement of partial beliefs in terms of subjective probability. This last point about beliefs is discussed in detail in Suppes (Forthcoming).

The present article is not focused on providing the more encompassing formal psychological theory of choice, which we are developing (Suppes, Drolet and Bodapati: 2005), but rather on the kind of concepts and empirical data that are central to our reconception of rationality and that properly ground the concepts of association and habit on which we are basing our current theoretical efforts. Fortunately, for us, neither of these basic concepts is new. There is much from the past we can use. The concept of association has had a prominent role in the development of psychology in the last three centuries, beginning especially with the work of Hobbes and Hume, before psychology became a discipline separate from philosophy. It has continued to occupy a central place in psychology and now such a position in neuroscience as well. Given this prominence, we shall not say as much about association in this article as about habit. But again, fortunately, we have much to use and digest from the past about the nature of habits. As we make clear in the next section, there is already to be found a detailed and rather sophisticated theory of habits in Aristotle. More particularly, Section 2 concentrates on the good and the bad, as advertised in the title, and what we have in mind are, above all, good and bad habits. We report the results of a fairly large empirical study to show how common and natural it is to think of behavior in terms of habits rather than preferences.

Section 3 is concerned with the second half of our title, the true and the false, where associations also have a role. We have less to say here, not because the truth is not almost as important as the good, but because we have concentrated in this article on the neglected topic of the good and the bad in most theories of rational choice.

Section 4 is about implications for rationality of the ideas and empirical data we have introduced. In Section 5, we return to the connection between our ideas of rationality and the classical Aristotelian view.

2 The Good and the Bad
2.1 Philosophical discussion
Beginning with Aristotle, the majority of accounts of habits distinguish between habits that are good and those that are bad:

> Presumably, then, *we* must begin with things known to *us*. Hence, any one who is to listen intelligently to lectures about what is noble and just and, generally, about the subjects of political science must have been brought up in good habits. For the fact is the starting-point, and if this is sufficiently plain to him, he will not at the start need to reason as well.... (Aristotle 1095b2-5: 937-38)

Aristotle connects many habit behaviors to virtue in character. He stresses in this connection the importance of learning.

> Virtue, then, being of two kinds, intellectual and moral, intellectual virtue in the main owes both its birth and its growth to teaching (for which reason it requires experience and time), while moral virtue comes about as a result of habit, whence also its name *ethike* is one that is formed by a slight variation from the word *ethos* (habit). From this, it is also plain that none of the moral virtues arises in us by nature; for nothing that exists by nature can form a habit contrary to its nature. For instance the stone which by nature moves downwards cannot be habituated to move upwards, not even if one tries to train it by throwing it up ten thousand times; nor can fire be habituated to move downwards, nor can anything else that by nature behaves in one way be trained to behave in another. Neither by nature, then, nor contrary to nature do the virtues arise in us; rather we are adapted by nature to receive them, and are made perfect by habit. (Aristotle 1103a14-24: 952)

But the outcome of learning can be either good or bad habits, as Aristotle makes clear in the following passage.

> Again, it is from the same causes and by the same means that every virtue is both produced and destroyed, and similarly every art; for it is from playing the lyre that both good and bad lyre-players are produced. And the corresponding statement is true of builders and of all the rest; men will be good or bad builders as a result of building well or badly. For if this were not so, there would have been no need of a teacher, but all men would have been born good or bad at their craft. This, then, is the case with the virtues also; by doing the acts that we do in our transactions with other men we become just or unjust, and by doing the acts that we do in the presence of danger, and being habituated to feel fear or confidence, we become brave or cowardly. The same is true of appetites and feelings of anger; some men become temperate and good-tempered, others self-indulgent and irascible, by behaving in one way or the other in the appropriate circumstances. Thus, in one word, states of character arise out of like activities. This is why the activities we exhibit must be of a certain kind; it is because the states of character correspond to the differences between these. It makes no small difference, then, whether we form habits of

one kind or of another from our very youth; it makes a very great difference, or rather *all* the difference. (Aristotle 1103a14-b25: 952-53)

Aquinas also offers a comprehensive view of how behaviors can be categorized as good or bad. According to Aquinas, 'A good habit is specifically distinct from a bad habit, since a good habit is one which disposes to an act suitable to the agent's nature, while an evil habit is one which disposes to an act unsuitable to nature' (*Summa Theologica II*, 1st Part of 2nd Part, Q54, p. 410). Aquinas analyzes many other aspects of habit. For example, in a passage very congenial to our view, he stresses, like Aristotle, the importance of actions being important to learning habits.

> *Like acts cause like habits.* Now things are like or unlike not only according to the sameness of diversity of their quality, but also according to the same or diverse mode of participation. For it is not only black that is unlike white, but also the less white is unlike the more white; since movement likewise takes place from the less white to the more white, as from one opposite to another, as is stated in *Physics* v.
> But since the use of habits depends on the will, as was shown above, just as one who has a habit may fail to use it or may act contrary to it, so he may happen to use the habit by performing an act that is not in proportion to the intensity of the habit. Accordingly, if the intensity of the act be in proportion to the intensity of the habit, or even surpass it, every such act either increases the habit or disposes to its increase, if we may speak of the increase of habits as we do of the increase of an animal. For not every morsel of food actually increases the animal's size, as neither does every drop of water hollow out the stone; but the multiplication of food results at last in an increase of the body. So, too, repeated acts cause a habit to grow.
> — If, however, the act falls proportionately short of the intensity of the habit, such an act does not dispose to an increase of that habit, but rather to its lessening. (Aquinas, *Summa Theologica II*, 1st Part of 2nd Part, Q. 52: 399)

Similar views, often from a somewhat different perspective, were held by William James. His account is similar to Aristotle's and Aquinas', inasmuch as he distinguishes between good and bad habits and also suggests that the development of good habits is essential to character improvement. James urges that, by developing good habits, we 'make our nervous system our ally instead of our enemy' (James 1890/1950: 122).

2.2 Behaviorism

In the behaviorism that dominated American psychology after James from roughly 1910 to 1970, the concept of good and bad reinforcement, i.e., positive and negative reinforcement, was central to learning. Behaviorists start with approach to, or avoidance of, a stimulus. Approach is a behavioral sign of the stimulus' being good or pleasurable for the organism. Avoidance is a behavioral sign of its being bad or unpleasurable. In a strictly behavioral approach, no other characterization, certainly no non-empirical characterization, is assumed in interpreting the experiments.

For example, consider the much studied case of conditioning the little worm Aplysia. Two kinds of conditioning are easy. The worm is conditioned to approach some stimuli and to avoid others. This approach-avoidance learning is central to the behavior of such simple organisms. There are some stimuli that such an organism will approach, and others that it will avoid instinctively i.e., without any conditioning. Conditioning uses these instinctive responses to get conditioning started. For example, suppose that an organism instinctively avoids stimulus S1 and that stimulus S2 occurs contiguously, both spatially and temporally with S1 in a series of trials. In many cases, the organism becomes conditioned to avoiding S2 and will do so when S2 occurs alone. The situation is similar for the conditioning approach to a stimulus. Pavlov's dogs conditioned to salivate at the ringing of a bell are an example of this in mammals.

Even so, from an external standpoint we can certainly judge that one stimulus that the organism is conditioned to is bad for its health, or certainly not as good as another to which it is also conditioned to approach. A study by Sheffield and Roby (1950) illustrates this nicely. Rats prefer water with saccharine in it, almost as much as they prefer water with sugar, even though the saccharine has no nutritional value. They easily become conditioned to always choose the water with saccharine in it over plain water. Of course, given the widespread predilection of humans for Diet Coke or Diet Dr. Pepper over plain water, this result is not surprising. However, such experiments are further testimony to the contextual character of the good. Diet Coke tastes good to us; water and saccharine taste good to rats. Nutritionists may even split the context further, while denying Diet Coke is at all useful nutritionally, some will maintain it is good because it replaces drinking something that is bad, namely, Classic Coke with lots of sugar, which promotes obesity.

2.3 Neuroscience of Conditioning

With respect to the neuroscience of such conditioning, starting with simple organisms, the first thing to note is that behaviorally the change brought about by conditioning is not necessarily permanent, but it can certainly last for some days. In the context of these simple organisms, this can mean for a lifetime. Successful conditioning is not something transient like remembering a telephone number or a numerical license plate for a few seconds or even minutes – usually seconds rather than minutes.

Unless one is a dualist about Aplysia and the like, this means that the existence of a long-term change in the physical structure of the nervous system of the Aplysia is accepted as a consequence of conditioning. The problem is to find it. There has been some progress by Kandel (1985) and others, but the results are as yet far from definitive. Better results were obtained in the 1950s and 1960s with EEG and single-electrode experiments of a variety of kinds. These experiments, of which there were many, did not identify the physical changes in the cell structure that were of a semipermanent nature as a result of the conditioning.

There were, however, many striking results at the level of the electric field, or more generally, at the level of the electric activity of single cells. For example, in some wonderful experiments, Doty and Giurgea (1961) showed the following. First, the stimulation of a given motor electrode, i.e., an electrode whose micro-tip was placed in a motor neuron, would lead to the natural limb movement of an animal. Now by the pairing (in the standard conditioning way) of sensory stimulation (the CS) with the natural US (the motor neuron), direct stimulation of the sensory neuron produced the limb movement. The logic of this is very similar to Pavlov's dog experiments, although the stimulation is directly delivered to the neurons. Important from our viewpoint, cutting the transcortical connections between the two electrodes, CS and US, did not disturb the conditioning. This appears to be good evidence for the field carrying the conditioning from CS to US.

This is just one example of many significant studies that are now rather neglected, but highly relevant to several subtle conceptual points about the mind and the brain. We give one human example. As long ago as 1935, Durup and Fessard, two French neurophysiologists, studied the interruption of EEG recorded alpha waves by the sudden introduction of a bright light as a stimulus. This phenomenon came to be known as the 'arousal pattern'. Durup and Fessard recorded their observations by photographing the blocked alpha wave. After a while, they noticed that the blocking began before the light was shown. It was triggered by the earlier auditory click of the camera shutter. Pavlovian conditioning once again, but this time observed at the level of electrical activity in the brain.

2.4 Conditioning at the Group Level

We can also observe Pavlovian conditioning at the group level. For example, macaque monkeys in the wild have at least six, and probably more, signals to warn each other of danger. From a conditioning standpoint, they can be thought of as working very much like Pavlovian conditioning from the standpoint of a single monkey. But when several are involved, there is a natural social interpretation in terms of a signal that can be true or false. For example, let Y1 be the yelp warning of a nearby snake climbing the tree. One monkey sees the snake and yelps Y1. Other nearby monkeys scramble to move away higher up in nearby trees. In contrast, the movement is downward or in hiding from Y2 which signals the presence of an eagle circling above. There is no interesting grammar attached to these signals, but the semantic interpretation is clear.

Interestingly, research indicates that a species can become conditioned to the alarm call system of another species. For example, hornbill birds understand Diana monkey warning yelps and respond accordingly (Rainey, Zuberbühler and Slater 2004). When prerecorded eagle shrieks or a monkey's eagle alarm calls are played, hornbills react defensively, producing their own noisy alarm calls. When prerecorded leopard growls or a monkey's leopard alarm calls are played, the hornbills rarely reacted. The relationship between the species is symbiotic: Diana monkeys use hornbill birdcalls as an early-warning system (Rainey, Zuberbühler and Slater 2004).

Neal Miller's (1959) prominent theory of approach-avoidance competition and conditioning can be used to account for such complex social-behavior situations. Miller's approach-avoidance analysis has close connections with the earlier introduction of good and bad habits discussed by Aristotle and others. We shall return to this in Section V.

In sum, behaviorists presuppose that people can assess the goodness or badness of options and act on these assessments. They approach the good and avoid the bad, and in social situations they develop the true and the false to help each other.

2.5 An Empirical Study of Habits

The idea that people's sense of what is true and what is false derives from their assessments of and reactions to the goodness or badness of options suggests that there is agreement among people's assessment of what options are good or bad. However, many scholars doubt there is or can be widespread agreement on what is good or bad. We test this apparently controversial suggestion in a study of habits.

Method

575 adults, age 18-99, were paid between $5 and $15 to participate in the study. Across ages, there were an approximately equal number of males and females. The study had two parts. In the first part, participants were presented with a list of 20 habits: 1) smoke regularly; 2) exercise regularly; 3) bite nails often; 4) regularly on time for appointments; 5) watch TV too much; 6) regularly meet deadlines; 7) drink too much (alcohol); 8) too critical of friends; 9) wear a seat belt regularly; 10) eat dessert regularly; 11) too argumentative in conversation; 12) go to the movies regularly; 13) too ungrateful of help; 14) leave a tip regularly; 15) shop at the same grocery store regularly; 16) too compulsively neat; 17) attend religious services regularly; 18) drive aggressively; 19) diet regularly; and 20) late for appointments. Participants were asked to indicate which three habits on the list they con-

sidered to be their worst and which three they considered to be their best. Specifically, participants read: 'Of the habits listed on the following page, which do you see as your worst habits?' and 'Which do you see as your best habits?' Participants were then asked to choose what they considered to be their three worst habits by putting an 'X' next to each of three habits on the list. They were also asked to choose what they considered to be their three best habits by putting an 'X' next to each of three habits on the list.

In the second part, we asked participants open-ended rather than close-ended questions for multiple reasons. First, we wanted to avoid the bias that might result from suggesting habits to participants. Second, we were curious about the *kinds* of good and bad habits participants would report as their best habits and worst habits. There may be widespread agreement about what are good habits and what are bad habits. However, the kinds of good habits and bad habits that participants report (e.g., habits that relate to self-control, successes or failures, vs. grooming, hygienic or unhygienic) might vary a lot. For example, they might vary with age. Participants were asked: 'In general (not including the above habits), what bad habits do you have that you would like to change?' and then 'What good habits do you have that you would like to keep?' Participants were told they could list as many bad and good habits as they liked.

Results

The first part of the questionnaire included close-ended responses. We calculated the frequency of different 'X' responses for the best and worst habits. Across all participants, there were a total of 2,606 Xs. An examination of the frequencies of Xs shows remarkably high agreement among participants as to which of their habits are good and which are bad (see Figure 1).

There are two things to note about Figure 1. First, some of the habits listed were relatively infrequent. That is, regardless of whether they are a good or a bad habit, participants generally did not indicate having them. For example, nearly all participants who put an X next to smoking agreed that smoking was one of their worst habits. However, relatively fewer participants smoked, for instance compared to participants who indicated they drink too much alcohol. Second, only for a few habits, e.g., regularly going to the movies, had a roughly even split of Xs between worst and best. However, few participants singled these habits out. Overall, these results suggest that there was a very high level of agreement among participants as to what behaviors are good or bad.

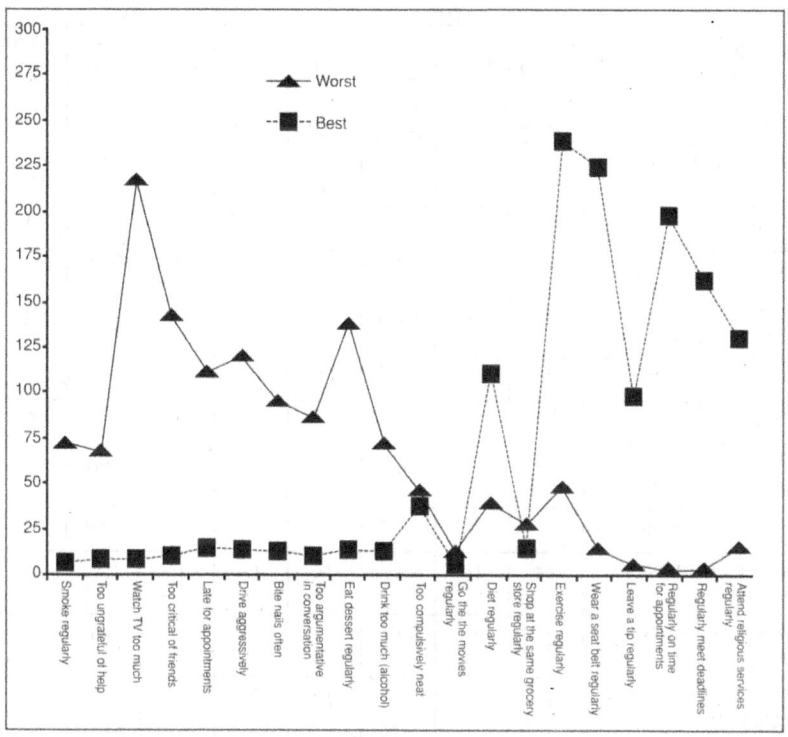

Figure 1: Number of Habits Checked 'Worst' and 'Best'

A stronger test of people's level of agreement about the good and the bad is to divide participants into subgroups based on factors known to affect judgments dramatically and compare the mean assessments of the subgroups. We assigned participants to groups depending on their age. Age is a variable that captures many socio-economic factors, e.g., income and generation, and individual differences, e.g., cognitive ability and emotionality, among people. Participants 50 years of age and over were assigned to the older adult group ($n = 178$; $M_{age} = 68$), while participants under the age of 50 were assigned to the young adult group ($n = 397$; $M_{age} = 21$). We then redid the above analyses on each age group separately. Table 1 shows the results of these analyses by age group.

Interestingly, even though they are on average nearly 50 years apart, the two groups gave strikingly similar responses. As Figure 2 shows, with only one or two exceptions, young adults' ranking of habits in terms of their goodness and badness mirrored that of older adults.

Habit	Young				Old			
	# Worst	# Best	% Worst	Rank Worst	# Worst	# Best	% Worst	Rank Worst
Smoke regularly	55	0	100	1	17	4	78.6	12
Too ungrateful of help	49	1	98.0	2	19	1	95.0	7
Watch TV too much	134	4	97.1	3	83	1	98.8	3
Too critical of friends	105	6	94.6	5	39	1	97.5	4
Late for appointments	88	5	94.6	5	24	4	85.7	10
Drive aggressively	97	8	92.4	6	23	1	95.8	6
Bite nails often	83	7	92.2	7	13	1	92.9	8
Too argumentative in conversation	57	7	89.1	8	30	0	100	1
Eat dessert regularly	55	8	87.3	9	83	3	96.5	5
Drink too much (alcohol)	55	10	84.6	10	18	0	100	2
Too compulsively neat	25	31	44.6	11	22	6	78.6	12
Go to the movies regularly	6	8	42.9	12	1	3	25.0	14
Diet regularly	16	28	36.4	13	24	81	22.9	15
Shop at the same grocery store regularly	4	12	25.0	14	24	4	85.7	10
Exercise regularly	17	144	10.6	15	32	93	25.6	13
Wear a seat belt regularly	6	126	4.6	17	8	96	7.7	17
Leave a tip regularly	3	63	4.6	17	2	33	5.7	18
Regularly on time for appointments	3	118	2.5	18	0	77	0	20
Regularly meet deadlines	3	136	2.2	19	1	24	4.0	19
Attend religious services regularly	1	64	1.5	20	14	64	18.0	16
TOTAL X's	1648				958			

Table 1: Number and Percent of Habits Checked 'Worst' and 'Best' by Age Group

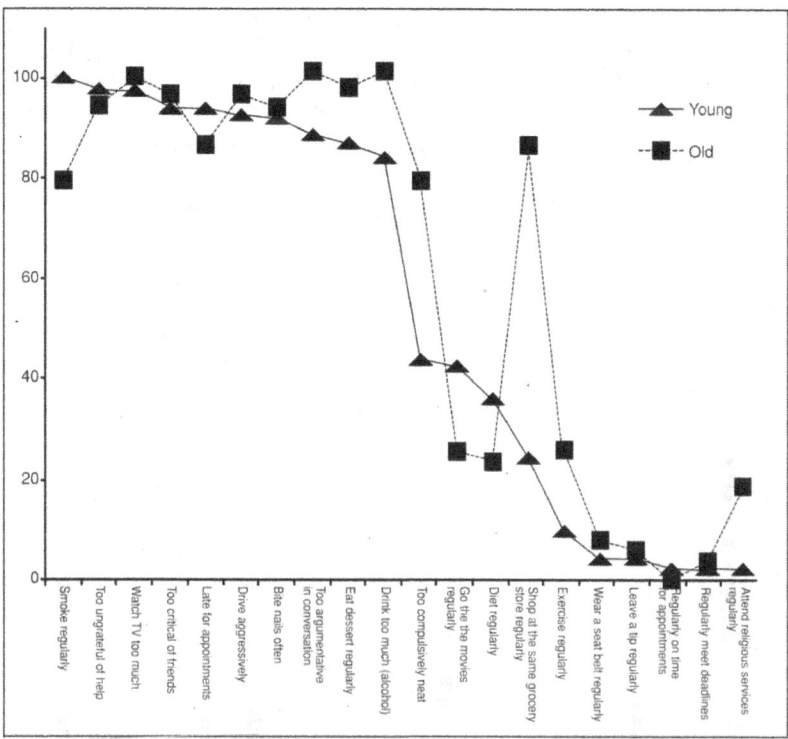

Figure 2: Percent Habits Checked 'Worst' by Younger vs. Older Adults

In summary, the results from analyzing the closed-response data indicate that there is a great degree of general recognition among people as to what is good versus bad, independent of age.

Across all participants, there were a total of 1,727 habit responses to the open-ended questions. On average, for the open-ended questions, participants gave on average 1-2 good-habits responses and 1-2 bad-habits responses. Two judges (an independent judge and one of the authors) coded the open-ended responses. The coding was done without the knowledge of participants' age, ethnicity, or gender. First, judges parsed participants' responses in order to identify separate habits. Second, habit responses were then categorized into specific groups of habits. These specific habit groups were partly based on past research on habits. For example, substance addiction has long been viewed as a habit. The protocol data itself also suggested specific habit groups. For example, many participants viewed aspects of interpersonal relationships as habits. For example, they viewed being kind to others as a habit behavior. Responses were assigned to the following 15 categories of habits: time management, grooming, exercise, diet, car, media (TV, web, etc.), money issues, substance addictions (smoking, drinking, and drugs), personality traits, nervous tics, sleep issues, work/school duties, religion, organization/cleanliness, and interpersonal relations.

As Figure 3 shows, participants' best habits appeared much more often in some habit groups and their worst habits appeared much more often in other habit groups. For example, bad habits appeared more frequently in the domains of time management ($F(1726) = 22.9, p < .0001$ and diet ($F(1726) = 11.24, p < .0008$) compared to good habits which appeared more frequently in the domain of exercise ($F(1726) = 15.62, p < .0001$).

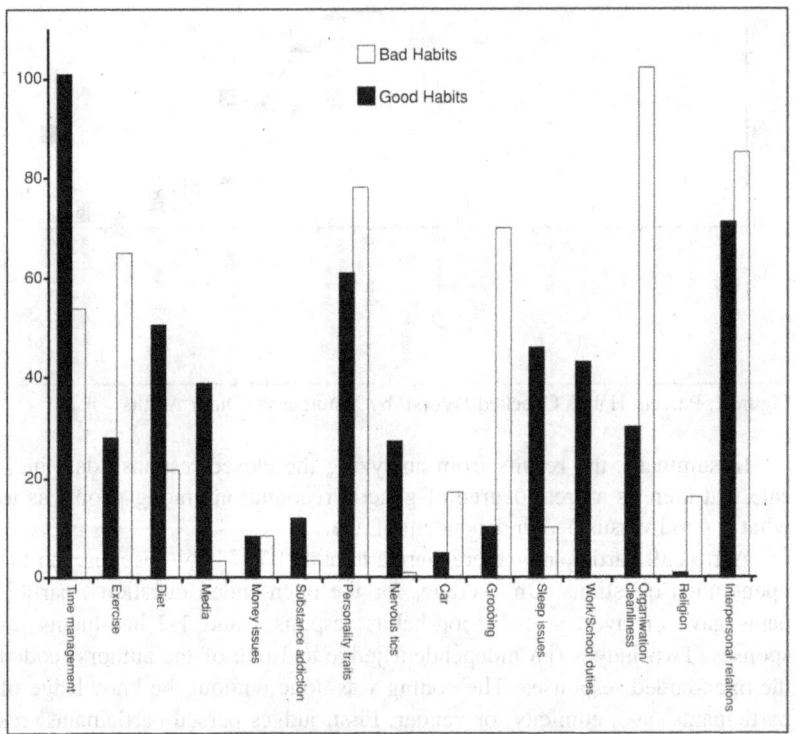

Figure 3: Percent Bad Habits and Good Habits by Habit Group

We also analyzed the open-ended responses of young versus older participants. We found some differences between age groups in terms of the kinds of habit behaviors they reported. Specifically, we found differences due to age in most (9) domains: time management, body care, diet, personality traits, nervous tics, car, sleep issues, organization and cleaning, and interpersonal relationships (all p's < .0005). Furthermore, we found significant interactions between age and whether a habit was reported as good versus bad for five domains: body care, personality traits, nervous tics, car, and organization and cleaning (all p's < .01), see Figures 4 and 5 for means and directions.

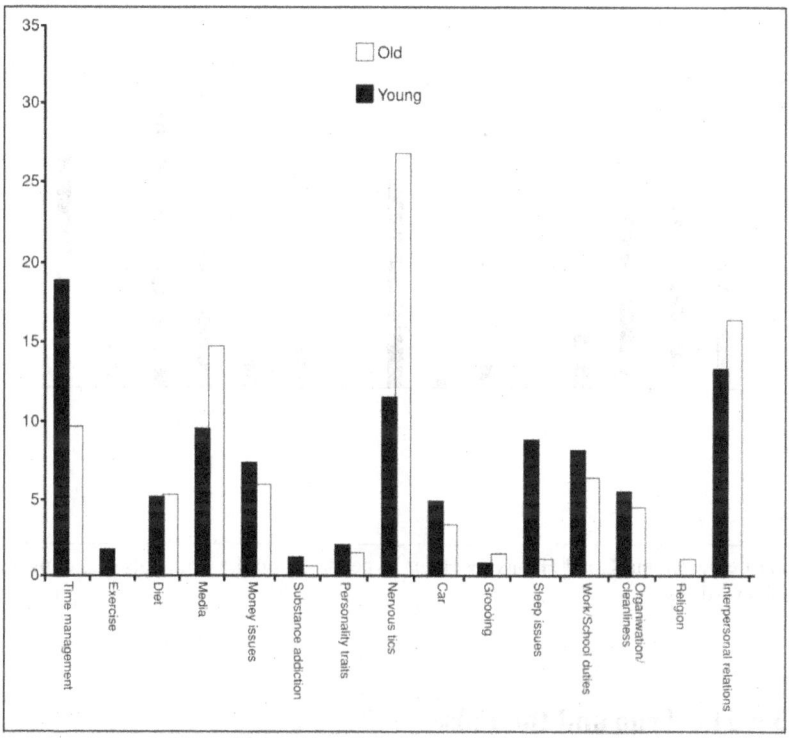

Figure 4: Percent Bad Habits by Habit Group Based on the Open-Ended Responses of Young vs. Older Adults

In summary, the results from analyzing the open-ended responses indicate that the kinds of good habits and bad habits that participants report (e.g., habits that relate to self-control, successes or failures, vs. grooming, hygienic or unhygienic) can vary a lot, but in contrast classification as being good or bad is relatively constant across the entire sample, young and old. This lends considerable credence to the claim that there is wide agreement on what is good and what is bad.

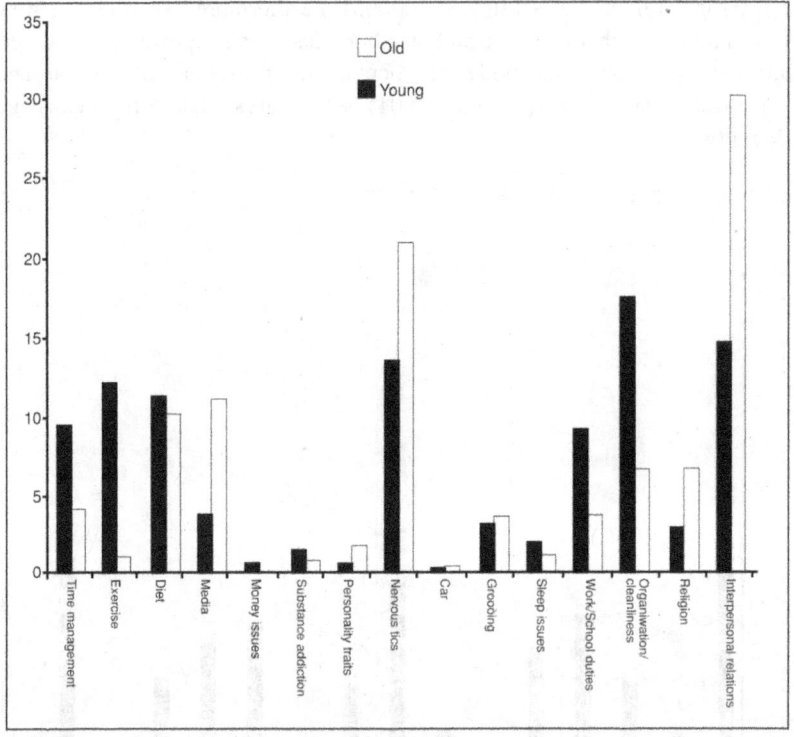

Figure 5: Percent Good Habits by Habit Type Based on the Protocols of Young vs. Older Adults

3 The True and the False
3.1 The Role of Associations

From the standpoint of learning, individual animals, such as Aplysia, which seem to communicate little to other members of their species, need only the concepts of approach, avoidance and conditioning. In species of a more complex nature, these concepts also lead up to the good and the bad. The need for a concept of truth seems minimal for Aplysia. But once animals of a given species begin to socialize with one another, simple signals but definite meaning, i.e. ones with little syntax, can have a natural interpretation as being true or false, as described earlier for macaque monkeys. And as also mentioned there, can even lead to signaling, e.g., warnings of predators, being understood across species.

Some philosophers, we are sure, would admit these simple cases of the true and the false, but not grant them any important epistemological or logical significance in giving an account of truth. One purpose of this section is to argue that this is a mistaken view. We review briefly the line of argument given in more technical detail by Suppes and Beziau (2003).

Philosophers discuss at length various theories of truth, – coherence theory, correspondence theory, problems of direct reference, sense and denotation, and so on –, but, curiously, do not give an account of how we actually perform truth computations, and even less why we are able to perform them so quickly. Philosophers who claim that 'Paris is the capital of France' is true because Paris is the capital of France are generally not interested in explaining how we actually compute the answer. But, since such sentences are almost never remembered, or even previously encountered, a computation is necessary.

Logicians also do not solve these problems. If we want to describe how one answers a question like 'Is 49 + 13 equal to 61?', it is certainly wrong to look at the logical foundation of arithmetic, whether it is proof-theoretical or model-theoretical. We answer such a question by using a series of small computational algorithms and tricks, not by looking for a formal proof from a set of axioms, or by finding a model in which the axioms are true and 49 + 13 = 61 is false. In the case of a question like 'Is Rome the capital of France?', it is even more doubtful that we are trying to deduce the truth or falsity of the sentence from a set of axioms, or by using a truth-table.

Moreover, it is misleading to say that we are making a *deduction* to arrive at the conclusion that 'Rome is the capital of France' is false, unless we strongly emphasize that deduction does not reduce to the narrow meaning of deduction in formal logic. To avoid misunderstanding, it is better to say that we are here trying to describe how we *compute* the truth and falsity of such a sentence.

In a recent work on computational semantics, the authors, Blackburn and Bos (1999), say:

> The book is devoted to introducing techniques for tackling the following two questions:
> 1. How can we automate the process of associating semantic representations with expressions of natural language?
> 2. How can we use logical representations of natural language expressions to automate the process of drawing inferences?
> (Blackburn and Bos 1999: iii)

Their idea is to find some algorithms to translate natural language into the language of first-order logic to represent the meaning of natural-language sentences, and then to find some additional algorithms to make inferences with these first-order translations. The two steps seem wrong for our purpose. It is doubtful that our brains use first-order logic to compute empirical truths. Both AI researchers and computational linguists have been over-influenced by formal logic. They do not deal directly with the problem of finding the obvious truth or falsity of atomic statements like 'Rome is the capital of France.'

We share with AI researchers an emphasis on *associations* (sometimes in AI, 'semantics networks' are also called 'associative networks'). When answering a question such as 'Is Paris the capital of France?', we are using notions which are associated with the input, like Eiffel Tower with Paris, or country with capital. Our purpose here is to try to explain the mechanism of such associations, in connection with the question of truth and falsity. But our description should not depend crucially on language, even though we are working with linguistic examples, since we think that this mechanism also has a common root in processes involving any language, nonverbal animal behavior, and stimulus-response phenomena in general.

The viewpoint here is that an associative network is a set of nodes with links between them. One central question is how an associative network is organized. We will not present any general theory of such organization, but will focus our attention on how truth computations fit into associative networks. For us 'true' is here no mysterious entity, but a word in the associative network, like 'Paris' or 'capital'. Our main task is to explain, given an input like 'Paris is the capital of France', what happens in the associative network. Our idea is that 'true' or 'false' become linked with 'Paris is the capital of France', on the basis of some already existing associative links. We suppose here that these links are fixed, that they correspond to associations already learned. Of course, for more general problems, the links have to be considered dynamically. For a detailed proof, for example, that grammars can be learned just from associations or conditioning connections, see Suppes (1969).

Our approach is similar to earlier work on semantic networks (Lehman 1992). The most important difference is the detailed consideration of the dynamics of the computation of truth, starting with the dependence on an explicit external cause of activation, i.e., an auditory or visual verbal stimulus being presented to a person. And this activation is followed by spreading activation internally to other nodes not directly activated by the stimulus.

Thus, ideas on which our model is based are the classical psychological concepts of association, activation, and spreading of activation. But these old ideas, which really go back to Hume, have not used by philosophers or logicians as a basis of natural psychological computation. This interlude on the true and the false has only meant to sketch how the basic concepts needed for a psychological theory of the good and the bad work very well for the true and the false. If you want, these ideas are easily extended to a similar associative psychological account of subjective probability, see Suppes (Forthcoming).

3.2 The Cognitive Revolution: From Behavior to Information

As discussed above, in the behaviorism that dominated American psychology from roughly 1920 to 1970, the concept of good and bad reinforcement, i.e., positive and negative reinforcement, was central to learning. Information about what is true was not explicitly emphasized. In contrast, the cognitive revolution of the 1960s and 1970s emphasized information rather than the behavior and the effects of reinforcement.

Indeed, one of the antecedents of the cognitive revolution was information processing theory. In the information processing view, people are seen as taking information into a perceptual system, selectively attending to some of it, encoding or transforming it for use by their cognitive faculties, storing it in memory, and later retrieving it from memory when an appropriate retrieval cue is activated (for a summary, see Brown and Craik 2000). Accordingly, as interest in information processing grew, so did interest in the analysis of perception, attention, immediate sensory memories, short-term memory, and the structure of long-term memory.

Researchers such as Newell and Simon (1961) developed computer models of cognition that incorporated the activities and structures involved in information processing. For example, their computer models included a central processor that corresponds to short-term memory in the human mind. Newell and Simon's computer programs attempted to simulate specific thought processes. Much good work was done by exploring this computer analogy, as a way to understand better the activities of brains (the hardware) and minds (the software). It is not our purpose to criticize it here, but only to note that it did not create a revolution in the theory of rationality, nor did it lead to any radical revisions of the rational theory of choice or decision much cherished by economists and statisticians. Again, we emphasize we believe there is much in this decision-theoretic work of permanent value. We only question its full adequacy as a theory of rationality.

4 Implications for Rationality

4.1 Limitations of Preference Theory

Past research has identified many limitations of preference theory. For example, contrary to preference theory, research in cognitive psychology demonstrates that people often do not have predefined preferences to refer to when making their choices. They do not know what they like beforehand.

Instead, people construct their preferences on-the-spot and as needed in order to solve choice problems (Bettman, Luce and Payne 1998).

Evidence for this constructivist view derives from many studies showing inconsistencies in people's choice behavior, so-called violations of rational choice. These studies identify numerous choice-problem factors (e.g., task and context; see Simonson and Tversky 1992 and Tversky, Sattath and Slovic 1988) that systematically, and often dramatically, influence choice making even though, according to principles of rationality, they should not. For example, the framing of choices can cause reversals in choice behavior even though the consequences of choices are formally identical. A classic example of framing is Tversky and Kahneman's (1981) 'lives saved' vs. 'lives lost' problem:

> Imagine that the U.S. is preparing for the outbreak of an unusual Asian disease, which is expected to kill 600 people. Two alternative programs to combat the disease have been proposed. Assume that the exact scientific estimates of the consequences of the programs are as follows. Which of the two programs would you favor?

Participants either viewed the lives-saved frame:

> If program A is adopted, 200 people will be saved. If program B is adopted, there is a one-third probability that 600 people will be saved and a two-thirds probability that no people will be saved.

Or the lives-lost frame:

> If program C is adopted, 400 people will die. If program D is adopted, there is a one-third probability that nobody will die and a two-thirds probability that 600 people will die.

In the lives-saved condition, 72% chose A, the safe-and-sure strategy, but only 28% chose program B, the risky strategy. In the lives-lost condition, 22% voted for the conservative strategy C while 72% opted for the risky strategy D. Although the objective information about choice outcomes (i.e., the truth information) is the same between frames, people's assessment of which plan is better differs between frames.

Research indicates that such inconsistencies in choice behavior and violations of preference theory that are due to factors such as decision frames are not mainly the result of people having bounded rationality (Simon 1955). The nonconformity of people's choice behavior is also driven by nonconscious as well as motivational forces, e.g., habits and emotions, respectively. Thus, the view that people's failure to adhere to the tenets of preference theory can be parsimoniously explained by their bounded rationality is simply wrong, minimally incomplete.

5 Our Aristotelian View of Rationality

We endorse the Aristotelian notion of rationality. For Aristotle, rationality is having good habits. In the introductory section, we quoted from a well-known passage of Aristotle (1095b2-5) in which he states, in language that is more familiar in discussions with our children than it is in the halls of psychology, about being 'well brought up in good habits if one is going to listen adequately to lectures about things noble and just.' But this is just a more or less literal translation of Aristotle's language. In modern terms it would be formulated in terms of the kind of environment in which the child had been raised and what kinds of habits had been inculcated in that environment. The point is one that is much neglected about Aristotle's conception of rationality. The most prominent classical view is that he is famous for having a view of rationality that centers on the giving of good reasons for an action. There is much is to be said for this view and it's important in the mature adult that such reasons are indeed used and play a role. What is neglected is Aristotle's clear understanding that it is not possible really to reach this position of maturity without developing, first, proper habits, so that one can learn and be taught in appropriate fashion. He is very clear also on the fact that it is not a matter of teaching explicit rules and giving specific explicit instructions, but it is the kind of learning that comes from being in proper circumstances, in for example, a proper sort of school or a proper family. Now put in such language of 'being proper' this sounds very inappropriate to our modern liberal and egalitarian culture, but translated, it is very much the kind of thing that has been attempted in all kinds of educational programs meant to shore up the background of young children. It is also clear to anyone the least bit familiar with modern conceptions of how nursery schools, day-care centers, and kindergartens are run, that explicit teaching of rules is not what is important but it is creating a kind of environment that leads to natural learning of appropriate habits. There is in fact in modern theories of learning, both for man and machine, a very natural distinction to be made here. It is that between supervised and unsupervised learning. It is a fact well recognized by Aristotle and much to be emphasized, we think, that many of the good habits that are important for all of us are ones that come not from supervised but from unsupervised learning. They come from those basic processes of association that work in appropriate ways given the opportunity. Creating the opportunity for unsupervised learning has been much of the focus of the deliberate educational framing of the early training of the young.

We have not developed anything like a theory of learning good habits, but we have stressed in our earlier discussion, and have brought out in the empirical study we conducted, how much agreement there is, in very broad terms, on the concept of a good or a bad habit. If you look at the list given earlier, it's also quite clear that this list primarily consists of habits that are unsupervised in their learning. Almost nothing occurs there that constitutes a formal part of the school curriculum, but they do constitute a part of the school environment. The students who, for example, do not know how to behave socially simply cannot be in a position to receive the regular school instruction. Such students, as is well known, are often placed in some kind of separate environment and given a great deal of special tutelage, in order to return them to the regular classroom after progress has been made, in the best sort of case, or as a necessary alternative, continue them in such special environments for many years.

What we are saying here about Aristotle's developmental outlook is one that we also endorse. There have been some nice recent studies of learning and habituation in Aristotle's thinking about the virtues. We mention especially Burnyeat (1999) and Sherman (1999). Of course the framework of this article is not such that we can pursue in depth the nature of learning that occurs in the acquisition of habits. We do this in a longer and more formal article now in progress (Suppes, Drolet and Bodapati 2005). Without going into detailed matters of learning, we do want to make more explicit in these final remarks the way in which we think habits replace the ordinary consideration of preferences and the maximization of expected utility. What we have to say is developed more thoroughly in Suppes (2001).

Habits constitute restraints, in the standard mathematical sense of constraints, on the choices we make. We do not consciously think of our habits in making choices, but concentrate, so far as we exercise conscious discrimination at all, in choosing one thing rather than another, in such a way as to satisfy the appropriate constraints. For example, Jones is at the stage of his life where he very much prefers wine to beer. At an ordinary dinner in a restaurant, faced with a menu, he only thinks about the choice of wine, and almost never considers beer. He doesn't go through any deliberate, rational analysis of the virtues of wine over beer, because of the constraint already established by long-settled habits. He accepts the constraint without even thinking or being conscious of it. He can, of course, at another time and for another purpose, make himself conscious of having this constraint. But the important point about habits is that in the act of choosing itself, we do not ordinarily pay conscious attention to the habits we have.

This is not to say that such conscious occasions can never occur. It is the stuff of family drama and the essence of many good novels for a person, real or fictitious, to face up to habits that must be broken, in order to make a choice that is much more important and meaningful to the person than any breaking of habits of old. But this is the exceptional situation—one that we can, of course, describe. Yet it is important to get the usual regime of choosing properly thought out. In fact, in the context of this article, we will not attempt to give a serious discussion of when we want to breach our constraints, that is, our habits, and go for something unusual, challenging or even frightening. This is an important topic, but one that can be left to the side, because of the low frequency of such choices, and the necessity of having a much better view of the usual kind of choices we make, from the dramatic ones of buying houses to the trivial ones of buying groceries.

So, we emphasize, the habits of a lifetime, as the saying goes, present constraints that are ordinarily satisfied. But the constraints do not fix the choice. Jones' strong constraint of always choosing wine, and never beer, does not in any way determine the particular choice of wine on a given occasion.

You may think that we are next going to say that we have come upon the proper role for maximization, namely, to maximize our choices subject to the constraints of habits. But we will not even accept the traditional theory of maximizing expected utility in this reduced role. To give you a sense of the organization of the ideas about rationality we are presenting, the next step after habits is to let the free associations of the moment make the choice as freely and as easily as possible. We won't say much about these associations here, but they are meant just to replace, not just maximization, but even Simon's (1955) satisficing of bounded rationality.

Let us be explicit about what we want to mean by *free associations*. We have in mind a hierarchical conception of how we make rational choices. To begin with, we must satisfy our habits. With satisfaction of the constraints given by habits we are then left with an unresolved set of choices. How should we choose from this set? The classical utilitarian method is by maximizing utility, but we have already expressed our skepticism about this classic theory. For us, the rational individual, who is choosing, is one who is freely associating and selecting that one of the available set that seems most attractive, because of the depth of past associations that are brought up, as can be the case in buying a house, or, in other instances, by the association to anticipated events. Often, a glimpse at something attractive nearby sets off the train of associations. Belief in the relatively high frequency of this last case is a fundamental tenet of advertising.

The immediate reaction of some readers may be to challenge this probabilistic mechanism of choice as normal. They may recall (perhaps we should say, *associate*) their earlier encounter with the literature of psychoanalysis and its emphasis on the central role of free association in interpreting dreams or analyzing repressions, slips of the tongue, and many other phenomena. But the central role of association in our mental life was not a

Freudian discovery. It goes back at least to Aristotle and was central to Hume's theory of human nature.

To make another point, we want to say something more explicit about what we mean by *free* associations, since the general theory of associations covers a large part of executing practical activities. In such activities the associations are not free, but strongly conditioned in a fixed sequence to accomplish the task at hand. As the standard phrase goes, they have become automatic. Free associations are of a different sort, weak rather than strong, used in search of memory, for example, but here just because the automatic method is not working. Free associations are more characteristic during moments of meditation or reverie, but also as unexpected intrusions of images unrelated to the task at hand, prompted by any of a great variety of possibilities.

The message we are trumpeting is that of learning to recognize the guidance and the help we can get from such associations, or perhaps even more, from those that do not rise to consciousness, but that are expressed in action by our actual choices. We often describe such choices as instinctual, as 'I like what I like and I can't say why', or as 'the one that seemed familiar but I can't explain why'. It is widely recognized that when such a response is given, it is artificial and inappropriate to insist on further explanation. It is a mark of the social habits Aristotle thought so important not to ask.

References

Aristotle 1941. *The Basic Works of Aristotle,* ed. R. McKeon, 397-98, 952-53. New York: Random House.

Aquinas, Saint Thomas. 1945. *Basic Writings of Saint Thomas Aquinas,* ed. A.C. Pegis, 399. Canada: Random House.

Blackburn, P. and Bos, J. 1999. *Representation and Inference for Natural Language: A First Course in Computational Semantics.* Stanford, CA: CSLI Publication.

Bettman, J.R., Luce, M.F. and Payne, J.W. 1998. Constructive Consumer Choice Processes. *Journal of Consumer Research* 25(4): 187-217.

Brown, S.C. and Craik, F.I.M. 2000. Encoding and Retrieval of Information. *The Oxford Handbook of Memory*, eds. E. Tulving and F.I.M. Craik, Ch. 6, 93-107. Oxford: Oxford University Press.

Burnyeat, M.F. 1999. Aristotle on Learning to Be Good. *Aristotle's Ethics*, ed. N. Sherman. New York: Rowman and Littlefield.

Doty, R.W. and Giurgea, C. 1961. *Brain Mechanisms and Learning.* International Symposium.

Durup, G., and Fessard, A. 1935. L'electroencephalogramme de l'homme. *Annual Psychology* 36: 266-81.

James, W. 1890/1950. *The Principles of Psychology*, Volume I. New York: Dover Publications, Inc.

Kahneman, D. and Tversky, A. 1979. Prospect Theory: An Analysis of Decision Under Risk. *Econometrica* 47: 263-91.

Kandel, E.R. 1985. Cellular Mechanisms of Learning and the Biological Basis of Individuality. *Principles of Neural Science*, eds. E.R. Kandel and J.H. Schwartz, 2nd edition. Elsevier: Amsterdam.

Lehman, F. 1992. Semantic Networks. *Semantics Networks in Artificial Intelligence*, ed. F. Lehman, 1-50. New York: Pergamon Press.

Miller, N.E. 1959. *Selected Papers*. Rockefeller University. Chicago: Aldine-Atherton Inc.

Newell, A. and Simon, H.A. 1961. Computer Simulation of Human Thinking. *Science* 134: 2011-17.

Rainey, H.J., Zuberbühler, K. and Slater, P.J.B. 2004. Hornbills Can Distinguish Between Primate Alarm Calls. *Proceedings of The Royal Society London B*, 271 (1540): 755-59.

Sheffield, F.D. and Roby, T.B. 1950. Reward Value of a Non-Nutritive Sweet Taste. *Journal of Comparative Physiology* 47: 471-81.

Sherman, N. 1999. The Fabric of Character. *Aristotle's Ethics*, ed. N. Sherman. New York: Rowman and Littlefield.

Simon, H. 1955. A Behavioral Theory of Rational Choice. *Quarterly Journal of Economics* 69: 99-118.

Simonson, I. and Tversky, A. 1992. Choice in Context: Tradeoff Contrast and Extremeness Aversion. *Journal of Marketing Research* 29: 281-95.

Suppes, P. 1969. Stimulus-Response Theory of Finite Automata. *Journal of Mathematical Psychology* 6: 327-55.

Suppes, P. 2001. Rationality, Habits and Freedom. *Cognitive Processes and Economic Behavior*. Proceedings of the Conference held at Certosa di Pontignano, Siena, Italy, July 3-8, 2001, eds. N. Dimitri, M. Basili and I. Gilboa, 137-67. New York: Routledge.

Suppes, P. Forthcoming. Where Do Bayesian Priors Come From? *Synthèse*.

Suppes, P. and J.-Y. Beziau. 2003. Semantic Computations of Truth, Based on Associations Already Learned. *Journal of Applied Logic* 2: 457-67.

Suppes, P., Drolet, A. and Bodapati, A. 2005. *A Theory of Choice, Normative and Descriptive, Based on Habits*. Working paper.

Tversky, A. and Kahneman, D. 1981. Judgment Under Uncertainty: Heuristics and Biases. *Science* 185: 1124-31.

Tversky, A., Sattath S., and Slovic, P. 1988. Contingent Weighting in Judgment and Choice. *Psychological Review* 95: 371-84.

2

Three Types of Decision Theory

NILS-ERIC SAHLIN AND NIKLAS VAREMAN[*]

1 Introduction

In his paper 'Truth and Probability' (1926) Ramsey laid the foundations of modern theory of subjective probability. He showed how, under ideal conditions, people's beliefs and desires can be measured with a betting method; and he demonstrated that if some intuitive principles of rational behavior are accepted, a measure of our 'degrees of belief' will satisfy the laws of probability. He was the first to state the Dutch book theorem, and he laid the foundations of modern utility theory and decision theory. In addition, he had a proof of the value of collecting evidence years before that became more widely known through the independent work of L.J. Savage and I.J. Good. He took higher order probabilities seriously; and in a derivation of the 'rule of succession' he introduced the notion of 'exchangeabilty' (without, however, giving it that name[1]).

The aim of 'Truth and Probability' is to analyze the connection between the subjective degree of belief we have in a proposition and the (subjective) probability it can be given, and to find a behavioral way of measuring degrees of belief. More precisely, Ramsey wants to show, first, that we can measure the degree of belief a subject has in a given proposition; and, second, that if the subject is rational, his or her degree of belief will have a measure satisfying the axioms of probability theory, a 'subjective' probability. Or, in other words, Ramsey shows that given his method of measuring

---

[*] The authors wish to thank Madison Williams, Christopher Pappas and Robin Stenwall for valuable comments.
[1] See Ramsey 1991 for a discussion.

strength of 'partial beliefs', the degrees of belief of a rational agent will obey the laws of probability.

Ramsey argues that people's beliefs and desires can be measured by a traditional betting method in which we measure a subject's belief simply by proposing a bet: we 'see what are the lowest odds which he will accept' (Ramsey 1990: 68). The strategy is to offer the agent a bet on the truth value of the proposition p involved in the belief. He took this method to be 'fundamentally sound', but argued that it nevertheless suffers from 'being insufficiently general, and from being necessarily inexact... partly because of the diminishing marginal utility of money, partly because the person may have a special eagerness or reluctance to bet...' (ibid.). If we ignore for a moment the problem of using sums of money as outcomes, a bet of this type is of the form: \$$x$ if p is true, \$$y$ if p is not true, when $x > y$. The traditional method now tells us that the agent's degree of belief in p is ($\$f - \$y$)/($\$x - \$y$), where $\$f$ is the greatest amount the agent is willing to pay for the bet. It should be noted that the smallest amount of money the agent is prepared to pay for the bet coincides with the smallest amount for which he will be willing to sell it. If the marginal utility of money is de-creasing, it is obvious that monetary outcomes will not give correct measures in cases of, for example, bets involving substantial sums of money. As Ramsey says, the method is sound, but not completely general and not very exact.

To have degree of belief ½ in an ethically neutral proposition is, according to Ramsey, to be indifferent to two options: a if p is true, b if p is not true; and b if p is true, a if p is not true ($a, b, c, ...$, denoting outcomes). 'This comes roughly to defining belief of degree ½ as such a degree of belief as leads to indifference between betting one way and betting the other for the same stakes' (ibid.: 74). An ethically neutral proposition of degree ½ comes close to something like the very idea of a fair coin.

This gives Ramsey an operational method, a way of measuring value differences. That the value difference between a and b is equal to the difference between c and d, simply means that if ep is an ethically neutral proposition believed to degree ½, the options [a if ep is true, and d if ep is not true] and [b if ep is true, and c if ep is not true] are equally preferable.

Ramsey then goes onto prove an important representation theorem. The theorem states that a subject's preferences can be represented by a utility function determined up to a positive linear transformation. It is the binary preferences that are represented, and the very goal of the theorem is to isolate the conditions under which such preferences can be seen as maximizing expected utility. The representation guarantees the existence of both a probability function and an unconditional utility function in such a way that the expected utility defined from this probability and utility represents the agent's preferences.[2]

Instead of a traditional betting method Ramsey can now use a refined betting method with differences in utilities rather than in money. In this way he can avoid some of the hitches with the traditional method – its being insufficiently general; necessarily inexact; distorted by the diminishing marginal utility of money; and vulnerable to problems relating to risk-aversion (risk-proneness). Thus, it should be remembered that it was in his efforts to avoid the difficulties he identified initially that he laid the foundations of the modern theory of utility.

It is then possible to define the degree of belief in p 'by the odds at which the subject would bet on p, the bet being conducted in terms of differences of value as defined' (ibid.: 76). If the subject is indifferent between a with certainty, and: b if p is true and c if p is not true (p not necessarily being an ethically neutral proposition, although p's truth cannot change the relative values of the outcomes), the subject's degree of belief in the proposition is defined as the difference in value between a and c divided by the difference in value between b and c. That is:

$P(p) = (u(a) - u(c)) / (u(b) - u(c))$,

where 'P(.)' denotes the subject's degree of belief function and 'u(.)' the subject's utility function. (However, it has not yet been shown that P(.) is a probability measure.) Ramsey also points out that the degree of belief in a proposition given another proposition can be defined along the same lines, using as lightly more complicated pair of bets.

Ramsey then proves that the obtained measure of degree of belief is a probability measure: it obeys the axioms of probability theory. The probability of any proposition is greater than or equal to 0; the probability of a proposition plus the probability of its negation equals 1; and, if two propositions are incompatible, the probability of the disjunction equals the sum of the probability of the disjuncts. Furthermore, Ramsey proves the Dutch book theorem: '[h]aving degrees of belief obeying the laws of probability

---

[2] Ramsey's utility theory is closely related to the theory developed by von Neumann and Morgenstern (1944) in *Theory of Games and Economic Behavior* about two decades later. Von Neumann and Morgenstern, however, assume 'objective' probabilities, prizes and lotteries in order to derive the utilities. Ramsey avoids these assumptions and thus avoids the need to postulate that subjects understand the information contained in a stated probability and that the probabilities are well-calibrated (i.e. that the subjective probabilities mirror the stated objective probabilities). Today it is well known that such a method does not work – that it does not avoid the type of problem Ramsey was aiming to sidestep. For example, robust empirical evidence shows that subjects have a tendency to overestimate very low (stated) 'objective' probabilities but underestimate all other probabilities – a type of behavior that will inevitably affect the measurement of utilities.

implies a further measure of consistency, namely such a consistency between the odds acceptable on different propositions as shall prevent a book being made against you' (ibid.: 79). Having degrees of belief obeying the axioms of probability, having a coherent set of beliefs, is simply a logically necessary and sufficient condition of avoiding a Dutch book. It should be noted that a subject can have more or less any degree of belief whatever in a proposition provided the set of beliefs to which it belongs is coherent (consistent). It is essentially this feature of Ramsey's theory that makes the theory subjectivist.

Ramsey was an open-minded subjectivist/Bayesian. He did not, for example, subscribe to de Finetti's dictum that objective 'probabilities do not exist'; rather he saw that some types of probability are a matter for physics and not logic. Ramsey would probably have argued that some probability assessments are not terrifically rational. If a subject has a degree of belief not reflecting the chances given by an accepted theory, then the subjective probabilities are clearly not well calibrated. Note that this suggests that two types of rationality need to be distinguished: external (how we relate to our surroundings) and internal (how our beliefs intertwine).

Ramsey's decision/probability theory is, then, close to being as complete as any such theory can be. He deals with, and provides answers to, the fundamental questions we have. But it is possible to cast doubt on the theory's assumptions; and the validity of its applicability can be questioned.

Ramsey's theory is descriptive rather than normative. Hence it is not the primary purpose of the theory to tell people what they ought to do (which is not to deny that the theory has normative ramifications.) It portrays the ideal decision-maker, and although it seems to raise a partly hidden *de dicto-de re problem*, the seriousness of this problem depends on what type of realist we are. To what extent does the theory tell us anything about human decision-making? Does it simply describe a surface phenomenon, failing to capture the underlying mechanisms of human decision-making? Are the concepts introduced appropriate for a theory of human decision-making? What type of character is Ramsey's ideal agent? From a psychological point of view the axioms he proposes are not entirely realistic.

Theories like Ramsey's and Savage's aim to represent a subject's state of belief with a unique probability measure, to any degree of precision. One class of examples shows that this aim leads to assumptions (axioms) that are far too strong.

Assume, for example, that the subject is offered two lotteries, and that the task is to choose the one considered most preferable. The first lottery gives 100 dollars if a white ball is drawn from an urn containing 30 white balls and 70 black balls; otherwise nothing. The second lottery gives 100 dollars if there is a transit strike in Verona, Italy, next week; otherwise nothing.

Assume that, after considering it carefully, the subject believes the probability that there will be a transit strike in Verona next week to be 0.30. Thus, provided dollars and utilities are exchangeable, the (subjective) expected utility of this lottery is 30 dollars. The second lottery has the same expected value as the first one. But although the two gambles have the same expected utility, the subject will trade the first gamble for the second. And this preference conflicts with the recommendations of the theories.

The subject prefers the first lottery to the second because he knows, or feels he knows, more about the urn than he does about Italian wages, working conditions and other factors that may provoke a transit strike in Verona. In some situations there are important differences in our knowledge of the various factors underlying our decisions, a difference in ignorance that cannot be mirrored by a unique probability measure.

The probabilities given by Ramsey's theory (and similar theories such as Savage's) are the result of the subject's inability to express fully his strength of preference. Ramsey's theory does not, however, take the second type of unreliability just indicated into account. The clarity of the subject's perception of uncertainty (in part caused by the quantity and quality of information he has) is not introduced.

Schervish, Seidenfeld and Kadane (1990) point to yet another problem for classical normative theories. They show that such theories, including those developed by Savage, von Neumann and Morgenstern, Anscombe and Aumann and de Finetti, all have a problem with state-dependent utilities. Theories using (horse) lotteries and prizes to derive probabilities cannot guarantee the existence of unique probabilities. The problem is that the utility of a prize is its utility given that a particular state of nature obtains. Even 'constant' prizes might have different values in different states of nature, and this means that the subject's preferences can be represented by far too many utility functions. As a consequence there is no unique subjective probability distribution over states of nature. Ramsey saw that his method of using preferences among bets to quantify value differences required the states defining the bets to be value-neutral. To this end, he proposed ethically neutral propositions. In his theory the outcomes have state-dependent utilities that can be measured through bets involving an ethically neutral proposition. The question, however, is whether we can understand and deploy the concept of an ethically neutral proposition without making use of lotteries. If we cannot, Ramsey's theory faces the same problems as the later theories with which it is associated.

In what follows we will discuss three types of decision theory – normative, descriptive and prescriptive. We shall use Ramsey's theory as a point of departure.

2 Normative Theories

In Book III of the *Topics* Aristotle hints at a logic of preference. He has two basic concepts. The concept of 'the worthier of choice', i.e. preferability, and its normative or ideal counterpart, the concept of 'better'. Unlike contemporary theorists, Aristotle works with two concepts of preferability. The first is situation-specific, the second absolute. He says, for example, '[s]ometimes better things are not also preferable; for it does not follow that, if they are better, they are also preferable' (118a8-10). To illustrate this he tells us that it is obviously better to be a philosopher than to make money, but that this is not preferable for a person 'who lacks the necessities of life'. To be a philosopher is better for a man, because it secures 'the actuality of a soul with respect to its function' (1098a16); it involves the consummation of his functions. This distinction is, no doubt, important if one wants to understand Aristotle's view on these matters. And it is also important in thinking about rational decision in general.

Throughout *Topics* Aristotle jumps back and forth between discussing material and formal principles. He says, for example, that 'to be a philosopher is better than to make money' (118a10-11), a perfectly sound material-principle. However, he also introduces formal principles such as: 'Also A is preferable to B, if A is an object of choice without B, while B is not an object of choice without A...' (118a20-22). In point of fact, this last principle – the Contraposition Principle – plays a central role in contemporary preference logic and decision theory. Other formal principles that Aristotle discusses include a substitutivity condition and a maxi-max principle.

What is interesting in this context is Aristotle's two perspectives. One reading is that he is dealing with two concepts of rationality: ideal rationality, expressed by the concept of better, and limited rationality, expressed by the concept of preferability, the notion that something is worthy of choice. But, if Aristotle's syllogisms are deductions rather than propositions, then his generic preference principles are no more than deduction patterns. The formalized syllogisms we find in Aristotle can be read as generalized material inferences. This hints at a distinction between norm and description (or perhaps norm and prescription): between 'better' and 'worthy of choice'.

A deeply entrenched misapprehension is that there is only one theory of rational decision-making – there is one and only one norm. And what people seem to have in mind when they refer to the norm is subjective expected utility theory; or, to be more precise, Savage's theory. This error has lead to endless and rather meaningless debates about rationality, to misinterpretations of empirical data, and to stagnation in the development of theory.

Ramsey's theory is not a normative theory; it is a narrative of an ideal agent. Nevertheless let us compare it with a couple of normative theories. After all, if we assume that the decisions of the ideal agent are the best that could be made, the normative interpretation of Ramsey is not so farfetched.

Ramsey's theory involves a set of eight axioms that can be divided into three groups depending on the job they do: behavioural, ontological and mathematical.[3] Behavioral axioms place restrictions on the agent's choices or preferences. For example, they require our preferences to be asymmetric and transitive. Ramsey's fourth axiom is a transitivity axiom which states that valued instances are transitive, and that in effect this is shown by transitive preferences among a set of games (involving an ethically neutral proposition such as a fair coin).

The ontological axioms tell us what the theory assumes exists. Ramsey's first axiom, for example, says that '[t]here is an ethically neutral proposition p believed to degree ½'. The ontological axioms of one theory can be rather different from the axioms of another theory. They may tell us, for example, that there are propositions of a kind, particulars we call events, what an act is, what we mean by an outcome or a state of affairs. These important axioms are not always fully spelt out.

The mathematical axioms are rather interesting. The general idea is that they are purely logical or mathematical, and that their sole function is to facilitate the derivation of desired representation theorems. Ramsey's list of axioms concludes with two mathematical axioms: a continuity axiom and an Archimedean axiom. Among other things these ensure that utilities are real numbers and not non-standard or p-adic numbers (which we could get if we 'reversed' the Archimedean axiom). Ramsey's sixth axiom – that '[a]ny progression has a limit (ordinal)' – and the proposition that the set of states is a Boolean algebra both seem to be mathematical axioms. But the well-known Archimedean axiom that if a is better than b, and b better than c, then the convex combination of a and c is better than b, for some weight between 0 and 1, and worse for some other probability, is not a purely structural axiom. It is an axiom tinted by independence, and it has clear behavioral consequences. Indeed there is a slippery slope between what we call structural axioms and ontological axioms.[4]

Ramsey thus sets up eight axioms that give us a utility function defined over consequences which is unique up to an affine transformation and a unique probability function. Savage, on the other hand, introduces seven

---

[3] See Suppes 1956 and Sahlin 1990.
[4] For a discussion of competing axiomatic systems, see Fishburn 1981.

axioms and shifts our focus from consequences and propositions to acts. Among his axioms is the now classic sure-thing principle. This says that the preference ordering on acts is independent of states that have identical consequences from two acts. If we add an independence axiom and a continuity axiom, it follows that there is a unique probability function defined over the set of states and a bounded utility function unique up to a positive affine transformation. Again, Jeffrey produces what has been called a mono-set theory in which propositions appear as primitives. The theory is, at one and the same time, both elegant and messy. The suggestion that we jettison the distinction between acts, states and outcomes, and assume instead that the agent orders complete packages, feels rather unintuitive. It also leads to complications. The representation theorems differ from those we are used to. We get conditional probabilities and the derived conditional expected utility function is unique up to a fractional linear transformation.

These three theories of rational decision-making are definitely not one and the same theory. The ontological assumptions are clearly different. The behavioral axioms are not identical. And they do not give identical representation theorems. But they are all theories of rational decision-making, and two of them are normally considered to be normative theories. What makes a normative theory normative?

The status of the axioms of classical logic has been discussed. Is it the fact that they are completely general, or is it rather their tautological character, that makes them axioms of logic or mathematics? Is it both of these features? We think of classical logic, first-order logic, as lying at the heart of logic because it has some attractive structural properties – for example, compactness, completeness and consistency. That is, classical logic is both simple and comprehensive. But what about the axioms of normative decision theory? The formalized syllogisms we find in Aristotle can be read as generalized material inferences. They are not all that different from some of the axioms of contemporary decision theory (whose contemporary counterparts are definitely not tautologies and have questionable generality). Transitivity and the Contraposition axiom are but two examples here.

We seem to regard a decision theory as normative in character when it has certain desired structural properties. First, the knowledge and beliefs of the decision-maker should be represented by a unique probability measure. Second, the decision-maker's preferences should be represented by a utility function (with some affinity), reflecting the costs and benefits of different outcomes. And, third, maximizing (conditional) subjective expected utility should be the decision maxim. This delivers benefits such as coherence and consistency (no Dutch books) and provides an argument for collecting evidence and updating beliefs according to basic principles. It also offers us a rather simple and comprehensive system that is suitable for mathematical treatment. In other words, we have some external, quasi-empirical reasons for preferring this set of structural properties.

3. Descriptive Theories

In the 1950s and early 1960s just a few devoted pioneers were doing empirical decision research. A few decades later, at the turn of the century, this field of research had become a scientific industry.

To begin with normative theories (including Ramsey's theory) were the source of inspiration. Are we rational? Do we follow the axioms and make decisions that accord with the decision maxims? It was found rather swiftly that we do not. Moreover, arguments for the ideal rarely convince those to whom they are put of the correctness and applicability of the theory. In fact arguments for the axioms seemed to have a direct and negative effect on 'rational' behavior.[5]

Daniel Kahneman and Amos Tversky have explored how people make decisions; and they have produced empirical evidence suggesting that people are not too impressive as decision-makers. We are 'irrational' in the sense that we do not follow the basic axioms and rules of traditional probability and decision theory. Their paper 'Prospect theory: An analysis of decisions under risk' (1979) is paradigmatic of contemporary descriptive research – a perfect case study.

Among psychologists (but also economists) expected utility theory is widely approved as *the* normative model of rational decision-making. The basic idea of expected utility theory is that two main types of factor determine our decisions: our *desires* and our *beliefs*. And that these determine the utilities and probabilities of the possible outcomes of our decisions, respectively. The expected utility theory provides us with a model showing how to handle our desires and beliefs, and an account of how these mental states combine in rational decisions. The fundamental decision rule of this model says that, in any given decision situation, we should choose the alternative with maximum expected utility (the principle of maximizing expected utility).

Psychologists have shown that there are several types of decision problem in which our preferences systematically violate the axioms of a generic expected utility theory. (This discovery appears to apply to the theories of Savage and Ramsey as well.) It has been argued, on the basis of this, that the theory offers an inadequate descriptive model of human decision behavior. Kahneman and Tversky suggest an alternative model: the Prospect Theory. What does this model tell us about human decision-making?

---

[5] See, for example, Slovic and Tversky 1974.

The *certainty effect* is one of the best-known violations of expected utility theory. In questionnaires used by Kahneman and Tversky subjects were asked to choose between:

	A:	2500 (Israeli pounds)	with probability .33
		2400	with probability .66
		0	with probability. 01
and	B:	2400 (Israeli pounds)	with certainty

Subjects also had to state a preference between:

	C:	2500	with probability .33
		0	with probability .67
and			
	D:	2400	with probability .34
		0	with probability .66

It was found that 82 per cent of the subjects preferred B to A, and that 83 per cent preferred C to D.

It is not too difficult (assuming that u(0 Israeli pounds) = 0, and that subjective probability assessments mirror stated probabilities) to see that these two choices, in combination, violate expected utility theory because together they imply a pair of incompatible utility inequalities. The pattern of preferences violates expected utility theory in a manner originally characterized by Maurice Allais.[6] It is the well-known sure-thing principle (or the 'independence' principle) that is put in question. This axiom asserts that if two alternatives have a common outcome for a particular state of nature, then the ordering of the alternatives should be independent of that outcome.

But what if gains are replaced by losses? Do we prefer a sure loss to a risk? Kahneman and Tversky found that when they switched to negative outcomes, a majority of their subjects preferred to gamble. Their results indicate that, when we reflect outcomes in 0, there is a *reflection effect* in which the preference order is reversed (at any rate, when all outcomes are negative or positive).

The third type of phenomenon reported by Kahneman and Tversky is that subjects dislike *probabilistic insurance*. The vast majority of their subjects preferred to pay the regular premium that eliminates all risks of loss rather than paying only half the premium so that 'there is a 50 per cent chance that you pay the other half of the premium and the insurance company covers all the losses; and there is a 50 per cent chance that you get

---

[6] See, for example, Allais 1979.

back your insurance payment and suffer all the losses' (Kahneman and Tversy 1979: 191).

This, and several similar results, indicates that probabilistic insurance is unattractive. But it is important to be aware that this type of preference *does not* violate expected utility theory. Expected utility theory does not say that probabilistic insurance is better than regular insurance. To demonstrate such superiority one would have to assume that the utility function is concave; and clearly this further assumption is empirical, not an axiom of the theory.

The same is true for the Allais-type of findings: these conflict with the utility theory only if we assume that the subject has the same utility function in the two choice situations. In the above-mentioned example of certainty effect, then, the conflict is neutralized if we assume that the subjects employ distinct utility functions in the two decision situations.

What Kahneman and Tversky call the *isolation effect* may, however, be inconsistent with expected utility theory, because 'a pair of prospects can be decomposed into common and distinctive components in more than one way, and different decompositions sometimes lead to different preferences' (ibid.: 192). In a multi-stage game, a game in which the first stage gives you nothing, or a new game, people tend to ignore the first stage of the game and concentrate on the outcomes, i.e. the final games. Thus they ignore the complete probability distribution. Presenting a multi-stage game in its normal form may therefore induce preference reversal of some sort. People's preferences may be altered not only by the representation of probabilities but also by the representation of outcomes.

The *Prospect Theory* is a two phase decision process: the decision problem is analyzed (this is the phase of prospect editing); then the decision alternatives are evaluated; then the alternative assigned the highest value is chosen.[7]

The expected utility theory tells us that our desires and our beliefs can be represented by a utility function u(.) and a probability function P(.), respectively; and that the decision-maker can compute the aggregated value of the various decision alternatives, i.e. their expected values (EU(a_i) = $P(s_1)u(o_{i1}) + \ldots + P(s_m)u(o_{im})$, where a_i, s_j, o_{ij} denote the action alternatives, the possible states, and the outcomes, respectively). The prospect theory, on the other hand, assumes the existence of two functions: the weighting function $\pi(.)$ and *the value function* $v(.)$. Jointly, these two functions give the value of an edited prospect.

---

[7] For the present discussion the editing phase is less important than the evaluation phase; let us so leave it for the time being. However, it should be remembered that the editing phase makes rather extensive psychological assumptions which, if they are not supported by a more general psychological theory, diminish the value of the Prospect Theory.

The weighting function π assigns a decision weight to the stated probabilities. It is not a subjective probability measure, nor is it a representation of a decision-maker's degree of belief. According to Kahneman and Tversky, decision weights 'measure the impact of events on the desirability of prospects, and not merely the perceived likelihood of these events' (ibid.: 203).

The experimental results give the weighting function a number of interesting properties. Small probabilities are over-weighted, i.e. $\pi(p) > p$. For small stated probabilities $\pi(.)$ is a sub-additive function of p, i.e. $\pi(rp) < r\pi(p)$. Moreover π is characterized by sub-certainty, since $\pi(p) + \pi(1 - p) < 1$, for all stated probabilities between 0 and 1 ($\pi(0) = 0$ and $\pi(1) = 1$). And π also has the property of sub-proportionality, i.e. for a fixed ratio of stated probabilities, the ratio of the matched decision weights is closer to unity when the probabilities are low than it is when they are high.

Given their descriptive aims, Kahneman and Tversky are able to ignore several problems connected with the requirement of logical coherence for normative or prescriptive theories. The problems connected with decision weights have been discussed by Bengt Hansson (1975), who discards the idea. Apart from the more or less obvious objection that arbitrary ways of splitting up outcomes may influence the decision unduly, there is a more profound result. The weight functions with a shape permitting them to explain archetypical psychological facts about people's perception of probabilities will also attach less weight to the expected value of a probability than the expected value of the weight of the probability, thereby implying behaviour that is the reverse of that found in Ellsberg-like cases.[8]

The traditional utility function is an assignment of value to outcomes or final states. The value function of Prospect Theory differs from this in that it assigns values, not to final states, but to changes in wealth or welfare – an assignment harmonizing well with the principles of perception and judgment. From this perspective, the adaptation level, reference point or level of aspiration become important bases for evaluation.

Besides this very important characteristic of the value function, the experimental findings indicate that the function should be generally concave

---

[8] That is, cases focusing on our beliefs rather than our preferences. In Ellsberg's example we imagine an urn containing 90 balls. In all, 30 are red and 60 are black or yellow, the latter colors in unknown proportion. One ball is to be drawn at random from the urn. There are two pairs of choice. First, a choice between A and B. A gives $100 if a red ball is drawn, nothing if a black or yellow ball is drawn. B gives the same amount of money if a black ball is drawn, nothing if a red or yellow ball is drawn. Second, a choice between C and D. C is identical to A and D is identical to B, but with an important difference: the drawing of a yellow ball gives $100. It is well-known that people prefer A to B and D to C, violating Savage's sure-thing principle.

for gains and convex for losses, and steeper for losses than for gains. This means that the experimental results are best characterized by an S-shaped value function (both for gains and for losses).

Note that when we define the value function in terms of deviations from the reference point, the prospect theory acquires properties which the utility theory lacks. But the same effect can be secured within the framework of expected utility theory if one makes the reasonable assumption that our utility function is context dependent. Furthermore, since expected utility theory conveys no information at all about the actual shape of an individual's utility function, the addition of such additional assumptions to the theory will significantly augment its explanatory power.

Does this type of research allow us to understand the psychological mechanisms of human decision-making? Does it indicate whether and how to replace or amend the theories used to predict the results of the experiments? We think not – at least, not in the way intended by those conducting the experiments. What this case study *does* show is that there is limited value in 'testing' a normative theory. These theories are not models of human decision-making. Ramsey's theory, for example, describes an ideal agent – i.e. portrays rational decision-making. In 'Truth and Probability' he says: 'I have not worked out the mathematical logic of this in detail, because this would, I think, be rather like working out to seven places of decimals a result only valid to one. My logic cannot be regarded as giving more than the sort of way it might work' (Ramsey 1990: 180). Reflection tells us that, as we are human beings, mathematical and structural axioms are not for us. Continuity axioms and Archimedean axioms are for those with far greater computational capacities. In Isaac Levi words, they are for 'rational an-gels' (Levi 1975:15). The ontological axioms structure the world in an ideal way; they formulate a playground beyond our ken. In any case, what reason do we have to assume that the rationality axioms – static as they are, and lacking both dynamic and evolutionary content – can be used to model human decision-making?[9]

Thus the discovery that expected utility theory lacks descriptive value has little value when it comes to developing a theory of human decision-making. The 'falsification' of expected utility theory does not help us towards a descriptive theory of analytical power and empirical resilience.

From a psychological perspective it is rather pointless to construct a descriptive theory by revising the concepts of a normative theory. The move from probability measures to weighting functions, and from utility measures

---

[9] According to Weirich 2004, Eells (in Eells 1994) sees static rationality as the kind presented in normative decision theory where only the agent's current cognitive resources are taken into account. Dynamic rationality, on the other hand, takes the agent's history into account.

to value functions, does not add a great deal of explanatory power to our descriptive theory. The explanation is still presented only at the level of separating beliefs and values, and of 'maximization of expected utility'.

To obtain real understanding of human decision-making epistemological and ontological assumptions are required. We need to say what a belief (a value or an expectation) is. To this end, theoretical concepts have to be introduced and linked together, resulting in explicit ontological commitments. What we lack is theories which, among other things, tell us what we can expect to exist and how these things are linked together. That is, we need to rethink the ontological basis of our descriptive decision models. We also require an understanding of how this rethinking will affect the experimental research currently being undertaken.

There is also a tendency to attach too much weight to mathematical descriptions. If these are competing descriptions, not *de re*, but merely *de dicto*, we are spending our time arguing about mathematical techniques rather than trying to understand human decision-making.

Finally, the case study illustrates something that is well-known: namely, that inductive methods do not deliver an *understanding* of, for example, human decision-making. The 'why?' here is left unanswered. What, however, inductive research can provide, and indeed has provided, is very good predictive models. The important question 'what?' can be given a limited answer. Thus, assuming that our descriptive aim is prediction and forecasting rather than understanding and explanation, empirical decision research will have value – as long, at any rate, as it can be used to predict human decision-making in real life situations.

It is far easier to grumble than to be constructive. What alternatives have we here? Not all empirical research on human decision-making is, or has been, of this kind. But normative theories have had, and continue to have, an unduly negative an effect on the development of descriptive theories of human decision-making. However, recently psychologists and other scientists have looked for new strategies, new models and new tools and techniques. Let us just mention one alternative strategy. Some psychologists are trying to use and develop so-called narrative methods.[10] Such methods have obvious drawbacks when compared with normative decision theories: notably, not being mathematical, they lack the systematic simplicity that is one of the most appealing properties of those theories. But they have the advantage of being, as it were, on their way to being a descriptive theory. If we want to understand why people take the decisions they take, and why we dread the risks we dread, we have to obtain a detailed understanding of the decision-maker's values, beliefs and expectations; we have to look at real-

---

[10] See Finucane and Satterfield 2005.

life situations. And narrative methods offer one way to do this. We are aware of the limitations of this type of research strategy. It cannot provide a miraculous remedy, and we need to be aware of the 'side-effects' or 'boundary-conditions'. However, the strategy allows us to cut away from the ballast of normativity.

4. Prescriptive Theories

Theories of decision-making can, as we have seen, meet rather different objectives. Some help to explain what a rational decision is (these are of interest mainly to philosophers). Others are designed more to predict decisions (economists). Yet others seek to find ways to counsel people to make better decisions (decision analysts). How the theory looks will depend on what one's interests are. A crude partition of the theories would of course be that philosophers formulate normative theories, economists formulate descriptive theories and decision analysts formulate prescriptive theories. This taxonomy may well be accurate, but we will see that among prescriptive theories there is also a partitioning.

When we ask what kinds of theory have been dubbed 'prescriptive decision theory' or 'prescriptive decision model' we see that initially the labels 'normative' and 'prescriptive' were more or less interchangeable. In the words of the statisticians French and Rios Insua (2000): '[u]ntil 10 or 15 years ago, "prescriptive" was generally used as a synonym for "normative".' (French and Rios Insua 2000: 5).

Kadane and Larkey (1983) distinguish two kinds of normative theory: '*Speculative* statements are non operational usually consisting of a goal or criterion (e.g., maximize utility or profit) with no precise instructions on how one might accomplish the goal or apply the criterion. *Prescriptions* are operational in that they give both a goal (or criterion) and feasible procedures (an algorithm) for accomplishing it' (Kadane and Larkey 1983: 1366). It seems the latter, operational feature was once attributed to the classical normative theories. A theory such as Savage's, which states that the rational agent maximizes utility and also tells us to separate beliefs from values and then compute expected utility, would qualify as a prescriptive theory in this sense, we may suppose.

However, according to French and Rios Insua, for more than 10 years now 'prescriptive' has involved something more than simply an operational normativity. Prescriptivity, in this new sense, is described in Bell, Raiffa and Tversky (1988): 'Loosely speaking, prescriptive analyses exploit some of the logical consequences of the normative theories and the empirical findings of the descriptive studies but, in addition, something else has to be added that is far from the spirit of normative or descriptive analyses' (Bell, Raiffa and Tversky 1988: 9).

The behavioral axioms of normative decision theories mirror (supposedly) fundamental intuitions about what our cognitive abilities would ideally be. To construe these theories as descriptive of human decision-making is to assume that our cognitive abilities really are those envisaged in the theory. Experimental findings that show where, in ordinary life, people violate the axioms are then naturally interpreted as the results of tests falsifying the theory. A new theory is then formulated. But as we have seen in the previous two sections, this path is by no means the most sensible one to take if our aim is to formulate a descriptive theory of human decision-making.

Another way to react to the experiments is to view them simply as tests of us rather than tests of the theory. When we violate the axioms, it is not the theory that is to blame. Instead the violation shows that we are irrational. And this should be handled not by constructing a new theory, but rather by finding ways to ensure that we are more rational – that is, ways to make our behavior accord more closely with the theory.[11] Proponents of this interpretation of the experiments, have objectives that are more pedagogical than theoretical. A prescriptive theory is, according to French and Rios Insua (2000), '[...] the application of normative ideas, mindful of the findings of descriptive decision studies, to guide real decision-making. Prescriptive analyses use normative models to guide the evolution of [the decision-maker's] perceptions in the direction of an ideal consistency, to which they aspire, recognizing the limitations of their actual cognitive processes' French and Rios Insua 2000: 5). This kind of theory can be dubbed, we think, 'Aristotelian prescriptivity'. Remember that Aristotle separates the absolute notion of 'better' and the situation- specific 'worthy of choice'. It seems, then, that while there is always a 'best' decision to be made, circumstance usually forces us to choose what is merely 'worthy of choice'. Given this, a theory of what is worthy of choice would, it seems, issue in recommendations that are consistent with our aim to do what is 'best'.

French and Rios Insua are not really describing a kind of theory. They are offering thoughts on how to present a given normative theory in such a way that decision-makers make their decisions in a manner they really aspire to do (assuming that there is 'an ideal consistency, to which they aspire'), much as an Aristotelian agent aspires to do what is 'best'. So Aristotelian prescriptivity presupposes an underlying normative theory; it is not a substitute for one. It seems the pedagogical element is what Bell, Raiffa and Tversky mean to indicate when they refer to the element of prescriptivity

---

[11] A whole industry of decision counseling and Multi Criteria Decision Analysis exemplifies the point in question: see French and Rios Insua 2000.

that is 'far from the spirit of normative or descriptive analyses' (Bell, Raiffa and Tversky 1988: 9).

But there is also, as is usually the case, a middle way. Here the experiments function as a kind of alarm bell telling us where to re-examine the axioms of the normative theory. They do not, as descriptive theorists would have it, automatically show that the theory should be altered. Neither do they leave the axioms intact without further inquiry – the view of Aristotelian prescriptivity theorists. Rather they tell us to examine the experimental results and the axioms in order to find which has the most leverage. Suppose that, in an experiment, we make choices that fail to accord with the theory, but on finding out what the theory tells us to choose we change our minds. So far, this would not give us reason to question the axioms of the theory. If, on the other hand, we persist in our choices even though we know they go against the theory, the axioms will have to be questioned (see Sahlin 1988).

This is a common problem in the analysis of normative concepts in general – a problem Rawls dealt with by stating that we should arrive at a reflective equilibrium between general principles and particular instances. In the context of rational decision-making we have, as general principles, the rationality axioms. These are justified by extrapolation from the features of a reasonable person. The particular instances should be individual decisions made by reasonable persons. The dynamics of the reflective equilibrium go something like this: starting from the general principles it is possible to deduce particular cases. If these cases conflict with actual cases it has to be decided whether the set of general principles should be altered or, perhaps, whether it can be shown that the actual case does not fall under the concept. Where the actual case is paradigmatic, the set of general principles has to be altered in some way. Where the actual case is not paradigmatic, our intuitions about what falls under the concept should perhaps be altered. And of course it may be possible to alter both the set of general principles and one's intuitions about extension of the concept.

Prescriptive theories viewed as theories of rational decision-making can therefore be construed as embodying a kind of reflective equilibrium between normative theories and descriptive ones. A recent example of such an attempt is Paul Weirich (2004). Weirich explicitly wants to find a reflective equilibrium between the general principles and the particular instances of a decision; the full title of his book is *Realistic Decision Theory: Rules for Nonideal Agents in Nonideal Circumstances*. The thought is that in any situation there is a rational decision to be made, i.e. an 'optimal' decision conditioned by our cognitive limitations and the complexity of the world around us. But, as Weirich himself acknowledges, his theory, having normative intent, does not come all the way to formulating non-ideal rules. Nevertheless he places himself very close to the descriptive end of the possible spectrum of theories. Our intuition is that rules formulated for an agent with all the cognitive limitations we possess will lack prescriptive value.

Weirich is interesting because he concentrates on the way in which the agent and the decision situation are to be characterized within a theory instead of on the decisions made by the agent in the decision situation. There are two ways to violate the axioms of normative decision theory. One is an *agent-centered way*. Here the agent violates the axioms because she is not cognitively equipped in the way the ideal agent is (i.e. does not know all logical consequences of her beliefs, lacks a simple ordering of preferences etc). This is the kind of violation Weirich tries to handle. But there is also a decision-centered way in which the axioms can be violated. Here it is discovered that most reasonable persons choose in ways that are in conflict with the way in which the ideal agent would choose. Of course, this means that if these violations are to be taken into account, some axioms of the theory will have to be altered. But they do not necessarily have to be altered the way Weirich has it – something that removes all idealizations of the theory. They just have to be altered in a way that makes the decisions 'come out right'. One characterization of this decision-centered view is that a prescriptive theory, with its underlying intent to provide us with a basis for sound behaviour, should be tested against *both* our intuitive understanding of what a sound decision is *and* what we actually do.

The decision-centered perspective then gives another meaning of 'prescriptive theory' in the framework of reflective equilibrium. This is that a prescriptive theory is simply one in which one or more axioms of normative theories are violated. As Ellsberg discovered, normative theories cannot effectively handle cases intermediate between decisions under risk and decisions under uncertainty (Ellsberg 1961). So, he concluded, normative theories are applicable in the areas in which they work; when they do not work, some theory violating one or more of the axioms of the normative theory may be appropriate. But if we allow that normative theories have limited scope and let prescriptive theories be defined simply by the fact that some axiom of a normative theory is violated, we open up a plethora of theories to be chosen from in a given decision situation. The relevant axioms here are behavioral in character. But even among these, perhaps no violation is acceptable. Some of these axioms may be such that their violation is always regarded as wrong, or irrational, even if empirical evidence shows that we actually do violate them. One such axiom, we believe, is the transitivity of preferences.[12] If we find ourselves in a situation where we have intransitive preferences, and if this cannot be explained away as a peculiarity of the situation,[13] we will try to change preferences so as to make them transitive.

Other axioms are less obviously important. We seem to be able to violate Savage's sure-thing principle without being accused of outright irrationality. So, some axioms seem to be more open to criticism by our intuitions than others. There are criteria governing when to abandon an axiom due to experimental findings describing our actual behavior. The evidence should be empirically and theoretically robust.

Robust empirical evidence has the following features. First, it is capable of comprehension. The subject should have a clear understanding of the task they are performing. Second, it is stable. The empirical results must not be due simply to the subject's inability to handle and process vast amounts of information. Third, there must be no alternative explanations. A simple shift of perspective (within a theoretical framework) should not make it possible to explain (away) the empirical results. Robust theoretical arguments, by contrast, have the following three characteristics. First, in them, the counter-arguments should not be such that they can, without much effort, be accommodated by the theory, given some reasonable auxiliary assumptions. Second, the arguments should 'prove' to us that one or other axiom of the theory is not as we first thought it was. Third, we want our arguments to point towards a new axiom, a new theory, which has the same analytic power (and empirical resilience) as the one being replaced (see Sahlin 1988).

It is clear that the paradoxes introduced by Allais and Ellsberg both give results satisfying all these criteria; but Aristotle's observations, like many other empirical results, do not do so.

Although the criteria determining the evidence that counts against axioms limit the number of possible prescriptive theories, they do not yield a unique theory. There can still be several theories, and these need not give the same advice in a given decision situation. Luce and von Winterfeldt have attempted to determine which axioms of some generic normative theory can most reasonably be given up and which axioms of Prospect Theory are most reasonable to keep in a prescriptive theory, so that we obtain, supposedly, the most reasonable prescriptive theory (Luce and von Winterfeldt

---

[12] More descriptively oriented theorists would choose to abandon the axiom: see, for instance, Tversky 1969.

[13] Imagine, for instance, that in the morning you prefer tea to ice cream to wine while in the afternoon you prefer ice cream to wine to tea and at dinner time wine to tea to ice cream. If the decision problem is formulated so that the time of day is not relevant, intransitive preferences can be exhibited.

1994). Perhaps we can find the most reasonable axioms *qua* axioms, but it is far from obvious that these axioms will yield the most reasonable *decisions* in specific situations – that is, will yield decisions we intuitively judge to be reasonable. This is reminiscent of cases in which there are several, quite different reactions to experimental findings. There, one can concentrate either on the reasonableness of the axioms, taking the experimental results to have no thing to do with the theory, or on the reasonableness of the actual decisions, arguing that the experiments have everything to do with the theory; or one can place oneself in the middle. Luce and von Winterfeldt concentrate on the axioms. They try to identify those that are most reasonable in the light of experiments. It turns out they give up the event monotonicity of normative theories and accept the duplex decomposition of Prospect Theory. This in turn yields a prescriptive theory which tells us what to do in a given context.[14] It is not directly evaluated in reference to what decisions it recommends.

An alternative to this approach would be to formulate a number of theories which violate different axioms of normative theories, and to treat, as most reasonable, the one that yields decisions most often in accord with our intuitions.

A third maneuver – a middle way – would perhaps be to accept a number of theories that violate some axiom of normative theory, and to determine which one is most reasonable in a given situation by analyzing their context and content. This would introduce a pluralist view of prescriptivity. An example of this is the theories of Levi (1980), Gärdenfors and Sahlin (1983) and Kyburg (1983). These theories can be shown to give different advice on what option to choose in certain decision problems. They involve different axioms (and have different decision maxims). Consequently, they recommend contrasting options (Gärdenfors and Sahlin 1988; Sahlin 1985).

How do we choose among these theories, then? Well, any violation of an axiom involves departure from the ideal, but the different theories will differ from the ideal in different ways. Just as we did earlier, we can here evaluate the theories either internally or externally. Internally, there could be an ordering of axioms by indispensability, depending on context. So in some contexts it is perhaps preferable to violate independence, while in others some other violation would be more attractive. Externally, we look instead at the decisions being made and see whether one or other theory gives,

---

[14] Prospect Theory values out comes in relation to a status quo instead of final wealth, and this is context dependent. The introduction of context dependence need not be the major alteration of normative theories Luce and Winterfeldt claim, since it is also possible to have different utilities for final wealth in different contexts. The abandonment of event monotonicity also leads to problems other than those discussed in Luce and Winterfeldt 1994: see Seidenfeld 1988.

in a given context, more reasonable recommendations than the others. Most probably, the internal evaluation is contingent on the external; whether we accept an axiom's violation or not, in a given context, is likely to be dependent on the decisions that are recommended in that context. But how do we identify the more reasonable recommendation? Circularity lurks here. We may need a normative meta-theory.

5 Rundown

We have briefly looked at how decision theory developed in the twentieth century, and at how different types of theory grow out of an ideal. We have also looked at some of the pros and cons of normative, descriptive and prescriptive theories. What lessons can be learned from these surveys?

One insight, we believe, is that if we are to obtain a true, descriptive theory of human decision-making – a theory, that is to say, which tell us what we do and why we do it – we will have to develop a theory that enjoys a certain autonomy vis-à-vis normative theories. We need theories incorporating concepts and laws that are independent of the idea of a norm and the notion of an ideal agent. We need theories which can be used to describe phenomena outside the psychology classroom, and explanations that are sound in evolutionary terms.

Another insight is that prescriptive theories cannot really be developed without an ideal, without a norm; but that, equally, it is far from clear what that norm is and thus how the tools should be devised. Are the prescriptive theories best viewed as evolving normative theories in the way the analogy with reflective equilibrium suggests? Or are they quite distinct from normative theories and such as to require an external norm? In addressing these issues it will be helpful, we think, to examine the feasibility of pluralist views of prescriptivity.

References

Anscombe, F.J. and Aumann, R.J. 1963. A Definition of Subjective Probability. *The Annals of Mathematical Statistics* 34(1): 199-20

Bell D.E., Raiffa H. and Tversky A. 1988. Descriptive, normative and prescriptive interactions in decision making. *Decision Making: Descriptive, Normative and Prescriptive Interactions.* eds. D.E. Bell, H. Raiffa and A. Tversky, 9-30. Cambridge: Cambridge University Press.

Allais, M. 1979. The so-called Allais Paradox and Rational Decision Under Uncertainty. *Expected Utility Hypotheses and the Allais Paradox*, ed. M. Allais and O. Hagen, 437-663. Dordrecht: Reidel.

Eells E. 1994. Bayesian Epistemology: Probabilistic Confirmation and Rational Decision. *Proto Soziologie* 6: 38-60.

Ellsberg, D. 1961. Risk, Ambiguity, and the Savage Axioms. *Quarterly Journal of Economics* 75: 643-69.

Finucane, M.L. and Satterfield, T. 2005. Risk as Narrative Values: A Theoretical Framework for Facilitating the Biotechnology Debate. *International Journal of Biotechnology* 7: 128-46.

Fishburn, P.C. 1981. Subjective Expected Utility: A Review of Normative Theories. *Theory and Decision* 13: 139-99.

French, S. and Rios Insua D. 2000. *Statistical Decision Theory*. London: Arnold.

Gärdenfors, P. and Sahlin, N.-E. 1983. Decision making with unreliable probabilities. *The British Journal of Mathematical and Statistical Psychology* 36: 240-51.

Gärdenfors, P. and Sahlin, N.-E. eds. 1988. *Decision, Probability, and Utility: Selected Readings*. Cambridge: Cambridge University Press.

Hansson, B. 1975. The Appropriateness of the Expected Utility Model. *Erkenntnis* 9: 175-93.

Hansson, B. 1988. Risk Aversion as a Problem of Conjoint Measurement. *Decision, Probability, and Utility: Selected Readings*, eds. P. Gärdenfors and N.-E. Sahlin, 136-58. Cambridge: Cambridge University Press.

Jeffrey, R.C. 1965. *The Logic of Decision*. New York: McGraw-Hill. 2nd revised edition 1983. Chicago: University of Chicago Press.

Kadane, J.B. and Larkey, P.D. 1983. The Confusion of Is and Ought in Game Theoretic Con-texts. *Management Science* 29: 1365-79.

Kahneman, D. and Tversky, A. 1979. Prospect theory: An Analysis of Decision under Risk. *Econometrica* 47: 263-91.

Kyburg, H. 1983. Rational Belief. *The Behavioral and Brain Sciences*, 6: 231-73.

Levi, I. 1980. *The Enterprise of Knowledge*. Cambridge, MA: The MIT Press.

Levi, I. 1997. *The Covenant of Reason*. Cambridge: Cambridge University Press.

Luce, D. and von Winterfeldt, D. 1994. What Common Ground Exists for Descriptive, Prescriptive, and Normative Utility Theories? *Management Science* 40: 263-79.

Ramsey, F.P. 1990. *Philosophical Papers*, ed. D.H. Mellor. Cambridge: Cambridge University Press.

Ramsey, F.P. 1991. *Notes on Philosophy, Probability and Mathematic*, ed. M.C. Galavotti. Napoli: Bibliopolis.

Sahlin, N.-E. 1985. Three Decision Rules for Generalized Probability Representation. *The Behavioral and Brain Sciences* 8: 751-53.

Sahlin, N.-E. 1988. The Significance of Empirical Evidence for Developments in the Foundations of Decision Theory. *Theory and Experiment*, eds. D. Batens and J.P. van Bendegem, 103-21. Dordrecht: Reidel.

Sahlin, N.-E. 1990. *The Philosophy of F.P. Ramsey*. Cambridge: Cambridge University Press.

Sahlin, N.-E. 1991. Baconian Inductivism in Research on Human Decision Making. *Theory & Psychology* 1: 431-50.

Sahlin, N.-E. 1993. Worthy of choice. *Theoria* 59: 178-91.

Savage, L.J. 1972. *The Foundations of Statistics*, London: Dover (1st edition, 1954, New York: Wiley).

Schervish, M., Seidenfeld T. and Kadane, J.B. 1990. State-dependent Utilities, *Journal of the American Statistical Association* 85: 840-47.

Seidenfeld, T. 1988. Decision Theory without Independence or without Ordering, what is the Difference? *Economics and Philosophy* 4: 267-315.

Slovic, P. and Tversky, A. 1974. Who Accepts Savage's Axiom? *Behavioral Science* 19: 368-73.

Suppes, P. 1956. The Role of Subjective Probability and Utility in Decision-making. *Proceedings from 3rd Berkeley Symposium on Mathematics, Statistics and Probability*, ed. J. Neyman, 61-73. Berkeley: University of California Press.

Tversky, A. 1969. Intransitivity of Preference. *Psychological Review*, 76: 31-48.

von Neumann, J. and Morgenstern, O. 1944. *Theory of Games and Economic Behavior*. Princeton: Princeton University Press.

Weirich, P. 2004. *Realistic Decision Theory: Rules for Nonideal Agents in Nonideal Circumstances*. New York: Oxford University Press.

3

Welfare, Voting and the Constitution of a Federal Assembly
Luc Bovens and Stephan Hartmann

This paper starts from the consideration that equal and proportional representation are two poles of a continuum of models of representation for the assembly of a federation of states. The choice of a model has repercussions on the welfare distribution in the federation. We determine, first by means of Monte Carlo simulations, what welfare distributions result after assemblies that were constituted on the basis of different models of representation have considered a large number of motions. We assess what model of representation is favored by a Rawlsian maximin measure and by the utilitarian measure and present matching analytical results for the utilitarian measure in a slightly idealized case. Our results show that degressive proportionality can be justified as a compromise between maximin and utilitarian considerations. There is little surprise in this result. What is more surprising, however, is that, within certain contexts of evaluation, degressive proportionality can also be justified on strictly utilitarian grounds.

1 Introduction

A federal assembly consists of a number of representatives for each of the nations (states, *Länder*, cantons) that make up the federation. In determining the constitution of such an assembly there is the following tension. On the one hand, we may think of the federation as a federation of nation states. This would support a model of equal representation, that is, a model in which each nation has the same number of representatives. On the other hand, we may think of the federation as a federation of people. This would support a model of proportional representation, that is a model in which the number of representatives for each nation is proportional to the number of its inhabitants. But presumably that is not the only motivation. What makes this issue worth quibbling about is that the model of representation that is introduced will have an impact on the welfare distribution over the nations in the federation that will ensue over due course. Welfare distributions can be evaluated in terms of various measures that correspond to different conceptions of justice. We will investigate which models of representation yield welfare distributions that score higher on the Rawlsian maximin measure and on the utilitarian measure. First, we construct a continuum of models of representation ranging from equal to proportional representation. In between these two extremes, we may identify models of *degressive proportionality*. On such models, the larger nations receive more representatives, but less than would be warranted by proportionality, whereas the smaller nations receive less representatives, but more than would be warranted by proportionality. We take the European Union as a paradigm case of a federation. We run a Monte-Carlo simulation in which a large number of motions are voted up or down within varying contexts of evaluation and investigate how well the resulting welfare distributions score on the Rawlsian maximin and on the utilitarian measures. Simulation results give us more leeway in specifying values for the parameters in the model, but they do not provide complete insight in the functional dependences of the measures on these parameters. We will provide analytical results for the utilitarian measure for a slightly idealized case.

Our study deals with a question in voting theory and theories of justice that has direct relevance for today's political world. With the increase in autonomous nation states across the world comes the need to design institutions for transnational political structures that are responsive to given conceptions of justice. With the projected extension of the European Union, there has been much discussion about how the various nations should be represented in the Council of the European Union. The Swedish proposal was for the number of representatives to be proportional to the square root of the population. This is a model of degressive proportionality. The French president responded that he failed to see *what was politically significant about the square root*. The question is of course what justification can be advanced for models of degressive proportionality. We will show that degressive proportionality can be justified as a compromise between maximin and utilitarian considerations. There is little surprise in this result. What is more surprising, however, is that, within certain contexts of evaluation, it can also be justified on strictly utilitarian grounds. We end with some suggestions about how our model could be made operational for empirical work.

2 The Federation, its Constituent Nations and Models of Representation

Let there be a federation that has a total population of S individuals. It is divided into N nations, some of which larger, some of which smaller. Each nation i has a population size s_i. The federal assembly is the decision-making organ for the federation. Our model can be readily generalized, but just to have some definite numbers, we will run our simulations with the actual population sizes of the European Union (see Table 1) and with the actual number of representatives in the Council of the European Union.

Austria	7.9	.0214
Belgium	10	.0271
Denmark	5.2	.0141
Finland	5	.0136
France	57.2	.1550
Germany	81.2	.2201
Greece	10.2	.0276
Ireland	3.5	.0095
Italy	57.8	.1566
Luxembourg	.3897	.0011
Netherlands	15.1	.0409
Portugal	9.8	.0266
Spain	39.1	.1060
Sweden	8.8	.0238
UK	57.6	.1561
Total	369	1

Table 1: Population sizes in Millions (Second Column) and Population Proportions (Third Column) of the Constituent Nations of the EU

To represent the continuum between equal representation and proportional representation in the assembly, we construct the following measure, which determines the proportion of representatives of nation i in the assembly:

$$r_i(\alpha) = \frac{x_i^\alpha}{\sum_{i=1}^{N} x_i^\alpha} \quad \text{for } x_i = s_i/S \text{ and } \alpha \in [0, 1] \tag{1}$$

where α is a measure of the degree of proportionality. If $r_i(0) = 1/N$, there is equal representation in the assembly. If $r_i(1) = x_i$, there is proportional representation in the assembly.[1] Intermediate values of α stand for models of representation of degressive proportionality that are located on the continuum between the two extremes. For example, $\alpha = \frac{1}{2}$ corresponds to the Swedish proposal. Obviously,

$$\sum_{i=1}^{N} x_i = 1 \text{ and } \sum_{i=1}^{N} r_i(\alpha) = 1 \text{ for any value of } \alpha.$$

How can we turn ratios of representatives into actual whole numbers of representatives for assemblies of particular sizes? This is a complex question in voting theory, but for our purposes the following simple system suffices. There are currently $N = 15$ nations in the European Union and $T = 87$ representatives in the Council of the European Union. To determine the number of representative for each nation i we multiply T with the ratio $r_i(\alpha)$. We assign, in a first step, $[r_i(\alpha)T]$—i.e. the whole number smaller than or equal to $r_i(\alpha)T$—representatives to each nation i. The number of remaining seats is

$$k(\alpha) = T - \sum_{i=1}^{N} [r_i(\alpha)T].$$

Clearly $k(\alpha) < N$. These $k(\alpha)$ seats are distributed as follows. We order the nations according to the relative sizes of the decimal parts $r_i(\alpha)T - [r_i(\alpha)T]$, going from larger to smaller. We now assign to each of the first $k(\alpha)$ nations in this ordering precisely one additional seat. Let $R_i(\alpha)$ be the number of seats that each nation i receives in the assembly on the proportionality measure α.

3 Voting on Motions

A motion affects the people of the respective nations in different ways. A motion to improve the defense of the federation may benefit each nation to the same extent. But a motion to improve the highway system in some nation on the periphery of the federation does little more than benefit the nation in question, while it constitutes a cost to the other nations. A motion can be thought of as a utility vector $<v_1, ..., v_i, ..., v_N>$ in which each v_i represents the expected utility that the motion will bring to an arbitrary person of nation i if the motion were adopted.

---

[1] When $\alpha > 1$, then the larger nations will get a disproportionately larger representation and the smaller nations a disproportionately smaller representation in the federal assembly. We will restrict α to the closed interval $[0,1]$, but our model can be readily extended to such models of representation.

There is a certain threshold value of utility so that all the representatives of a nation will vote in favor of the motion if the utility that this motion will bring to the nation in question exceeds the threshold value. They vote against the motion if the utility drops below the threshold value. They will abstain if the utility equals the threshold value. Let us say that the threshold value is the point at which the costs balance out against the benefits for the nation of question. Costs and benefits should be understood broadly. They may also reflect feelings of altruism between the nations in question.

David Hume (1888 [1739]: Book III, Part II, Section II) notoriously believed that questions of justice only arise if we can expect moderate selfishness (and not benevolence or extreme selfishness) and in times of relative scarcity (and not in times of extreme scarcity or abundance). We will not follow Hume's contention as to when questions of justice arise, but his taxonomy comes in handy in distinguishing between alternative *contexts of evaluation*:

(i) *Benevolence and Abundance*. In times of economic prosperity, or amongst nations that genuinely care about the well being of the other nations, the benefits that nations receive when a motion is adopted tend to outweigh the costs more often than not. There is money enough to go around so that costs matter minimally and there is a positive disposition towards political initiatives in general so that each nation's utility from a motion receives an added bonus. To model this situation, we let the utility values in the vector that represents a motion be random numbers generated under a uniform distribution over the range $[-.5, 1]$ and we set the threshold value for acceptance at $v_t = 0$. Hence, the chance that an arbitrary nation will vote for a motion is 2/3. As a mnemonic aid, let us name this the context of *generous* voters.

(ii) *Extreme Scarcity and Extreme Selfishness*. In times of economic recession, or amongst nations that are strictly concerned with their own welfare, the costs of a motion tend to outweigh the benefits more often than not. The nations are wary of expenditures and they only benefit from the implementation of motions in support of projects that directly affect their own welfare. We let the utility values be random numbers generated under a uniform distribution over the range $[-1, .5]$ with $vt = 0$. Hence, the chance that an arbitrary nation will vote for some motion is 1/3. This is the context of *stingy* voters.

(iii) *Moderate Selfishness and Relative Scarcity*. This context is intermediate between the previous two poles of the continuum. We let the utility values be random numbers generated under a uniform distribution over the range $[-1,1]$ with $v_t = 0$. The chance that an arbitrary nation will support a motion is 1/2. This is the context of *balanced* voters.

Some observations are in order. First, in our model, the utility values are independent of each other. Alternatively, one could model, say, these contexts by stipulating different degrees of dependency between the utility values in a motion. Positive dependencies hold between nations that are in a close bond with one another. Or it may also be the case that the nations are sensitive to the common good of the federation. An extreme case would be the one in which all nations would receive the same utility value from all motions. We will address the challenge of modeling dependencies in Section 6. Second, we chose uniform distributions. But the distributions do not need to be uniform. Our analytical results will show that the utilitarian measure remains invariant under an alternative choice of distribution as long as we keep constant a limited set of parameters that characterize the distribution. Third, we vary the range of the utility values and keep the threshold values fixed. Alternatively, one could keep the range fixed and change the threshold value, but this does not make any difference to our results.

4 Evaluating Models of Representation

Models of representation in a federal assembly are social arrangements. Each value of α constitutes an alternative social arrangement. We start with the model of equal representation ($\alpha = 0$) and increase the value of α with increments of $\Delta\alpha$ (which we set in our computer simulation at .01) until we reach the model of proportional representation ($\alpha = 1$). We consider m motions for some sufficiently[2] large m, say $m = 10,000$, in our calculations. That is, we generate m n-dimensional vectors $<v_1^k, ..., v_i^k, ..., v_N^k>$ for $k = 1,..., m$ with random numbers in the ranges that correspond to the respective contexts of evaluation. For each motion, a vote is taken by an assembly whose constitution is based on a particular value of α. The representatives of a nation i will all vote for a given motion if v_i^k exceeds the threshold value v_t which we take to be the same for all nations; they will all vote against the motion if v_i^k is lower than v_t; and they will abstain if v_i^k equals v_t. If the motion k is accepted, each nation i is assigned a utility value v_i^k. If the motion is not accepted, each nation remains unaffected by the motion. After the m motions have all been considered, we divide the sum of the utilities that each nation has accrued by m: the resulting vector $u(\alpha) = <u_1(\alpha), ..., u_i(\alpha), ..., u_N(\alpha)>$ contains the utilities $u_i(\alpha)$ that a person in nation i can expect from a motion, given a particular model of representation represented by a specific value of the parameter α. At the end of this process we have a vector of utility distributions associated with the values of α, viz. $<u(0), u(\alpha), u(2\alpha),..., u(1)>$, or, more specifically, in our computer simulation, $<u(0), u(.01), u(.02), ..., u(1)>$.

---

[2] 'Sufficiently' means that higher values of m do not change our results.

In formal terms, $u_i(\alpha)$ is constructed as follows. Let the function[3] $g(y)$ equal 1 if $y > 0$ and 0 if $y \leq 0$ and let $sign(y)$ be the standard function in mathematics which equals 1 if $y > 0$, 0 if $y = 0$, and -1 if $y < 0$. The *decision function* $D_k(\alpha)$ yields 1 if the majority supports motion k and 0 if the majority does not support such a motion:

$$D_k(\alpha) = g\left(\sum_{i=1}^{N} R_i(\alpha) \ sign \ (v_i^k)\right) \qquad (2)$$

We can now express $u_i(\alpha)$, i.e. the expected utility of a motion for nation i, as the sum of the utilities that a nation i receives from accepted motions over the numbers of motions considered:

$$u_i(\alpha) = \frac{1}{m}\sum_{k=1}^{m} v_i^k D_k(\alpha) \ i = 1, ..., N. \qquad (3)$$

Following Harsanyi (1976), the model of representation α that is supported by utilitarianism is the model that maximizes expected utility. Hence, the measure that is to be maximized is the sum of the component utility values $u_i(\alpha)$ in the utility vector $u(\alpha)$ weighted by the respective population proportions x_i:

$$M^{util}[u(\alpha)] = \sum_{i=1}^{N} x_i u_i(\alpha) \qquad (4)$$

The model of representation α that maximizes this measure is the social arrangement that is supported by the utilitarian conception of justice.

Following Rawls's difference principle (or rather, the difference principle substituting utilities for primary goods) the distribution which maximizes the minimum expected utility $u_i(\alpha)$ of a person in nation i is the fairer distribution (1971: 125f.). The measure to be maximized is the minimum utility value in $u(\alpha)$:

$$M^{min}[u(\alpha)] = Min(u_i(\alpha)) \text{ with } i \in \{1,...,N\}. \qquad (5)$$

The model of representation α that maximizes this measure is the social arrangement that is supported by the Rawlsian conception of justice.

---

[3] g is similar to the Heaviside function, except that the Heaviside function is undefined for 0.

5 A Justification for Degressive Proportionality

Figure 1 presents the graph of the Rawlsian measure for the context of *balanced* voters. This measure supports a model of representation in the neighborhood of equal representation. It behaves in a similar manner for *generous* and *stingy* voters as for *balanced* voters except that the values of the measure are lower for *stingy* voters and higher for *generous* voters (graphs omitted). Figure 2 presents the graph of the utilitarian measure for the context of *balanced* voters. This measure supports a model of proportional representation within a context of *balanced* voters. But surprisingly, Figures 3 and 4 show that, in contexts of *stingy* and of *generous* voters, the utilitarian measure supports a degressively proportional model of representation.

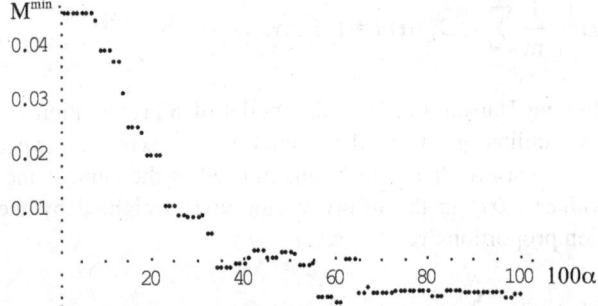

Figure 1: The Rawlsian Measure for *Balanced* Voters for Europe and 87 Representatives

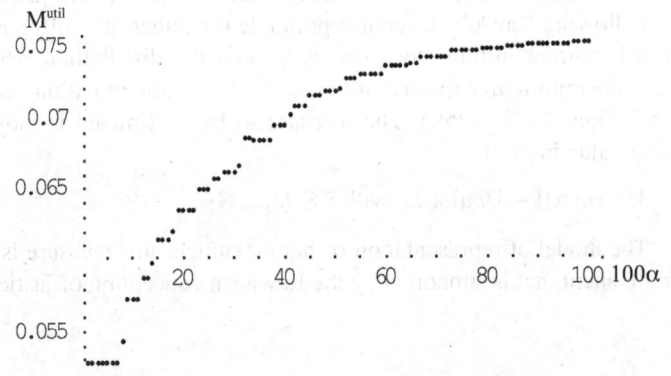

Figure 2: The Utilitarian Measure for *Balanced* Voters for Europe and 87 Representatives

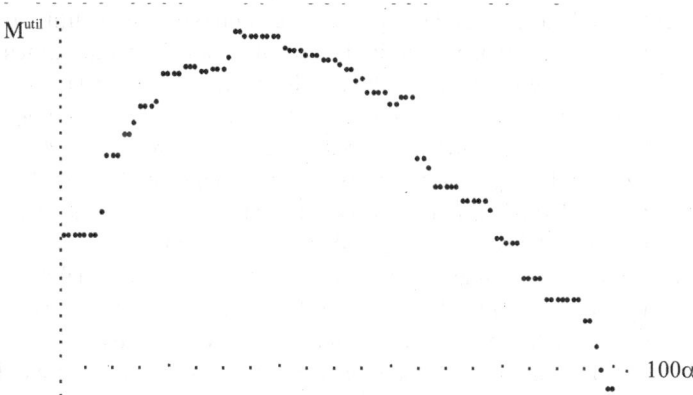

Figure 3: The Utilitarian Measure for *Generous* Voters for Europe and 87 Representatives

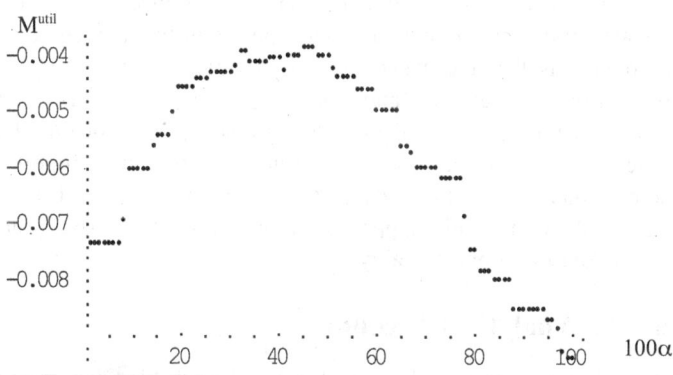

Figure 4: The Utilitarian Measure for *Stingy* Voters for Europe and 87 Representatives

There are two good reasons why one might favor some degressively proportional model on welfarist grounds. One might defend a welfare distribution that combines utilitarian with Rawlsian considerations. Independently of the context of voting, striking a balance between these considerations favors a degressively proportional model of representation. This is not unsurprising. The Rawlsian measure is motivated by certain egalitarian concerns. One can only move away from an egalitarian welfare distribution if it is the case that introducing some inequality does not make anyone worse off. If all the nations have an equal input in the vote, then the inhabitants of all nations can be expected to end up with equal utility. But if larger nations have a greater input in the vote than smaller nations, then larger nations will outvote smaller nations. The welfare levels of larger nations will gain as a consequence, whereas smaller nations will be outvoted and their welfare levels will suffer as a consequence. So the inequality that is introduced by allotting larger nations a greater input in the vote does make inhabitants of smaller nations worse off, which is not tolerated by a Rawlsian conception of justice. On the other hand, this inequality will be less of a concern for the utilitarian, since the chance of being an inhabitant of a larger nation is greater than the chance of being an inhabitant of a smaller nation. Thus, inequality may actually increase expected utility, which entails that there is nothing objectionable for the utilitarian in introducing at least some proportionality into the constitution of the assembly. To conclude, if we want to strike a balance between Rawlsian and utilitarian considerations, one may reasonably expect that some model of degressive proportionality will be favored.

But how much proportionality can we introduce into the constitution of the assembly and still maintain that expected utility is likely to rise? What *is* surprising is that the answer to this question depends on the context of evaluation. For *generous* and *stingy* voters, expected utility is at its maximum when there is some degree of degressive proportionality. For *balanced* voters, expected utility is maximum in the case of full proportionality. Assuming that a context of *balanced* voters is not the norm, it turns out that a strict utilitarian should support some model of degressive proportionality, rather than full proportionality.

6 An Analytical Account

We will derive analytical results for the more striking results of our simulation, that s, for the behavior of the utilitarian measure.[4] The measure M^{util} is an expectation, viz. the expected utility $E[U]$ from an arbitrary motion. We shall compute this expectation by conditioning on the propositional variables A and C. The variable A equals A when the motion is accepted and $\neg A$ when the motion is not accepted. To define the variable C, construct all the combinations of i nations voting for the motion and $N - i$ nations voting against it. From combinatorial analysis, we know that there are

$$\sum_{i=0}^{N} \binom{N}{i} = 2^N$$

---

[4] The analytical work in this section can be directly extended to the Rawlsian measure as well.

such combinations. The variable C equals C_1 when all the nations vote for the motion, C_2 when all nations except N vote for the motion, ..., and C_2^N when all nations vote against the motions. By probability calculus,

$$E[U] = \sum_{A=A,\neg A} \sum_{C=C_1,...,C_{2^N}} E[U|A, C]P(A, C). \tag{6}$$

Notice that $E[U|\neg A, C]$ equals 0 for any values of C, since the expected utility of a rejected motion is 0. Furthermore, by the chain rule, $P(A, C) = P(A|C)P(C)$. Hence,

$$E[U] = \sum_{C=C_1,...,C_{2^N}} E[U|A, C]P(A|C)P(C). \tag{7}$$

In Table 2 we illustrate this calculation for a federation of two nations named '1' and '2'. Each row lists the factors within each term of the sum in (7). First, let u^+ be the utility that a nation derives from an accepted motion assuming that they voted for the motion. u^+ equals 1/2 for *generous* and *balanced* voters and 1/4 for *stingy* voters. Let u^- be the utility that a nation derives from an accepted motion assuming that they voted against the motion. u^- equals –1/2 for *generous* and *balanced* voters, and –1/4 for *stingy* voters. On row 2 of the table, nation 1 voted for and nation 2 voted against. Hence, assuming that the motion is accepted, the expected utility from this motion is the sum of the u^+ and u^-, weighted by the population proportions of the respective nations. Second, the chance that the motion will be accepted depends on the proportion of the representatives in the assembly. The function $g(y)$ is defined as before, i.e. it equals 1 if $y > 0$ and 0 if $y \leq 0$. The chance that a motion is accepted equals 1 if a majority supports the motion, i.e. if $R_1 - R_2 > 0$, and equals 0 if the majority does not support the motion, i.e. if $R_1 - R_2 \leq 0$. Note that the values of R_i are a function of x_i and α for $i = 1, 2$. Third, let p be the chance that an arbitrary nation will vote for a motion. We have seen above that p equals 1/2 for *balanced* voters, 2/3 for *generous* voters and 1/3 for *stingy* voters. On row 2, the chance that the particular combination of nation 1 voting for and nation 2 voting against the motion equals $p(1-p)$. In the last column we show the product of these factors on each row, while on the last row we show the sum of these products.

	1	2	$E[U\|A, C_i]$	$P(A\|C_i)$	$P(C_i)$	Π
C_1	+	+	$u^+x_1 + u^+x_2$	$g(R_1 + R_2)$	p^2	
C_2	+	−	$u^+x_1 + u^-x_2$	$g(R_1 - R_2)$	$p(1-p)$	
C_3	−	+	$u^-x_1 + u^+x_2$	$g(-R_1 + R_2)$	$(1-p)p$	
C_4	−	−	$u^-x_1 + u^-x_2$	$g(-R_1 - R_2)$	$(1-p)^2$	
						Σ

Table 2: Construction of the Function $E[U]$ in Equation (7)

The computational time in constructing a plot for $\alpha \in [0, 1]$ can be substantially reduced by assuming that the assembly has an infinite number of members, so that we can actually conduct a vote by means of the ratios $r_i(\alpha)$. This may seem unrealistic, but the fact of the matter is that such an assumption makes very little difference as long as the assembly is sufficiently large. We calculate $E[U]$ for *stingy*, *generous* and *balanced* voters in the European Union for ($\alpha \in [0, 1]$) and plot these functions in Figures 5, 6 and 7.[5] Note that the function is smoother, i.e. less of a sequence of step functions, than the simulation results in Figures 2, 3 and 4 would suggest. This is because the steps come about due to the relatively small size of the Council of the European Union. In Figure 8 we have simulated the utilitarian measure for the European Parliament with 626 representatives. Notice how this function virtually coincides with the function that is represented in Figure 5. This function is calculated with proportions of representatives, which is tantamount to calculating the function for an assembly with an infinite number of representatives.

It is worth noting that the function $E[U]$ is fully determined by the parameters u^+, u^- and p for a particular federation. In our simulation we specified a uniform distribution for v_i for $i = 1,..., N$. But the only features of this distribution that are relevant are the probability p that an arbitrary nation will accept a motion, the expected utility u^- of an accepted motion for a nation that voted against the motion and the expected utility u^+ of an accepted motion for a nation that voted against the motion. As long as we keep these

---

[5] The reader will notice that the function $E[U]$ for *generous* voters equals the function $E[U]$ for *stingy* voters plus 1/4. This can be proven to be the case by replacing the function $g(y)$ by the Heaviside function and by appealing to the integral representation of the Heaviside function, which is a common technique in mathematical physics. (Proof omitted.) However, unlike the g function used in (2), the Heaviside function is not defined for 0, i.e. when the numbers of votes for the motion equals the numbers of votes against the motion. The theorem does not hold for instance when $\alpha = 0$ and there is an equal number of nations, since in this case it may be the case that the number of representatives voting for the motion equals the number of representatives voting against the motion.

parameters fixed, the particular shape of the distribution is of no consequence for the quantities of interest in this paper.

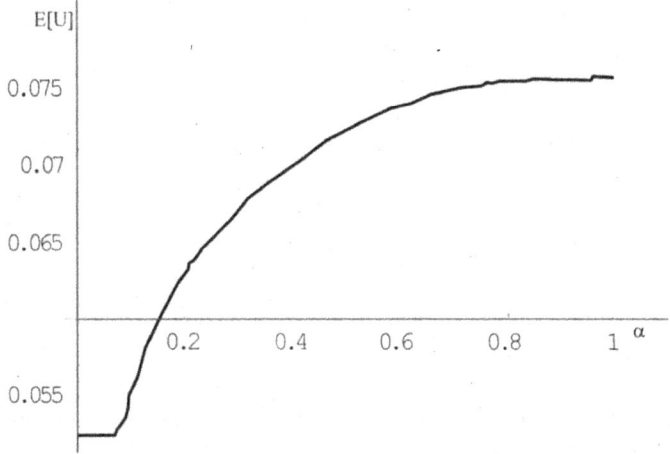

Fig. 5: The function E[U] for *Balanced* Voters for Europe and an Infinite Number of Representatives

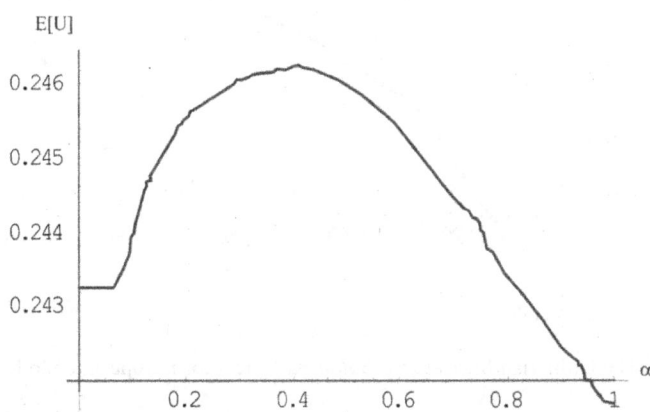

Fig. 6: The function E[U] for *Generous* Voters for Europe and an Infinite Number of Representatives

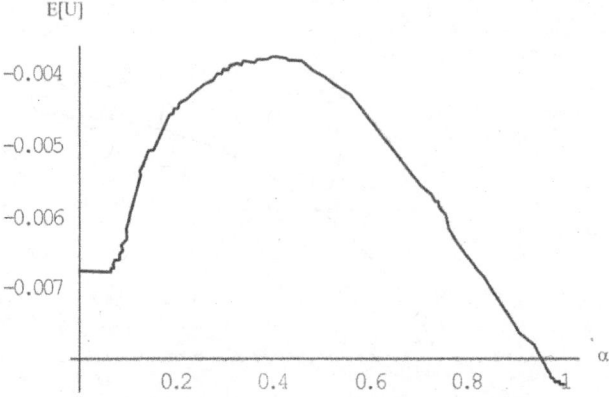

Fig. 7: The function E[U] for *Stingy* Voters for Europe and an Infinite Number of Representatives

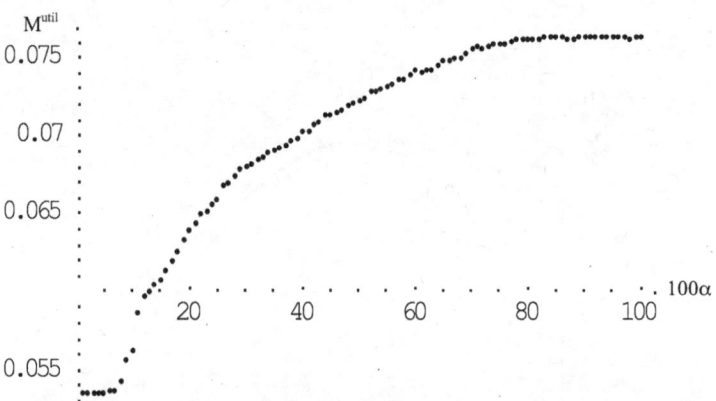

Fig. 8: The Utilitarian Measure for *Balanced* Voters for Europe and 626 Representatives

We can also explain why the function $M^{util}[u(\alpha)]$ remains constant for low values of α within each context. The value of $M^{util}[u(\alpha)]$ is determined by the values of x_i and the values of R_i for $i = 1,..., N$ nations assuming a particular context of evaluation. For a given federation the values of x_i are fixed. The values of R_i are determined by the values of x_i and α. Set the value of α at 0. As we increase the value of α nothing will happen to $U(\alpha)$

unless there is some change in one of the g functions. Let's return to the European Union with $N = 15$ as an example. When α equals 0 then the 8 smallest nations can outvote the 7 largest nations, since they have a majority of representatives. The lowest value of α for which a change occurs in one of the g functions is when there is sufficient degressive proportionality so that the 8 smallest nations can no longer outvote the 7 largest nations. Order the nations according to size so that (1) refers to the smallest nation and (15) to the largest nation in the European Union. When $\alpha = 0$, then $g(R_{(1)} + \ldots + R_{(8)} - R_{(9)} - \ldots - R_{(15)}) = 1$. But as we allow for more proportionality in the system, i.e. as we increase the value of α, then $g(R_{(1)} + \ldots + R_{(8)} - R_{(9)} - \ldots - R_{(15)})$ will eventually flip to 0. For what value of α does this change occur? The change in the g function occurs precisely when $R_{(1)} + \ldots + R_{(8)}$ no longer exceeds $R_{(9)} + \ldots + R_{(15)}$. If the number of representatives is infinite, then R_i equals r_i and this condition is equivalent to the condition that

$$x^\alpha_{\pi(1)} + \ldots + x^\alpha_{\pi(8)}$$

no longer exceeds

$$x^\alpha_{\pi(9)} + \ldots + x^\alpha_{\pi(15)}.$$

To find this value we solve the following equation for α:

$$x^\alpha_{\pi(1)} + \ldots + x^\alpha_{\pi(8)} = x^\alpha_{\pi(9)} + \ldots + x^\alpha_{\pi(15)}. \tag{7}$$

With the proportional population sizes for the European Union this yields $\alpha \approx .065$. And indeed the function $M^{util}[u(\alpha)]$ is constant roughly over the interval $[0, .065]$ in Figures 1 through 8. (For finite numbers of representatives, the value .065 is only an approximation and this approximation is the more accurate, the greater the number of representatives.) There are also other less perspicuous plateaus in the curve representing function $M^{util}[u(\alpha)]$, which are due to various combinations of possible coalitions.

7 Further Questions

We have made the simplifying assumption that the utility levels of the various nations for any given motion are independent and identically distributed variables, that the distribution in question is uniform, and that the threshold level for voting for a particular motion is kept constant across all nations. To give empirical content to this study in institutional design, many of these assumptions will need to be relaxed. In particular, the assumption of independence may need to be dropped: it may well be the case that a number of nations have common interests – for example, motions dealing with agriculture will often elicit strongly correlated utility levels for Mediterranean nations in the EU. The assumption of identical distribution may have to be relaxed: some nations tend to benefit more while others benefit less from motions that affect the whole federation. Also the assumption of uniformity may need to be relaxed. For it may well be the case that benefits and cost are less weighty for some nations, so that a normal distribution with mean at the threshold value and a fairly low standard deviation is more characteristic. Finally, the assumption of a constant threshold level may need to be dropped. Certain nations may, for example, be more picky and only vote for a motion if they stand to benefit substantially. It is easy to build any of these adjustments into the code of the simulation. The easiest way to do so is to generate random numbers for the utility values of the nations under a multivariate normal distribution. We can set different bounds and different means for each nation, increase or decrease the variance as we want the distribution to be more or less uniform for some nation, and specify covariance measures that express a commonality of interests between the nations. Of course, to construct a multivariate normal that characterizes the impact of different motions on the welfare of nations in the federation would be a serious empirical challenge. But to substitute this multivariate normal in our simulation is straightforward.

An alternative to degressive proportionality is to demand that the motion be approved both by an assembly with proportional representation and by an assembly with equal representation. In the United States, the House of Representatives and the Senate approximates this model. Or one may obtain similar results by demanding from a single assembly that the votes of the representatives reflect the majority of the population in the federation as well as the majority of the nations. It is an open question whether there exists a model of regressive proportionality that yields values on the Rawlsian maximin measure and the utilitarian measure with a single majority vote that are Pareto optimal relative to the values on a double majority vote. Is the answer to this question stable across different contexts of evaluations? Is it stable when we relax the assumptions in various ways? These are some of the questions for future research.

References

Harsanyi, J. 1976. *Essays on Ethics, Social Behavior and Scientific Explanation*. Dordrecht: Reidel.

Hume, D. 1888 [1739]. *A Treatise of Human Nature*. Oxford: Clarendon Press.

Rawls, J. 1971. *A Theory of Justice*. Cambridge, MA: Harvard University Press.

4

Acting Rationally with Irrational Strategies. Applications of the Parrondo Effect
DAVID ATKINSON AND JEANNE PEIJNENBURG

When the Parrondo effect was discovered a few years ago (Harmer and Abbott 1999a, 1999b), it was hailed as a possible mechanism whereby, in a kind of collaboration of failure, losing strategies could be combined to yield profit. The precise relevance of the Parrondo effect to natural and social phenomena is however still unclear. In this paper we give specific examples, first in the artificial setting of a gambling machine, and then in more natural applications to genetics and to environmental policies. This last example touches questions of rational behavior and expected utility in a novel setting.

1 Introduction

Ever since it was formulated, the rationality ideal of the *homo economicus* has been subjected to criticism. Psychologists have argued that individual agents do not, and in fact should not, rigorously maximize expected utility; and sociologists have claimed that the same goes for groups of agents. Many have stressed the important role of intuition and of uncertainty in decision-making, and in the wake of Herbert Simon it has been argued that our actions are, and should be, aimed at 'satisficing' rather than maximizing (Simon 1957).

The main point of all these criticisms was clear enough: true rationality is richer than the anemic model presented by Economic Man. But whereas the model was generally deemed too simple and too unrealistic, closer to the *modus operandi* of a robot than to that of a living being of flesh and blood, none of the critics contested its clarity and transparency. In fact, however, the model has a strange and obscure feature. This feature was first formulated in 1999 in a different context (namely information theory) and it is known as the Parrondo effect, after its discoverer, the Spanish physicist Juan Parrondo. Briefly, the Parrondo effect – some speak of the 'Parrondo paradox' – consists in the fact that two losing strategies can, under certain special conditions, be combined counterintuitively to yield success. In such special cases it might be rational, according to the standards of Economic Man, to combine two clearly irrational strategies.

In most of the formulations of the Parrondo effect, the mechanism is capital dependent, the outcome being a function of the player's current capital. While this property seems natural enough in a gambling casino, it is not very appealing in other applications. This shortcoming has however been alleviated by the introduction of games that are not capital dependent, but rather history dependent. In these games, the next move depends (deterministically or probabilistically) on the previous two (Parrondo, Harmer and Abbott 2000; Iyengar and Kohli 2004; Harmer, Abbott and Parrondo 2005). In this paper we shall give examples of this history dependent scheme, first in the artificial setting of a gambling machine (Sect. 2), and then in more interesting applications to genetics (Sect. 3) and environmental policies (Sect. 4).

The purpose of our examples is to show, in not wholly unrealistic situations, how the Parrondo effect could function. We do not arrogate to ourselves the expertise necessary for the true specification of the circumstances and parameters relevant to an empirical example, this being properly the purview of the scientific specialist. Nor do we argue that the Parrondo effect is omnipresent in nature or in society. Nevertheless it can and presumably does occur, and while the scenarios sketched below are fanciful, it is hoped that they carry the germ of a structure that is viable in the hurly-burly of the field and laboratory.

2 Crazy Horse Saloon

In the Crazy Horse Saloon there are two one-arm bandits (fruit machines) that the customers call Buffalo Bill and Calamity Jane. The rules are simple, as befits the Wild West. You put one dollar into the slot of one of the machines and pull the arm. If you win, you get two dollars back, but if you lose, you get nothing.

Gambling with Buffalo Bill generally leads to loss: on average, for every 9 pulls only 4 are wins, yielding $8, a net loss of $1. Calamity Jane is even more of a swindler, for very few pulls give wins and, in the long run, almost all the stake is lost. Nevertheless a gambler who emulates the ambidextrous Jesse James and pulls randomly, sometimes on Buffalo Bill and sometimes on Calamity Jane, wins in the long run. On average, for every 9 pulls there are 6 wins and 3 losses, yielding $12, a net gain of $3.

How is this possible? How can random switching between two losing strategies result in a long term win? The secret of the one-arm bandits is that they give varying odds, depending on the results of the previous two pulls. After two successive losses (*LL*), Buffalo Bill always concedes a win (*LLW*), but after a loss and a win (*LW*), it always gives a loss (*LWL*). On the other hand after a win, followed either by a loss or a win, (*WL*) or (*WW*), the next pull results in a win 75% of the time, (*WLW*) or (*WWW*). Summarizing,

Buffalo Bill
(*LL*) leads to (*LLW*) and (*LW*) leads to (*LWL*) 100%
(*WL*) leads to (*WLW*) and (*WW*) leads to (*WWW*) 75%

In effect, in the cases (*WL*) or (*WW*), a computer simulates the throwing of a biased coin that, when tossed, yields a head (win) three quarters of the time. In the same vein, case (*LL*) corresponds to the simulated tossing of a coin with two heads, case (*LW*) to the simulated tossing of a coin with two tails.

The other one-armed bandit, Calamity Jane, works in a similar way, the only difference being that the two-headed and the two-tailed coins exchange their roles. That is, in the case (*LL*) the next pull always gives a loss, and in the case (*LW*) the next pull always gives a win. Summarizing,

Calamity Jane
(*LL*) leads to (*LLL*) and (*LW*) leads to (*LWW*) 100%
(*WL*) leads to (*WLW*) and (*WW*) leads to (*WWW*) 75%

It is easy to see why Calamity Jane is such an unfavorable machine, for eventually two losses will occur in a row, and then all subsequent pulls result in loss.

What are the odds when a gambler switches randomly from one machine to the other? It is understood that both one-armed bandits are run by the same computer, so that when the gambler changes from one machine to the other, the information about the results of the previous two pulls, (*LL*), (*LW*),(*WL*), (*WW*), is not lost. The 75% probability of a win in the latter two cases is unchanged. After two losses, (*LL*), since on average Buffalo Bill is used for half of the time and Calamity Jane for the other half of the time, in one half of the cases there is a win, and in one half there is a loss. Thus the probability of a win is 50%. Similarly, after a loss and a win (*LW*), since Buffalo Bill yields a loss and Calamity Jane a gain, the probability of a win is also 50%. In summary, the result of an even-handed use of both one-armed bandits is as follows:

Jesse James
(*LL*) leads to (*LLW*) and (*LW*) leads to (*LWW*) 50%

(WL) leads to (WLW)	and	(WW) leads to (WWW)	75%

In effect, random switching between the machines amounts to the simulated tossing of a fair coin in the cases (LL) and (LW). It is therefore clear why Jesse James is a winning strategy, for the simulation is equivalent to using sometimes a fair coin and sometimes a coin that is biased towards a win.

Figure 1 is a plot between P_{LL}, the probability of a win in the case (LL), and P_{LW}, the probability of a win in the case (LW), given that the probability of a win in the cases (WL) and (WW) is ¾. The curve separating a win from a loss in the long term is convex downwards, so that the straight line from the point $P_{LL} = 0$ and $P_{LW} = 1$ (Calamity Jane, CJ) to the point $P_{LL} = 1$ and $P_{LW} = 0$ (Buffalo Bill, BB), both in the region of long-term loss, passes through the point $P_{LL} = ½$ and $P_{LW} = ½$ (Jesse James, JJ), in the region of long-term win.

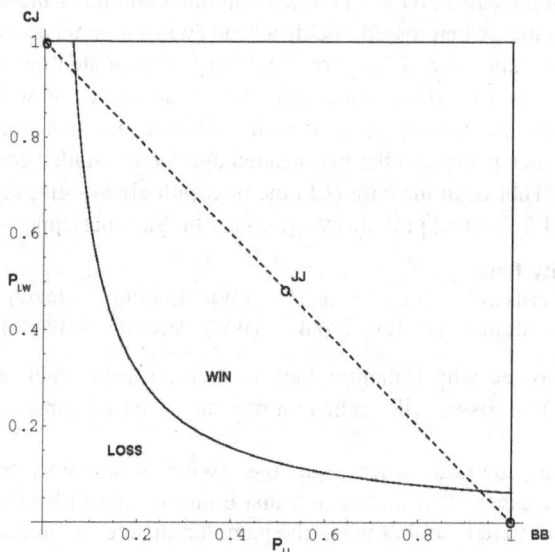

Figure 1: Win-loss curve and the 3 points BB, CJ and JJ

3 Genetic Disorder

Let us now transfer the same structure to a biological setting. In an isolated tribe of Aborigines the number of individuals remains steady over the millennia. Some of the females suffer from a genetically determined mitochondrial disorder (D) that is passed from maternal grandmother to mother to daughter, along the female line. A daughter whose mother and grandmother had the disorder will certainly have it too. If only her grandmother had it, her mother being healthy (H), she will be healthy. In summary,

(DD) leads to (DDD) and (DH) leads to (DHH) 100%

which may be read as follows: if the disorder is present in, say, generations g and $g + 1$ in a given family, then it will be present in generation $g + 2$ too, whereas if it is present in generation g but absent in generation $g + 1$, then it will be absent in generation $g + 2$.

It is discovered, on the other hand, that if the grandmother was healthy, then the probability that the daughter will be healthy is ¾, irrespective of whether the mother herself has the disorder. This may be symbolized as

(HD) leads to (HDH) and (HH) leads to (HHH) 75%

The above probabilistic system is precisely that of the one-armed bandit Calamity Jane, with the following translation key: 'D' for 'L' and 'H' for 'W'. As we know, the long-term expectation with this machine is certain loss, which translates into the certainty of eventual disorder. Indeed, it is easy to see that, in any genealogical line, there will eventually be two succeeding generations in which the females have the disorder, after which all female descendants will also have the disorder. After some time there will never again be a healthy female in the tribe. Such is the sad conclusion, so long as the tribe remains isolated.

In another isolated tribe, there is also incidence of the same mitochondrial disorder in the female population, but the difference is that the males carry a special gene that is missing in the first tribe. This gene affects the working of the gene responsible for the mitochondrial disorder. It interferes with the expression of the defective gene in the maternal grandmother in such a way that a daughter whose mother and grandmother had the disorder will *not* have the disorder. On the other hand, if her grandmother had the defect, but her mother did not, and if her father is from her tribe, and so carries the special gene, she will indeed have the disorder. The situation in the cases (DD) and (DH) is therefore

(DD) leads to (DDH) and (DH) leads to (DHD) 100%

In the case that the grandmother does not have the disorder, the situation is as it was in the first tribe, namely

(HD) leads to (HDH) and (HH) leads to (HHH) 75%.

This probabilistic system is the same as that of Buffalo Bill, resulting in a steady-state population, after many generations, in which, of every 9 females, 5 have the disorder and 4 do not.

On a propitious day in the outback the two tribes meet and mingle amicably, not to say amorously. The consequence is that, in a given genealogical line, sometimes the male partner carries the special gene, and sometimes he does not. If the two tribes are of the same size, and the intermingling of the populations over the generations is thorough, then

(*DD*) leads to (*DDH*) and (*DH*) leads to (*DHH*) 50%

as in the case in which there was randomization between the machines Buffalo Bill and Calamity Jane, the situation that we called Jesse James. After many generations, there will be two healthy females for every one that carries the defective gene, a significant improvement over the state of health of the second tribe, and a very great improvement over that of the first.

4 Pollution of the Environment

Is the Parrondo effect relevant only to the blind workings of natural processes, or could it also be germane to rational decision-making? Imagine a world of the near future, slowly warming as a result of its own industrial CO_2 production. In this world there are two superstates, Emarica and Cathay, co-existing in a delicate balance of power. In an attempt to cope with the effects of global warming, the leaders of Emarica and Cathay, after marathon meetings at diplomatic and ministerial level, eventually agree to sign a treaty. The treaty includes a list of Environment-Friendly Actions (EFAs) and Environment-Hostile Actions (EHAs). EFAs are for example the reafforestation of a denuded area of specified minimum size, the introduction of traffic-free Sundays in a sufficiently populous town, the recycling of effluent from particular kinds of factories, and so on. The stripping of a primeval forest is an EHA, as would be the abolition of the speed limit on the motorways of a county, and so is the building of a dirty factory or power station.

The treaty's protocol entails that, in each superstate, central governmental permission and financing for an EFA or an EHA should depend on the nature of the two previous projects that had been approved by its own leader. The first half of the protocol specified what to do when an EFA was followed by either another EFA of an EHA. An accord was reached that the next project to be permitted would be an EFA in three out of every four cases of this type. In only one case in the four would an EHA be allowed, however urgent the need. In this way, both leaders could announce to the world that, while national economic requirements were not being stifled, the long-term health of future generations would be adequately protected.

Unfortunately the other half of the protocol, namely the specification of the action to be taken after an EHA had been followed either by another

EHA or by an EFA, was never ratified by the superstates. The *sous-entendu* was that each superstate would have to decide for itself what policy to adopt in these cases. With an eye on his Green lobby, and in order to minimize further bookkeeping, the president of Emarica decreed that an EHA followed by another EHA should always be followed by an EFA, thus redressing the balance between environment friendly and unfriendly actions. However, an EHA followed by an EFA would, he proclaimed, always be followed by permission for an EHA. In this way the president could claim that the pre-eminent industrial strength of his great nation would be safeguarded. The electorate was however deceived by a false notion of responsibility, for the Emarican strategy is precisely mirrored by the one-armed bandit Buffalo Bill of Section 2, under the mapping 'EHA' for 'L' and EFA for 'W'. With this strategy, in the long term, for every four EFAs there will be five EHAs, and so the Emarican environment will inexorably, if slowly, deteriorate. A very few Greens recognized this fact, but they were outvoted by the rest of the Emarican people.

The chairman of Cathay was even less considerate of the environment and its defenders. He chose to ignore the remonstrations of political dissidents and to use the leeway in the treaty to sanction a new EHA whenever two EHAs had occurred in succession, this being advantageous to heavy industry. He agreed to enforce an EFA after an EHA had been followed by an EFA, in order not to appear wholly antithetical to the purpose of the international treaty. In this way, as his inner council of advisors assured him, he could reach the goals of the current five-year plan, and at the same time earn the respect of the international community. Since the Cathayan strategy mirrors that of Calamity Jane, however, we know that, as time goes on, there will more and more EHAs and fewer and fewer EFAs: the air will become unbreathable and the environment irreversibly ruined.

However, in another part of that future world there is a third state, not a superstate, but a loose confederation of old colonial powers called Commarket. Commarket has also signed the treaty, but cannot agree internally on the policy to be followed in the cases not covered by the protocol. Some of the countries favored the Emarican option and some the solution adopted by Cathay. After much currying of favors and lobbying of interests, a compromise was reached within Commarket: sometimes EHA-EHA was to be followed by EHA and sometimes by EFA, and similarly for EHA-EFA, but with this rider: central permission and financing for an EFA or an EHA was to be random. After EHA-EHA or EHA-EFA, and averaged over a long time, about the same number of EHAs as EFAs were to be permitted. This strategy is precisely that of Jesse James, and so the people of Commarket took advantage (advertently or inadvertently – that always remained unclear) of the Parrondo effect: for every EHA there would be on average two EFAs, and on the old continent the milieu would improve with each passing year.

5 Is the Parrondo Effect Paradoxical?

For reasons of expository simplicity, the imaginary scenarios sketched in Sections 3 and 4 have both been based on the one-armed bandits of Section 2. Before considering in Section 6 how realistic systems might be susceptible to more general manifestations of the Parrondo effect, let us first try to answer the question: 'How surprising is it that Buffalo Bill (BB) and Calamity Jane (CJ) are losing strategies, whilst their average, Jesse James (JJ), is a winning one?' This question is opportune, for some scholars find the fact so surprising that they call it a paradox, whilst others believe that it is merely counterintuitive.

As we already indicated in Section 2, it is obvious that JJ wins on average, for it is simulated by sometimes tossing a fair coin, and sometimes one that is loaded 3 to 1 in favor of a win. Moreover, it does not require much insight to come to the conclusion that CJ is a losing strategy, for (WL) gives, after a new toss, (WLL) 25% of the time, that is to say (LL), if we include only the last two results after the new toss. Moreover, (LL) remains in this state for all subsequent tosses. Since (WW) leads to (WL) 25% of the time, and (LW) always to (WW), it is clear that, in the course of time, it is more and more likely that the cul-de-sac of the (LL) state will be entered, resulting in uninterrupted loss.

It is not quite so easy to understand why BB is a losing strategy. In terms of what we shall call the diachronous probability, the chance that the state (WW) leads again to (WW) is ¾, as the one-armed bandit Buffalo Bill is played, one pull after another. However, another way of describing the situation is by talking about synchronous probabilities in a large ensemble of BB machines, n_1 of which are in the state (LL), n_2 in the state (LW), n_3 in the state (WL) and n_4 in the state (WW), all at the same time, $t = 0$. At $t = 1$, the arm of each bandit in the ensemble is pulled once, resulting in a new configuration of states, with occupation numbers $\underline{n}_1$, $\underline{n}_2$, $\underline{n}_3$, $\underline{n}_4$. This way of looking at the matter is more suited to the genetic example of Section 3, where a whole population of female Aborigines was involved. Here indeed we can consider the relative numbers of the four states synchronously, i.e. at one time. Now the only way that (WW) can be produced at $t = 1$ for a given machine is if its state at $t = 0$ was also (WW), since (LW) always evolves into (WL). Hence the number of (WW) states at $t = 1$ is on average three-quarters of the number of (WW) states at $t = 0$, the number at $t = 2$ nine-sixteenths of that number, and so on. In short, the (WW) states will die out as time progresses, and, for sufficiently large times, we can safely ignore n_4 compared with n_1, n_2, and n_3.

The only way that (LL) can be produced at $t = 1$ is from a state (WL) at $t = 0$, and this occurs with probability ¼, so $\underline{n_1} = n_3/4$. At $t = 1$, (WL) can be produced from either (LW) or (WW) at $t = 0$, but we agreed to neglect the latter, on the grounds that the number of (WW) states will rapidly become negligible. Since (LW) becomes (WL) with certainty, $\underline{n_3} = n_2/4$. In the course of time, the relative populations of the four states stabilize, and at equilibrium we may omit the underlining, so $n_1 = n_2/4 = n_3/4$ and $n_4 = 0$. The total number of machines is $n = n_1 + n_2 + n_3$ and thus $n_1 = n/9$, $n_2 = n_3 = 4n/9$ and $n_4 = 0$. Since the n_1 (LL) states and the n_3 (WL) states have just resulted from losses, while the n_2 (LW) states have resulted from a win, the average number of losses is $n_1 + n_3 = 5n/9$, whereas the average number of wins is only $n_2 = 4n/9$. This concludes the demonstration that BB is indeed a losing strategy. Inasmuch as the losing nature of the BB strategy is not obvious, we conclude that the occurrence of the Parrondo effect is surprising.

One puzzling aspect of the Parrondo effect deserves closer attention, since it is easily neglected. It may seem odd, especially in the diachronous interpretation, why it should make a difference whether one adopts the JJ strategy or simply takes BB and CJ to constitute one entity. For example, consider all the actions of Emarica and Cathay together over a certain period of time. Does this not amount to averaging, and should not the Parrondo effect imply that there will be twice as many EFAs (i.e. wins) as EHAs (i.e. losses)? The answer is no, for what is missing in such a spurious averaging on paper is the bookkeeping involved in keeping track of the two previous actions. For example, if the last two actions were both EFAs, then the next will be an EHA, only if *all three* actions appertain to Emarica. If, in the attempted averaging on paper, the list includes an EFA by Emarica, followed by an EFA by Cathay, then the probability that the next action will be an EHA, whether by Emarica or Cathay, is not determined by the given data. If all the actions were those of Commarket, on the other hand, the probability in question would be ½.

6 Generalization

The probabilities that were chosen for BB and CJ were very special, indeed extreme examples. A generalization consists in taking different points in the 'loss' region of Figure 1 to define the probabilities for BB and CJ. For example, BB could be moved to $P_{LL} = 0.8$ and $P_{LW} = 0.05$, and CJ might be placed at $P_{LL} = 0.03$ and $P_{LW} = 0.6$. Both of these new points are in the 'loss' region, but the mid-point of the straight line drawn between them is still in the 'win' region, so there is still a Parrondo effect. The precise position of the rectangular hyperbolic curve that separates the 'win' and the 'loss' regions is dictated by the common probability that was chosen for the transitions (WL) to (LW) and (WW) to (WW). In Sections 2-4 this was assumed to be ¾, but it can be changed to any value strictly between 0 and 1. For example, if it is ½, corresponding to simulation by a fair coin, the hyperbola passes through the point $P_{LL} = ½ = P_{LW}$, but a Parrondo effect is still possible by astucious choice of the BB and CJ probabilities. Further, the probabilities for the two transitions (WL) to (LW) and (WW) to (WW) need not be equal, in which case the model is more complicated. Finally, the restriction that the probabilities associated with the next step depend only on the last two steps, while that may be natural enough in the genetic context, is an unnecessary simplification in certain other applications. Relaxation of this restriction is possible, leading to a richer Parrondo structure. In short, much generalization is possible: the occurrence of the counterintuitive Parrondo effect does not depend on the fine tuning of parameters, and it may well be a more common phenomenon than we presently realize.

References

Harmer, G.P. and Abbott, D. 1999a. Parrondo's Paradox. *Statistical Science*, 14(2): 206-13.

Harmer, G.P. and Abbott, D. 1999b. Losing Strategies Can Win by Parrondo's Paradox. *Nature*, 402(6764): 864.

Harmer, G.P., Abbott, D. and Parrondo, J.M.R. 2005. Parrondo's Capital and History Dependent Games. *Advances in Dynamic Games: Applications to Economics, Finance, Optimization and Stochastic Control*, eds. A.S. Nowack and K. Szajowski, 635-48. Boston: Birkhauser.

Iyengar, R. and Kohli, R. 2004. Why Parrondo's Paradox Is Irrelevant for Utility Theory, Stock Buying, and the Emergence of Life. *Complexity*, 9(1): 23-27.

Parrondo, J.M.R., Harmer, G.P. and Abbott, D. 2000. New Paradoxical Games Based on Brownian Ratchets. *Physical Review Letters*, 85(24): 5226-29.

Simon, H.A. 1957. *Models of Man*. New York: Wiley and Son.

5

In- and Ex-probabilities: Keynes and Econophysics

DOMENICO COSTANTINI AND UBALDO GARIBALDI

1 Preliminary Remarks

In this essay we argue that it is possible to deal with economic issues by making use of probabilistic notions only. To achieve this, we shall describe macroeconomic variables in terms of the probabilistic behavior of large systems of economic agents. Such an approach requires us to specify the way in which agents interact at the micro-level, where interactions are described by probability conditions. Economic agents are supposed to change from one state to another. This change is described by transition probabilities. The perspective from which we shall tackle economics could be called a probabilistic agent-based approach. Customarily similar attempts are referred to probability models. As a consequence, most authors speak of probabilistic or statistical modeling. We prefer to avoid this terminology and to speak of fragments of a probabilistic economic theory. The reason is that this theory, of which we shall give some examples, is intended to describe and interpret economic phenomena by leaving out non probabilistic notions altogether.

One could object that theories of this type already exist. To ask for a statistical perspective may seem redundant to econometricians because they maintain that econometrics already deals with economics in a stochastic framework. Thus, at a first sight, one might regard econometrics as the best example of a probabilistic economic theory. We do not share this conviction, and in what follows we shall briefly justify this view. But the main point is that our probabilistic agent-based approach deals with macroeconomics variables in the same way as statistical mechanics intends observable quantities such as temperature and pressure. This is surely not the case of econometrics.

As is well known, probability notions were first used for solving problems related with games of chance and insurance. In spite of this, the works of J. Bernoulli and P.S. Laplace were an early indication of the application of probability notions to the social sciences. With A. Quételet, the dissemination of these notions into the social sciences became a vigorous one. This happened about two centuries ago. But it did not happen in economics. The reason of this rejection has been convincingly explained by Mirowsky (1989). We refer the interested reader to his work. Here we only recall Mirowski's main thesis: in different periods, economic thought fully adopted the conception of the world typical of the physical sciences of the time. This is the case for both classical and neoclassical economics that took physics as the archetype of a scientific theory.

The notion of economic equilibrium adopted in different periods is in tune with the corresponding equilibrium notion in mechanics. To limit our attention to classical and neoclassical economics, some authors uphold that there is a sharp distinction between the notions of equilibrium characterizing these schools of thought. For instance, P. Garegnani (1976, quoted by Mirowski 1979: 238) maintains that the classical notion of equilibrium is associated with the concept of center of gravity. This analogy is intended to describe the supposed gravitation of the market price around the natural price. Neoclassical economics tried to overcome the riddle posed by the classical notion of economic equilibrium by considering temporary equilibrium, that is, by taking into account a sequence of market-clearing prices. In this way, neoclassical economics claimed to have solved the problem by collapsing natural price onto market price. It is worth to point out that in both theories the notion of economic equilibrium pertains to the equivalences in the economic system. Equilibrium is conceived as a property of the state of the system. It regards the way in which things are in the economy. At most, one considers fluctuations but not the probabilities of fluctuations. This deserves some emphasis since, in what we shall do, equilibrium does not pertain to facts but to the probability with which facts may occur.

The time in which classical mechanics could be the paradigm for a deterministic market economics came to an end. The ideal of determinism clashed with two great revolutions in classical physics. First, the kinetic theory of gases provided explanation of the second law of thermodynamics in terms of collisions of a myriad of microscopic particles, whose complex dynamics could only be investigated by using probability notions. Second and more decisive, the birth and growth of quantum mechanics, especially the interpretation of the new mechanics, as irreducibly stochastic. Probability and statistical notions had become absolutely necessary in physics. Economic theorists could not ignore this great transformation. This is a critical point. It amounts to an alternative reading of the role of econometrics, which we regard as the attempt to superimpose probability upon a strongly deterministic ideal of explanation. This attempt was just like the one performed by the nineteenth century classical mechanics. The rise of econometrics can be seen as a consequence of Laplacean deterministic metaphysics as well as of the Gaussian theory of errors (both associated with the deterministic bias typical of eighteenth century thought). We shall return to this theme. Econometrics is an updated way to look at the theory of errors, with which it is indissolubly tied. The deterministic bias economics took from classical physics is responsible for the fact that the introduction of probability notions in economics, granting that it has taken place, has begun in a spurious and crude mode.

2 Keynes and Probability

The explicit introduction of stochastic concepts in economics is almost as old as in physics. As matter of fact, L. Bachelier in 1900 applied the stochastic process now called Brownian motion to the study of the random character of changes in stock-market prices. His work did not attract much attention. This is undoubtedly an irony of history. But let us stress another puzzling episode. We refer to the work of J.M. Keynes on the foundations of probability and statistics.

His well-known book *A Treatise on Probability* was written more than ten years before publication in 1921. In this work, Keynes made an original contribution to the philosophy of probability, provided a comprehensive and deep review of inferential statistics as it was understood in the nineteenth century and, what is more important for us, presented a penetrating analysis of probability notions. From our perspective, the following aspects should be emphasized: (i) the notion of 'probability' as an essentially relative concept (see Keynes 1921: 7); (ii) the notions of 'average' and of 'expectations' considered as intrinsically probabilistic; (iii) the introduction of the notion of 'coefficient of influence' or 'dependence'. On this notion we have based our discussion of probability in relation to economics.

Now a question arises: was this long and accurate research completely forgotten by Keynes the economic theorist? Our opinion is that it was not. In his economic theorizing, Keynes used many mathematical concepts forged in the physical science. However, he also extensively used probability notions. His investigations on the foundations of probability and statistics prove to be of fundamental importance in his economic theory. His work on money, wealth and the general theory of employment cannot be fully understood without looking at his *Treatise on Probability*.

In his work on economic theory, however, Keynes did not make explicit reference to probability foundations. Only on very few occasions he explicitly mentioned probabilistic notions. We focus on some of these. First, in dealing with long-term expectations, Keynes refers to that balance between amounts of relevant knowledge and relevant ignorance that he called the 'weight' of an argument. Second, his analysis and revision of the principle of indifference, the new name he gave to the old Bernoullian principle of non-sufficient reason. Third, his discussion of various types of risks, which can hardly be understood without having in mind his probabilistic definition of risk. Even apart from all this, an accurate reading of Keynes' economic writings reveals a deep probabilistic foundation. As a matter of fact, in these works we often find concepts such as expectation, mean value, propensity, possibility, incentive to buy or to sell, changes in prediction, which are all probabilistic in character. Furthermore, one should not forget that a probabilistic notion cannot be absolute (given once for all), as it is relative to a given evidence. As a consequence, many economic concepts are also relative in character.

We have previously said that Keynes did not explicitly use the notion of probability in his economic analysis. This is only partially true. It would be better to say that Keynes did not explicitly formulate his economic theory in probabilistic terms. Often the use of probability notions is so manifest that only a deterministic prejudice can obscure it. This is the case with Keynesian concepts such as aggregate supply function, aggregate demand function and effective demand. Before undertaking the analysis of such concepts, we shall examine two alternative ways of using probability notions.

3 In- and Ex-probabilities

Since its emergence, probability has been interpreted in two distinct ways. One pertains to knowledge of facts, the other to the facts themselves. The first way regards the formation of an opinion about facts of which one has partial knowledge. With reference to the results of previous observations, probabilities are allotted to hypotheses whose truth is unknown. The other approach has been introduced in order to account for chance phenomena. Having recognized the indeterministic nature of some aspects of the world, one appeals to probability in order to describe, explain and predict phenomena. To exhibit the above difference, someone has used the terms 'epistemic probability', for the first, and 'ontological' probability, for the second. This terminology may engender philosophical misunderstanding and we shall not use it. Referring to the first use of probability, we introduce the neutral term of *ex-probability*, which refers to occasions in which probability is external to the theory. Probability results from ignorance of the real way in which the external world, usually intended as governed by deterministic laws, works. This is the case of the molecules governed by Newton's laws of motion. As already noticed by Laplace, we cannot know the positions and momenta of all particles, thus we resort to probability. Nobody can deny the existence of a widespread use of ex-probabilities. We maintain that, besides this old notion, there exists a true factual aspect, which we shall call *in-probability*. This is far from being new. Within quantum mechanics, it has become common to acknowledge the existence of 'objective probabilities', as physicists, by using a misleading term, name the in-probabilities. We deny that the only factual use of probability is associated with quantum mechanics. In-probabilities appear owing to the non deterministic character of a theory. This was clearly shown by P. and T. Ehrenfests' interpretation of the work of L. Boltzmann, especially his theorem on the probable increase in entropy with time. In genetics, the factual character of probability has been accepted since Mendel. This is not the case with economics. In general, economists do not recognize the fundamental non deterministic relations of the external world and the associated unpredictability of the future.

In our opinion, this was not Keynes's view. We maintain that, on many occasions, Keynes took the indeterministic character of the economy for granted and, at least in an informal way, extensively referred to in-probability. We are aware that to locate the factual aspect of probability in Keynes's economic writings is not easy. This is due to various reasons. First, at the beginning of last century, only few examples of the use of in-probability were known. These were Bachelier's treatment of stock-market prices; Einstein's probabilistic explanation of Brownian motion; the vindication of Boltzmann's *H*-theorem accomplished by means of a stochastic process, the dogs and fleas process of the Ehrenfests.

Stochastic processes play an essential role in the factual use of probability. Keynes was not aware of this revolutionary turning-point, which made it possible to obtain an insight into entangled phenomena. In the bibliography of his *Treatise on Probability*, Keynes quoted about ten works of Markov; nonetheless he was not really acquainted with the revolutionary work of this author. But what is more puzzling is that on many occasions, Keynes referred to Bachelier's contributions. In particular, he mentioned two of his books, i.e. *Calcul des probabilités,* 1912 and *Le jeu, la chance et le hasard,* 1914. However, Keynes only considered some suggestions given by Bachelier to solve specific problems, such as the use of prior probabilities in the Bayes-Laplace rule (see Keynes 1921: 351), or a form of Laplace's rule of succession (see Keynes 1921: 379). Keynes did not mention Bachelier's approach to the random evolution of stock-market prices. In this respect, it should not be forgotten that the work of Einstein on Brownian motion, as well as that of the Ehrenfests, had an impact strictly confined to physics, while Bachelier's seminal contributions on finance were completely ignored till the last decades of the twentieth century. Second, as we have already mentioned, Keynes's economics is not a formal theory. In his theory neither stochastic processes nor transition probabilities are explicitly dealt with. Third and most importantly, in the *Treatise on Probability* Keynes based his formal theory on propositional calculus and could not account for individual components of any given statement (or strategy).

At this point, the following question arises: what about probability in the *Treatise*? Or: is the notion studied in the *Treatise* an ex- or in-probability? Our answer is straightforward: neither of both. The reason is simple. In the *Treatise*, Keynes dealt with probability in a formal way. In stating the fundamental theorems of probability Keynes clearly asserts that he is dealing with the formal logic of probable knowledge (Keynes 1921: 115). Following Leibniz, he thought of probability calculus as a branch of logic. From this viewpoint, the probability relation is a primitive notion and as such it does not need any explicit definition. All that Keynes did was to introduce some axioms – like sum and product rules – to be used in dealing with conditional probabilities. Being a notion implicitly defined through the axioms, it can be considered both as an ex-probability or as an in-probability. In Part V of the *Treatise*, which is devoted to the foundations of statistical inference, probability is clearly intended to result from ignorance. It is thus an ex-probability.

But this is not the case for some probability notions used in Keynes' *General Theory of Employment, Interests and Money* (Keynes 1973 [1936]). We have already noted that on many occasions Keynes used notions of the 'ex-probability' type. But there are other occasions in which Keynes explicitly refers to in-probabilities. We consider only three cases. First, Keynes' use of the principle of indifference. In section IV of Chapter 12 of the *General Theory* Keynes, when discussing the results of an investment over a long time period writes:

> Nor we can rationalise our behaviour by arguing that to a man in a state of ignorance errors in either direction are equally probable, so that there remains a mean actuarial expectation based on equi-probabilities. For it can easily be shown that the assumption of arithmetically equal probabilities base on a state of ignorance leads to absurdities. (Keynes 1973: 152)

Here the sentence 'it can easily be shown' refers to the analysis of the principle of indifference in the *Treatise*. The reference to the contradictoriness of this principle in order to reject the hypothesis of the equiprobability of errors in either direction is clearly relevant to economic theory. Hence Keynes is using in-probabilities.

Second, in Chapter 3 of the same volume Keynes states that

> the amount of employment, both in each individual firm and industry and in aggregate, depends on the amount of the proceeds which the entrepreneurs expect to receive from the corresponding output.[3] (Keynes 1973: 24)

and the important footnote 3 makes explicit the probabilistic meaning of the notion 'amount of the proceed':

> An entrepreneur [...] does not, of course, entertain a single undoubting expectation of what the sale-proceeds of a given output will be, but several hypothetical expectations held with varying degrees of probability and definiteness. By his expectation of proceeds I mean, therefore, the expectation of proceeds which, if it were held with certainty, would lead to the same behaviour as does the bundle vague and more various possibilities which actually make up his state of expectation when he reaches his decision. (Keynes 1973: 24)

As a consequence, the 'amount of the proceed' is a mean value, and as such it may vary according to the probability distribution used to calculate it. However, the second part of the footnote partially obscures the meaning of the first part. For it is very difficult, at least for people thinking in probabilistic terms, to understand what an expectation held with certainty is. In any case, Keynes is using in-probabilities.

4 Effective Demand

Third, and more important, in the following passage Keynes defined the central notions of aggregate supply and demand functions

> Let Z be the aggregate supply price of the output from employing men, the relationship between Z and N being written $Z = \varphi(N)$, which can be called *the aggregate supply function*.[1] Similarly, let D be the proceeds which entrepreneurs expect to receive from the employment of N men, relationship between D and N being written $D = f(N)$, which can be called the *aggregate demand function*. (Keynes 1973: 25)

And, finally, he gave his definition of effective demand

> The value of D at the point of the aggregate demand function, where it is intersected by the aggregate supply function, will be called *the effective demand*. (Keynes 1973: 25)

In order to understand the concept of effective demand one must make clear the meanings of Z and D. To this respect, first of all we note that the aggregate supply price Z might be intended as a deterministic quantity. In fact, if one assumes that both the values of N and that of the output of each employed man are exactly known, the aggregate supply function $f(N)$ allows us to determine the exact value of Z. But nobody exactly knows either the amount of the output of any employed man or that of any given number of employed men. Such an exact knowledge may only be assumed on the ground of a metaphysical prejudice. The exact output has the same nature of the true value of a quantity. There is no exact amount as there is no true value. A lot of deviations are always to be taken into account. In the best case, these deviations are to be handled with ex-probabilities, for example by using the Gaussian theory of errors. But, if we take Keynes's philosophy of probability into account, it is much more satisfactory to think that Keynes conceived of the amount of output as a stochastic notion. Hence Z is not a fixed quantity but a stochastic variable. *Mutatis mutandis* the same holds true for D. Due to the fact that Z and D are random variables defined on the sets of their possible values, there are two probability distributions. As a consequence, the 'point of intersection' of these (distribution) functions is a two-dimensional interval whose points are allotted probabilities. Strictly speaking, the 'intersection' is a probability distribution too.

The consequences of this are not slight, as effective demand is a central concept of Keynes's economic analysis

> Since this [the effective demand] is the substance of the General Theory of Employment, which will be our object to expound, the successive chapters will be largely occupied with examining the various factors upon which these two functions depend. (Keynes 1973: 25)

The stochastic aspect we have just emphasized has a great influence on notions such as equilibrium prices, demands and so on. As a consequence of this stochastic approach, equilibrium is turned into a notion which is probabilistic in character. Equilibrium points do not exist. There are only equilibrium probability distributions. We shall come back to this issue. For the time being we stress that concepts such as aggregate supply function, aggregate demand function and effective demand are probabilistic in character. As we have just seen, Keynes himself said that effective demand is probabilistic in character. And, of course, Keynes himself considered effective demand to be the substance of his theory. Thus the core of his theory is a probabilistic one.

5 Econometrics

From this perspective, the rationale of Keynes's sharp criticisms of the way in which cyclical fluctuations were submitted to statistical tests becomes clear. The route followed by econometricians was far removed from that hinted at by Keynes. The refusal to accept the non deterministic character of economic relationships affected the use of probability notions in the first half of last century. This is the very reason that brought probability in economics close to a notion intrinsically based on ignorance. Econometricians confined the use of probability to hypothetical probability, that is likelihood: this is the notion, strongly influenced by frequentist philosophy, which was adopted by Ronald Fisher. This is also the case with estimation, which mainly aimed at specifying the values of deterministic quantities by means of the method of maximum likelihood. An econometric model, such as a linear equation characterized by a set of previously estimated parameters, has to be tested against data. When testing and/or estimating, econometricians aim at the values of parameters, they want to find out the true description of a world imagined as a deterministic one. Within econometrics, probability notions are nothing but tools to be used in a state of partial ignorance of the actual characteristics of the system. In our view, this attitude clashes with Keynes's philosophy of probability. The notion of probability used by Irving Fisher, Ronald Frisch and Joseph Alois Schumpeter within economics was in full agreement with that of Laplace and Gauss.

We are convinced that Keynes's criticism does not regard probability as such, but the way in which probability has been used in econometrics. The contrast disappears when we reflect upon the role Keynes assigned to probability in economics. Our distinction between ex- and in-probability was unknown to Keynes. Partially for this reason he did not introduce a formal probabilistic theory. In the following, we argue that this formal development could be performed, at least in some cases, by supplying a form of knowledge which can provide understanding of both the microscopic and macroscopic sides of the non deterministic world in which we live. The failure to appreciate the factual and relative character of probabilities is the true reason why probabilistic explanations have not been considered as good explanations. The passages below point to the role of conditional probabilities in economics, which was clearly seen by Keynes.

Let us recall the final words of Keynes's *Treatise on Probability*:

> The physicists of the nineteenth century have reduced matter to the collisions and arrangements of particles, between which the ultimate qualitative differences are very few; and the Mendelian biologists are deriving the various qualities of men from the collisions and arrangements of chromosomes. In both cases the analogy with a perfect game of chance is really present; and the validity of some current modes of inferences may depend on the assumption that it is to material of this kind that we are apply to them. Here, though I have complained sometimes at their want of logic, I am in fundamental sympathy with the deep underlying conceptions of the statistical theory of the day. If the contemporary doctrines of Biology and Physics remain tenable, we may have a remarkable, if undeserved, justification of some of the methods of the traditional Calculus of Probabilities. [...] and it may turn – reversing Quételet's expression – that 'La nature que nous interrogeons c'est une urne.' (Keynes 1921: 427-8)

Since the beginning of last century, the statistical approach to biology and physics has remained not only 'tenable', as Keynes thought, but has grown in an impressive way. The contemporary biological and physical understanding of the external world is essentially and irreducibly a probabilistic one. The 'fundamental sympathy with the deep underlying conceptions of the statistical theory of the day' that Keynes expressed almost a century ago reveals his confidence in the role of probability in science. However, this 'fundamental sympathy' did not induce economists to understand economic phenomena as 'collisions and arrangements' of economic agents. In what follows we show that this is possible.

6 Econophysics

The use of in-probabilities in economics is made explicit in the literature on 'econophysics'. This term denotes work done in economics by means of physical methods, that is, by employing a variety of notions and tools forged in theoretical physics, and more specifically in statistical mechanics. Interest is focused on the interactions of a large number of economic agents, characterized by different behaviors. Econophysics follows two main approaches. The first, which is more widespread, essentially refers to financial markets and is descriptive in character (Mantegna and Stanley 2000). In a sense, studies in this area follow the approach of Pareto and Gibrat. Much of this research refers to the power-law distribution, of which Pareto's law is a special case. Financial markets are monitored to a time scale of seconds. Almost every economic transaction is recorded and data are available. Various researchers became interested in these data in the conviction that they can lead to a deeper understanding of financial phenomena. Such researchers believe it useless to try to explain the temporal development of financial events, that is, the time series obtained from market data. They think it is more useful to specify the atemporal statistical distributions of data. This is done by analyzing the frequencies of financial events in an attempt to derive the probability properties of statistical distributions. A consequence of this approach is the great interest in statistical distributions, scaling and other similar notions.

As we noted above, the starting point of this approach are Pareto's investigations on wealth. Of great interest are also the writings of Lévy on probability distributions apt to fit the market data better than the bell-shaped Gaussian distribution. The traditional way of analyzing time series, of a Gaussian character, is unable to give a good description of financial phenomena, because the development of prices through time gives rise to irregular trajectories. The frequency distributions drawn from these trajectories exhibit heavy tailed distributions with large kurtosis. In order to enlarge fat-tailed distributions, one might focus on power law distributions and hence scale-invariant correlations in the way suggested by Benoît Mandelbrot. This is the case of economic time series like stock market indices, or currency exchange rates, that is, phenomena depending on the evolution of a large number of strongly interacting agents. Following Bachelier, Einstein and Wiener, stochastic processes, too, play a central role in this research.

Let us consider the latter approach, which we shall follow. A common tradition in economic writings is based on the concept of representative agent. This concept has a lot to do with the concept of 'average man' of Quételet. This agent is a fictional being able to summarize anthropometric data for the purpose of investigating the characteristics of clusters of people, for instance the average chest circumferences of a group of Scottish soldiers. By using an average, that is a single intermediate value, one pretends to represent large collectives. The concept of representative agent is ultimately based on that of average man. One assumes that the actions of a great number of agents, say a group of firms or consumers taken together, may be conflated into the action of a single agent endowed with appropriate characteristics.

Instead of the representative agent, we shall consider economic systems whose agents are actually interacting with each other. Statistical physics deals with the study of macrophysical systems with a very large number of microcomponents. A typical task of this branch of physics is to deduce the observable properties of a volume of gas by assuming some statistical characteristics of the behavior of its particles. Of course, particles interact with each other, for instance they collide with other particles. Statistical physics may also be regarded as the discipline that can analyze the global behavior of populations, by drawing appropriate inferences from probabilistic properties of the population components. A well-known phenomenon in statistical mechanics is the fact that the interacting particles of a physical system may give rise to a collective behavior different from that of individuals. This is true even in the case in which the population is homogeneous. The study of such interactions is the route we shall follow to build some fragments of a probabilistic agent-based economics.

To base macroeconomic theories on the interactions of a large number of heterogeneous economic agents is a new way to see economic phenomena. In the second half of the nineteenth century, the first explanation of mass behavior in terms of interacting elements was offered by statistical mechanics. In the last century, this approach became central in population genetics. With great delay, the same route is being followed in economics too, and the leading scholar in this field is Masanao Aoki. His research tries to explain the behavior of economic macrovariables, such as prices, trading volumes and so on, by specifying the probabilistic behavior of microvariables such as individual economic agents. Aoki writes that his work is an attempt to reformulate macroeconomics, and

> discusses model composed of a large number of microeconomic agents. That a large number of microeconomic agents interact [...] has several important consequences. The most important is undoubtedly the fact that a large number of microeconomic states are compatible with a given macroeconomic state. [...] Although this fact is completely ignored in the existing macroeconomic literature, it has profound effect on the behavior of the macroeconomic model that we construct by aggregating models of microeconomic agents. (Aoki 2002: 2)

The effect of microeconomic agents on macroeconomic behavior is described as follows

> At any given point in time, microeconomic agents have chosen some decisions, typically from finite-choice set. Joint effects of their choices affect the economic environments in which they perform and make further choices in the future, that is, there is feedback from aggregate decisions to individual choices. Therefore, the agents operate in endogenous stochastic and dynamic environments (Aoki 2002: 5)

With a large number of interacting economic agents, one obtains scenarios similar to those considered in statistical mechanics, for instance in research dealing with the thermodynamics limit. This means that macroeffects are governed by deterministic laws. One must keep in mind, however, that all economic effects are stochastic in character, being achieved thanks to the fact that one treats

> all micro- and macroeconomic variable as random variables or stochastic processes, although macroeconomic variables become deterministic in the limit of the number of microeconomic units approaching infinity. Relationships among economic variables are statistical in an essential way, and are not made so by having additive disturbance or measurement errors superimposed on deterministic relationships. (Aoki 2002: 10)

Instead of adopting the metaphysical notion of an agent producing a single good that can be consumed or invested s a capital asset, we shall consider a variety of agent types. In the economic systems there are agents that share the same behavioral rule or strategy. Agents of the same type cluster together. Hence market agents tend to form clusters characterized by the fact that all agents belonging to the same group share the same property. As is well known, the meaning of the term economic agent varies according to context. It may refer to single individuals trading in a stock market, individuals trading a given commodity, workers of a given firm, unemployed people, households, firms, national economies, and so on. However, not only individual agents but also clusters of agents may be of interest, owing to the fact that a few agents may approximately determine the excess demand for goods on the market. The important fact is that an agent following a given strategy may change it, and adopt a different one. Such changes ensue from the interactions with agents following different strategies, and this determines the evolution of the over-all economic system.

Another important problem we shall consider is related to equilibrium. From the period of Classical Economics onwards, exactly like in the physics of that time, equilibrium has been understood as a special state of a system which exhibits a balance of forces. Hence equilibrium is intended as a given state or, better, as a given disposition of the components of the system. For instance, a market reaches the equilibrium state when his aggregate properties satisfy certain conditions. This way of regarding equilibrium changed when the kinetic theory of gases was introduced. Such a theory features a dynamical mechanism that changes the clusters (or 'types') to which the elements of the system belong, in the same way as collisions change the states of the colliding particles. In general, the evolution of the system as a whole, that is the joint evolution of all its elements, results from microscopic changes governed by statistical laws. In economic terms, as held by Aoki (see quotations above), this amounts to account for macroeconomic variables in terms of the probabilistic behavior of a large collection of agents. The macroeconomic evolution of the economic system results from the innumerable actions of the economic agents belonging to the system, and such actions are probabilistically governed.

7 A Formalization

In what follows, we shall outline some fragments of a probabilistic agent-based economic theory. Probability accounts for the single elements (economic agents) of any given system. The changes which take place in the strategy of individual agents are described by probabilistic laws. The question we shall have to answer is the following: what is the probability of choosing a new strategy when an agent gives up the old one? The macroscopic properties of the economic system result from the statistical behavior of agents, expressed by means of transition probabilities. More importantly, the analysis we shall perform leads to probability distributions that characterize the equilibrium state of the system.

The laws describing the behavior of agents are probabilistic in character. In order to make this clear, we shall start with a brief description of the probabilistic behavior of the elements belonging to the system. Besides the basic rules of probability, that is the sum and the product rules, we introduce the conditions of exchangeability and invariance. The first condition is well known, the second states that the relevance quotient, which is the modern name for Keynes's 'coefficient of influence', is a function of the number of elements under consideration. (For details see Costantini and Garibaldi 2004.)

Before proceeding with the analysis, it is necessary to recall a result which will be useful in what follows. Let $Y_1, Y_2, ..., Y_n ...$ be a sequence of random variables whose range is $\{1, ..., j, ..., g\}$, $n_j \equiv \# \{Y_i = j; I = 1,2, ...n\}$ the *occupation number* of j in the first random variables, $\mathbf{n} \equiv (n_1, ..., n_g)$, $\sum_{j=1}^{g} n_j = n$, the corresponding *occupation vector*, and $P(.|.)$ an *exchangeable* and *invariant* probability-function. It can be proved (see for example [2]) that if $E \equiv Y_1 = j_1, ..., Y_n = j_n$ and $I > n$, then for all j

$$P(Y_i = j | E) = P(j | \mathbf{n}) = P(j | n_j, n) = \frac{\lambda p_j + n_j}{\lambda + n}, \qquad (1)$$

where

$$p_j \equiv P(j) \equiv P(Y_i = j) \text{ and } \lambda \equiv \frac{P(Y_i = j | Y_o = h)}{p_j - P(Y_i = j | Y_o = h)}, j \neq h, i \neq 0$$

are free parameters to be fixed in order to reach the value of the probability function $P(.|.)$. Sometime, with respect to the *initial probability* p_j, we shall use a new parameter defined as $w_j \equiv \lambda p_j$. When this is the case, $w \equiv \sum_{j=1}^{g} w_j = \lambda$. From (1) it follows that: if $\lambda > 0$, the probability function $P(.|.)$ is positively stochastic dependent; if $\lambda < 0$, the probability function $P(.|.)$ is negatively stochastic dependent; if $\lambda \to \infty$, the probability function $P(.|.)$ is stochastic independent. Hence the value of (1) depends upon the initial probabilities of $\mathbf{p} \equiv (p_1, ..., p_g), \sum_{j=1}^{g} p_j = 1$, and the stochastic (in)dependence fixed by λ.

Now we consider a system **S** consisting of N elements and g *cells* (predicates, strategies) 1, ..., g. The state of the system is its *occupation vector* $\mathbf{N} \equiv (N_1, ..., N_j, ..., N_g)$, that is, the vector of the occupation numbers of the predicates of **S**. **N** may be considered as the set of all the *individual descriptions* of **S**, $E \equiv X_1 = j_1, ..., X_n = j_n, ..., X_N = j_N$, for all n, $j_n \in \{1, 2, ..., g\}$, whose occupation numbers are those of **N**. We shall denote by $\mathbf{N}^{(g,N)}$ the set of all occupation vectors of **S**.

The simplest change in **S** occurs when one of its element changes its strategy, or, as we shall also say, when an element of **S** moves from one cell to another. For instance, an element belonging to cell k moves to cell j. If this is the case, the occupation number N_k decreases by one unity becoming $N_k - 1$, while N_j is increased by one unity becoming $N_j + 1$. Following the physicists' convention, we shall call such events *destructions* and *creations* respectively, of course within a given cell. As a consequence of a destruction in cell k, the state of **S**, which before the destruction is $\mathbf{N} \equiv (N_1, ..., N_k, ..., N_g)$, $\sum_{k=1}^{g} N_k = N$, becomes $\mathbf{N}_k \equiv \mathbf{N} - \mathbf{e}(k) = (N_1, ..., N_k - 1, ..., N_g)$, and the size of the system becomes $N-1$, while after creation in cell j, it becomes $\mathbf{N}_k^j \equiv \mathbf{N}_k + \mathbf{e}(j) = (N_1,...,N_k-1,...,N_j+1,...,N_g)$, whose size is again N. We shall focus on destruction and creation probabilities. These are $P\{\mathbf{N}_k | \mathbf{N}\}$, i.e. the probability that, being $\mathbf{N}$ the state of the system, it becomes $\mathbf{N}_k$, respectively $P\{\mathbf{N}_k^j | \mathbf{N}_k\}$, i.e. the probability that having the system suffered a destruction in k, and thus being $\mathbf{N}_k$ its state, it will enjoy a creation in j. The reason of this is that we aim at determining the probability that the system undergoes a transition from $\mathbf{N}$ to $\mathbf{N}_k^j$.

When $\mathbf{N}$ is the state of $\mathbf{S}$, we look for the probabilities of destroying an element in k and of creating an element in j. To this purpose we assume the following conditions:

C (*general condition*) Destruction and creation probability are exchangeable and invariant.

DC (*destruction condition*) If the state of $\mathbf{S}$ is $\mathbf{N}$, for the destruction sequence $D_1, D_2,,..., D_n, n \le N$, the parameters of (1) take the values $\lambda^D = -N$ for all k,
$$p_k = \frac{N_k}{N}.$$

CC (*creation condition*) If the state of $\mathbf{S}$ is $\mathbf{N}$, for the creation sequence $C_1, C_2,,..., C_n, n \le N$, the parameters of (1) take the values $\lambda^C = \lambda + N = w + N$ and for all j,
$$p_j = \frac{\lambda g^{-1} + N_j}{\lambda + N} = \frac{w g^{-1} + N_j}{w + N}.$$

From **C** it follows that, in order to determine both destruction and creation probabilities, we have to fix g free parameters. **DC** accomplishes this task for the destruction probability. On the contrary, this is not the case for **CC**. This condition fixes only partially the probability of creating an element in a given cell.

In the system we are considering, creation may occur only after destruction, moreover the number of creations must equal that of destructions. In other words, sequences of destructions and creations do not change the size of the system. In what follows we shall assume that any given destruction is immediately followed by a corresponding creation. According to **C**, **DC** and **CC** the probabilities of these events are

$$P(D_1 = k; \mathbf{N}, \lambda^D) = \frac{N_k}{N}, \tag{2}$$

$$P(C_1 = m; \mathbf{N}_k, \lambda^C) = \frac{\lambda g^{-1} + N_m}{\lambda + N - 1}, \tag{3}$$

The **N** and λ^D after the semicolon ';' in (2) and $\mathbf{N}_{kl}$ and λ^C after the semicolon ';' in (3) denote that the free parameters have been determined after taking into account the context in which destructions and creations take place. For the sake of simplicity we have considered destructions and creations occurring in different cells. Using the Kronecker's function it becomes possible to take the general case into account (see Costantini and Garibaldi 2004).

7.1 Stochastic dynamics

Let us consider the stochastic dynamics of **S**, that is $\mathbf{X}(0)$, $\mathbf{X}(1)$, ... $\mathbf{X}(t)$, $\mathbf{X}(t+1)$, ..., such that at time t the state of **S** is **N**. We assume that during the time interval $[t, t+1)$ one element is destroyed in k and immediately afterwards another element is created in m. By (2) and (3) the probability of this transition is

$$P(\mathbf{N}_k^m \mid \mathbf{N}) = \frac{N_k}{N} \cdot \frac{\lambda g^{-1} + N_m}{\lambda + N - 1}. \tag{4}$$

A probability distribution $\pi(\mathbf{N})$ defined on $\mathbf{N}^{(g,N)}$ is an equilibrium probability distribution for **S** when, whatever may be the initial state $\mathbf{N}(0)$, $\lim_{t \to \infty} P(\mathbf{X}(t) = \mathbf{N}(t) \mid \mathbf{X}(0) = \mathbf{N}(0))$ exists, and this limit distribution does not depend either upon time or upon the initial state of the system. A probability distribution on the states of **S** is stationary if it does not change with time. If a set of states is ergodic, for this set there exists a stationary distribution. Furthermore, if this set is aperiodic, then the stationary distribution and the equilibrium distribution coincide. We are looking for the stationary distribution $\pi(\mathbf{N})$ of the Markov chain whose transition probability is (4). The probabilistic time evolution of the system is given by the Chapman-Kolmogorov equation, that is

$$P(\mathbf{X}(t+1) = \mathbf{N}) = \sum_{\mathbf{N}'} P(\mathbf{X}(t+1) = \mathbf{N} \mid \mathbf{X}(t) = \mathbf{N}') P(\mathbf{X}(t) = \mathbf{N}'), t = 0,1,2,\ldots,$$

which may be written as

$$P(\mathbf{X}(t+1) = \mathbf{N}) - P(\mathbf{X}(t) = \mathbf{N}) =$$
$$\sum_{\mathbf{N}'} P(\mathbf{X}(t+1) = \mathbf{N} \mid \mathbf{X}(t) = \mathbf{N}') P(\mathbf{X}(t) = \mathbf{N}') - \sum_{\mathbf{N}'} P(\mathbf{X}(t+1) = \mathbf{N}' \mid \mathbf{X}(t) = \mathbf{N}) P(\mathbf{X}(t) = \mathbf{N}).$$

This is the discrete 'Master Equation'. When for any pair $\mathbf{N}' \neq \mathbf{N}$, the equality

$$P(X(t+1) = N \mid X(t) = N')P(X(t) = N') =$$
$$= P(X(t+1) = N' \mid X(t) = N)P(X(t) = N)$$

holds, then

$$P(X(t+1) = N) = P(X(t) = N) = \pi(N). \tag{5}$$

This equality asserts that the distribution $\pi(N)$ does not change over time. Hence a distribution satisfying (5) is invariant. The set of equations (5) expresses the detailed balance between pairs of occupation vectors belonging to the same ergodic set. Roughly speaking, the meaning of (5) is that the probability flux from N to N' equals that from N' to N.

Considering the detailed balance conditions and the transition probability in the opposite direction, that is, that from N_k^m to N, we can determine the equilibrium probability distribution we are looking for, i.e.

$$P(N;\lambda) = \frac{N!}{\lambda^{[N]}} \prod_{j=1}^{g} \frac{\left(\frac{\lambda}{g}\right)^{[N_j]}}{N_j!} = \frac{N!}{w^{[N]}} \prod_{j=1}^{g} \frac{\left(\frac{w}{g}\right)^{[N_j]}}{N_j!}, \tag{5 bis}$$

where $x^{[y]} \equiv x(x+1)...(x+y-1)$ is the Pochhammer symbol, or ascending factorial.

If one considers different values of λ, that is $\lambda = g$, $\lambda \to \infty$ and $\lambda = -g$, thus different types of creation probabilities, one obtains different equilibrium distributions for S. For example: by putting $\lambda = g$ one obtains the Bose-Einstein statistics, that is, a uniform probability distribution on $N^{(g,N)}$; by putting $\lambda = -g$ one obtains the Fermi-Dirac statistics, that is, a uniform probability distribution on $N^{(g,N)}$ when the vectors of this set have occupation numbers 0 or 1; by putting $\lambda \to \infty$ one obtains the Maxwell-Boltzmann statistics, that is, the symmetric multinomial distribution on all occupation vectors. Values of λ different from those just considered have no physical meaning. However, they can be profitably used in our approach to economics.

8 Fragments of Probabilistic Economics

In this paper we do not wish to outline a purely indeterministic economic theory. For the time being we shall attempt to give a hint of the way in which in-probabilities may enter an agent-based economic theory. The distinctive mark of such an approach is to give up any attempt to deal in a deterministic mode with the way in which changes of the strategy of economic agents take place. A second distinctive feature is that one should study from a probabilistic perspective the economic behavior of individual economic agents. For this reason we shall consider an economic system consisting of N *economic agents* and g *strategies*. Hence the state of the system, $\mathbf{N} = (N_1,...,N_j,...,N_g)$ is the list of agents following g possible strategies. On the contrary, an individual description of the system $\mathbf{E} \equiv X_1 = j_1, ..., X_n = j_n, ..., X_N = j_N$ specifies the strategy followed by any given economic agent.

8.1 Herd Behavior: Kirman's Ants

The first fragment we would consider is a well known property of financial markets. One might take as an example the case of financial traders that may buy or sell shares. The issue regards the behavior of trading agents that cluster together by choosing the same strategy. A phenomenon of this kind is usually called herd behavior or herding. This collective or aggregate behavior arises from the interaction among agents whose individual courses of action seem to be simple. This means that the grouping together cannot be deduced from certain characteristics of the behavior of individual agents but emerges from their interactions. Herding is responsible of the effect known as 'fat tail'. The tentative explanation we shall give rests on the theoretical tools developed in the previous section. It is purely theoretical and makes no references to any specific situation. But the same holds true for the first seminal attempt that has been suggested to explain herd behavior.

This attempt is the well-known explanation of herding behavior suggested by Kirman (1993), who considered the collective behavior of ants. The problem setting is the following. Two almost identical sources of food are located at the same distance from an ants' nest and the ants go to both sources for feeding. The two sources are supplied with food in such a way that, notwithstanding what ants take away, they always maintain the same level of food. Some ants forage to one source, say source A, and some others go to the other, say source B. The percentages of ants foraging at A and B change over time but most of the time ants distribute themselves between the two sources in a very unequal manner. Sometime almost all ants forage at A whilst the remaining few do the same at B. After a period of time in which this proportion is maintained, and without any obvious change of context, the percentage suddenly reverses in the sense that now almost all ants go to B and only few go to A. Such abrupt changes occur repeatedly. As a consequence, taken collectively, ants spend the most of the time in percentages near 1 and 0 at one or the other source, while only a small fraction of time is spent at percentages very different from 1 or 0. Considering a long period of time and plotting the percentage of ants arriving at one source, the other percentage is obtained by difference. One may describe the above situation by means of a U-shaped histogram showing a series of frequencies, of which the highest are either close to 1 or to 0, while only few frequencies are associated with percentages significantly different from 1 or 0. In an apparently symmetrical situation ants behave in an asymmetrical way. Kirman noted that this behavior is similar to the herding behavior observed in assets markets as well as in other economic situations.

Kirman considers N ants and two sources of food A and B. For short, we call A-*ant* one that is foraging at A and B-*ant* one that is foraging at B. As in the case of the Ehrenfest urn model, the state of the system is determined by the number of ants feeding at B, say $n = 0, 1, ..., N$. The model assumes that ants go to one of the two sources, forage there and come back to the nest. However, it is also assumed that sometime two ants meet at random, say a A-ant meets a B-ant. As Kirman himself stressed by referring to the drawing of two marbles from an urn filled with black and white marbles, he is considering two composite events whose joint probabilities satisfies the multiplication rule. The choice of the ants is supposed to be random. In explicit terms, this means that each ant has the same probability of being chosen for meeting another ant, so that

$$\frac{N-n}{N}$$

is the probability that an A-ant meets a B-ant. When this happens, the A-ant might become a B-ant. The probability of this event is

$$\left(a + (1-b)\frac{n}{N-1}\right).$$

Kirman explains the above probability as follows. In the case of a meeting such as the one considered here, $1 - b$ is the probability with which the B-ant recruits the A-ant, in the sense that the latter becomes a B-ant. There is, furthermore, a small probability a that the A-ant becomes a B-ant without having met any B-ant. The economic interpretation given by Kirman is that the self-conversion to the opposite strategy of an agent may be caused by the arrival of some information coming from outside the market. Whatever the interpretation of a, it is manifest that the role of this small probability is to ensure that the process does not stop when either $n = 0$ or $n = N$.

Kirman's model also provides a reverse event, which is what happens when a B-ant meets an A-ant and possibly becomes a A-ant. The probabilities involved in this second composite event are similar to those of the first event. We have thus two possible events that may be expressed by saying that the system undergoes a transition: first, from n to $n + 1$ in the case in which an A-ant becomes a B-ant; second, from n to $n - 1$ in the reverse case in which a B-ant becomes an A-ant. Kirman, however, does not suppose that these two events are exhaustive. By putting $P(n+1|n) + P(n-1|n) \leq 1$, he introduces the possibility that the state of the system does not change. The probability of this third event is obviously equal to $1 - P(n+1|n) - P(n-1|n)$. This possibility is guaranteed if $N > 2$ and $a \ll 1$. Summing up the transition probabilities considered by Kirman, one has the following scheme:

$$P(n+1|n) = \frac{N-n}{N}\left(a + (1-b)\frac{n}{N-1}\right)$$
$$P(n-1|n) = \frac{n}{N}\left(a + (1-b)\frac{N-n}{N-1}\right) \qquad (6)$$
$$P(n|n) = 1 - P\{n+1|n\} - P\{n-1|n\}$$
$$P(r|n) = 0 \text{ for } r \neq n-1, n, n+1$$

After determining the transition probability of the relevant Markov chain, Kirman considers two special cases: the Ehrenfest model, when $a = 1/2$ and $b = 1$; and a martingale with final absorption in $n = 0$ or $n = N$, with $a = b = 0$. Then Kirman examines the equilibrium probability distribution of the Markov chain defined by (6). We shall soon return to this distribution. Following Kirman, we shall now focus on the asymptotic form of the equilibrium probability distribution when the number of agents is large. In this respect, the argument of Kirman is not very clear. Anyway he maintains that if

$$N \to \infty, a = \frac{c}{N} \text{ and } b = \frac{2c}{N}, \qquad (6 \text{ bis})$$

the limit distribution on $x = n/N$ is a symmetric beta with both parameter equal to c, that is

$$\frac{\Gamma(2c)}{\Gamma(c)\Gamma(c)} x^{c-1}(1-x)^{c-1}, 0 < x < 1. \qquad (7)$$

For small values of c, (7) is U-shaped, that is it allots great probabilities to the extreme value of x, i.e. 0 and 1. Kirman's conclusion is that the above stochastic process determines the transition probability of moving from one state of the system to another. As a result of these transitions, the system sooner or later reaches all its possible states; moreover every state is revisited again and again. When the limit is reached, what does not change is the equilibrium probability distribution.

Before looking with more attention into Kirman's model, it is worth considering again the meaning of equilibrium when this is seen from a probabilistic point of view, that is, when a system reaches an equilibrium probability distribution. A probabilistic equilibrium does not determine a state in which the system will stay for ever. In Kirman's model, the equilibrium state is not a fixed percentage of ants that indefinitely forage at a given source of food, say A. From a probability perspective, such a constant behavior does not exist. There is not a single state that the system attains and never leaves. In this model, ants unceasingly change their strategies. This means that they forage sometime at A and sometime at B, and these changes follow one another perpetually. But all this does not happen in a chaotic mode, rather changes occur according to a well defined stochastic law. This, when (6 bis) holds, is the Beta distribution.

8.1.1 A Reconstruction of Kirman's Model

It may be shown that transition probabilities (6) are a special case of the stochastic process considered in the previous section. Before doing this, however, we may note that in (6 bis) N (the number of ants) tends to infinity, whereas $a = c/N$ and $b = 2c/N$ tend to zero as both parameters are function of N. We shall come back to this issue after examining the role of these parameters.

It is not difficult to recognize that in the transition probabilities of the first two rows there are two steps referring to destruction and creation probabilities. As a matter of fact $N - n/N$ and n/N are destruction probabilities. On the contrary, at least at first sight, it is not easy to realize that one may give the form of (3) to the creation probabilities of the rows of (6). But this is actually the case. As a matter of fact, we have

$$w = \frac{b}{1-b}(N-1), \text{ that is, } b = \frac{w}{w+N-1} = w_1 \text{ and } a = \frac{b}{2},$$

and thus $a = \dfrac{w}{2(w+N-1)} = w_2.$

This implies that the creation probabilities of the first two rows of (6) become

$$\frac{w}{2(w+N-1)} + \left(1 - \frac{w}{w+N-1}\right)\frac{n}{N-1} = \frac{\frac{w}{2} - n}{w+N-1}. \tag{8}$$

In a similar way, we see that the other creation probability becomes

$$\frac{\frac{w}{2} + N - n}{w + N - 1} \tag{9}$$

Equations (8) and (9) show that Kirman's stochastic process is a special case of the process considered in section 4. In other words, the transition probabilities of Kirman's model may be written as

$$P(\mathbf{N}_k^j \mid \mathbf{N}) = \frac{N_k}{M} \frac{\dfrac{w}{2} + N_j}{w + N - 1}, j = 1,2 \text{ and } k = 1,2, \qquad (10)$$

where $N_1 = n$ and $N_2 = N - n$. The argument in section 4 ensures that these are the transition probabilities of an exchangeable and invariant process satisfying **C, CD** and **CC**.

An immediate consequence of what we have seen is that the stochastic process has an equilibrium probability distribution as shown by (5 bis), which is a bivariate Polya distribution with both parameters equal to $w/2$. It follows that both parameters of that distribution are

$$\frac{N-1}{2} \frac{b}{1-b},$$

that is, they are both function of the size of the system. As a consequence, as $N \to \infty$, the Polya distribution does not converge to a beta distribution but to a δ function. Or, what is the same, according to the degenerated equilibrium probability distribution, the state $N/2$ has a probability equal to 1. This makes clear that in Kirman's model the growth without limit of the number of ants is not sufficient to reach the beta distribution. In order to reach the beta distribution Kirman was compelled to consider limit (6 bis). From our point of view, the matter is much simpler. In order to reach the same result, we do not need any other assumption. As a matter of fact, when $N \to \infty$, the Polya distribution arising from (10) approaches a symmetric beta distribution. The form of this distribution is specified by w. Choosing $(w/2) > 1$, the equilibrium probability distribution is a symmetric U-shaped distribution.

8.1.2 Towards an Economic Interpretation: Fundamental and Technical Propensities

When $j \neq k$, the creation probability of the transition probability (10) may be written as

$$P(\mathbf{N}_k^j \mid \mathbf{N}_k) = \frac{w}{w+N-1}\frac{1}{2} + \frac{N-1}{\lambda+N-1}\frac{N_j}{N-1}, k \neq j = 1,2. \qquad (11)$$

This is the weighted mean of two distributions: a theoretical one, the probability distribution

$$\left(\frac{w}{2}, \frac{w}{2}\right)$$

and an empirical one, the relative frequencies distribution

$$\left(\frac{N_1}{N}, \frac{N_2}{N}\right).$$

The weight of the first distribution is w and that of the second is $N-1$. This value accounts for the fact that, after one agent has taken the decision to change strategy, the number of agents following any strategy is no more N but $N-1$. The theoretical and empirical distributions are the extreme points of a simplex. This accounts for independence, $w \gg n$, and extreme correlation, $w \ll N$. Both points have an interesting meaning. Referring to choice among alternative strategies, a choice made by taking only the theoretical distribution into account is not affected by the occupation number of the strategy. Such a choice is stochastically independent of the behavior of the other agents in the market, as it is only determined by something that could be described as the basic attitude of the agent. On the contrary, a choice made by taking only the empirical distribution into account only look at the behavior of the other agents. From a stochastic perspective, such a choice fully depends on the behavior of the other agents. It reveals the existence of extreme herding propensity.

From the perspective of a probabilistic economic theory, transition probability (11) may be interpreted in an interesting way by supposing that any given economic agent shows two attitudes, which we shall call fundamental and technical propensities respectively. These attitudes might be displayed by referring to two ideal types of economic agents: the fundamental person or 'fundamentalist' F, and the technical person or 'chartist' C. A fundamentalist is a trader who bases his strategy of buying or selling, on the objective situation of the firm whose assets he is trading. He looks at interest rates, dividends, balance sheets in order to estimate the value of financial assets. His aim is to go as close as possible to an objective evaluation of a company and thus of its assets. A fundamentalist disregards the fleeting state of the market. The behaviors of other agents is irrelevant to him. On the contrary, a chartist looks mostly at the recent history of market prices. By using interpolative methods he tries to predict the future values of the assets. He is a trader who, after suitably plotting the past evolution of the value of an asset, bases his strategy on predicted future evolution as it may be associated with the charts by which he has represented the past. Therefore for a chartist the behaviors of the other agents is all what he is considering. He does not care about the 'objective value' of an asset, as he is interested in the expected short-run path of its price.

Obviously, fundamental and technical people are ideal types. An economic agent acting in a financial market is both a fundamentalist and a chartist in the sense that, in order to select a course of action, he takes both types of propensity into account. Equation (11) is a way to quantify the balancing an agent performs in order to choose his course of action. Equation (11) may be regarded as the formalization of a two-stage choice: being F or C, followed by a course of action, to buy 1, or to sell 2. We are thus faced with four possibilities: to be a fundamentalist and buy, $1|F$; to be a fundamentalist and sell, $2|F$; to be a chartist and buy, $1|C$; to be a chartist and sell, $2|C$. These four possibilities must be probabilistically valued. By the basic rules of probability theory we have, for $j = 1, 2$,

$$P(j) = P(j \wedge (F \vee C)) = P(j|F)P(F) + P(j|C)P(C). \quad (12)$$

This equality is identical to (11) by substituting in (12) the following values:

$$P(F) = \frac{w}{w+N-1}, P(C) = \frac{N-1}{w+N-1}, P(j|F) = \frac{w_j}{w}, P(j|C) = \frac{N_j}{N-1}.$$

The values of the free parameters of (12), that is w, w_j, N_j and N, determine the strategy of the economic agent. For instance, large values of w and w_j and small values of N associated with large values of $N_1 \leq N$, give rise to a high probability to buy.

We are now in the position to examine the model of Kirman in the light of (12). We focus on the creation probability of the second equation of (6) supposing that n is the occupation number of the cluster of buying persons. This means we are considering the creation probability after a buying person has decided to change his strategy. By substituting in (11)

$$P(F) = b, \ P(C) = 1-b, \ P(2|F) = \frac{1}{2}, \ P(2|C) = \frac{N-n}{N-1} \quad (13)$$

we have

$$\frac{b}{2} + (1-b)\frac{N-n}{N-1}.$$

We know that $a = (b/2)$, so that the last expression is the creation probability of $P(n-1|n)$.

8.1.3 Further Remarks on Kirman's model

The transition probabilities of (6) suggest that 'destructions' occur at random. This has been clearly shown by Kirman himself when he linked the meeting of two ants with the drawing of two marbles from a bag. On the contrary, it is really difficult to imagine the rationale behind Kirman's creation probabilities. As a matter of fact, he gave no justification for the form of these probabilities. We have shown how creation probabilities can be dealt with in our framework. Our reconstruction highlights a specific feature of Kirman's creation probabilities. This is the equality of initial weights. But it is equation (13) that makes this peculiarity clear. Looking at the matter from our perspective, one realizes that b and $1 - b$ are the probabilities of F and C. Since b is a free parameter, the two probabilities are not fixed by Kirman's model. This notwithstanding, these probabilities point out that the choice between fundamental and technical propensities does not depend upon the size (N) of the financial market, but is a choice made by any given agent independently of other agents' behavior. On the other hand, what is fully clear is the meaning of

$$P(2 \mid F) = \frac{1}{2} = P(1 \mid F).$$

This shows that the equality of initial weights for a fundamentalist is the same as the equality of the probabilities of buying and selling. In other words, when Kirman's model is applied to the financial market, it suggests that a fundamentalist decides at random whether to buy or to sell. This means that his choice is fully independent of his attitude. This contrasts with the expectation one generally has about the behavior of a fundamentalist. Finally, and coming back to (11), we see that a change of strategy, which in Kirman's model always happen at random, in our approach is first of all determined by a balance between fundamental and technical propensities (whose weights are respectively w and $N - 1$). The probability of buying or selling only plays a secondary role, as it is a conditional probability that varies according to the nature of the propensity one is considering.

8.2 Stock Price Dynamics

The second fragment of probabilistic economics we shall examine is close to the approach suggested by Kirman. In a sense, what we are doing is a continuation and enlargement of Kirman's model. Our work, however, remains at a very abstract level as we take many simplifications for granted. The relationship of our model with that of Kirman becomes clear if one assumes that the two sources of food correspond with the two alternative strategies to buy or to sell. However, we shall now consider another strategy different from the previous two. Each agent may choose among three different strategies, which constitute a class of exclusive and exhaustive courses of actions: either to buy a given stock, or to sell it, or to abstain from trading. Hence we introduce the 'abstainer', that is, an agent who takes the decision to 'wait and see'. Referring to Kirman's model, the abstainers might be regarded as ants stopping to forage in order to look at the development of the situation. In what follows we shall discuss the advantages associated with the new assumption.

Following Cont and Bouchaud (2000), we consider a stock market with N agents labeled by $1 \le i \le N$, whose names are $X_1, ..., X_i, ..., X_N$. Such agents are assumed to trade in a single asset, whose price logarithm at time t is $x(t)$. During each time period, an agent may choose to buy, to sell or not to trade. At any given time, any given agent may choose from among the three following strategies: to buy, +1, to sell, –1, to abstain, 0. These are the cells we want to consider. At any given time, the description of the market is as follows:

$$X_1 = +1, \ X_2 = 0, \ ..., \ X_n = -1, \ ..., \ X_N = +1,$$

that is, the agent denoted by X_1, for short the first agent, buys, the second abstains, the nth sells, up to the last that buys. An occupation vector of the system is

$$\mathbf{N} = (N_+, N_-, N_0), \ N_+ + N_- + N_0 = N. \tag{14}$$

Thus N_+ agents buy, N_- sell and N_0 abstain from trade. Expression (14) describes the state of the system.

For the sake of simplicity, we analyze the change of strategy of a single agent by noting, however, that we could also consider the strategy changes of a finite number of agents. The demand for stock of agent i is represented by a random variable Y, which can take three values $\{+1, -1, 0\}$. The aggregate excess demand for the asset at time t is $D(t) \equiv \sum_{i=1}^{N} Y_i(t)$. We assume that price is proportional to $D(t)$, i.e. $\Delta x(t) = x(t-1) - x(t) = \eta^{-1} D(t)$, where η is the excess demand needed to shift the percentage return of one unit. For the sake of simplicity, we assume $\eta = 1$. At time t, the state of the system is $N(t) \equiv (N_+(t), N_-(t), N_0(t))$ and the excess demand is $D(t) = N_+(t) - N_-(t)$. The parameters (our *initial weights*) associated with the three strategies w_+, w_-, w_0, (such that $w = w_+ + w_- + w_0$) determine the transition probability of the Markov chain.

The economic interpretation of the above scheme is straightforward. At any given step an agent may change strategy. For positive values of parameters, agents are inclined to join the majority; for negative values, agents are inclined to be at odds with the majority; when the parameters become very large (go to infinity) the agent is not influenced by the environment.

When conditions **C**, **CD** and **CC** hold, the equilibrium distribution is (5 bis), which in the case we are considering becomes

$$P(N_+, N_-, N_0) = \frac{N!}{N_+! N_-! N_0!} \frac{w_+^{[N_+]} w_-^{[N_-]} w_0^{[N_0]}}{w^{[N]}}. \tag{15}$$

It is worthwhile to give an interpretation for the three parameters of (15). At each time t, an agent may change her strategy, for example being a '+' / '−' she may become a '−' or a '0', but she might also maintain her initial strategy. As we have seen, the change amounts to a destruction followed by a creation. Destructions do not depend upon any parameter, that is, in all cases the probability of giving up a strategy for a new one is given by

$$\frac{N_j}{N}, j \in \{+,-,0\}.$$

In other words, this probability is the same for all agents independently of the strategy they follow. The decision to change a strategy is taken at random. Therefore, it is more likely that the decision to change strategy will be taken by agents belonging to the cluster whose size is largest.

The probability of adopting a new strategy is of special interest, and we shall spend a few words trying to explain it. But in order to avoid misunderstanding, we should make clear the sense in which we are using the term 'new' with respect to a strategy. This should also clarify the meaning of a strategy change. A new strategy is not necessarily different from the old one, that is, from the strategy the agent followed till now. For 'new strategy' we simply mean the strategy the agent accepts after having taken the decision to reconsider the strategy he has till now followed. In other words, having given up the current strategy, the agent has before him three possible strategies, i.e. +,− and 0. Being the choice among them probabilistic in character, it may happen that the strategy he will accept is the same as that he has just given up. Briefly, the 'new' may possibly be identical to the 'old'. Obviously, when this is the case, the agent does not change his strategy in practice.

The probability of the creation we are considering depends upon the values of w and $w_j, j \in \{+,-,0\}$. These parameters are free, in the sense that their values must be fixed in order to arrive at the equilibrium distribution. For $w > 0$, we have positive stochastic dependence. The probability that the agent adopts a new strategy, not necessarily different from the old one, is given by

$$\frac{w_j + N_j}{w + N - 1}, j \in \{+,-,0\}.$$

This means that this probability increases both with w_j and N_j. The effect of this, roughly speaking, is that agents incline to follow the majority. But this propensity decreases with a growing w. When $w \to \infty$, we have stochastic independence. If this is the case, the probability we are considering becomes

$$p_j = \frac{w_j}{w}, j \in \{+,-,0\},$$

that is, such a probability only depends upon the parameter values and not upon $N_j, j \in \{+,-,0\}$. In this case, the probability of a strategy change is not affected by the size of the three agent groups. Roughly speaking, the behavior of any given agent is not affected by the behavior of the other agents trading in the market. But there is another aspect of the initial weights that is worth stressing. For w_+ can be interpreted as the propensity of agents to buy, w_- as the propensity to sell, and w_0 as the propensity to abstain from trade. If, for example, w_0 is much greater than both w_+ and w_-, agents are inclined to wait and see.

We are now ready for the study of the price dynamics of the asset under consideration. To begin, we suppose that, as w_+, w_-, N_+ and N_- have finite values, the values of w_0 and N_0 grow without limit. Formally we assume the 'thermodynamic limit', which is a name for the limits $w_0 \to \infty$, $N \to \infty$ when

$$\frac{N}{w} \to \chi \text{ (constant)}.$$

In this case, the limit means that we keep constant the subsystem including buying and selling people whose occupation vector is (N_+, N_-), while the size of the market tends to infinity for any given density of agents with respect to the total weight. Clearly this situation is not the one considered in the case of the thermodynamic limit. This is because the joint distribution of + and − tends (in distribution) to the product of two distributions, that is, the Polya distribution factorizes, i.e. $P(N_+, N_-, N_0) \to P(N_+)P(N_-)$. As a result, the two equilibrium probability distributions are stochastic independent. Moreover, they are both negative binomial distributions, that is

$$P(N_+;\chi) = \frac{w_+}{N_+!}\left(\frac{1}{1+\chi}\right)^{w_+}\left(\frac{\chi}{1+\chi}\right)^{N_+},$$

$$P(N_-;\chi) = \frac{w_-}{N_-!}\left(\frac{1}{1+\chi}\right)^{w_-}\left(\frac{\chi}{1+\chi}\right)^{N_-}.$$

A more interesting economic interpretation of the above limit is as follows. For the limit corresponds to an increase in the number of agents associated with an increase in the propensity to wait and see, when both increments are carried out in such a way that the mean values of bulls and bears are constant, that is

$$E(N_+) = N\frac{w_+}{w_+ + w_- + w_0} \to w_+\chi \text{ and } E(N_-) = N\frac{w_-}{w_+ + w_- + w_0} \to w_-\chi.$$

If this is the case, the cluster of abstainers may be considered as a reserve of potential traders, in the sense that this cluster may both supply active agents and admit agents that stop trading.

A moment reflection persuades that the equilibrium distributions depends upon $w, w_j, j = +, -$ and χ, that is

$$E(N_j) = w_j\chi \text{ and } V(N_j) = w_j\chi(1-\chi),$$

while for kurtosis we have

$$K(N_j) = \frac{1}{w_j}\left(6 + \frac{1}{\chi(1+\chi)}\right),$$

which shows that the kurtosis of the negative binomial distribution is large for small values of w_j.

The probability characteristics of price increments for the item under consideration may be determined as follows. We know that

$$E(\Delta x) = E(N_+ - N_-) = (w_+ - w_-)\chi.$$

Moreover, due to the stochastic independence of the distributions of N_+ and N_-, we have:

$$V(\Delta x) = V(N_+ - N_-) = (w_+ - w_-)\chi(1+\chi),$$

and

$$K(\Delta x) = \frac{(V(N_+))^2 K(N_+) + (V(N_-))^2 K(N_-)}{(V(N_+) + V(N_-))^2} = \frac{1}{w_+ + w_-}\left(6 + \frac{1}{\chi(1+\chi)}\right).$$

It is worth noting that the three equations above relate the momenta of the distribution of price increments to the three parameters w_+, w_- and χ, which characterize the state of the market. It follows that, by using methods of statistical estimation, from the mean value, variance and kurtosis of the observed frequencies distribution, it is possible to determine the values of the three parameters. This would enable a test of proximity of the dynamics suggested by our theoretical framework with the actual dynamics of the price of any given stock.

References

Aoki, M. 2002, *Aggregate Behavior and Fluctuations in Economics*, Cambridge and New York: Cambridge University Press.

Costantini, D. and Garibaldi, U. 2000. A Purely Probabilistic Representation for the Dynamics of a Gas of Particles. *Foundations of Physics* 30(1): 81-99.

Costantini, D. and Garibaldi, U. 2004. The Ehrenfest Fleas: From Model to Theory. *Synthèse* 139(1): 107-42.

Cont, R. and Bouchaud, J.P. 2000. Herd Behavior and Aggregate Fluctuations in Financial Markets. *Macroeconomic Dynamics* 4(2): 170-96.

Garegnani, P. 1976. On the Change in the Notion of Equilibrium in Recent Work on Value and Distribution. *Essays in Modern Capital Theory*, eds. M. Brown, K. Sato and P. Zarembka, 25-45. Amsterdam: North Holland.

Keynes, J.M. 1921. *A Treatise on Probability*, London: Macmillan.

Keynes, J.M. 1973. *The General Theory of Employment Interest and Money. The Collected Writings of John Maynard Keynes, vol. VII*. London: MacMillan.

Kirman, A. 1993. Ants, Rationality and Recruitment. *The Quarterly Journal of Economics* 108(1): 137-56.

Mantegna, R.N. and Stanley H.E. 2000. *An Introduction to Econophysics. Correlations and Complexity in Finance*. Cambridge: Cambridge University Press.

Mirowski, P. 1989. *More Heat than Light*. Cambridge: Cambridge University Press.

II Mental Frames and Cognitive Abilities

6

Reasoning to be Rational
JOHN BROOME

1 The Problem of Motivation

Suppose you believe you ought to do something. Very often, a belief of this sort will cause you to do what you believe you ought to do. But many philosophers find this puzzling. They wonder how a belief can 'motivate' an action, as they put it. This puzzle has driven a great deal of recent moral philosophy.

Noncognitivists deny that your state is a genuine belief. This offers one solution to the puzzle. When you apparently believe you ought to do something, noncognitivists think you are actually in some other sort of a state, which already incorporates a motivation in some way. Perhaps, say, it is really a sort of intention.[1] Other philosophers accept that a normative belief is a genuine belief, and then are then faced with the need to explain how a genuine belief can cause a person to act.

Whether or not this seems puzzling, it is not really very hard to explain. We can simply say that people are naturally disposed to do what they believe they ought to do. This is not a universal or infallible disposition, but most of us most of the time are inclined that way. Furthermore, this easy explanation is surely correct; we do indeed mostly have this disposition. We can add that we have been caused to have it by processes of natural selection. But this explanation still leaves a lot to be explained. Through what process does the disposition work, exactly? *How* does our belief cause us to act, when it does?

An answer might be that people who have the disposition just do what they believe they ought to do; it just happens through some unconscious causal process within them. But this answer is unsatisfying. Some people

---
[1] For example, see Gibbard 2003.

have the disposition, and others do not. We can classify them accordingly; let us call the first sort 'sheep' and the second sort 'goats'. But unless we are inclined to Calvinism, we shall not be content with merely classifying. We should expect goats to be able to make themselves sheep: we should expect that people by their own efforts can actually bring themselves to intend to do what they believe they ought to do. And we should expect to be able to produce an account of how they can do so.

We can call in rationality to help. We can say that rationality requires you to do what you believe you ought to do, from which it follows that the goats are irrational. No doubt this is correct too, and it gives us a criticism to throw at the goats. But it does not help explain how the goats can turn themselves into sheep. We need an account of how people can bring themselves to satisfy requirements of rationality. Till we have that, we still lack an explanation of how they can bring themselves to do what they believe they ought to do. Our story remains unsatisfactory.

However, calling in rationality is a genuine step forward, because people have a means of bringing themselves to meet some of the requirements of rationality. Our means is reasoning. Reasoning is something we do. It is a mental activity of ours that can bring us to satisfy some of the requirements of rationality.

Suppose you believe it is raining and that if it is raining the snow will melt. Plausibly, rationality requires you to believe what is entailed by things that you believe – in this case that the snow will melt. But suppose you do not yet believe the snow will melt. (Suppose you have just woken up. You have noticed the rain, and you know that rain causes snow to melt, but you have not yet thought about the snow.) You can bring yourself to believe it by undertaking a process of reasoning. This process will start from your initial beliefs and it will conclude with your believing the snow will melt. In doing this reasoning you are mentally active, and you bring yourself to satisfy a requirement of rationality.

Now suppose you believe you ought to stand for parliament. Plausibly, rationality requires you to intend to do what you believe you ought to do. You can bring yourself to satisfy this requirement, too, by a process of reasoning. So I claim, at least. I call this *kratic reasoning*. The process will start from your initial belief that you ought to stand for parliament, and conclude with your intending to stand for parliament. Intending to do something normally causes you to do it, so normally you will end up standing for parliament.

In your reasoning you are active; you bring yourself to satisfy the requirement of rationality. It is because you reason that you are disposed to do what you believe you ought to do. This is the answer to the question I asked. How does your disposition work? It works through this activity of yours. You are not merely passive.

I am talking about explicit, conscious reasoning. That is something we do. Very often, we come to satisfy various requirements of rationality through unconscious, automatic processes. We might well call those processes unconscious reasoning. But I am not counting them as reasoning in this paper. In this paper, I am concerned only with reasoning as activity, and that is conscious reasoning.

Reasoning offers the best answer to the question of how we can be motivated by our normative beliefs, because it is an answer that recognizes we are active. That explains my interest in kratic reasoning, and the motivation for this paper. I need to demonstrate that there is indeed such a thing as kratic reasoning. I cannot achieve that much in this paper. This paper is merely the beginning of a movement in that direction. It examines the nature of reasoning in general, and particularly of practical reasoning. It end by saying a little about kratic reasoning in particular.

2 Types of Reasoning

Reasoning is a process that starts from some mental states of yours, and brings you to a new mental state. These states are of the sort that are called *attitudes*, which means they have a *content*. The attitude is an attitude towards its content. A belief is an attitude; the content of a belief is the proposition that is believed. An intention is another type of attitude; its content is what is intended. Philosophers generally assume that the content of any attitude – not just a belief – is a proposition, and they give the name 'propositional attitude' to all attitudes. But I think we have to recognize that some attitudes have contents that are not propositions,[2] my term is simply 'attitude'.

Reasoning sets out from some premise-attitudes and brings you to a conclusion-attitude. In the first example above, your two premise-attitudes are a belief that it is raining and a belief that if it is raining the snow will melt. Your conclusion attitude is a belief that the snow will melt. In the second example, your premise-attitude is a belief that you ought to stand for parliament, and your conclusion-attitude is an intention to enter parliament.

Traditionally, reasoning has been divided into two types: theoretical and practical. We can classify reasoning into types by the nature of its conclusion-attitude. Theoretical reasoning is reasoning that concludes in a belief; practical reasoning is reasoning that concludes in an intention. There may

---

[2] See my 'The unity of reasoning?' (Forthcoming) for an explanation of why.

also be other types, such as reasoning that concludes in a desire, but this paper is concerned with theoretical and practical reasoning only.

3 Requirements of Rationality

Reasoning is an activity by means of which we can bring ourselves to satisfy some of the requirements of rationality. In a sense, this is its purpose. I therefore need to start by describing some requirements of rationality. Here are three examples:

Modus ponens. Rationality requires of N that, if N believes that p and N believes that if p then q, and if it matters to N whether q, then N believes that q.

End-means. Rationality requires of N that, if N intends that e, and if N believes that e will be so only if m is so, and if N believes that m will be so only if she intends that m, then N intends that m.

Krasia. Rationality requires of N that, if N believes that she ought that p, and if N believes that p will be so if and only if she intends that p, then N intends that p.

These are rather formally set out, using schematic letters. They are technically requirement-schemata. To generate a specific requirement, for 'N' substitute a term that designates a person, and for the other letters substitute terms that designate propositions. The ungrammatical 'ought that' is employed as a technical device in the statement of *Krasia*; its meaning it clear.

The formulae say, roughly, that rationality requires you to believe what follows by modus ponens from things that you believe, that rationality requires you to intend what you believe is a necessary means to an end that you intend, and that rationality requires you to intend to do what you believe you ought to do. The more precise formulations include a number of qualifying clauses, without which the requirements would not be accurately stated. The qualifying clauses in *Modus ponens* and *Krasia* do not matter for my purposes in this paper, and I shall leave you to work out for yourself why they are needed. However, I do need to give some attention to the formal specification of *End-means*, because my rough description of this requirement could be misleading.

First, *End-means* contains the clause 'if N believes that m will be so only if she intends that m'. Suppose you intend to win a race, and suppose that you believe you will not win it unless you breathe. But suppose you believe you will breathe anyway, whether or not you intend to breathe. You believe that breathing is something you do automatically. Then, even though you intend to win the race and believe that breathing is a necessary means of doing so, you may be perfectly rational even if you do not intend to breathe. Hence the need for this qualifying clause.

Next look at the other conditional clause in *End-means*: 'if N believes that e will be so only if m is so'. My rough description of *End-means* suggests the clause is 'if N believes that m is a necessary means to e', but actually it is not. That is why the rough description can be misleading. The actual, formal condition is different in two respects. First, N is not required to believe m is a means to e. It might be a consequence of e, for example. The presence of that second condition 'if N believes that m will be so only if she intends that m' allows me to formulate *End-means* with this extra little bit of generality. However, as it happens, this bit of generality plays no part in this paper. The other difference is much more important.

The other difference is that the condition requires N to believe only that: If e then m. It does not require her to believe, more strongly, that: Necessarily, if e than m. In a sense, N has to believe that m is a necessary condition for e, but only in a weak sense of 'necessary condition'. It will emerge in section 9 that this extra generality very much increases the importance of *End-means*.

I cannot enter into the grounds of requirements of rationality in this paper, and I cannot try to justify the formulations I have given. I think they are all intuitively satisfactory. For example, *End-means* is a rendering of Kant's famous remark:

> Who wills the end, wills (so far as reason has a decisive influence on his actions) also the means which are indispensably necessary and in his power. (Kant 1948: 80-81)

I shall accept these requirements simply on intuitive grounds. Nevertheless, in fairness I ought to mention that each is controversial to some degree; I shall have to ignore the controversy.

4 Theoretical Reasoning: the Second-Order Model

I shall start my investigation of reasoning with theoretical reasoning because it is easier to understand than other types. I shall use it to draw out some of the central characteristics of reasoning. Practical reasoning will come later.

Modus ponens is a requirement on your beliefs. You can be brought to satisfy it by theoretical reasoning. So I shall start with that requirement. How can you come to satisfy *Modus ponens* by reasoning? Two very different models of reasoning are available; I call them respectively the second-order model and the first-order model. I shall start with the second-order model, but only in order to reject it.

I call it the 'second-order model' because it assumes that second-order beliefs participate in your reasoning. I can explain it most easily using the example I have already introduced. You wake up hearing rain. Because of what you hear, you believe it is raining. You have a long-established belief that, if it is raining, the snow will melt. Moreover, it matters to you whether the snow will melt. However, because you are sleepy and have not yet thought about the snow, you do not yet believe the snow will melt. So you do not satisfy the requirement *Modus ponens* in this instance. You believe it is raining; you believe that, if it is raining, the snow will melt; but you do not believe the snow will melt. By reasoning, you can surely bring yourself to satisfy the requirement. How will your reasoning proceed?

According to the second-order model, it will set out from a belief in the requirement itself. The model assumes you believe the relevant instance of *Modus ponens*. That is, you believe rationality requires of you that: you believe the snow will melt if you believe it is raining and you believe that, if it is raining the snow will melt. According to the second-order model, starting from this belief in the requirement, you reason your way to satisfying the requirement.

This is an example of theoretical reasoning, but the second-order model can be applied to reasoning of any sort. In general, it supposes that your reasoning starts from your believing some requirement of rationality in some instance, and concludes with your satisfying that requirement in that instance. The requirements I am concerned with are requirements on your attitudes of the sort I described in section 3. So when you believe a requirement, your belief is about your attitudes – specifically about what rationality requires of them. I therefore call it a 'second-order belief'. The model supposes that your reasoning sets out from a second-order belief of this sort.

I think the second-order model fails, and I shall next explain why. My explanation will be brief.[3]

The model requires you to progress from believing in a requirement of rationality to satisfying that requirement. How might that happen? I see two possible routes. One is that it might happen through some unconscious process. You might be so constituted that, when you believe rationality requires you to be in such-and-such a mental state, you tend to enter that state without thinking about it. I find it implausible that this sort of thing would happen reliably. But I am anyway not interested in this route because a process of this sort would not be reasoning, even if it did happen. At least, it would not be conscious reasoning, which is what concerns me in this paper.

---

[3] For a fuller explanation see Broome 2006.

The second possible route goes through an intention. When you believe you ought to be in such-and-such a state, this belief might first bring you to form the intention of being in that state. Then, second, the intention might cause you to be in it.

The first stage of this process is forming the intention. This is the sort of thing that can happen through conscious reasoning. At least I think so. I think that reasoning can bring you to satisfy the requirement *Krasia*. That is to say, when you believe you ought to do something, reasoning can bring you to intend to do it. I have already called this type of reasoning 'kratic reasoning'. It is described in section 10. We might suppose that, when you believe rationality requires you to be in a particular mental state, kratic reasoning could bring you to intend to be in that state. At least for the sake of argument, I shall grant that this is possible.

But the second stage of the process can rarely succeed. Intending to be in a mental state is rarely successful; it rarely causes you to be in that state. I am speaking only of the sorts of mental states that rationality requires of you. These are complexes of attitudes, as my examples show. You can rarely alter your attitudes by intending to.

Sometimes you can. Sometimes you have a means available of coming to have a particular attitude. For example, going regularly to church may be a means of coming to believe there is a God. If so, an intention to believe there is a God might be effective. It might cause you to believe there is a God, through causing you to go regularly to church. But for most attitudes, no such means is available.

Without a means, you cannot alter your attitudes by intending to. You can do some things by intending to, without using a means. For example, you can raise your arm by intending to, without using a means. But we do not have that sort of control over our attitudes. I cannot support this claim here; I simply assert it.[4] It means the second-order model of theoretical reasoning cannot work through this second route, because we do not have the sort of control over our attitudes that it would require.

We do not have that sort of control over any of our attitudes, not just our beliefs. The second-order model therefore fails, not just as a model of theoretical reasoning, but as a model of reasoning in general. It will not appear again in this paper.

5 Theoretical Reasoning: the First-Order Model

The first-order model is very different. To describe it I shall continue to use the same example. Suppose you believe it is raining, and that if it is raining

---

[4] It is supported by Hieronymi 2006. My own arguments are different from hers.

the snow will melt. But suppose you do not believe the snow will melt. Then you do not satisfy requirement (2). But you might bring yourself to satisfy it by reasoning. To do so, you would say to yourself that:

It is raining
If it is raining the snow will melt.
So, the snow will melt.

I have written down a sequence of sentences, which designate propositions. You do not necessarily say these sentences to yourself; you might reason in Italian, say. But you do say to yourself the propositions that these sentences designate. You say to yourself *that* it is raining, and *that* if it is raining the snow will melt, and then you say *that* the snow will melt. I shall mention the word 'so' later.

You initially believe the first two of these propositions; in saying them to yourself you are expressing your beliefs. You do not initially believe the third. But when you say it to yourself, you express a belief in it. By the time you come to say it, your reasoning has brought you to believe it. By this time, you satisfy *Modus ponens*. That is how your reasoning works.

The propositions you say to yourself constitute the contents of your beliefs. You can reason with beliefs only because they are attitudes, which are states that have contents. Their contents give you something to reason with.

Saying to yourself is an act. Sometimes no doubt, you say things to yourself out loud, but more often you do it silently. In that case, I could alternatively have said you call the proposition to mind; 'saying to yourself' is a more graphic way of describing what you do. One thing it does it bring the beliefs together, if you have not previously done that in your mind. In any case, whether you speak silently or out loud, you are acting. So you are literally active when you reason. This partially explains how reasoning is a way to be active in satisfying the requirements of rationality. It is an activity. It is an activity in a further way I shall describe later.

Your acts of saying to yourself are part of your reasoning, but not the whole of it. Your reasoning is the causal process whereby some of your beliefs cause you to acquire a new belief. It includes a sequence of acts, and it is itself a complex act. To be reasoning, the process must involve acts of saying to yourself. Some of your beliefs cause you to acquire a new belief, through some acts of this sort. The process ends when you acquire your new belief.

The acquisition of this belief is an act. Described one way, the acquisition is something you intend. When you embark on your reasoning, you intend to come to believe whatever is the conclusion that emerges from the reasoning: you intend that, if p is the proposition that emerges from the reasoning, you believe p. However, you do not intend to believe the specific proposition that emerges. In the example, you do not intend to believe the snow will melt. Coming to believe the snow will melt is an act like finding your glasses under the bed, after looking for them. You intend to find your glasses, and this makes it the case that your finding them under the bed is an act. But you do not intend to find them under the bed.

Since reasoning is a process whereby some of your beliefs give rise to a new belief, acts of saying to yourself can only form a part of it when they express beliefs. In the example, in saying to yourself that it is raining, you must express a belief of yours that it is raining. When you say to yourself that the snow will melt, you must express a belief of yours that the snow will melt, and so on. In the context of belief, saying to yourself is asserting to yourself. True, you could say to yourself the sequence of sentences

'It is raining.
If it is raining the snow will melt.
So the snow will melt.'

even if you did not have the corresponding beliefs. But in doing that you would not be reasoning because you would not be going through a process whereby some of your beliefs give rise to a new belief.

In the course of your reasoning, you do not say to yourself any second-order propositions about your mental states; you say to yourself the propositions that constitute the contents of your mental states. In the example, you do not say to yourself that you believe it is raining, nor that you ought to believe the snow will melt, nor anything else about your beliefs. You reasoning is not *about* your beliefs. We may say you reason *with* your beliefs. It is *about* the contents of your beliefs.

(The word 'belief' is ambiguous. It sometimes refers to a mental attitude, and sometimes to a proposition that is a content of a mental attitude. I use it in the former sense only.)

The second-order model of reasoning fails because we do not have the sort of control over our beliefs that it demands. On the other hand, the process I am now describing directly modifies your beliefs, because it works on the contents of beliefs. When you conclude that the snow will melt, in doing that you are directly acquiring a new belief.

I have not yet said enough to characterize reasoning even for the paradigmatic example of theoretical reasoning. My description so far has only been this: you say to yourself some propositions that you believe, and this causes you to acquire a new belief. But some processes that fit this description would not be reasoning. For example, suppose you believe it is raining and that if it is raining the snow will melt. Suppose you say to yourself that it is raining and that if it is raining the snow will melt, and suppose this causes you to believe you hear trumpets. That bizarre process is probably not reasoning.

What distinguishes true reasoning from bizarre processes like this? You might think it is the presence of a second-order belief. In my example of genuine reasoning, you moved from believing it is raining and believing that, if it is raining the snow will melt to believing the snow will melt. You might think this process is reasoning only if you have the second-order belief that: rationality requires you to believe the snow will melt if you believe it is raining and you believe that if it is raining the snow will melt. The presence of that belief is needed to make it reasoning.

Even if this was so, it would not restore the second-order model of reasoning. The reasoning is still conducted at the first order, even if you need a second-order belief in the background to make it reasoning. But actually I think it is not so. A sophisticated reasoner may have this second-order belief, but I do not see why you need so much sophistication in order to reason. I do not see why you need to have the concept of a rational requirement, or even the concept of a belief.

It is more plausible that a different sort of background belief is needed to separate your reasoning process from others such as the bizarre one. You might need to believe that, from the proposition that it is raining and the proposition that if it is raining the snow will melt, it follows that the snow will melt. That is to say, you might need in the background, not a second-order belief about what rationality requires of your beliefs, but a belief about the inferential relations that hold among the propositions that constitute the contents of your beliefs. I do not deny that a belief such as this may be a necessary condition for you to reason. But even if it is necessary in the background, it is not itself a part of the reasoning; its content does not constitute an extra premise. That is the lesson taught us by Lewis Carroll in 'What the tortoise said to Achilles' (1985). So the first-order model of reasoning is not affected, even if this belief is necessary in the background.

My own view is that reasoning processes are computational. This is what characterizes them as reasoning and distinguishes them from bizarre processes such as the one I described. If I am right, it adds to the ways in which reasoning is an activity, since computation is something you do. You operate on the contents of your attitudes computationally. The content of your first premise-belief – that it is raining – is the antecedent of the content of your second premise-belief – the conditional proposition that if it is raining the snow will melt. You apply the modus ponens rule, which tells you in these circumstances to form a proposition that is the consequent of the conditional: that the snow will melt. You end up believing this consequent. According to this model, that word 'so' indicates your working through the rule-governed process. Computation is too big and difficult a topic for me to broach in this paper. I shall simply allow myself the assumption that reasoning is an operation on the contents of your attitudes.

To summarize the description of reasoning that has emerged from this paradigmatic example: reasoning is a process whereby some of your attitudes give rise to another attitude; in reasoning you say to yourself the contents of these attitudes, and you reason about these contents, operating on them computationally. Reasoning is an operation on contents.

6 Theoretical Reasoning in Reverse

Theoretical reasoning often does not proceed in a neat linear fashion as it did in my example. In the example, your reasoning sets out from some initial beliefs and concludes with a new belief. But actual theoretical reasoning will often lead you to drop one or more of your initial beliefs, rather than acquire a new one. Dropping a premise-belief will equally successfully bring you to satisfy the requirement of rationality *Modus ponens*. But how does reasoning of this sort work?

Suppose you embark on the process of reasoning I described, but do not conclude it. I shall change the example. You believe that whales are fish and that if whales are fish then whales have gills. You say to yourself that whales are fish and that if whales are fish then whales have gills, but you find you do not end up believing whales have gills. You have failed in what you intended, which was to come to believe a new proposition.

You remain in violation of the requirement *Modus ponens*. But you may yet be able to achieve rationality through reasoning. You may not be able to do so if it is some irrational obstruction that prevents you from believing the conclusion. But normally, when you cannot believe the conclusion of reasoning you embark on, it is because you believe the negation of the conclusion. In the example, you believe whales do not have gills. For example, you may have seen pictures of whales, and seen that they do not have gills.

This means you can continue with your reasoning in another direction. You can say to yourself that whales do not have gills. You might conclude your reasoning by saying to yourself that whales are not fish. You now have a new belief that whales are not fish. In the course of your reasoning, you say to yourself in sequence that

Whales are fish.
If whales are fish, then whales have gills.
Whales do not have gills.
So, whales are not fish.

Each time, you express a belief. This is peculiar at first sight. It is a single sequence of reasoning, but it contains two contradictory beliefs. How is this possible? Because the process of reasoning takes time. At the outset, you believe whales are fish, but by the end of your reasoning you no longer believe this and instead you believe its negation.

Rationality requires you not to believe both a proposition and its negation. This is a requirement I have not mentioned yet, because it is not one that we can come to satisfy by reasoning. We are caused to satisfy some requirements of rationality by unconscious processes, and this is one of them. Unconscious processes will normally not allow you to believe both a proposition and its negation. Given that, you will not be able to come to believe whales are not fish whilst still believing whales are fish. So for you to complete your reverse reasoning, two things must happen: you must come to believe whales are not fish, and you must stop believing whales are fish. Provided both do happen, you will end up satisfying *Modus ponens* and also its cousin – yet another requirement of rationality – *Modus tollens*.

Since reasoning is not necessarily linear, it might go in either of two directions. In the example, it could have gone forward and brought you to believe whales have gills, but actually it went backward and brought you to believe whales are not fish. This raises a new question. What controls the direction of your reasoning?

In the example, you start with competing beliefs: that whales are fish, that if whales are fish then whales have gills, and that whales do not have gills. In a sense, the direction of your reasoning must be determined by the relative robustness of these beliefs. How convinced are you that whales are fish, or that they have no gills? Robustness in this context is a complex notion. Consequently, to give a proper account of the direction of reasoning would be a substantial undertaking, which I cannot embark on here.

7 Intention and Beliefs

So much for theoretical reasoning. I am about to turn to practical reasoning, but I need to mention a crucial preliminary first. Practical reasoning is reasoning that concludes in an intention. Before we can understand it, we need to notice something about the way we express intentions. In expressing an intention we also express a belief. When you say 'I shall wake up at 5.00', expressing an intention, your are saying that you will wake up at 5.00. If a prospective burglar overhears what you say, she may well conclude she had better finish burgling your house before 5.00. To her it does not matter whether you are expressing an intention or merely a belief that you will wake up at 5.00. Either way, what you say constitutes an assertion.

This is puzzling. How can the expression of an intention also express a belief? It means that, when you express an intention sincerely, you must have the corresponding belief. But does anything guarantee that is so?

Something does. There is a connection between the belief and the intention that makes this possible. It is sometimes thought that, if you intend to do something, you must believe you will do it. This is not exactly true, because you may have an intention without believing you have it. For example, suppose you have arranged to go to a meeting in Pisa on 21 May, but have temporarily forgotten your appointment. You still intend to be there, but you have forgotten you intend it. In that case, though you do intend it, you may not believe you will be in Pisa on 21 May. However, if you *believe* you intend to do something, in that case you must believe you will do it. This is the intimate connection between an intention and the corresponding belief, which allows both to be expressed by the same sentence. Although you can have an intention without believing you have it, you cannot *express* an intention without believing you have it. Consequently, when you express an intention, you must believe you will do what you intend.

I recognize this is a strong claim, and very controversial in the philosophy of action. The evidence I offer for it is that the expression of an intention is also an expression of a belief. Both take the form of saying an indicative sentence. So you cannot express an intention without expressing a belief that you will do what you intend, which you cannot do sincerely without having the belief. This should not be surprising. One purpose of forming an intention is to settle something about what is going to happen. You decide to be in Pisa on 21 May, and that settles it that you will be in Pisa on 21 May. In your subsequent thinking you can use the information that you will be in Pisa on 21 May. For example, it may become a premise in your theoretical reasoning. You may conclude that you will not be in Bologna that day. Since this is one of the purposes of an intention, it is unsurprising that expressing an intention is also expressing a belief.

8 Instrumental Reasoning

Now at last I arrive at practical reasoning. I shall start with instrumental reasoning, and specifically with reasoning that can bring you to satisfy the requirement of rationality *End-means* stated in section 3. This is the requirement (roughly) that you intend what you believe is a necessary means to an end that you intend. I repeat the precise formula here:

> *End-means.* Rationality requires of N that, if N intends that e, and if N believes that e will be so only if m is so, and if N believes that m will be so only if she intends that m, then N intends that m.

Suppose you intend to visit Stockholm, and believe you cannot do so except by buying a ticket. Suppose at present you do not intend to buy a ticket. Suppose, moreover, that you believe you will not buy a ticket unless you intend to do so. Then at present you do not satisfy *End-means*; you do not intend what you believe is a necessary means to an end that you intend. But you can bring yourself to satisfy this requirement by a piece of practical reasoning. You can say to yourself:

> I shall visit Stockholm.
> I shall not visit Stockholm if I do not buy a ticket.
> So I shall buy a ticket.

When you say the first of these sentences, you express your initial intention to visit Stockholm. When you say the second, you express your initial belief that buying a ticket is necessary for doing so. When you say the third, you expresses an intention to buy a ticket. You did not have this intention initially, but you acquire it by means of your reasoning.

This is an intuitively satisfying example of practical reasoning. Let us see if we can give a satisfactory account of how it works. When you say to yourself 'I shall visit Stockholm', whatever else you do, you say to yourself that you will visit Stockholm. In your reasoning as a whole, you are asserting three propositions to yourself in sequence. You are saying that:

> You will visit Stockholm.
> You will not visit Stockholm if you do not buy a ticket.

And finally that

> You will buy a ticket.

When you say you will visit Stockholm, whatever else you are doing, you are expressing a belief that you will visit Stockholm. You have this belief only because you intend to visit Stockholm. Consequently, what you say expresses your intention as well as your belief. You next say to yourself that you cannot visit Stockholm except by buying a ticket. This expresses a straightforward belief. You have now expressed two beliefs, and from their content it *follows* that you will buy a ticket. If you do not believe you will buy a ticket, you are in violation, not just of the practical requirement *End-means*, but also of the theoretical requirement *Modus ponens* or rather of its cousin *Modus tollens*.

Compare my paradigm example of theoretical reasoning. You start by saying to yourself that

> It is raining
> If it is raining, the snow will melt

You now operate on these propositions and end up believing that

> The snow will melt

You could do exactly the same with the Stockholm case. After saying to yourself that you will visit Stockholm and that you will not visit Stockholm if you do not buy a ticket, you could operate on these propositions and end up believing that you will buy a ticket.

However, the process of coming to believe you will buy a ticket is not as simple as it is in the theoretical case. Remember you believe you will not buy a ticket unless you intend to do so. Consequently, you will not be able to acquire the belief that you will buy a ticket unless you also acquire the belief that you intend to buy a ticket. In normal circumstances, you can only come to believe you intend to buy a ticket by actually coming to intend to buy one. So, in order to acquire the belief that you will buy a ticket, which your theoretical reasoning leads you to, you need also to acquire the intention of buying a ticket.

To complete your reasoning two things must click into place: the intention and the belief. Provided the reasoning proceeds smoothly, they will do so. You may then say to yourself 'I shall buy a ticket', thereby expressing both a newly-acquired intention to buy a ticket and a newly-acquired belief that you will buy a ticket. Your reasoning is practical because it concludes in an intention, and it is theoretical because it concludes in a belief. It brings you to satisfy both the practical requirement *End-means* and the theoretical requirement *Modus tollens*. It is a single piece of reasoning that has theoretical and practical aspects.

The practical and theoretical aspects cannot be separated. You might think that the theoretical reasoning leads the practical reasoning: that you first come to believe you will buy a ticket through some theoretical reasoning, and this belief then causes you to intend to buy a ticket. But that is not so. Merely believing you will do something will not cause you to intend to do it. The causal connection is the other way round: intending to buy a ticket causes you to believe you intend to buy a ticket, which causes you to believe you will buy a ticket. Given that you believe you will not buy a ticket unless you intend to, no purely theoretical reasoning can take you from your premise-beliefs – that you will visit Venice and you will not visit Venice if you do not buy a ticket – to a conclusion-belief that you will buy a ticket. You acquire that belief only by acquiring the intention of buying a ticket.

Like theoretical reasoning, this piece of practical reasoning may not proceed in a linear fashion. Your acquisition of a new belief might be blocked. You might find you cannot believe you will buy a ticket. Perhaps you believe you do not have enough money, so you cannot form the intention of buying one. If you do not form it, you remain in violation of requirements *Modus tollens* and *End-means*. But you have an alternative way to satisfy these requirements by reasoning: you can throw your reasoning into reverse. You may say to yourself that you will not buy a ticket. Then you might conclude your reasoning by believing you will not visit Stockholm. In this case, your reasoning goes:

> You will visit Stockholm
> You will not visit Stockholm if you do not buy a ticket
> You will not buy a ticket
> So you will not visit Stockholm

This reverse practical reasoning is not as straightforward as reverse theoretical reasoning. If you are to reach the end point of believing you will not visit Stockholm, you will have to drop your belief that you will visit Stockholm. This is turn requires you to drop your intention of visiting Stockholm. To be successful, your reverse reasoning must cause you to drop that intention. Once you have done that, you satisfy *Modus tollens* and *End-means*.

9 Two Objections and a Generalization

This account of instrumental reasoning to a means you believe is necessary is a development of an earlier account of mine (Broome 2002). That earlier account attracted some accurate criticism from Jay Wallace, in his paper 'Normativity, commitment, and instrumental reason' (Wallace 2001). My new amended account owes a lot to Wallace's paper. I am not yet confident it is correct, but I think it survives a couple of objections, which I shall now describe.

The first is that it makes practical reasoning too close to theoretical reasoning. In my account, theoretical and practical reasoning are inextricably entangled. The practical reasoning that brings you to intend to buy a ticket is also theoretical reasoning that brings you to believe you will buy a ticket. In one way, this is a valuable feature of the account. It makes it a good antidote to skepticism about practical reasoning. Skepticism has been rife since David Hume announced that 'reason is the discovery of truth and falsehood'.[5] Practical reasoning is plainly not the discovery of truth and falsehood, so if Hume was right, there is no practical reasoning. But I think no one should doubt that you can reason from an intention to achieve an end to an intention to take a means. The Stockholm example is an intuitively attractive example of this sort of reasoning, even if my account of how it works is mistaken. Furthermore, if my account is not mistaken, it shows that this sort of reasoning is made correct by the same valid syllogism as makes the corresponding theoretical reasoning correct. This strengthens the example as an antidote to skepticism.

---

[5] Hume 1978, book 3, part 1, section 1.

However, the close entanglement of theoretical and practical reasoning is a disadvantage in another way. Intuitively, there should be more independence between theoretical and practical reasoning. As Michael Bratman put it to me, this account of practical reasoning is 'just too cognitive'. Bratman's objection is included in his paper 'Intention, belief, practical, theoretical' (Forthcoming).

My present view is that practical and theoretical reasoning are indeed genuinely entangled to the extent described in my account. That is my response to this objection. The argument is set out in detail in my paper 'The unity of reasoning?' (Broome 2006) I shall not rehearse it here.

The second objection is that the account is too special to be interesting. It is an account of reasoning that can bring you to satisfy the requirement *End-means*. As I described it informally, *End-means* is the requirement to intend what you believe is a necessary means to an end that you intend. It is a requirement of instrumental rationality, and the reasoning that brings you to satisfy it is instrumental reasoning. It is reasoning from an end to a means. This already makes it a special, limited sort of reasoning. But, more than that, it is reasoning from an end to a means that you believe is necessary to that end. This makes is very special indeed. A worthwhile account of practical reasoning has to be wider than this. That is the objection.

It is founded on a misunderstanding. Informally, I described the requirement *End-means* as the requirement to intend what you believe is a necessary means to an end that you intend. But I explained in section 3 that this is not a very accurate statement of the formal requirement. The example shows why not. In the example, you believe buying a ticket is a necessary condition for your visiting Stockholm, but only in a weak sense of 'necessary condition'. You believe you will not visit Stockholm if you do not buy a ticket. You do not believe that you *cannot* visit Stockholm if you do not buy a ticket. That strong belief is not required to make your reasoning work.

You will rarely believe a means to an end is necessary in the strong sense. For example, you probably do not believe that buying a ticket is a necessary means, in the strong sense, of visiting Stockholm. You probably believe you can get to Stockholm in other ways – perhaps by walking and swimming, or perhaps by stowing away on a ship. So if the reasoning I described required that sort of a belief, it would be so special as to be uninteresting. The objection would be a real one.

On the other hand, you will very commonly believe a means to an end is necessary in the weak sense. Unless you live in Sweden, you probably do believe that, actually, you will not visit Stockholm unless you buy a ticket. Because this type of belief is so common, my account of instrumental reasoning has a very wide field of application.

Indeed, I hope it may even be developed into the core of an account of instrumental reasoning in general. At present I can offer only a rough outline of how I hope the development may be achieved. Here it is.

Instrumental reasoning in general is reasoning that takes you from intending an end to intending some means of achieving it. Suppose you intend an end, and you believe there is a range of alternative means available. Suppose you intend to visit Stockholm, and you see various alternative ways of getting here. Here is how I suggest your reasoning proceeds. It goes through several stages.

At the first stage, you evaluate the alternative means. Your evaluation will be a piece of theoretical reasoning whose details do not concern me here. It may be long drawn-out and complex. I am only concerned with the conclusion-attitude that will eventually emerge from it. I suggest it will be a normative belief that has a conditional content. I suggest you conclude this theoretical stage of your reasoning by coming to believe that you ought, if you achieve the end, to take a particular means. For example, you come to believe you ought, if you visit Stockholm, to buy a ticket. This stage of reasoning is theoretical because the conclusion-attitude is a belief; that is how theoretical reasoning is identified.

Suppose you have acquired a normative belief of this sort. According to the requirement of reasoning *Krasia*, rationality requires you, if you believe you ought to do something, to intend to do it. In this case, rationality requires to have a conditional intention corresponding to your conditional normative belief. I have already assumed there is a process of reasoning, which I called kratic reasoning, that can bring you to satisfy this requirement. I shall say more about it in section 10. If this is right, then the next step of your reasoning is to form a conditional intention, through kratic reasoning. In the example, through kratic reasoning, you come to intend, if you visit Stockholm, to buy a ticket. That intention is the conclusion-attitude of this second stage of your reasoning.

You acquire this intention by reasoning, which means you must believe you have it. As I explained in section 7, this means you must acquire at the same time the belief that you will carry it the intention out. You come to believe that, if you visit Stockholm, you will buy a ticket – in other words, that you will not visit Stockholm if you do not buy a ticket. You believe that your buying a ticket is a condition of your visiting Stockholm that is necessary in the weak sense. This is exactly the premise-belief of the instrumental reasoning that I described in section 8. Since you intend to visit Stockholm, you are now able to go through the reasoning I described there. You will emerge with the intention to buy a ticket.

My suggestion is that this multi-stage process is the activity of reasoning that can bring you to intend a means to and end that you intend, when there is a choice of means. You might take a short cut through it. You might cut out the theoretical reasoning that leads you to a conditional normative belief, and the kratic reasoning that takes you from there to a conditional intention. You might choose a means is some other, less reasoned, way. That is to say, you might arrive by some other route at the conditional intention to take a particular means if you achieve the end. Once you have that conditional intention, so long as you believe you have it, you can then do the last stage of the reasoning I described. Through the process instrumental reasoning set out in section 8, you can arrive at an unconditional intention to take the means.

If all this is correct, it means that the account I gave of instrumental reasoning represents the core of all instrumental reasoning. At first it may have seemed to have a very limited application. Instead it may be entirely general.

If all this is correct, it also means that kratic reasoning is at the heart of instrumental reasoning. In the course of instrumental reasoning, you may take a short cut that cuts out the stage of kratic reasoning. But full-blooded, complete instrumental reasoning requires it. This makes kratic reasoning even more important than it may have seemed at first. We very badly need an account of it.

10 Kratic Reasoning

But I have to confess that I am not yet in a position to provide much of an account. I think the outline of it is plain. Kratic reasoning is reasoning by means of which you can bring yourself to satisfy the requirement *Krasia* set out in section 3. I repeat it here.

> *Krasia*. Rationality requires of N that, if N believes that she ought that p, and if N believes that p will be so if and only if she intends that p, then N intends that p.

Roughly, *Krasia* requires you, if you believe you ought to do something, to intend to do it. Suppose you believe you ought to stand for parliament. You can say to yourself:

> I ought to stand for parliament
> So, I shall stand for parliament.

Your first statement expresses your normative belief that you ought to stand for parliament. Your second statement expresses an intention to stand for parliament. You do not have this intention when you start your reasoning, but by the time you conclude your reasoning, you have it.

This process satisfies the description of reasoning that emerged in section 5. It is a process that takes place among your attitudes, which have contents. It is an activity of yours. It is computational: the content of your concluding attitude can be computed from the content of your initial belief. It is an operation on contents, then. So it satisfies the description. Moreover, it is intuitively plausible as a piece of reasoning.

So there is an outline of kratic reasoning. However, I would hope to be able to say more than this to justify the claim that it is genuine reasoning.[6] Compare the account I gave of instrumental reasoning in section 8. I there explained in detail the process by which your conclusion-intention arose during the process of the reasoning. But in the case of kratic reasoning, I have so far left that mysterious. Explaining it is a task for the future.

References

Bratman, M. Forthcoming. Intention, belief, practical, theoretical, in *Spheres of Reason*, eds. S. Robertson, J. Skorupski and J. Timmerman.

Broome, J. 2001. Normative practical reasoning. *Proceedings of the Aristotelian Society*. Supplementary Volume 75: 175-93.

Broome, J. 2002. Practical Reasoning. *Reason and Nature: Essays in the Theory of Rationality*, eds. J. Bermúdez and A. Millar, 85-111. Oxford: Oxford University Press.

Broome, J. 2006. Reasoning with Preferences? *Preference Formation and Well-Being*, ed. S. Olsaretti, 183-208. Cambridge: Cambridge University Press.

Broome, J. Forthcoming. The Unity of Reasoning? *Spheres of Reason*, eds. S. Robertson, J. Skorupski and J. Timmerman.

Carroll, L. 1895. What the Tortoise Said to Achilles. *Mind*, 4: 278-80.

Gibbard, A. 2003. *Thinking How to Live*. Cambridge, MA: Harvard University Press.

Hieronymi, P. 2006. Controlling Attitudes. *Pacific Philosophical Quarterly* 87: 45-74.

Hume, D. 1978. *A Treatise of Human Nature*, eds. L.A. Selby-Bigge and P.H. Nidditch. Oxford: Oxford University Press.

Kant, I. 1948. *The Moral Law (Groundwork of the Metaphysic of Morals)*, transl. H.J. Paton. London: Hutchinson.

Wallace, R.J. 2001. Normativity, Commitment, and Instrumental Reason. *Philosophers' Imprint* 1(3), www.philosophersimprint.org/001003/.

---

[6] My 'Normative practical reasoning' is a step in that direction, but it mainly answers possible objections, rather than giving a proper positive account of kratic reasoning (Broome 2001).

7

Pragmatic Arguments for Rationality Constraints*
WLODEK RABINOWICZ

This paper discusses pragmatic arguments for 'rationality constraints' on a decision-maker's state of mind – on her beliefs or preferences. Arguments of this kind purport to show that a violator of a given constraint can be made to act to her guaranteed disadvantage. To put it dramatically, she can be exploited by a clever bookie, who doesn't need to know more than the agent to be exploited in order to set up his exploitation scheme. The *locus classicus* for such arguments is Frank Ramsey's essay on 'Truth and Probability', where the general idea is floated for the first time:

> If anyone's mental condition violated these laws [= the laws of probability], ... [h]e could have a book made against him by a cunning bettor and would then stand to lose in any event. (Ramsey 1990 [1926]: 78)

Well-known examples of pragmatic arguments are synchronic Dutch books, for the standard probability axioms, diachronic Dutch books, for the

---

* This paper is an expanded and extensively revised version of my contribution to a collection of essays on Isaac Levi's philosophy (cf. Rabinowicz 2006). Along with several other changes, it responds to some criticisms made by Levi in his reply (cf. Levi 2006). I am indebted to several people for comments and discussion. Luc Bovens and John Broome have been especially helpful in this respect. My work on this subject was supported by a research grant from The Bank of Sweden's Tercentenary Foundation and was partly conducted during my stay at The Swedish Collegium for Advanced Study in the Social Sciences (SCASSS) in Uppsala. I am indebted to the participants of my seminar at SCASSS in 2004, for their useful comments. Some of the material in this paper was presented at the Ramsey Centennial conference in Cambridge in 2003, at a workshop on philosophy and probability in Bielefeld that same year, at a workshop on logic in games, language and computation in Amsterdam in 2004, at a conference on rationality and patterns of reasoning in Bertinoro that same year, and at seminars in Canberra (Social and Political Theory, Research School for Social Sciences), Stanford (department of philosophy) and Lund (departments of philosophy and economics). I would like to thank the organizers and the participants of these events.

more controversial principles of reflection and conditionalization, and Money Pumps, for the acyclicity requirement on preferences.

When one examines these examples, one thing stands out: The proposed exploitation set-ups share a common feature. Suppose an agent is logically and mathematically competent. Assume also that she prefers being better off than worse off and acts accordingly. Then, as we shall see, even if she violates a given constraint, she cannot be exploited unless she is *disunified* in her decision-making. By this I mean that exploitation is possible only if the agent makes decisions on various issues she confronts one by one, rather than on all of them together. Instead of deciding on the whole package, she proceeds in a piecemeal fashion and decides on each component in the package separately.

The kind of disunification I have in mind is not a form of schizophrenia. It is not that one 'part' of the agent decides on one issue and another 'part' on another issue at hand. Instead, the disunification is in the *object* of decision-making: Different issues are addressed by the agent separately rather than together.

Any given agent can be disunified in this sense either synchronically or diachronically. In the synchronic case, she is simultaneously presented with a number of opportunities, each of which she can accept or reject, and she deals with each of these opportunities separately. A unified decision-maker would instead consider all the offers together and make a single choice of a particular *configuration* of the opportunities. In the diachronic case, the opportunities are offered at different times, with the schedule of offers known beforehand by the agent. She is diachronically disunified if she defers her choices to the times at which the different offers will be made. A unified approach would again involve one decision on the whole package of opportunities, i.e. a single choice of a particular configuration of opportunities, present and future. Thereby, the need for piecemeal decisions is being pre-empted.

This sort of unity in decision-making requires overview and consideration of complex choice alternatives. This may be costly and inconvenient. For various reasons, we may find it easier to deal with different issues separately, rather than in a wholesale manner. Furthermore, in diachronic cases, pre-commitments might sometimes be difficult or impossible: We might be unable to pre-determine our future actions. This sets significant practical limitations on unified decision-making.

Since the exploitation set-ups only work for disunified agents, pragmatic arguments for various constraints on beliefs and preferences should be seen as delivering *conditional* recommendations: 'If you are going to make your decisions in a disunified way, then you'd better satisfy these constraints.' In other words, arguments of this kind fail to establish the inherent rationality of the constraints under consideration. Some of these constraints, such as the acyclicity of preference or standard probability axioms, do have an intuitive claim for being categorical requirements of rationality. But other principles for which pragmatic arguments have been provided, such as the principle of reflection, do not seem to have any inherent rational pull. However, on the view I want to defend, there still is something to be said for pragmatic arguments: They allow us to identify conditions that *level the ground* for disunification in decision-making.

In this paper, I will not try to provide a conclusive defense of my interpretation of pragmatic arguments. I will, however, support it by illustrating in some detail the intimate connection between exploitability and disunification.

Note that on the reading I suggest, diachronic arguments come out as somewhat *stronger* than the synchronic ones. The reason should be clear from what was pointed out above: Unified decision-making is more difficult to manage diachronically than synchronically. Consequently, there are stronger reasons for the agent to satisfy the constraints that would level the ground for diachronic disunification.

Isaac Levi has a very different view of the status of pragmatic arguments (cf. Levi 2002). In a way, his position is opposed to mine. According to him, it is only synchronic pragmatic arguments that have a good claim to validity. The diachronic ones, he argues, are worthless. Before I explain why he takes this view and why I think he is mistaken, I need to rehearse some examples of the arguments of both kinds, in order to provide a background for the discussion.

1 A Synchronic Dutch Book Argument for Probability Laws

In this argument, it is assumed that an agent's probability assignments – her degrees of belief – are her guides to action. As such, they are related to her betting dispositions or, in another version of this subjective approach to probabilities, to her betting commitments. On that version, the agent who assigns a probability for a proposition is committed to a specific *betting rate* for the proposition in question.

To see what this means, consider a bet on a proposition A that costs C money units to buy and pays S units if won. S is the *stake* of the bet, while C is its *price*. A bet is said to be *fair* if the agent is equally prepared to take each of its sides: to buy it or to sell it, depending on what she is asked to do. To pronounce a bet as fair, for a given agent, is thus to ascribe to the agent a commitment to a certain betting behavior. Assume now that for different fair bets on A, with varying stakes and prices, the *ratio* between their prices and stakes remains constant. If the stake increases or decreases, the price has to increase or decrease in the same proportion for the bet to remain fair. This simplifying assumption, which would follow if we supposed that the agent is seeking to maximize his expected monetary payoff, is reasonable at least within a certain range, in which the monetary amounts S and C are not too high. Within that range, the assumption of the constant ratio for the fair bets on a given proposition is not especially problematic, since for small amounts we may safely assume that utility is proportional to money.

We shall call this constant ratio the *betting rate* for A. The betting rate for a proposition A is thus the quotient C/S for a fair bet on A. The agent's *probability* for A, $P(A)$, is identified with her betting rate. For a bet on a proposition A with a given stake, the higher the price the agent is willing to pay (or the higher the price she demands), the higher is her probability for A.

Example: If a bet on A with a stake $S = \$20$ and a price $C = \$9$ is fair for the agent, then her betting rate for A equals $9/20 = .45$, which means that we can set her probability for A as equal to .45.

Note that, given this interpretation of probabilities as betting rates, the expected monetary value of buying a fair bet on A with price C and stake S is zero:

$$[P(A) \times S] - C = [C/S \times S] - C = 0.$$

Similarly, selling such a bet has the expected value zero:

$$C - [P(A) \times S] = C - [C/S \times S] = 0.$$

We can also look at this in another way. If we assume that the agent's betting commitments are determined by her beliefs, we can take it that her probabilities (= degrees of belief) are reflected in her betting rates. We could express this by saying that a bet is fair if and only if the expected value of buying that bet or of selling it is equal to zero given the agent's probabilities.[1]

---

[1] However, this informal motivation for the identification of probabilities with betting rates, while reasonable for agents who can be assumed to be expected-utility maximizers, is problematic in the present context. If an agent violates some of the pre-conditions of expected utility maximization, if, for example, her beliefs do not satisfy some of the standard probability axioms, then justifying the identification of probabilities with betting rates on the basis of expected-utility considerations does not seem to be appropriate.

Also, it should be mentioned that there is a troublesome existence assumption lurking behind this whole approach to probabilities in terms of fair bets. It is by no means obvious that fair bets exist in the first place. Note that the highest price the agent is willing to pay for a bet on A with a given stake may be lower than the lowest price for which she is willing to sell it. If this

A *Dutch book* is a system of bets on various propositions such that, if the agent accepted all the bets in the book, they would together give her a positive loss whatever happens. A *synchronic* Dutch book is a system of simultaneous bet offers of this kind, while in a *diachronic* Dutch book, bet offers are made at different points in time.

As is well known, if the agent violates the standard probability laws, he is vulnerable to a synchronic Dutch book. This provides a pragmatic argument for obeying the laws in question.

As an example, consider the addition axiom for probabilities,

$P(A \vee B) = P(A) + P(B)$,

if propositions A and B are logically incompatible.

Suppose the agent's probability assignments violate this axiom. For example, suppose that $P(A) = \frac{1}{2}$, $P(B) = \frac{1}{2}$, but $P(A \vee B) = \frac{3}{4}$. This makes her vulnerable to a Dutch book: We can offer her bets on A and on B, each with a stake S, which she can *buy* at a price $\frac{1}{2} S$ for each bet. At the same time we can ask her to *sell* a bet on the disjunction A or B with the same stake and a price $\frac{3}{4} S$. Given her probabilities, all these bets are fair. As can be seen from Table 1, if all the bet offers are accepted, the agent's guaranteed loss is $\frac{1}{4}S$.[2]

---

is the case for all stakes, then for no bet on A the agent would be willing to take both of its sides. If the constancy assumption still holds (for small stakes at least), the agent will then have two betting rates for A instead of one, the buying rate (= the highest price-stake ratio she is willing to accept as a buyer) and the selling rate (= the lowest price-stake ratio she is willing to accept as a seller). Under such circumstances, probabilities could no longer be identified with betting rates (unless we are prepared to work with probabilities understood as pairs of numbers, rather than as single numbers, with one number corresponding to the buying rate and the other to the selling rate), but they could still be seen as *partial* determinants of the agent's betting dispositions. The agent's probability for A could then be assumed to lie somewhere between the two rates in question. This, however, would create problems for the Dutch-book arguments, as will be shown in the next note.

[2] If the exploiter is not supposed to know more that the agent herself, then we must assume that the agent knows her own probability assignments. (Otherwise, the bookie who lacks superior knowledge would not know them either, which would hinder him from setting up the exploitation scheme.) Needless to say, this is a rather problematic assumption.

There is another complication as well. If an agent's buying rate and her selling rate need not coincide (see the preceding note), then this example only shows how one can exploit an agent whose selling rate for $A \vee B$ is lower than the sum of his buying rates for A and for B. If – as is reasonable to assume – the buying rate does not exceed the selling rate and the probability of a proposition lies somewhere in-between the two, then an agent like this violates the addition axiom for probabilities. But the opposite does not hold: The agent's probability for $A \vee B$ may be lower than the sum of his probabilities for A and for B, but his selling rate for the disjunction still need not be lower than the sum of his buying rates for the disjuncts. Such an agent

Possibilities	Bought bet on A	Bought bet on B	Sold bet on $A \vee B$	Total
$\underline{A}$	$S - \frac{1}{2}S$	$-\frac{1}{2}S$	$\frac{3}{4}S - S$	$-\frac{1}{4}S$
$\underline{B}$	$-\frac{1}{2}S$	$S - \frac{1}{2}S$	$\frac{3}{4}S - S$	$-\frac{1}{4}S$
$\neg(A \vee B)$	$-\frac{1}{2}S$	$-\frac{1}{2}S$	$\frac{3}{4}S$	$-\frac{1}{4}S$

Table 1: The agent's gains and losses

It is easy to see that the violator of the addition axiom is being exploited in this set-up only because her decision-making is disunified: She decides on each bet separately, rather than on all the three bets together. If she did the latter, then – assuming she is logically and mathematically competent – she would certainly not choose to accept the whole bet package: A simple calculation would show that refusing all the bets would be better for her whatever happens. Of course, in this unified mode, she might still decide to accept one or two bet offers, say, she might decide to buy the bets on A and on B. But this would not give her a guaranteed loss.

Many years ago, Brian Skyrms suggested that that an agent who is vulnerable to a synchronic Dutch book must be logically confused. Such an agent seems to evaluate one and the same betting arrangement differently depending on the way it is presented: as a set of three bets, or as one composite opportunity of making a loss whatever happens (cf. Skyrms 1980). In this suggestion, Skyrms was influenced by Frank Ramsey's remark on this issue:

> If anyone's mental condition violated these laws [= the laws of probability], his choice would depend on the precise form in which the options were offered him, which is absurd. (Ramsey 1990 [1926]: 78)

However, this suggestion of the underlying logical confusion cannot be right, as far as I can see. It is true that the agent we consider views each bet in the set as attractive and yet assigns a negative value to the bet package as a whole. This does not mean however, that she evaluates the same betting arrangement differently under different logically equivalent descriptions. It only means that her valuations are not additive: The value she ascribes to the whole package is lower than the sum of the values she ascribes to its parts. But this, by itself, need not be questionable. One doesn't need to be logically confused to have non-additive valuations. (Cf. Schick 1986)

On the betting interpretation of probabilities, the agent *can* be considered to be logically muddled, however, if she violates another probability

---

will not be exploited by the set-up we have described. The same remarks apply, mutatis mutandis, to the diachronic exploitation scheme that will be described in the next section.

law: the law that requires logical truths to be assigned probability one. Let A be a logical truth and suppose that the agent's probability for A differs from one. If it exceeds one, the agent is willing to buy a bet on A with a price that is higher than the stake to be won. If it is lower than one, she is willing to sell a bet on A for a lower price than the stake she will have to pay out. Thus, in each case, she is exploitable. Note that this exploitation set-up, in order to work, does *not* require the agent to be disunified in her decision-making: After all, the betting arrangement consists of one bet only. But the exploitation in this case is possible only if the agent is logically confused or does not mind making sure losses. This means that the exploitation set-up under consideration is consistent with the claim we are defending: Disunification is a necessary pre-requisite of exploitability for a logically and mathematically competent agent, who prefers to be better off rather than worse off.

2 A Diachronic Dutch Book Argument for Reflection

The principle of Reflection expresses a requirement that current probability assignments reflect one's expectations concerning one's future probabilities. Thus, in particular, one's current conditional probability for a proposition A given the supposition that one's future probability for A will at most be k, should itself be k at the most.

Reflection: $P(A/P'(A) \leq k) \leq k$, provided that $P(P'(A) \leq k) > 0$,

where P is the agent's current probability at time t, and P' is her probability assignment at an arbitrary future point of time t' ($t' \geq t$).

It is a standard objection to Reflection that this principle is intuitively implausible if the agent has a reason to distrust her future cognitive abilities. Under such circumstances, she might be well-advised to have non-reflective probability assignments. To illustrate this possibility, suppose she has grounds to believe that her future probability for A, at $t' > t$, might be excessively low: too low given the evidence she expects to have at that time. To take an extreme case, suppose she expects to be subjected to a brainwash that will at t' make her unreasonably skeptical of A. Under these circumstances, we would want to say that her current conditional probability for A on the hypothesis that $P'(A) \leq k$, where k is low, should be higher than k.

Clearly, an expected brainwash is just one possible example of a situation in which Reflection seems to be an unreasonable demand. Any other example of expected cognitive deterioration would do to make this point. Still, as has been shown by van Fraassen (1984), an agent whose probability assignments violate Reflection is *ipso facto* vulnerable to a diachronic Dutch book, quite independently of what grounds she might have for violating this constraint. That is, for any case of violation of Reflection, we can set up a system of bets to be offered to the agent at different times, such that (i) each bet is fair when it is being offered, in terms of the agent's probabilities at that time, but (ii) together, all bets taken together guarantee her a certain loss.

Here is an example (cf. Christensen 1991). Suppose that an agent's probability assignment P at t violates Reflection. For example, suppose that

(i) $P(A/P'(A) \leq \frac{1}{2}) = \frac{3}{4}$.

Let E stand for the proposition that $P'(A) \leq \frac{1}{2}$, and suppose that

(ii) $P(E) = 1/5$.

At t, a bookie offers the agent two bets:
(1) a bet on E that costs 1 unit and pays 5 if won;
(2) a *conditional* bet on A given E, that costs 15 and pays 20 if won.

In a conditional bet, the price of the bet is refunded if the condition fails to materialize. Conditional probabilities give betting rates for conditional bets. Therefore, given our assumptions about the agent's probabilities, it is easy to see that bets 1 and 2 are fair.

Then, at t', *if E is the case* at that time, the bookmaker offers to *buy* from the agent a third bet:
(3) a bet on A that costs 10 and pays 20 if won.

Selling this bet will be fair or 'more than fair' in terms of the agent's probabilities at t', if E will then be the case, i.e., if the agent's probability for A at t' will at most be equal to $\frac{1}{2}$.

If the agent accepts all these bet offers, she will lose 1 unit whatever happens. If E will not be the case, she will lose her bet on E and no other money will change hands: The conditional bet on A given E will be called off and no bet offer will be made at t'. On the other hand, if E will be the case, the agent will win the bet on E and her conditional bet on A will be on. But then, at t', the bookie will be able to buy back the bet on A *at a lower price* (bet 3). Since the price difference $(15 - 10 = 5)$ exceeds the net gain from the bet on E $(5 - 1 = 4)$, the agent will again suffer a total loss.

Possibilities	Bet on E – bought at t	Bet on A given E – bought at t	Bet on A – sold at t'	Total
$E \wedge A$	5 – 1	20 – 15	10 – 20	–1
$E \wedge \neg A$	5 – 1	– 15	10	–1
$\neg E$	–1	Called off	—	–1

Table 2: The agent's gains and losses

There is an obvious objection to this line of reasoning. A pragmatic argument for a constraint on the agent's probability assignments is supposed to demonstrate that violations of this constraint would lead to a guaranteed loss by her own lights. To be effective, such an argument should therefore be based on the assumption that the agent to be exploited knows at least as much as her would-be exploiter. Consequently, insofar as the latter acts on a definite plan of action, this plan must also be known by the agent. In other words, the agent must have *foresight*.

But surely, the objection continues, if the agent has foresight and thus knows what bet offer is kept in store for her at t' if E will then be the case, she can at t stop the whole exploitation process from the start by simply refusing to take the earlier bets. Thereby, she can upset the bookie's designs and the whole book will crumble: By refusing the earlier bets, she prevents getting bet opportunities at t' that she would then be willing to accept, but that she now – by her *present* lights – finds unattractive (cf. Levi 1988, and Maher 1992).[3]

Skyrms (1993) shows how this objection can be met. Suppose the bookie is *persistent* in his exploitation scheme and the agent knows this. Persistency means that the later bet offers are not conditioned on the acceptance of the earlier ones. In particular, if E will materialize at t', the bookie can be relied on to offer to buy the bet on A at that time, even if the agent were to refuse the bets at t. Suppose also that the bookie makes all the three bets 'more than fair': For each bet offer she accepts, the agent gets a small reward ε. Assume, however, that $3\varepsilon < 1$. Then, even with the extra rewards, the agent will suffer a total loss if she accepts every bet offer she receives. She will lose at least one unit minus 3ε.

In terms of her probabilities at t, selling bet 3 is unattractive for the agent. Were that opportunity offered at t, conditionally on E, she would never accept it. At t', however, if E will be the case, selling this bet on A will become attractive in the light of the probabilities she will have at that time. Since she knows this beforehand, the agent can use backward-induction reasoning to solve her decision problem. Insofar as she trusts her future practical rationality, she can at t predict she will sell the bet on A at t' if E will then be the case.[4] She will do it, whatever bets she might have ac-

---

[3] Note that, in terms of the agent's *prior* probabilities (at t), bet 3 has negative monetary value: $P(A/E) \times (C(\text{bet } 3) - S(\text{bet } 3)) + P(\neg A/E) \times C(\text{bet } 3) = ¾ \times (10 - 20) + ¼ \times 10 = -5$.

[4] Backward-induction reasoning is based on trust in one's future rationality. The agent expects to act rationally in the future, which allows her to predict her future behavior and then to make her current choices in the light of these predictions. One might therefore wonder whether this kind of reasoning is available to agents who violate Reflection because they mistrust their own cognitive rationality in the future. The answer is that a violator of Reflection can well make use of backward induction as long as she expects to be *practically* rational in the future, i.e., ra-

cepted earlier on. But then accepting the conditional bet on A given E at t doesn't make things worse in any way. In fact it makes them better, by an extra ε. Similarly for the bet on E, and even more so for both these bets taken together. (This improves the agent's prospects by 2ε.) Thus, if the bookie is known to be persistent, backward-induction reasoning leads the agent to accept all the bets on offer, at t and t', even though she knows this will give her a certain loss.

As a matter of fact, backward induction is not needed in this case, to establish the point.[5] Simple dominance reasoning would suffice. For the agent to conclude that she has no reason to abstain from the bets offered at t, she need not assume she will do the rational thing at t'. It is enough if two conditions are met. (i) She believes her actions at t won't influence the potential bet offer at t'. (ii) She expects to deal with that offer at t' in the same way independently of what she might do at t. As (i) and (ii) imply that her present actions won't influence her behavior in the future, she can conclude that buying bets at t is preferable to abstaining, as it improves her prospects by 2ε independently of what she will do at t'.

All this assumes, however, that the bookie is known to be persistent. This assumption of persistency was never explicitly stated in van Fraassen (1984). Nor was it emphasized in the well-known diachronic Dutch book argument for conditionalization, due to David Lewis (cf. Teller 1973). As a result, Levi (1988) was able to argue that, in the case of diachronic Dutch books, the process of exploitation could be stopped at the outset, by refusal to accept the initial bets. He thought this would let the agent off the hook, as no subsequent bet offers would then be forthcoming (cf. Levi 1988: 204f). Levi's suggestion was further developed by Maher (1992).

That the persistency of the exploiter closes this gap in van Fraassen's and Lewis' arguments has been pointed out by Skyrms (1993). As the latter puts it:

> Why is it assumed [by Maher and Levi] that the cunning bettor will just go home if [the agent] refuses to bet today? [...] Even though [the agent] will see it coming, she will prefer the sure loss [...] because doing so looks strictly better to her than the alternative. (ibid.: 323f)

And he concludes: 'Seeing it coming does not help.' (ibid.: 326).

As in the example in the previous section, it is easy to see that the violator of Reflection is being exploited in this kind of set-up only because her

---

tional in what she does *given* what she then believes and prefers. That she expects those future beliefs to be unfounded is another matter: One can become cognitively irrational and still remain a practically rational agent.

[5] Backward-induction reasoning plays a more essential role in connection with money pumps; see next section. There, we shall characterize this reasoning model in more detail.

decision-making is disunified: She decides on different bets separately, at the times they are being offered, instead of making decision on all the three bets together. If she did the latter, then – assuming she is logically and mathematically competent – she would certainly not choose to accept the whole bet package, since a simple calculation would show that refusing the three bets would be better for her whatever happens.

The salient feature of this case is the agent's disunification over time: Even if she were synchronically unified and thus even if she made a joint decision on the two bets offered to her at t, she would still be exploited as long as her decision on the bet offer at t' were left to that future occasion. The two bets offered at t, if considered together, promise the agent a positive expected profit (of 2ε),[6] and thus represent together an attractive opportunity. The same applies to the third bet, if and when it is offered at t': Its expected value at that time is positive. Together, however, these two opportunities guarantee a sure loss.

3 Money Pumps Against Agents with Cyclical Preferences

Suppose the agent's preferences with respect to alternative outcomes x, y, and z are cyclical: She prefers x to z, z to y, and y to x. In symbols,

$$x \prec y \prec z \prec x.$$

Let x be the *status quo* alternative that will be realized if no action is taken by the agent. She is offered y in exchange for x. The exchange costs her a certain amount, ε, where ε is too small to reverse her preferences over outcomes. After this exchange, she is offered to trade y for z, if she pays an additional ε. When she does this, she is offered to trade z for x, if she again pays ε. After the three exchanges, the agent is back to where she started, minus 3ε. She has been used as a money pump. Isn't it irrational to be vulnerable to such a predicament? (Cf. Davidson, McKinsey and Suppes 1955, and Raiffa 1968).[7]

---

[6] Here, we assume that the agent satisfies the standard probability axioms. Then her expected monetary value for the two bets offered at t equals
$P(E \wedge A) \times (S(\text{bet 1}) - C(\text{bet 1}) + S(\text{bet 2}) - C(\text{bet 2}) + 2\varepsilon) + P(E \wedge \neg A) \times (S(\text{bet 1}) - C(\text{bet 1}) - C(\text{bet 2}) + 2\varepsilon) + P(\neg E) \times (-C(\text{bet 1}) + 2\varepsilon)$
$= 3/20 \times (5 - 1 + 20 - 15 + 2\varepsilon) + 1/20 \times (5 - 1 - 15 + 2\varepsilon) + 4/5 \times (-1 + 2\varepsilon) = 2\varepsilon.$

[7] Sometimes it is claimed that money pumps can be used against any agent with *non-transitive* preferences, whether these preferences happen to be cyclical or not. This, however, is not quite correct. Non-transitivity by itself is not enough: To be vulnerable to a pump, it is not enough that the agent prefers z to y, y to x, but does not prefer z to x. In addition, she must either prefer x to z (the case of a cycle) or at least be *indifferent* between the two alternatives. In the former

In *indefinite* money pumps, the process of exchange continues until the agent is ruined. Here, I only consider *finite* pumps, in which the exploitation stops after a certain number of full rounds, with each round bringing the agent back to the basic alternative with which she started. For simplicity, assume that there are three basic alternatives in the cycle (as in our example above, with $x \prec y \prec z \prec x$) and that there is only one round, i.e., the pump stops after three exchanges. For this short pump to work, the extra payment of ε should not reverse the agent's preferences at any stage, at least up to 3ε. Thus, we need to assume that

$$x \prec y - \varepsilon \prec z - 2\varepsilon \prec x - 3\varepsilon.$$

The money-pump argument, as described above, has met with an obvious objection: For the pump to work, the agent mustn't know she is being taken for a ride. Otherwise, if she knew that further trades are being kept in store for her, she would refuse to trade (cf. Schick 1986, and Schwartz 1986). The point of the objection is that the important condition of foresight, which should be satisfied in diachronic pragmatic arguments, is not satisfied in the money pump in its traditional version.

The common view is therefore that a prudent agent with foresight would avoid to be pumped, because she would see what's coming. She would realize that the first trade would lead to the second one, which would lead to the third, which would get her back to where she started, minus the payments. At some point, therefore, before completing the full circle, she would refuse making an exchange.

As we have already seen, this idea of foresight prudently employed as a shield against exploitation can be made more precise in terms of backward-induction reasoning. When an agent confronts a sequential choice problem and has a robust trust in her future practical rationality, she can solve the problem reasoning backwards. Thus, she can first determine what move it would be rational for her to make at the last choice node at each branch of her decision tree, where it is clear what payoff each move would result in.

---

case, she can be subjected to the standard money pump, while in the latter case we can offer her a small reward δ to get her to trade z for x, instead of exacting a payment ε in that step. This reward should be enough to get her to make the exchange, given that she is indifferent between z and x. Since we collect 2ε from her other two trades (x for y and y for z), she will still be exploited as long as $\delta < 2\varepsilon$. But if she neither prefers x to z nor is indifferent, i.e., if her preference ordering contains a *gap* with respect to these two alternatives, then a money-pump set-up is unavailable. In the case of a preferential gap, there is no guarantee that a small δ will be sufficient to tip the scale and get the agent to make a trade. This means that money pump arguments can be used as a support for the transitivity requirement on preferences only if it is assumed that we are dealing with an agent whose preference ordering is complete (= non-gappy).

Relying on her future rationality, she can predict she would make that move if she were to reach the node in question. Taking her trust in her future rationality to be robust, she expects to hold on to these predictions upon reaching the next-to-last choice node on each branch. This allows her to determine what move would be rational at each such penultimate node and thus, again relying on her future rationality, to predict her own behavior at that node. Continuing in this way, from the end-points of the tree to its beginning, such a sophisticated chooser finds out what moves are rational at each choice node of the tree. To put it shortly: At each choice node, the backward-induction move is the one that would be optimal on the assumption that any move made at that node would be followed by the backward-induction moves at all the later choice nodes.

Backward-induction reasoning is readily applicable to money-pump problems: As has been argued by McClennen (1990: section 10.2), a sophisticated chooser avoids being pumped. I have argued for the same claim myself in Rabinowicz (1995). As McClennen's argument is slightly flawed, the presentation below follows my 1995 paper.

As before, we assume that the agent's preferences with respect to x, y and z are cyclical, that they are constant throughout the process of exchange, that they are not reversible by extra payments, and that $x - 3\varepsilon \prec x$, which means that the agent who starts with x and ends up with $x - 3\varepsilon$ will suffer a definite loss from her own point of view. In fact, we take it that $x - 3\varepsilon$ is dispreferred by the agent not just to x but also to any alternative she prefers to x. Thus, in particular, since $x \prec y - \varepsilon$, it also holds that $x - 3\varepsilon \prec y - \varepsilon$. Finally, we suppose that the agent knows the preferences she has.

We now consider the agent's sequential choice problem that consists of three trade offers:

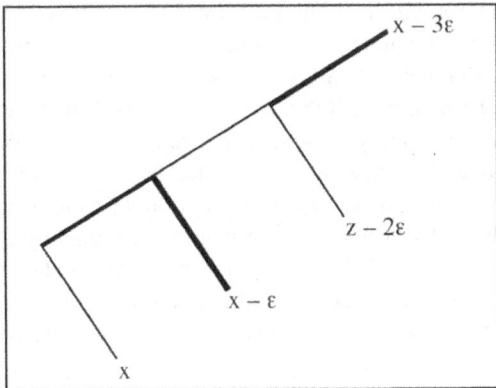

Figure 1: Money Pump

The forks in this tree are the agent's choice nodes. Going up means trading, going down means refusing to trade. The final outcome is specified at the end-point of each branch in the tree. The *status quo* alternative is x, which means that x will be the final payoff if the agent at the starting-point refuses to trade, i.e. goes down in the first node. If he instead goes up but then stops trading, she ends up with $y - \varepsilon$. If she trades twice and then stops, she ends up with $z - 2\varepsilon$. And if she trades thrice, she arrives at $x - 3\varepsilon$.

The bold lines in the tree represent backward-induction moves. At the third node, the agent's preferences dictate *trading*, since she prefers $x - 3\varepsilon$ to $z - 2\varepsilon$. Given that she expects to trade at the third node if she were to come that far, her choice at the second choice node should be to *refuse* to trade: This refusal gives her $y - \varepsilon$, which she prefers to $x - 3\varepsilon$. But then, given that she expects to refuse at the second node, her choice at the first node should be to *trade*, since she prefers $y - \varepsilon$ to x. Thus, the sophisticated chooser will make just one exchange and then stop. Even though her preferences are cyclical, she will not be pumped.

A pump like this may in general involve any number n of basic cycling alternatives, $x_1, \ldots x_n$ ($n = 3$ in our example, in which the basic alternatives are x, y and z), and any number k of full rounds (in our example, $k = 1$). It is easy to see that, for any pump of this kind, the sophisticated chooser will never end up with an alternative she disprefers to the *status quo* alternative (= the alternative she starts with). The reason is simple: If she trades at her first choice node, this move will be followed by a series of moves dictated by backward induction. And she must expect this to be the case. Thus, she has a definite and correct expectation as to the final outcome of her trading move. If she nevertheless does trade, it must be because she prefers the outcome in question to the *status quo* alternative. It follows then that she either refuses to trade at all or, if she does trade, she will sooner or later end up with an outcome she prefers to the one she has started with.[8]

Backward-induction reasoning is not without its problems. It presupposes, as we have seen, that the agent takes herself to have a robust trust in her own future rationality – robust in the sense that it would survive even at the choice nodes that can only be reached by a series of irrational moves. But, as the well-known objection goes, wouldn't the agent at such nodes have grounds to doubt whether she would act rationally at the *subsequent* choice nodes? If she didn't do it earlier, why expect she would do it later? To put it differently: If backward induction is supposed to codify rationality and some choice nodes in the decision tree can only be reached by moves

---

[8] More precisely, it can be proved that the agent will stop the pump at some point before the completion of the first round. For the proof, see Rabinowicz 2000.

prohibited by backward induction, wouldn't the agent at such nodes have grounds to doubt whether her subsequent moves would be as backward induction requires? However, in the presence of such doubts, backward-induction reasoning would crumble.[9]

This objection does not apply to the short money pump described above. There, it is only the third choice node that cannot be reached without a move prohibited by backward induction. But that node is terminal: It is not followed by any further occasion for choice. What is rational to do at a terminal choice node, however, does not depend on what one expects to do afterwards: There aren't any subsequent choice nodes to consider. Thus, continued self-trust has no role to play at that point. On the other hand, at the non-terminal choice nodes in this short money pump, the agent has no evidence about any prior backward-induction violations on her part and thus has no grounds for doubts about her future rationality.

The objection does apply, though, to more complicated money pumps, which involve several rounds or are based on cycles that consist of more than three alternatives. Still, if a money pump is not too long, and if the sophisticated agent starts out with a very firm conviction about her commitment to the backward-induction procedure, the evidence about her past deviations from that commitment might never be extensive enough to shatter this initial conviction. She might be able to explain them away as isolated mistakes that would not be repeated in the future.[10]

Are we then out of the woods, at least as far as relatively short money pumps are concerned? Is foresight, coupled with sophistication, sufficient to stop the pump? Not quite, I am afraid. What follows is a description of a money pump that can be used against a sophisticated chooser (cf. Rabinowicz 2000).

In the money pumps discussed up to now, the series of trades terminates as soon as the agent refuses to make yet another exchange. No further trade offers are forthcoming. Suppose we change this feature of the decision problem and assume the exploiter to be *persistent*: If you refuse a trade offer, he comes back with the same offer at the next stage.[11] There are three stages at which offers are made. The decision tree for this new money pump looks as follows:

---

[9] Cf. Binmore 1987, Reny 1988 and 1989, Bicchieri 1989, Pettit and Sugden 1989. For some defenses of backward induction, either general in scope or limited to a specific class of cases, see Sobel 1993, Aumann 1995 and 1998, Rabinowicz 1998 and Broome and Rabinowicz 1999.
[10] These remarks also apply to the modified money pump that I am going to consider below.
[11] Obviously, it is a variant of the same idea that was exploited by Skyrms 1993 in his treatment of diachronic Dutch books (cf. the preceding section).

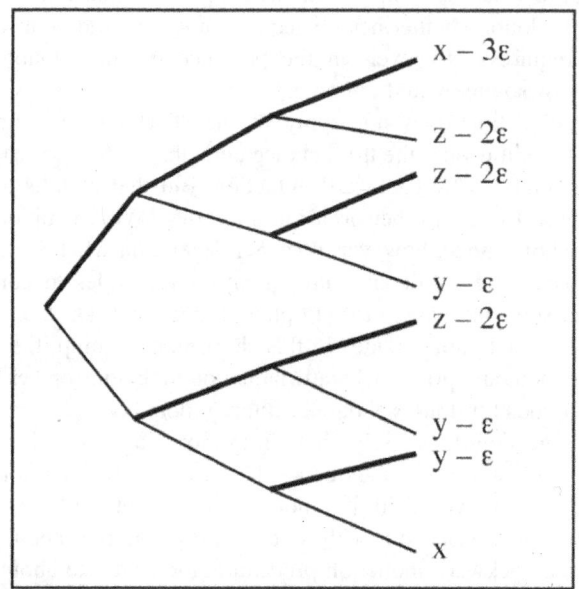

Figure 2: Money Pump with Persistent Offers

As before, trades and refusals to trade are represented as upward and downward moves, respectively. If the agent each time refuses to trade, she ends up with x. If she trades just once (at whatever stage), she ends up with $y - \varepsilon$. If she trades twice, she receives $z - 2\varepsilon$. Finally, if she trades three times, she receives $x - 3\varepsilon$, i.e. gets back to what she has started with minus extra payments.

The bold lines again stand for the backward-induction moves.

(i) Clearly, at each terminal choice node, backward induction prescribes trading, as this gives the agent her preferred alternative and she knows that her choice is final: No further trade offers will be forthcoming.

(ii) Since she predicts she will trade at each terminal node, she should also trade at each penultimate node. For the upper penultimate node, she predicts that trading would eventually lead to $x - 3\varepsilon$ while refusal to $z - 2\varepsilon$, which she disprefers. Analogously, for the lower penultimate choice node, she predicts that trading would eventually lead to $z - 2\varepsilon$ while refusal to $y - \varepsilon$, which she disprefers.

(iii) Given that she predicts she will trade at each node after the first one, she should trade at the first node as well. Trading at that node would eventually lead to $x - 3\varepsilon$, while refusal would lead to $z - 2\varepsilon$, which she disprefers.

We conclude, then, that in this modified money pump, a sophisticated chooser with cyclical preferences will be pumped: She will trade each time, which will get her back to the *status quo* alternative minus extra payments. The reason is obvious. The exploiter, being persistent in his offers, never lets the agent off the hook. Refusing to trade at an early stage does not terminate the pump: The trade offer will instead be repeated.

Despite obvious similarities having to do with the persistency of offers, there is an important difference between this money pump and Skyrms's exploitation set-up, which was devised for a violator of Reflection. In Skyrms's set-up, backward induction is unnecessary for the resolution of the agent's decision problem. Dominance is enough, as we have seen. In the money pump, however, dominance reasoning is inapplicable, for two reasons. (i) The agent's choices at the earlier stages influence the opportunities she will confront later: Depending on whether she trades at a given stage or not, she will be offered different trade opportunities at the subsequent stage. (ii) Her current trading decisions crucially depend on her expectations about her trading decisions in the future.

That backward induction implies repeated trading, if the exploiter is persistent, is a robust result, which can be generalized to pumps with an arbitrary number of stages (for the proof, see Rabinowicz 2000). Such pumps may be based on any number n of basic cycling alternatives, $x_1, ..., x_n$ (in our example, $n = 3$), and they may involve any number k of full rounds (in our example, $k = 1$). The only extra assumption we need to obtain this result is that the small payment required by each trade never reverses the agent's preference with regard to the basic cycling alternatives, independently of how many such payments she has already made.

As in the set-ups in the two preceding sections, the agent with cyclical preferences is being exploited because her decision-making is disunified. More precisely, she is disunified over time: She decides on each exchange separately, at the stage when it is being offered, instead of making a single choice on all the three stages together. If she did the latter, then, we may safely assume, she would certainly not choose to accept all the three exchanges, since a simple calculation would show that refusing the three trades would get her the same outcome (x) without any extra costs.

As her preferences are cyclical, it is not determined by our description of the case what particular outcome the unified agent *would* choose in such a situation. But this cyclicity in her pair wise preferences does not imply that she would be unable to make a rational choice, when she considered all the alternatives together. Cyclicity in pair wise preferences over a set of alternatives is compatible with the possibility that the agent finds some of the alternatives in the set unequivocally choice worthy, while she rejects other alternatives. In our example, we may assume that $x - 3\varepsilon$ will be among the rejected alternatives, while x might well be one of the alternatives that will be considered choice worthy.

Let C be a choice function that picks out subsets from sets of alternatives in a given domain. Intuitively, for any such alternative set S, the alternatives in C(S) are the ones that the agent would view as choice worthy when confronted with S as the set of alternatives to choose from. We allow C(S) to be empty for some non-empty sets S in the domain. Pair wise preference can then be analyzed in terms of C: An alternative i is preferred to an alternative j if and only if C$\{i, j\}$ = $\{i\}$. Analogously, indifference between i and j means that C$\{i, j\}$ = $\{i, j\}$. If C$\{i, j\}$ is empty, there is a gap in the agent's preference ordering as far as the comparison between i and j is concerned.

The distinction between the two types of cyclicity – the benign and the vicious one – is important when it comes to the discussion of the rationality of cyclical preferences. Benign cyclicity allows for a rational choice from the cycle as a whole. But even if the sophisticated agent's cyclical preferences are benign, she can *still* be subjected to a money pump.

I mention this possibility, because Levi (2006) does not take it into consideration. He thinks there is no need for resorting to money pumps in attacking cyclical preferences. What makes such preferences unacceptable in his view is the agent's predicament when it comes to a choice from the whole set of cycling alternatives:

> Suppose the agent X with cyclic preference over x, y and z is confronted with a choice between these three prizes. There is no optimal option in the three way choice. X should eliminate the cyclicity from X's preference so that X's preference can function as a guide in optimizer X's deliberations. Cyclic preferences are irrational precisely because X cannot choose rationally in some decision problems. Were X confronted with a three way choice between x, y and z, X could not follow the policy of choosing an option that is ... optimal according to some permissible ranking and, indeed, could not follow the slightly different policy of choosing an option that is maximal in the sense that no option is strictly preferred to it. I am convinced by this argument that cycles should be avoided. Rabinowicz's argument [= my money pump with persistent trade offers] seems far less compelling.

It should be clear, however, why Levi's criticism of cyclicity is unconvincing if pairwise preference is analyzable in terms of an underlying choice function. When there is a cycle, there is room for a money pump. But even though every option in the cycling set is dispreferred to some of its competitors, it may well be that the cycle in question is benign. In that case, the choice from the whole set is unproblematic, contrary to what Levi suggests.

4 Levi's Criticism of Diachronic Pragmatic Arguments

In *Money Pumps and Diachronic Dutch Books* (2002), Levi considers my money pump with persistent trade offers and Skyrms's version of the diachronic Dutch book against violators of Reflection. He argues that there exists a decisive difference between these exploitation set-ups and the synchronic Dutch books. The difference has to do with the range of options that are available to the agent. An agent who is vulnerable to a synchronic exploitation set-up acts in a way that is *dominated by some option that stands at her disposal*. Something must be deeply wrong with a person who behaves like this. She can't be rational if she instead of what she does could have chosen an option that would give her better results under all possible circumstances. Thus, to give an example, in a synchronic Dutch book against a violator of the addition axiom for probabilities, the agent accepts each bet that is being offered, even though she has at her disposal the option of refusing all of them. The latter option *dominates* what the agent does: It would yield better results whatever happens.

By contrast, in a diachronic set-up, think of the agent at the initial choice node. She 'has no control then over what [she] will choose later. [She] can only predict what [she] will do.' (Levi 2002: 239) As a consequence, when she is exposed to my Money Pump and ends up making the three trades, '[she] is not choosing [at any point] an option dominated by another *available as an option* to [her]' (ibid.: 241, Levi's emphasis). In particular, at the initial choice node, refusing to trade at any of the three stages is not an option that stands at the agent's disposal. Because of this absence of a dominating option, she cannot be charged with irrationality.

To be sure, Levi writes, a Money Pump like mine shows that an agent with cyclical preferences can be taxed for having preferences of this kind. The extra payments she incurs may be seen as such a tax. If her preferences weren't cyclical, she would not have to pay just to get back to her *status quo* alternative. But vulnerability to taxation is not irrationality. Levi concludes:

> Money Pump arguments were designed initially to show that individuals who violate certain canons of rationality will end up choosing options that are dominated by other options available to them just like synchronic arguments do. Showing that violating these canons is one way, that in the face of other assumptions, makes one vulnerable to taxation, is no substitute. Those who use money pump arguments to defend acyclicity of preference have failed to show that decision-makers who violate acyclicity are driven to choose dominated options. (ibid.: 241f)

Levi's diagnosis of Skyrms's version of the diachronic Dutch book against a violator of Reflection is exactly similar. Vulnerability to diachronic exploitation does not show that the agent is irrational and, again, the reason for this is to be found in the range of options that are at the agent's disposal. The agent lacks control over her future choices; she can only predict what she will do. She cannot at t decide not to accede to the bookie's offer at t'. Consequently, she cannot at t decide to refuse all the bets offers she expects to receive. But this means that she cannot be accused of acting in a way that is being dominated by some of her available options.

> According to Skyrms's scenario, X is worse off, no matter how X chooses, than X was in the initial status quo. If X has the option of remaining in the status quo position, X should do so [rather than act as she does]. But by hypothesis X does not have this option. X is not rationally compelled to choose an option dominated by *other available options* ... Buying [the bet on A conditional on E] at the initial stage is not dominated by refusing to buy it at that stage. Since these are the only two options, where is the beef? (ibid.: 247, Levi's emphasis)

5 My response

Indeed, where is the beef? Levi is quite right that, in my money pump and in Skyrms's diachronic set-up, both of us have assumed that the agent at the initial stage cannot control what he will do in the future. As Skyrms puts it: 'Deciding not to bet ever is not an option.' (Skyrms 1993: 323) Consequently, the agent's course of action is not dominated by any of the options that stand at her disposal. It is only dominated by a certain *sequence* of options, each of which is available to the agent at some time. In the set-ups under consideration, such a dominating option sequence consists in declining each opportunity when that opportunity is being offered. But the times at which different options in the sequence become available are not the same and the sequence as a whole is not an option for the agent, at any time.

I cannot speak for Skyrms, but as for myself, I assumed these limitations in the agent's diachronic self-control in order to make the exploitation unavoidable from the point of view of the agent. I thought the diachronic case was in this way more worrisome than the synchronic one. In the latter, it certainly would be extremely unrealistic to suppose that the agent is bound to be disunified – that she can separately decide on each of the bet opportunities, but cannot decide jointly on all of them together.

However, to deal with the issue raised by Levi, we can simply modify the diachronic set-up so as to put the two kinds of arguments, of the synchronic and the diachronic kind, on an equal footing. Let us assume, therefore, that the agent at the initial stage *can* decide on the whole temporal sequence of her actions, but, as a matter of fact, she does not deliberate on the sequence as whole but instead makes her decisions one by one: She decides on different bet offers separately, at the time when they are made. However, if she did view her decision-problem in a unified way, which she could, her prior decisions would make an impact on her subsequent behavior.

In this way, it seems, the synchronic and the diachronic exploitation set-ups become analogous. In the synchronic case, the agent is also assumed to engage in a disunified decision-making: She makes decisions on each bet separately. (Otherwise, as we have seen, no exploitation would take place.) But, if she viewed the situation in a unified way, she would then make a single choice as to which bets to accept and which to reject. It is in this sense that she has at her disposal the option of declining all the bets, which dominates her actual behavior. This option is available to her, since it would figure in her deliberation as one of the alternatives if she were unified and nothing hinders her from being so. In this respect, then, the synchronic set-up is similar to the diachronic one, after we have modified the latter to make the two set-ups comparable.

One might perhaps argue that there still is this difference between the synchronic and the diachronic case: In the diachronic case, when I consider each offer separately, I predict my future choices in order to determine what will be the final outcome of my current choice. In the synchronic case, however, when considering a particular bet offer, I don't make any predictions about the decisions I take about other offers in the package. As long as each of these other offers still is under my deliberation, I cannot – it seems – relate to them in a predictive mode. At least on one interpretation of Levi's thesis that deliberation crowds out prediction, this is, I guess, what he would want to say.[12] But then disunification in the synchronic case involves more than just making a separate decision on each bet offer. It would also seem to involve some form of abstraction: While considering whether to accept a given bet, the agent abstracts from his decisions on the other bets on the table. (Indeed, without some assumption like this it is difficult to see how an agent who violates standard probability axioms could be exploited in a synchronic set-up to begin with.)

However, this potential difference between the diachronic and the synchronic case does not affect the issue of the availability of a dominating option. The two set-ups can be analogous in the latter respect. In each set-up, the dominating option can be available to the agent but is not an alternative she considers in her (disunified) deliberation. If this analogy is possible, then Levi has no grounds for his claim that the synchronic pragmatic arguments have a bite which diachronic arguments lack. Rather, it seems, the two kinds of arguments are on the same footing.

---

[12] For his exposition and defense of that thesis, see Levi 1989, 1991, 1997. For a critical discussion, see Joyce 2002 and Rabinowicz 2002.

In the synchronic set-up, the presence of the option to refuse all the bets does not, it seems, make it irrational for the agent to decide to accept any particular bet, when she considers whether to accept it or refuse it. She considers this question in a disunified fashion, in which the option of the wholesale refusal does not figure as one of the alternatives. The same applies to the diachronic case. In the diachronic set-up, the mere presence of the option to refuse all the offers, current and future ones, does not make it irrational for the agent to accept any particular offer in the exploitation sequence, when she considers whether to accept that offer or to refuse it. For, again, she considers this question in a disunified fashion, in which the option of the wholesale refusal does not figure as one of the alternatives.

In his recent comment, Levi disagrees with me on this point. Using my money pump with persistent trade offers as an example, he argues that the disunified form of practical deliberation must be irrational if it is not inescapable:

> A possible way to understand Rabinowicz's suggestion is that X has control *at the initial node* over which of the eight paths X will choose. [Here, 'the eight paths' refers to the eight branches in the decision tree for the money pump in question.] But X deliberates in a 'disunified' way so that at each node he deliberates between the 'sell-don't sell' options available then.
>
> If X refuses to consider all the options that are available to X according to X's beliefs and goals, X's deliberation is irrational. Indeed, this is so whether or not the options that are not considered dominate the one chosen from the options that are. Such disunity is to be avoided. This is so whether X is offered a set of gambles at the same time or is offered a sequence of options where X regards X to be in control of the path X will take. (Levi 2006)

Levi's point, then, is that any deliberation that ignores some of the options available to the agent is *ipso facto* irrational. Since disunified deliberation by necessity has this feature (as it ignores the 'wholesale' options), it is always irrational, whether or not the ignored options dominate the chosen ones and quite independently of whether the decision set-up is diachronic or synchronic.

If Levi is right, pragmatic arguments for various constraints on the agent's beliefs and desires would all seem to be ill-conceived. We have seen that such arguments presuppose not only that the agent violates the relevant constraints but also that she makes her decisions in a disunified fashion. But then, if disunification *itself* turns out a form of irrationality, the arguments lose their bite: They provide no reasons for upholding the relevant constraints. Instead, disunification could then be blamed for everything. Note also that, if Levi is right in what he now suggests, then synchronic and diachronic arguments would again be put on equal footing, as I have been arguing and contrary to his earlier claims. There would be no reason to suggest that synchronic arguments somehow are better or more compelling than the diachronic ones.

But is Levi right in his underlying assumption? Is it always irrational to ignore some of the options that are available for choice? It seems to me that this is to go much too far. It is one thing to require the considered alternatives to be *jointly exhaustive* in the sense that the agent would do one of them in every possible development. It is quite another thing to demand that the agent should consider every available alternative. When I deliberate, in a disunified fashion, whether to accept a certain opportunity or not, the alternatives I consider are jointly exhaustive, despite the fact that I ignore the more extended options, which concern the whole package of opportunities. This, I imagine, is how things are with all of us, most of the time. In practically every choice situation, the alternatives that figure in our deliberation admit of versions and extensions that we do not reflect upon. However detailed our deliberation might be, there is nearly always room for even more detail and elaboration. I think, therefore, that Levi demands too much. Consequently, the same applies to his suggestion that disunification as such is to be avoided, whether or not the options that are not considered dominate the ones that are being chosen.

It is time to sum up the main claims of this paper. As intimated in the introduction to this paper, I do not think that pragmatic arguments of any variety are able to establish the inherent rationality of constraints on the agent's state of mind. Instead, their perspective on constraint violations is purely instrumental: Their proper function is to identify conditions that the agent has reason to comply with if she wants to afford disunified decision-making. In Levi's terminology, it is just a matter of 'tax avoidance': Pragmatic arguments identify constraints one needs to satisfy to avoid paying tax for disunification. But I share Levi's view that avoiding tax at all costs is unreasonable, especially if we are dealing with constraints that do not seem to be inherently compelling. (The principle of reflection is surely a case in point.) In this respect, synchronic and diachronic pragmatic arguments are on a par. However, to the extent that synchronic unification is much easier to achieve that its diachronic counterpart, diachronic arguments provide us with stronger instrumental reasons for compliance. This is rather ironical. The most classical and influential pragmatic arguments – synchronic Dutch books – are considerably less compelling than their younger diachronic cousins.

References

Aumann, R. 1995. Backward Induction and Common Knowledge of Rationality. *Games and Economic Behavior* 18: 6-19.

Aumann, R. 1998. A Note on the Centipede Game. *Games and Economic Behavior* 23: 97-105.

Bicchieri, C. 1989. Backward Induction with Common Knowledge. *Proceedings of the Philosophy of Science Association* 2: 329-43.

Binmore, K. 1987. Modelling Rational Players: Part 1. *Economics and Philosophy* 3: 179-213.

Broome, J. and Rabinowicz, W. 1999. Backwards Induction in the Centipede. *Analysis* 59: 237-42.

Christensen, D. 1991. Clever Bookies and Coherent Beliefs. *The Philosophical Review* 50: 229-47.

Davidson, D., McKinsey, J.C.C., Suppes, P. 1955. Outlines of a Formal Theory of Value, Part I. *Philosophy of Science* 22: 140-60.

Joyce, J.M. 2002. Levi on Causal decision Theory and the Possibility of Predicting One's Own Actions. *Philosophical Studies* 110: 69-102.

Levi, I. 1988. The Demons of Decision. *The Monist* 70: 193-211.

Levi, I. 1989. Rationality, Prediction, and Autonomous Choice. *Canadian Journal of Philosophy* 19(suppl.): 339-63.

Levi, I. 1991. Consequentialism and Sequential Choice. *Foundations of Decision Theory*, eds. M. Bacharach and S. Hurley, 92-122. Oxford: Blackwell.

Levi, I. 1997. *The Covenant of Reason*. Cambridge: Cambridge University Press.

Levi, I. 2002. Money Pumps and Diachronic Dutch Books. *Philosophy of Science* 69(suppl): S235-S247.

Levi, I. 2006. Reply to Rabinowicz. *Knowledge and Inquiry: Essays on the Pragmatism of Isaac Levi*, ed. E.J. Olsson. Cambridge: Cambridge University Press.

Maher, P. 1992. Diachronic Rationality. *Philosophy of Science* 59: 120-41.

McClennen, E. 1990. *Rationality and Dynamic Choice*. Cambridge: Cambridge University Press.

Pettit, P., and Sugden, R. 1989. The Backward Induction Paradox. *Journal of Philosophy* 86: 169-82.

Rabinowicz, W. 1995. To Have One's Cake and Eat It, Too: Sequential Choice and Expected Utility Violations. *The Journal of Philosophy* 92: 586-620.

Rabinowicz, W. 1998. Grappling with the Centipede. *Economics and Philosophy* 14: 95-125.

Rabinowicz, W. 2000. Money Pump with Foresight. *Imperceptible Harms and Benefits*, ed. M.J. Almeida, 123-54. Dordrecht: Kluwer.

Rabinowicz, W. 2002. Does Practical Deliberation Crowd Out Self-Prediction? *Erkenntnis* 57: 91-122.

Rabinowicz, W. 2006. Levi on Money Pumps and Diachronic Dutch-Book Arguments. *Knowledge and Inquiry: Essays on the Pragmatism of Isaac Levi*, ed. E.J. Olsson. Cambridge: Cambridge University Press.

Raiffa, H. 1968. *Decision Analysis: Introductory Lectures on Choice under Uncertainty*. Reading, MA: Addison-Wesley.

Ramsey, F.P. 1990 [1926]. Truth and Probability. *F.P. Ramsey: Philosophical Papers*, ed. D.H. Mellor, 52-94. Cambridge: Cambridge University Press.

Reny, P. 1988. *Rationality, Common Knowledge and the Theory of Games*. PhD thesis. Princeton, NJ: Princeton University.

Reny, P. 1989. Common Knowledge and Games with Perfect Information. *Proceedings of the Philosophy of Science Association* 2: 363-69.

Schick, F. 1989. Dutch Bookies and Money Pumps. *The Journal of Philosophy* 83: 112-19.

Schwartz, T. 1986. *The Logic of Collective Choice*. New York: Columbia University Press.

Skyrms, B. 1980. Higher Order Degrees of Belief. *Prospects for Pragmatism*, ed. D.H. Mellor, 109-137. Cambridge: Cambridge University Press.

Skyrms, B. 1993. A Mistake in Dynamic Coherence Arguments? *Philosophy of Science* 60: 320-28.

Sobel, J.H. 1993. Backward Induction Arguments In Finitely Iterated Prisoners' Dilemmas: A Paradox Regained. *Philosophy of Science* 60: 114-33.

Teller, P. 1973. Conditionalization and Observation. *Synthèse* 26: 218-38.

van Fraassen, B. 1984. Belief and the Will. *The Journal of Philosophy* 81: 235-56.

8

Rationality and Prediction in the Sciences of the Artificial: Economics as a Design Science[*]

WENCESLAO J. GONZALEZ

Within the realm of the sciences of the artificial, which may be understood as 'design sciences,' rationality and prediction have a central role. Both — rationality and prediction — are needed for scientific design, and they have tasks on different levels. On the one hand, a design is made by means of rationality, which involves the cognitive, practical, and evaluative spheres;[1] and, on the other hand, scientific design also requires predictions regarding possible aims, processes, and results (where accuracy and precision may be relevant criteria).

Furthermore, rationality and prediction may have an influence on the prescriptions of design sciences, insofar as these disciplines are applied sciences requiring the knowledge of the possible futures (in the short, medium or long run) before any decision is made (this is true in subjects such as economics). Moreover, design sciences may also have consequences for the possible technological devices based on scientific knowledge, insofar as technology is built by using scientific knowledge (know that) in addition to specific technological knowledge (know how).

In particular, rationality and prediction are key factors in the science of economics, which is one of the sciences of the artificial, and it works with design activities in applied economics. Microeconomics and macroeconom-

---

[*] This paper was prepared at the Center for Philosophy of Science (University of Pittsburgh) in 2005. It belongs to the research project 'Bounded Rationality and Design Sciences: The Role of Prediction and Prescription' (HUM2004-06846/FISO) supported by Spanish Ministry of Education and Science.

[1] From Kant onwards, the philosophical tendency is to consider the three following major contexts of choice: beliefs, actions, and values (see Rescher 1988: 2-3).

ics deal with agents and institutions that introduce new products (above all in the more creative areas of applied economics, such as business firms and financial markets) according to some rationality standards and according to predictions (for the short, medium or long run). For this reason, this paper will pay special attention to the case of economics. The philosophical and methodological analysis carried out below will examine in turn the following issues: (i) the realm of the sciences of the artificial; (ii) the design sciences as characteristic sciences of the artificial; (iii) the kinds of rationality most relevant in these sciences, through the study of the case of economics; and (iv) the role of prediction in the sciences characterized by the use of designs.

1 The Realm of the Sciences of the Artificial

It seems clear that the sciences of the artificial are a domain of 'human-made' products. But this ontological feature can be understood in different ways, which converge towards two possible kinds of 'sciences of the artificial'. On the one hand, the type of studies that, starting from *professional practices* of some accumulative sort (such as pharmacology, librarianship, management, and so on), later on become scientific studies (here design guides the process of global achievement, rather than the expertise and techniques previously learned by the agents in the profession). On the other hand, the scientific research of *the artifacts* (the human-made objects), which may follow the patterns of the natural sciences (such as physics, chemistry, biology) or of the social sciences (such as sociology, economics, psychology),

In the first brand of the sciences of the artificial, the configuration of the new subject-matter is usually by a 'scientification' of a profession (Niiniluoto 1993: 9), which transforms it according to the problem-solving approach of the applied sciences. The contents often remain in the scientific domain, even though scientific knowledge is often used for technological purposes (as in the case of pharmacology and the pharmaceutical industry). Meanwhile, in the second type of studies, the sciences of the artificial often focus on the properties (physical, chemical, biological) of technological artifacts. Then, research is commonly seen as the scientific foundation of technological knowledge, serving the aims of technology, as is the case with the 'science of materials'. In the case of the social sciences, the latter approach can lead to a new branch inside the discipline (sociology, economics, psychology, and so on), as with the sociology of industry or in the economics of technological innovation.

After Herbert A. Simon's work (Simon 1996 [1969]), the characteristic 'sciences of the artificial' appear to be of the first kind, and they are described by the model of the 'design sciences'. Thus, in the study of human-made products, the starting point normally involves the use of design to solve a particular problem. This conception of 'design',[2] which includes the utilization of scientific prediction and some kind of rationality, contributes to making the sciences of the artificial different from other sciences, either of the formal or of the empirical type. In general, the genuine aims, processes, and results of the design sciences are different from those of the other sciences. Nonetheless, there are sciences, such as economics, which can be at the same time a science of the artificial and a social science.

Even though design sciences share with the formal sciences (logic and mathematics) the idea of models as 'constructions', the difference between them due to their characteristic elements is clear: in the sciences of the artificial the aim of design, the processes that are developed to solve concrete problems, and the final results are – or may be – tangible ones[3] (e.g., the composition of a medical drug or a new monetary innovation). At the same time, the sciences of the artificial share with the natural sciences and the social sciences the notion of model as a 'representation' or 'resemblance' of empirical reality[4] (as in pharmacology or in experimental economics). But again, commonly, the typical aims, processes, and results of design sciences are different from those of the natural sciences and social sciences. The sciences of design deal with kinds of objects that are *artificial* (human-made) rather than natural items or social events. That explains why the sciences of the artificial have been proposed only after the development of the natural sciences and the social sciences.

Nevertheless, for a methodological appraisal, scientific activities – natural, social and artificial – share a common sphere of empirical testing, insofar as their statements can be assessed by observation or experimentation. Even so, the contents of the sciences of the artificial require a specific consideration, since they consist of objects, procedures, and outcomes intentionally originated by *human design*. Therefore, they are ontologically different from natural items or social events. Moreover, the feature of being based on human design makes that, *de facto*, the sciences of the artificial are closer to technology than to other empirical sciences. They are many times used as a necessary foundation for some technologies (such as pharmacol-

---

[2] An overview of different conceptions of 'design' is provided in Atwood, McCain, and Williams 2002: 125-32.

[3] This difference – to be tangible – is related with the distinction between 'calculus' and 'experiments', which is basic to Wittgenstein's views on prediction in mathematics: in an experiment we have something tangible, whereas calculus is only an ability to do something. Cf. Gonzalez 1996a: 299-332, section 3.

[4] On models as 'constructions' as well as 'representations' or 'resemblance'. and their use in connection to economic predictions, see Gonzalez Forthcoming: sections 12.3 and 13.1.

The role of models in science is analyzed in Morgan and Morrison (eds.) 1999. On the case of economics, Turner 2001: 42-53.

ogy in the case of pharmaceutical companies). Yet 'design sciences' belong to a realm that is *scientific* rather than technological, and they have a scientific rationality that is different from technological rationality,[5] even though there is an interaction between science and technology, which could be very strong indeed in some cases.

Simon insists on a close connection between the sciences of the artificial as human-made undertakings and the technological doings, because they are both goal-oriented and share the need for designs to achieve their goals:

> we speak of engineering as concerned with 'synthesis,' while science is concerned with 'analysis.' Synthetic or artificial objects – and more specifically prospective artificial objects having desired properties – are the central objective of engineering activity and skill. The engineer, and more generally the designer, is concerned with how things *ought to* be – how they ought to be in order to *attain goals*, and to *function*. Hence a science of artificial will be closely akin to a science of engineering. (Simon 1996 [1969]: 4-5)

At the same time, Simon highlights the distinction between the artificial and the natural, while laying less emphasis upon the distinction between the artificial and the social, which has methodological consequences for cases such as economics (e.g., in social planning). Thus, he goes so far as to hold that 'economics exhibits in purest form the artificial component in human behavior, in individual actors, business firms, markets, and the entire economy' (ibid.: 25). This view of economics as a science is clearly different from that of other Nobel Prize winners, such as Milton Friedman, John Hicks and James Buchanan, and has clear repercussion for the role of scientific prediction.[6]

When Simon establishes the *boundaries* for the sciences of the artificial, his approach is a combination of epistemological, methodological and ontological elements:

> 1. Artificial things are synthesized (though not always or usually with full forethought) by human beings. 2. Artificial may imitate appearances in natural things while lacking, in one or many respects, the reality of the latter. 2. Artificial things can be characterized in terms of functions, goals, adaptation. 4. Artificial things are often discussed, particularly when they are being designed, in terms of imperatives as well as descriptives. (ibid.: 25)

These properties of the artificial world are at the interface between the *internal* natural laws (e.g., the resistance of materials) and the *external* natural

---

[5] On the features of 'technology' in comparison with 'science', see Gonzalez 2005: 3-49, especially: 11-12.
[6] Cf. Gonzalez 1998a: 321-345, especially: 322-29.

laws of the environment. In addition, they belong to a society that gives them a certain *value* (for example in economics, especially in the case of scarcity).

Taking into account Herbert Simon's analysis of the boundaries of the sciences of the artificial, it seems that their study requires consideration of these sciences as 'design sciences', and therefore as fields of inquiry different from the 'descriptive sciences'. This must be understood before undertaking the philosophical examination of the kinds of rationality more relevant for the sciences of the artificial and before examining the role of prediction in these sciences as developed through the use of design.

2 The Sciences of the Artificial as Design Sciences

Nowadays, at the core of the sciences of the artificial is still 'design science', a branch that has been emerging since the mid-1970s. Around 1975 a Design Research Center was created at Carnegie Mellon University, and since 1985 it became the 'Engineering Design Research Center'. Thus, this field started in the domain of the science of the artificial:

> In substantial part, design theory is aimed at broadening the capabilities of computers to aid design, drawing upon the tools of artificial intelligence and operations research. Hence, research on many aspects of computer-aided design is being pursued with growing intensity in computer science, engineering and architecture departments, and in operations research groups in business schools. (Simon 1996 [1969]: 114)

It is a teleological activity: design 'is concerned with how things ought to be, with devising artifacts to attain goals' (ibid.). The number of alternatives is not unlimited and optimization can be a serious problem. Hence, according to Herbert A. Simon, 'we cannot within practical computational limits generate all the admissible alternatives and compare their respective merits' (ibid.: 120).

Before this idea of 'design science' as connected with computers was brought up, a broad notion of 'design' was available, which was linked with other types of technologies, where rationality and prediction were also in place:

> Up until about 1950' a rational step-by-step approach to design served adequately for those artifacts being created. Technical knowledge about the properties of materials was well known and the step-by-step traditional rational approach for solving problems in a coherent manner was adequate. Research and scientific knowledge was familiar with the composition of materials and designers could adequately predict the outcomes for their artifacts given that no other known variables or principles of design were violated. (Atwood, McCain, and Williams 2002: 126)

Following that historical background, it seems clear that there are two approaches to 'design', which are different from the conceptual point of view: the scientific perspective and the technological approach. Nevertheless, due to the interaction between the sciences of the artificial and the diverse branches of technology (industrial, naval, aeronautic, civil, and so on), these two kinds of designs – scientific and technological – are not clearly distinguished in different methodological approaches (see Cross, ed. 1984). However, it is philosophically important to differentiate between them, not only because 'technique' becomes 'technology' when there is scientific support, but also because technological design adds new factors – regarding the artifact – that are not included in scientific design (for example, in the case of artifacts made by NASA, where the scientific design precedes methodologically the technological design).

In the *scientific perspective*, the design is a central element of a science related to aims, processes and results connected to human activities, a science which may eventually lead to human-made products (for example, to get a new medical drug, an innovation for business firms or a new computer program). Then, design is linked to applied knowledge in order to solve concrete problems. Thus, it includes both cognitive content and practical utility. Moreover, scientific design is tested using the kind of methodological tools adequate to other empirical sciences (among them, prediction), that is, processes that involve both observation and experimentation. Meanwhile, in the *technological orientation* design is aimed at a creative transformation of existing reality (natural, social, or artificial) in order to produce new results (normally, a kind of human artifact, such as a bridge, an aircraft, a ship, a computer, a cell phone); and the objects produced can directly affect the lives of the members of society. Of course, technological changes may promote social development or they might be against the common good of the citizens.[7]

The scientific perspective and the technological orientation follow different kinds of rationality, because, in principle, science and technology seek different aims, processes and results. These differences are important from the 'internal' point of view (for example, semantical, logical, epistemological, or methodological), but also from the 'external' viewpoint (for example, social, cultural, or political) (Gonzales 1998b, especially 95-107). On the one hand, scientific rationality has several aims, mainly in the cognitive sphere, and they can be pursued in order to *increase our knowledge* (basic science) or to *resolve practical problems* in a concrete area (applied science) (Niiniluoto 1993: 3-6; Niiniluoto 1995). On the other hand, techno-

---

[7] There are also philosophical reflections on present phenomena in comparison to the past, such as in the case of the Luddites, cf. Graham 1999: ch. 1; Kitcher 2001, ch. 13: 167-80.

logical rationality is oriented towards a *creative transformation of reality* (natural, social, or artificial) according to a given design, which is followed by some specific doings in order to get a posterior artifact or a final product.

Where cognitive contents and practical utilities do have a key role is in applied science, which frequently includes an interaction between scientific knowledge and the material support given by technology. From a conceptual point of view, there is an understandable difference with respect to basic science: applied science involves the *practical orientation* of scientific knowledge. Thus,

> besides epistemic utility, the knowledge provided by applied science is expected to have *instrumental value* for associated human activity. Applied science is thus governed by what Habermas calls the 'technical interest' of controlling the world. (Niiniluoto 1993: 6. See also Habermas 1968)

Design sciences, which belong to the sciences of the artificial, are a clear example of the scientific interest in how the things *ought to be* to in order to reach certain goals (Simon 1996 [1969]: 4). It seems rather obvious that the sciences of the artificial are, in general, applied sciences.[8]

Moreover, besides the distinction between science (basic and applied) and technology from the *internal* point of view (i.e., semantic, logical, epistemological, methodological, ontological and axiological), there are differences between scientific activity and technological doing from the *external* perspective. The above difference ordinarily comes from the *complexity* and the *level of repercussion* of the values that intervene (such as ethical, social, cultural, political, ecological, aesthetic, economic values). Usually, these *external values* influence technology more deeply than science, and technology is generally more intelligible than science, insofar as it is completely human-made.[9] As a matter of fact, technological design, the process of developing it, and its outcome – an artifact – are all made by human beings, who are trying to creatively transform some available reality.

3 Kinds of Rationality in the Sciences of the Artificial

On the whole, in the sciences of the artificial it is possible to distinguish three successive *epistemological levels* of rationality, which have a methodological repercussion. Such levels are:

---

[8] 'It is important to distinguish *applied* science from the *applications* of science. The former is a part of knowledge production, the latter is concerned with the use of scientific knowledge and the methods for solving of practical problems of action (e.g., in engineering or business), where a scientist may play the role of a consult' (Niiniluoto 1993: 9).

[9] Herbert Simon made explicit this point to me in a conversation.

(i) the rationality of being a science, considering its characteristic features ('artificial' versus 'natural' or 'social') as well as the differences of this activity respect to other human doings, such as technology;

(ii) the rationality of the specific discipline under consideration (for example, pharmacology, library science, economics, materials science), which reflect the designs, processes and possible outcomes associated with each one of them;

(iii) the rationality of the agents who are involved in the sphere of these sciences, taking into account their particular need for decision-making (this has a clear repercussion upon social institutions).

These three epistemological levels of rationality can be seen in a science like economics. Firstly, rationality of *science as such*, which is the widest possible scientific realm, is shared by the different scientific disciplines (at least, by those that have an empirical character, such as the natural sciences, the social sciences and sciences of the artificial). Secondly, rationality of economics *as a scientific endeavor* within the social sphere and the artificial realm, which is connected with other disciplines (such as psychology, sociology, political science). Thirdly, the rationality of economic *undertakings of agents* in particular cases (for example, the situations in which the economic agent needs to make a decision and to develop a kind of action in that regard).

3.1. Simon's Framework on Rationality

De facto, Herbert Simon has made contributions to all the three levels of rationality (Gonzales 2003a). However, his main emphasis is on the rationality of economic agents, which he connects with his vision of economics as interwoven with psychology. His cognitive interest also has influenced his view of economics as a science of understanding economic processes rather than a science focused upon successful predictions (Simon 1989). Thus, when he conceives *rationality*, the third level is particularly relevant, as can be noticed in his definition of 'rationality'. In his view, this term 'denotes a style of behavior that is appropriate to the achievement of given goals, within the limits imposed by given conditions and constraints' (Simon 1972: 161; see Simon 1982 [1964]: 405). The elements of this definition may receive more exact specification in particular contexts. Moreover, there are – for him – important specialized uses of rationality following those factors (style of behavior, goals, conditions and constraints) (Gonzales 2003a: 75-76).

According to Simon, there are several *uses of rationality*, which influence the way of *achieving goals*. We shall consider these in turn. First, within the sphere of the *utility function*, commonly subject to the idea of maximization, Simon points out the existence of two types of rationality: i) the strict species of rationality, customarily understood in terms of *optimality* (for example, the rational consumer of formal economic theory maximizes his expected utility, or the rational entrepreneur maximizes his expected profit); and ii) the more general kinds of rationality, called *adaptiveness* or *functionality*, where it is assumed that the pursuing of one's goals may not take the form of maximizing the expected value of a utility function – or, in game theory, minimizing the expected value of a loss function. Second, regarding the *type of criteria* that are to be fulfilled in order to obtain any given goal, rationality can be seen in *dualistic* terms: the criteria should be consistent with the idea of the *all-or-none* way, as in the case of attainment of aspiration, which is obtained or not obtained. Third, according to the *level of the goals* mentioned in Simon's definition, rationality can take different forms: a) goals of the choosing individual, b) goals of the social system to which he or she belongs, or c) goals imputed by the observer (Simon 1982 [1964]: 405).

From the point of view of the *conditions and constraints* that appear in Simon's definition of rationality, he maintains that they are of two different kinds: i) the rationality associated with *objective* conditions and constraints (that is, objective characteristics of the environment external to the choosing organism); and ii) the rationality associated with *subjective* conditions and constraints, or *bounded rationality* (that is, the rationality that is associated with perceived characteristic or characteristics of the organism itself, which could be taken as fixed or beyond its own control). This last option corresponds plainly to Simon's conception of human rationality as limited. In any case, he considers that an unambiguous use of the term 'rationality' requires a specification by the user of the assumptions being made about goals and conditions (ibid.).

The above elements of the definition of rationality – the style of behavior, the achievement of goals, and the limits due to conditions and constraints – are pointed out before the specific case of economics comes out.[10] For, as Simon recognizes, 'rationality' is a philosophical term previous to the emergence of the social sciences as independent disciplines (and, therefore, previous to the sciences of the artificial). Moreover, he considers that 'the modern usage of rationality is very close to Aristotle's concept of calculative or deliberative intellectual virtue' (Simon 1982 [1964]: 406). This kind of rationality emphasizes the *process* of choice (to pick out or to single out an option among several) that requires the employment of the intellec-

---

[10] Frequently Simon insists on the need of a broad concept of 'rationality' and criticizes 'economic rationality' – the neoclassical model – insofar as it is associated with a very particular and special form of rationality: the rationality of the utility maximizer, cf. Simon 1978: 1-16; especially: 2-3.

tive faculty (to think about ends and means). This view has a direct influence on the subjects that have their roots in Aristotle: logic, ethics and psychology; whereas in other subjects, such as economics or sociology, the prevailing kind of rationality prefers the emphasis on the *choices* themselves (that is, the emphasis on the outcomes rather than on the processes).

In the fields that Simon has explored in greater depth (psychology and economics),[11] there is a difference in the predominant kind of rationality. This divergence is extremely relevant for him, and it is the starting point for one of his main contributions to economics: the distinction between *substantive rationality* and *procedural rationality*. Thus, Simon points out that 'substantive rationality' is the concept of rationality that grew up within economics, while 'procedural rationality' is the concept that developed within psychology (Simon 1976: 130). Although he recognizes that the two fields – economics and psychology – address two significantly different sets of research questions, and that each one has adopted a view of rationality which, in principle, is more or less appropriate to its own research concerns, he criticizes substantive rationality in economics and stresses the importance of procedural rationality for this science.

When these concepts of rationality – the prevailing ones in economics and psychology – are compared and contrasted, several new differences appear, because economics has almost uniformly treated human behavior as rational, whereas psychology has always been concerned with both the irrational and the rational aspects of behavior. Simon is aware of this and pays attention to rationality instead of considering irrationality as well. Nevertheless, he frequently points out that economics sometimes uses the term 'irrationality' rather broadly (mainly, in Gary Becker's contribution)[12] so that the meaning of the term 'rationality' is correspondingly narrowed. As a matter of fact, this restricted use of 'rationality', which is dominant in the neoclassical economics – especially, in the Chicago school –, excludes from the domain of the rational many phenomena that psychology would include.

---

[11] In fact, Simon began with political science, which connects with psychology and economics. His first book, which he quotes very frequently, is in that field: *Administrative Behavior* (Simon 1997b). He is also very well known for his contributions to computer science, cf. *The Sciences of the Artificial* (Simon 1996 [1969]).
On the biographical aspects of these intellectual interests, cf. Simon 1991: ch. 4, 9, 10, 12, 16 and 21. A complete enumeration of his intellectual activities is in that book: 'the political scientist, the organization theorist, the economist, the management scientist, the computer scientist, the psychologist, the philosopher of science' (Simon 1991: xviii).

[12] Cf. Becker 1962 and 1974. However, Simon has pointed out that what G. Becker calls 'irrationality' in the first article, would be called 'bounded rationality' in his own paper, cf. Simon 1978: 2, note 2. The argument is clear: Becker indicates that he denotes as *irrational* any deviation from utility maximization; thus, Simon's bounded rationality is 'irrationality' in Becker's terminology, cf. Simon 1979: 497, footnote 2.

Consequently, he prefers to use the broader conception of rationality common in psychology (Simon 1987: 25). This view of economic science as connected to psychology has influenced Simon's approach to design sciences, where economic rationality has a key role.

Economics, if it is understood as a science of the artificial, may basically be considered in dualistic terms. This is true both if we consider its structure (outer environment and inner environment), and if we examine the kinds of rationality (substantive and procedural) to be used in order to deal with the economy as a complex system:

> the outer component is defined by the behavior of other individuals, firms, markets, or economies. The inner environment is defined by an individual's, firm's, market's, or economy's goals and capabilities for rational, adaptive behavior. Economics illustrates well how outer and inner environment interact and, in particular, how an intelligent system's adjustment to its outer environment (its *substantive rationality*) is limited by its ability, through knowledge and computation, to discover appropriate adaptive behavior (its *procedural rationality*) (Simon 1996 [1969]: 25).

Thus, the ontological and epistemological components (environments and rationalities) are combined with a kind of methodology that is of the adaptive type: economic processes are adaptive artifacts brought about in order to achieve human goals through evolutionary adjustment.[13]

To put it differently: there is a difference in dealing with economics as an artificial system, depending upon the kind of rationality that is used. When rationality is *substantive*, we can predict the economic behavior of the system without knowing how to actually compute the optimal output, because the goal – such as maximizing the difference between income and expenditure – completely defines the firm's inner environment. On the other hand, when rationality is *procedural*, there is economic uncertainty (that is the usual case), and we are dealing with the complexities of real firms in the real world of business. Thus we need to find a way of calculating, although in an approximate way, where a good course of action lies. This leads to a theory of estimation under uncertainty and a theory of computation (Simon 1996 [1969]: 25-27).

Even though the latter conception of procedural rationality is more realistic – it has a better empirical grounding – than substantive rationality, it involves an important problem, which is both epistemological and axiological: Simon reduces rationality to the relation between means and ends, and therefore he *de facto* assumes the ends as given. For him,

---

[13] The evolutionary character of human reason is stressed in Simon 1983.

> we see that reason is wholly instrumental. It cannot tell us where to go; at
> best it can tell us how to get there. It is a gun for hire that can be employed
> in the service of whatever goals we have, good or bad. (Simon 1983: 7-8)

This conception leads to a clear limitation of his view of economics as a science of the artificial, since the evaluative rationality of ends is very important for design, in addition to the instrumental rationality, which deals with the means-to-end connection and seeks effectiveness and efficiency.

3.2. From Instrumental Rationality to Evaluative Rationality

Evaluative rationality has a key role for scientific designs, since the sciences of the artificial are goal-oriented, and we need an evaluation of the inherent appropriateness of goals (Rescher 2003: 25-26; Rescher 1999: 25, 39, 81-83, 87, 91-93, 172). This rationality of ends is different from instrumental rationality, which deals with the effectiveness and efficiency of means (that is, with the efficacy of getting the job done and the efficiency in using less or more simple means). The relevance of evaluative rationality could be seen when the rationality of economic agents (that is, the third level on the scale already introduced) is analyzed, by also taking into account the rationality of economics as a scientific endeavor (that is, the second level).

For what concerns the distinction and complementarity of evaluative rationality and instrumental rationality, the contribution of experimental economics is of special interest.[14] Experimental economics is a branch of economic science in which the artificial elements are clearly in view, since in this case the feature of 'artificiality' can be considered from the point of view of design, the processes in use and also the outcome. As a matter of fact, the artificiality of a laboratory situation raises the question of the methodological evaluation, which involves a tension with respect to validity (internal versus external) (Schram 2005). In addition, the feature of *artificiality* is explicit in 'artificial economics' (agent-based computational economics), another branch of this discipline, which deals with 'the computational study of economies as complex adaptive systems implying interacting agents with cognitive skills', and in which research work 'intensively use[s] computer simulation as well as artificial intelligence concepts mostly based on multi-agents systems. In this context, the most used models come from game theory'.[15]

Experimental economics, which in 2002 received public recognition in the form of a Nobel Prize (Vernon Smith and Daniel Kahneman), is a field of investigation that has been a focus of increasing attention since the mid-

---

[14] In this regard, the analysis follows Gonzalez 2003b: 71-83, especially: 74-76.
[15] 'Artificial Economics' 2005.

1980s. Several Nobel laureates, who have worked on game theory (such as John Nash and Reinhard Selten, both awarded in 1994), have also developed economic experiments (Gonzales 2007: 300-301). Philosophically, Selten's contribution to the analysis of rationality in economics is particularly relevant: he assumes the need for evaluative rationality, and he is also well aware of the methodological distinction between 'descriptive economics' and 'normative economics', which is important if we want to analyze economics as a scientific activity.

The concept of 'rationality' plays a key role in experimental economics. Initially, at the level of economic agents, *rationality* is a notion that is closely linked to 'choice' and 'decision-making'. But when that level is connected with the dual framework of economics as a scientific discipline (descriptive–normative), it is customary in economics to present rationality in twofold terms: on the one hand, *normative rationality*, which points to what one should do in order to attain some specific aim and, on the other hand, *descriptive rationality*, which is used to reflect human endeavors in order to explain them or to predict them. Both aspects – normative and descriptive – assume that human behavior – the conduct of *homo economicus* – is goal oriented, and the emphasis is usually laid upon the relation from means to ends. Thus, a rational economic choice appears frequently as a selection of *adequate means* to attain *given ends*.

If the ends have more weight in the characterization of rationality and we understand that 'rationality consists in the intelligent pursuit of appropriate ends' (Rescher 1988: 1), then the notion of *rationality* becomes wider than in the dominant tendency of mainstream economics. As a matter of fact, there are three different *dimensions of rationality* regarding choice and decision-making: (i) cognitive rationality, (ii) practical rationality, and (iii) evaluative rationality. They are related to

> three major contexts of choice, those of *belief*, of accepting or endorsing thesis or claims, of *action*, of what overt acts to perform, and of *evaluation*, of what to value or disvalue. These represent the spheres of cognitive, practical, and evaluative reason, respectively (ibid.: 2-3).

Hence, not all deliberative reasoning – including the economic one – is a 'means-end' reasoning. There are three kinds of rationality according to the objects of rational deliberation: *cognitive rationality*, which deals with what is possible to believe or accept in the realm of knowledge; *practical rationality*, which decides regarding actions; and *evaluative rationality*, which judges what to prefer or prize (it assesses values, goals or ends). Thus, Simon's framework on rationality is insufficient, as the third aspect – evaluative – does not appear in his conception. This is a limitation in his view of economics as a science of the artificial.

When the analysis is focused on economic agents, and follows the assumptions concerning rational choice (especially of a single-agent) common in the mainstream tendency of economics, there is first an attribution of *practical rationality* (the optimality of one's action is assumed, given one's desires and beliefs: if agent a desires d and believes that action r will secure d, the agent is practically rational in choosing r); and there is a second attribution of *cognitive rationality* to the actor (in this case rationality is an attribute of belief, and consists in recognizing its correctness, given the evidence at the actor's disposal) (Bicchieri 1992: 155-88, especially 161-62). But ordinarily there is no mention at all of *evaluative rationality*: the ends are given – they are not evaluated – and a rational agent is instrumentally rational, that is, he or she should make practical decisions on means to attain the given ends.

Simon's conception of rationality follows that instrumental line as well (Simon 1983: 7-8), in spite of his being unmistakably critical of the outlook on rationality of mainstream economics. However, a new step towards the understanging of rationality has been made thanks to experimental economics: Reinhard Selten's views on economic rationality, which is also based on bounded rationality. Selten goes beyond Simon's instrumental rationality, insofar as he accepts the presence of *evaluative rationality* in addition to practical rationality and epistemic rationality. Even though he does not use that terminology, it seems to me that these three dimensions of rationality underlie what he calls 'three stages of reasoning', which he finds in the bounded rational strategy: i) superficial analysis, ii) goal formation, and iii) policy formation (Selten 1990: 656; see also Selten 1998 and 2001).

Following his distinction, we have 'superficial analysis' when there is easily accessible information, and the reasoning is of the qualitative rather than quantitative type. Here the presence of *cognitive rationality* is undeniable. The 'goal formation' seems to make implicit (or even explicit) use of evaluative rationality: when some concept of 'fairness' intervenes (be it in terms of equal profits, profits proportional to 'Cournot profits', and so on) in order to determine the quantities for players which can be called 'an ideal point' (a cooperative goal), then a *rational evaluation* of the aim is made. Finally, 'policy formation' looks at the means to reach the end: it is necessary to determine a way in which the goal (cooperative at the ideal point) can be achieved. This case is a characteristic use of *practical rationality*.

A few years ago, Selten has offered us a good example of *evaluative rationality* through an experimental solidarity game (Selten and Ockenfels 1998). In this case, the 'non self-interested' motivations of the players can include reasoning about the *ends* themselves. On the one hand, solidarity aims at a reciprocal relationship, but it is a more subtle relationship than giving after one has received. Solidarity is different from reciprocity, insofar as the gifts made are not reciprocated. On the other hand, the subjects have to decide how much, in the case of their winning, they are willing to give to a loser, when he or she is the only one in the group, or to each one of the losers, when these are two.

What has been found is quite different from utility maximization: the players have

> a decision process which first fixes the total amount to be sacrificed for solidarity, and then distributes it (up to rounding) among the losers regardless of their number (Selten and Ockenfels 1998: 525).

The decision process that deliberates on the aim is based on the value of solidarity and is different from practical rationality of an instrumental kind. This finding is made through an experimental design, within an environment that is not the usual social environment, but it is relevant for grasping the actual rationality of economic agents. Furthermore, to show the insufficient character of instrumental rationality contributes to viewing rationality in economics as a scientific activity. For it is shown that economic processes cannot be reduced within the framework of mainstream economics.

4 The Role of Prediction in the Sciences of the Artificial

Methodologically, prediction has a crucial role within science, in general, and in economics, in particular. When the focus moves to the sciences of the artificial and to economics as one of them, the following appear to be the most characteristic roles of prediction: i) it may be used as a tool for testing theories; and ii) it may be used as an instrument for policy-making. Methodologically, the first goal is very common in any basic science, be it a natural science (such as physics, chemistry, geology) or a social science (be it economics, sociology, psychology). On the other hand, the orientation towards public policy involves a connection between prediction and prescription (Simon 1990), which is very noticeable in some applied sciences, such as economics, where the solution of concrete problems requires the discovery of patterns to guide social action.[16]

In the case of economics as a scientific activity, the use of prediction as a tool for testing theories, in general, and hypotheses, in particular, is normally associated with 'descriptive science', whereas the utilization of prediction as an instrument for policy-making is seen as part of 'normative science'. But an overall picture gives us a broader distinction: 'basic science' involves the first methodological use of prediction, while 'applied science'

---

[16] There is a large amount of publications on the use of prediction as basis for economic prescription (see Ascher 1978; Burns 1986; Llewellyn, Potter, and Samuelson 1985; and Pagan and Robertson 2002).

includes the second utilization of prediction. This requires considering the status of 'predictive science' in its relation to fundamental and applied research.

Predictive science has a rather complex position, which includes basic research and applied research (see Gonzalez Forthcoming). On the one hand, prediction can have the descriptive aim of a basic science (for example, in astronomy); on the other hand, predictive science is essential for applied science that works on design (as in applied economics or pharmacology). Following this twofold status, both aspects should be emphasized. First, predictive science as basic research offers *descriptive knowledge* about the future. Thus,

> many 'ordinary' scientific disciplines — like physics ..., psychology, and economics — have futuristic relevance in the sense that their theories, together with initial conditions about the present and boundary conditions about the environment, yield predictions about observable events in the future (Niiniluoto 2001: 372).

Second, predictive science in the area of *applied research* is based on interest in successful predictions for various practical reasons. Thus,

> a scientific theory, which is able to produce reliable predictions about future events, has *predictive power*. Practical astronomy, meteorology, and social statistics are examples of applied sciences which have predictive power as their central epistemic utility (Niiniluoto 1993: 7)

Thus, predictive science can progress in both cases (i.e., basic science and applied science). Regarding the first aspect, it seems to me that there are no good reasons to distinguish between *basic research* and *predictive science* as separate endeavors that are associated under the label of 'descriptive science'.[17] On the one hand, the possible difference between 'basic research' and 'predictive science' within 'descriptive science' is not sufficiently clear. On the other hand, the expression 'descriptive science' is not good enough to reflect the kind of activity carried out by the scientists. The aim of this type of research and the structure of knowledge claims in this domain are more 'explanatory' or 'predictive' than 'descriptive'. To explain (to answer 'why-questions') is certainly a more complex activity than to describe, and to predict usually has more aspects than to describe (to test, to control, and so on).[18]

---

[17] This is the proposal made in Niiniluoto 1993: 14.

[18] According to Wesley Salmon, 'there are at least three – probably more – legitimate reasons for making predictions. First, we are sometimes curious about future happenings, and we want to satisfy that curiosity without waiting for the events in question to transpire. ... Second, we sometimes make predictions for the sake of testing a theory. ... Third, we sometimes find ourselves in situations in which some practical action is required, and the choice of an optimal decision depends upon predicting future occurrences' (Salmon 1981: 115-16).

In this regard, the distinction that is sometimes used to evaluate research projects may be useful: 'non-oriented basic research' (this is a kind of research that ultimately will not lead to applied research) and 'oriented basic research' (this is a type of research that may eventually lead to applied research). This distinction, which is common to science policy, encompasses not only internal factors (such as epistemological, methodological, ontological aspects) but also external values (such as social, economic, cultural criteria). The reason is clear: *oriented basic research* can lead to applied science and, in some countries, receives more attention than basic science; consequently, these countries are reluctant to support *non-oriented basic research*, and give a higher value to pragmatic aims over cognitive aims. In spite of this external consideration, it seems obvious that certain predictions are 'non-oriented basic research' (such as predictions on 'black holes' in distant galaxies) while others are 'oriented basic research', which is usually the case with economic predictions.

Undoubtedly, future studies cannot be limited to the sphere of 'descriptive science', as *applied science* also deals with future phenomena (unobserved events) and should consider what should be done ('prescription'). In this regard, the object to be studied in *future studies* is like a branching tree with different possibilities, where chance events and human choices have a role towards a future that is still open. Thus, the study of alternative scenarios to be realized or to be avoided should consider several aspects, such as i) how to *construct alternative* possible futures, ii) how to *assess the probability* of alternative futures, and iii) how to *evaluate the preferability* or desirability of alternative futures (Niiniluoto 2001: 373). These aspects should be considered in the sphere of the aims of the sciences of the artificial, when the designs are prepared.

Concerning to the realm of *applied research*, prediction appears as a common methodological tool: the need for anticipating knowledge of what seems possible should precede the rules of what should be done (this is the case in applied economics, which depends on economic forecasting made by the predictive techniques of statistical economics and econometrics).[19] Progress in scientific prediction is central to improvements in the area of prescription. This can be seen in any *design science* and, therefore, in economics too, if the latter is considered as a design science. The emphasis would be on the relationship between prediction and prescription. In order to carry out a design activity in science, the common path is to consider in advance whether the project is feasible (prediction), before we give indications about how to solve the problem that is foreseen (prescription). Thus,

---

[19] On the methods of prediction in economics and the role of models in them, cf. Gonzalez Forthcoming: chapter 10.

to make a prediction is, in principle, chronologically prior to establishing a prescription when the problems involved are in the realm of design science (a good example would be operations research in business).

Noticeably, the science of design is directly connected to prescribing: design looks for courses of action whose aims are to change existing situations into preferred ones, and those processes require identification of some prescribed paths to be followed. This characteristic affects prediction, since 'design like science is a tool for understanding as well as for acting' (Simon 1996 [1969]: 164). In both cases – understanding and acting – design has consequences affecting the future. Thus, it seems that *prediction* is an unavoidable part of every design process and

> the quality of design is likely to depend heavily on the quality of the data available. The task is not design without data but to incorporate assessments of the quality of the data, or its lack of quality, in the design process itself (ibid.: 146).

This is the case of data for social planning as in the much discussed world dynamics of the 1972 Club of Rome report (Meadows, D.L., Behrens, Meadows, D.H., Naill, Randers, Zahn 1974), where the understanding of phenomena and the suggestions for acting have not been successful.

Clearly, Simon thinks that the main failure concerns what the Club of Rome predicted.[20] For him,

> good predictions have two requisites that are often hard to come by. First, they require either a theoretical understanding of the phenomena to be predicted, as a basis for the prediction model, or phenomena that are sufficiently regular that they can simply be extrapolated. ... The second requisite for prediction is having reliable data about the initial conditions – the starting point from which the extrapolation is to be made. Systems vary in the extent to which their paths are sensitive to small changes in initial conditions (Simon 1996 [1969]: 147).

On the one hand, Simon thinks that the condition for extrapolation (that is, the observation of sufficiently regular phenomena) is seldom satisfied by data about human affairs; on the other hand, he considers that we have reasons to admit that social phenomena are also sensitive to initial conditions.

Ilkka Niiniluoto sees Simon's account as ambiguous, insofar as he does not clearly distinguish between 'design' (which appears in many professions) and 'scientific design' (which adds new factors):

> Scientific design is a species of design, i.e., the activity of solving design problems by using scientific methods and scientific knowledge. Operations Research (OR) provides methods for finding optimal or satisfactory solutions to design problems (e.g., game theory, decision theory, linear

---

[20] Cf. Simon 1996 [1969]: 146-47. The Club of Rome report is also analyzed in Simon 1997a [1947]: 110-11, 118-19, 123, and 419.

programming). In this sense, scientific design is the result of the 'scientification' of art, technology, management, or development (Niiniluoto 1993: 8-9).

In this regard, there is initially a professional activity and, later on, the emergence of scientific design within a scientific context. This type of design belongs to applied research: scientific design generates

> instrumental knowledge for the production and manipulation of natural and artificial systems. Design science produces knowledge which may then be applied within scientific design (ibid.: 9).

When Niiniluoto analyzes the relationship between design science and prediction in the context of future studies, he considers that *future studies* are seeking their identity as a new academic discipline (Niiniluoto 2001: 371-77). It seems clear that future studies cannot be reduced to the model of descriptive science, since they require that design sciences (that are at the core of the sciences of the artificial) be also included. But 'design' should not be identified with 'planning in the broad sense', as there are conceptual and pragmatic differences between them, especially when planning emphasizes the role of direction of human action and the temporal dimension of the activities to be developed.[21] In addition, Simon rightly points out that human rationality follows the 'satisfacing' rather than the 'optimizing' path in order to reach accepted ends in a systematic way.

Nowadays it is clear that progress in applied sciences should include the development of design sciences, whose aim is not, strictly speaking, to tell how things are but how they *ought to be* in order to achieve certain goals. This involves a relation between means and ends (that is, efficiency and effectiveness), which should be considered in sciences, such as economics, that deal with human and social practice. Design science always looks at the future and requires prediction and prescription: it belongs to the field of *future studies*, which combine the tasks of exploring *probable* and *preferable* futures. In addressing both tasks, design science is a mixture of theoretical and empirical research. Moreover, design science can go beyond the philosophical-methodological analysis to reach out into the sphere of political action (Niiniluoto 2001: 377). This is the case with economics, in which applied research deals with phenomena searching for what should be done regarding public policy (in the nationa and international economy).[22]

---

[21] On the notion of 'planning' and its differences with 'foresight', 'prediction', and 'forecasting' see Gonzalez 1996b: 201-28, especially: 215-16.

[22] The relationship between applied economics and political action has been emphasized by Joseph E. Stiglitz, Nobel Prize in 2001 (see Stiglitz 1991).

References

Artificial Economics. http://cisco.univ.lille1.fr/ae2005/ (08/22/2005).

Ascher, W. 1978. *Forecasting: An Appraisal for Policy-makers and Planners*. Baltimore: J. Hopkins University Press.

Atwood, M.E., McCain, K.W. and Williams, J.C. 2002. How does the Design Community Think about Design? *Proceedings of the Conference on Designing Interactive Systems: Processes, Practices, Methods, and Techniques*, 125-32. New York: ACM Press.

Becker, G. 1962. Irrational Behavior and Economic Theory. *Journal of Political Economy* 70: 1-13.

Becker, G. 1974. A Theory of Social Interactions. *Journal of Political Economy* 82: 1063-93.

Bicchieri, C. 1992. Two Kinds of Rationality. *Post-Popperian Methodology of Economics*, ed. N. de Marchi, 155-88. Boston: Kluwer.

Burns, T. 1986. The Interpretation and Use of Economic Predictions. *Predictability in Science and Society*, eds. J. Mason, P. Mathias and J.H. Westcott, 103-25. London: The Royal Society and The British Academy.

Cross, N. ed. 1984. *Developments in Design Methodology*. Chicester, UK: J. Wiley and Sons.

Gonzalez, W.J. 1996a. Prediction and Mathematics: The Wittgensteinian Approach. *Spanish Studies in the Philosophy of Science*, ed. G. Munevar, 299-332. Dordrecht: Kluwer.

Gonzalez, W.J. 1996b. On the Theoretical Basis of Prediction in Economics. *Journal of Social Philosophy* 27(3): 201-28.

Gonzalez, W.J. 1998a. Prediction and Prescription in Economics: A Philosophical and Methodological Approach. *Theoria* 13(2): 321-45.

Gonzalez, W.J. 1998b. Racionalidad científica y racionalidad tecnólogica: La mediación de la racionalidad económica. *Agora* 17(2): 95-115.

Gonzalez, W.J. 2003a. Racionalidad y Economía: De la racionalidad de la Economía como Ciencia a la racionalidad de los agentes económicos. *Racionalidad, historicidad y predicción en Herbert A. Simon*, ed. W.J. Gonzalez, 65-96. A Coruña: Netbiblo.

Gonzalez, W.J. 2003b. Rationality in Experimental Economics: An Analysis of Reinhard Selten's Approach. *Observation and Experiment in the Natural and Social Sciences*, ed. M.C. Galavotti, 71-83. Dordrecht: Kluwer.

Gonzalez, W.J. 2005. The Philosophical Approach to Science, Technology and Society. *Science, Technology and Society: A Philosophical Perspective*, ed. W.J. Gonzalez, 3-49. A Coruña: Netbiblo.

Gonzalez, W.J. 2007. The Role of Experiments in the Social Sciences: The Case of Economics. *Handbook of the Philosophy of Science: Focal Issues*, ed. T. Kuipers: 299-325. Amsterdam: Elsevier.

Gonzalez, W.J. Forthcoming. *Scientific Prediction and Economics: A Philosophic - methodological Analysis of Prediction and its Role in Economics*. Pittsburgh: University of Pittsburgh Press.

Graham, G. 1999. *The Internet: A Philosophical Inquiry*. London: Routledge.

Habermas, J. 1968. *Erkenntnis und Interesse*. Frankfurt: Suhrkamp.

Kitcher, Ph. 2001. *Science, Truth, and Democracy*. Oxford: Oxford University Press.

Llewellyn, J., Potter, S. and Samuelson, L. 1985. *Economic Forecasting and Policy – The International Dimension*. London: Routledge and K. Paul.

Meadows, D.L., Behrens, W.W. III, Meadows D.H., Naill R.F., Randers, J. and Zahn E.K.O. 1974. *Dynamics of Growth in a Finite World*. New York: J. Wiley and Sons.

Morgan, M. and Morrison, M. eds. 1999. *Models as Mediators. Perspectives on Natural and Social Science*. Cambridge: Cambridge University Press.

Niiniluoto, I. 1993. The Aim and Structure of Applied Research. *Erkenntnis* 38: 1-21.

Niiniluoto, I. 1995. Approximation in Applied Science. *Poznan Studies in the Philosophy of the Sciences and the Humanities* 42: 127-39.

Niiniluoto, I. 2001. Future Studies: Science or Art? *Futures* 33: 371-77.

Pagan, A.R. and Robertson, J. 2002. Forecasting for Policy. *A Companion to Economic Forecasting*, eds. M. Clements and D.F. Hendry, 152-78. Oxford: Blackwell.

Rescher, N. 1988. *Rationality. A Philosophical Inquiry into the Nature and the Rationale of Reason*. Oxford: Oxford University Press.

Rescher, N. 1999. *Razón y valores en la Era científico-tecnológica*. Barcelona: Paidós.

Rescher, N. 2003. *Rationality in Pragmatic Perspective*. Lewinston, NY: The Edwin Mellen Press.

Salmon, W.C. 1981. Rational Prediction. *British Journal for the Philosophy of Science* 32: 115-25.

Schram, A. 2005. Artificiality: The Tension Between Internal and External Validity in Economic Experiments. *Journal of Economic Methodology* 12(2): 225-37.

Selten, R. 1990. Bounded Rationality. *Journal of Institutional and Theoretical Economics* 146(4): 649-58.

Selten, R. 1998. Features of Experimentally Observed Bounded Rationality. *European Economic Review* 42: 413-36.

Selten, R. 2001. What is Bounded Rationality? *Bounded Rationality: The Adaptive Toolbox*, eds. G. Gigerenzer and R. Selten, 13-36. Cambridge, MA: The MIT Press.

Selten, R. and Ockenfels, A. 1998. An Experimental Solidarity Game. *Journal of Economic Behavior and Organization* 34(4): 517-39.

Simon, H.A. 1972. Theories of Bounded Rationality. *Decision and Organization*, eds. C.B. McGuire and R. Radner, 161-76. Amsterdam: North-Holland.

Simon, H.A. 1976. From Substantive to Procedural Rationality. *Method and Appraisal in Economics*, ed. S. Latsis, 129-48. Cambridge: Cambridge University Press.

Simon, H.A. 1978. Rationality as Process and as Product of Thought. *American Economic Review* 68(2): 1-16.

Simon, H.A. 1979. Rational Decision Making in Business Organizations. *American Economic Review* 69(4): 493-513.

Simon, H.A. 1982 [1964] *Models of Bounded Rationality*. Vol. 2: *Behavioral Economics and Business Organization*, 405-407. Cambridge, MA: The MIT Press.

Simon, H.A. 1983. *Reason in Human Affairs*. Stanford: Stanford University Press.

Simon, H.A. 1987. Rationality in Psychology and Economics. *Rational Choice. The Contrast between Economics and Psychology*, eds. R.M. Hogarth and M.W. Reder, 25-40. Chicago: The University of Chicago Press.

Simon, H.A. 1989. The State of Economic Science. *The State of Economic Science. Views of Six Noble Laureates*, ed. W. Sichel, 97-110. Kalamazoo, Michigan: W.E. Upjohn Institute for Employment Research.

Simon, H.A. 1990. Prediction and Prescription in Systems Modeling. *Operations Research* 38: 7-14. Reprinted in Simon, H.A. 1997. *Models of Bounded Rationality*. Vol. 3: *Empirically Grounded Economic Reason*, 115-28. Cambridge, MA: The MIT Press.

Simon, H.A. 1991. *Models of my Life*. New York: Basic Books-HaperCollins.

Simon, H.A. 1996 [1969]. *The Sciences of the Artificial*, 3rd ed. Cambridge, MA: The MIT Press.

Simon, H.A. 1997a [1947]. *Administrative Behavior*, 4th edition. New York, NY: The Free.

Simon, H.A. 1997b. *Models of Bounded Rationality*. Vol. 3: *Empirically Grounded Economic Reason*. Cambridge, MA: MIT Press.

Stiglitz, J.E. 1991. The Economic Role of the State: Efficiency and Effectiveness. *Efficiency and Effectiveness in the Public Domain, The Economic Role of the State*, eds. T.P. Hardiman and M. Mulreany, 37-59. Dublin: Institute of Public Administration.

Turner, P. 2001. Economic Modeling for Fun and Profit. *Understanding Economic Forecasts*, eds. D.F. Hendry and N.R. Ericsson, 42-53, Cambridge, MA: The MIT Press.

9

Context, Congruence and Co-ordination
ROBERTO SCAZZIERI

1 Preliminary Remarks

Rational arguments may be assessed from a variety of viewpoints, ranging from the perfect rationality framework to circumscribed rationality and other patterns of focused reasoning and choice. A critical feature of rationality assumptions in economic theory is their association with the way in which reasoning and decisions by heterogeneous and independent individuals (or collective agents) may be made consistent with one another within a congruent structure (that we may associate with social equilibrium). Neo-classical general equilibrium is a pattern by which independent agents come up with mutually compatible choices in the case of a parametric environment. Nash equilibrium is a classical pattern by which 'free' agents may settle to a set of consistent choices when their respective environments are interdependent and actually known to be such[1]. Models of limited rationality may be associated with a variety of co-ordination patterns by which agents generate some degree of congruence as a result of the partial similarity of focusing devices[2]. In this latter case, social equilibrium results from the ability to identify common co-ordination images, and a congruent structure often emerges from tacit co-ordination, and agents' active participation 'in the creation of *traditions*' (Schelling 1960: 106). Patterns of social congruence may be radically different from one another depending upon the

---

[1] This means that the environment of choice for agent Ai depends (and is known to depend) upon the actual choice(s) of agent Aj and vice versa.

[2] The central epistemic features of bounded rationality are discussed in Simon 1983. A philosophical perspective on meanings of rationality under conditions of uncertainty is proposed in Suppes 1984: 184-221.

underlying conception of rationality. Perfect rationality under parametric environment is associated with 'atomistic' social equilibrium, that is, with a congruent structure in which mutual consistence is achieved in spite of minimal social interaction. Perfect rationality under a non-parametric environment may be associated with a 'strategic' social equilibrium, in which consistence is achieved by virtue of more intense social interaction (actual or regarded as probable). Limited rationality takes most choice environments to be of the non-parametric type. However, the route to effective decisions is associated with the ability to 'filter' abundant information and to focus upon a manageable knowledge set. In this case, congruence may emerge as a result of a more complex, but often more realistic, process of adjustment and fine tuning. The reason is that the individual filtering of information may be significantly different from one individual (or social group) to another, so that the likelihood of social congruence is enhanced by individuals' ability to spot features of partial similarity across a variety of contexts. Here, we may informally describe a *social context* as the set of conditions under which any specific co-ordination pattern (or *set* of co-ordination patterns) is feasible[3]. A remarkable consequence of the shift of emphasis to co-ordination contexts is that, in a social universe characterized by a sufficient degree of internal differentiation, limited rationality makes congruence more likely (see below). A necessary condition for that is that individuals should be *skilled* social actors, so as to be able to identify similar attributes across a large number of individual (or social) types. This suggests that social equilibrium may be the unintended outcome of multiple cases of 'niche co-ordination'. In this case, however, the different niches should belong to a social *continuum* in which individuals (or groups) share

---

[3] This description of a social context is compatible with J. McCarthy's view of cognitive context as the set of conditions under which any given formula is true (see McCarthy 1993). It is also compatible with F. Giunchiglia's formalization of context as the 'local theory' relevant for the solution of a specific cognitive problem (or set of problems) (see Giunchiglia 1993). Any given social context may also be considered as the 'current state' of a pragmatic representation (see, for a discussion of this view in the case of design contexts, Richards and Simoff 2001). This suggests the view of social contexts as recorded memory of (past) co-ordination experience (see also Richards and Simoff 2001: 121). It is noteworthy that, according to Mark Crimmins, it is often impossible to identify a particular context without at the same time identify the cognitive attitudes of agents within that context: 'many attitude statements report not only the objects and properties the agent's attitude is claimed to be about, but also something more internal about the agent's cognitive fixes on the properties and objects' (Crimmins 1991: 187). Crimmins then describes 'cognitive fixes' as 'token mental representations, concrete particulars analogous to file folders or concrete nodes in concrete networks [...] A token representation can belong only to a single agent, persists through time, and is at any one time involved in various beliefs, desires, intentions and so on, but it is not individuated by the contents of these attitudes any more than a file folder is individuated by the stuff in it' (ibid.: 188).

certain features with adjacent individuals (or groups) though by no means with all agents in the same social set. Social congruence may be differently construed depending upon the rationality framework in which interaction takes place. A cognitive setting characterized by the ability to detect unusual connections in a diverse social universe is one in which rationality is practical rather than 'universal'. In this case, multiple foci breed distinct perspectives from which co-ordination may be sought. Limited rationality suggests inferential diversity. The latter expresses itself by means of manifold attitudes to similarity and conceptual association. Indirect social knowledge may be derived from direct experiences as a result of lateral exploration (exploration within a *continuum* of partial similarities). And this process normally follows a different route depending upon the specific context in which each individual elaborates her (his) own cognitive endowment. This approach makes congruence an unintended outcome of social diversity, provided the latter follows the pattern of partial similarity and limited (local) difference described above.

2 Virtual and real co-ordination

Contexts suggest a shift from virtual to realized co-ordination. This means that the reasons for co-ordination are found in contingent sets of circumstances, rather than in general dispositions or structures. Co-ordination may be analyzed by following one or the other of the two following routes: (a) the *top-down route*, which takes us from general principles to the circumstances of realized co-ordination; (b) the *bottom-up route*, which takes us from a description of realized co-ordination to the discovery of general principles. The top-down route has been central to economics and decision analysis and has become closely associated with the standard theory of rational choice. The bottom-up route is associated with the view that rationality is circumscribed (bounded), but is less clearly associated with any specific theory of reasoning and rationality. This approach suggests that standard theory is inadequate (unduly restrictive) but is far from providing a new general account of reasoning processes that we may want to call *rational*. I want to suggest that it is time to take stock of the impressive body of literature on circumscribed rationality and to ask whether it is possible to identify a number of core questions that a *theory* of circumscribed rationality is most likely to ask.

Let us start with a few stylized facts. Most accounts of circumscribed rationality seem to share the following set of characteristics: (i) they presuppose a description of *context*; they view context as a set of *salient features*; they suggest the need of some *distancing* from a naive instrumentalist conception of rationality. Is it possible to make sense of this set of features in terms of a more general account of rationality and reasoning? It is worth recalling that, according to Aristotle, the practice of reason presupposes the ability to *distance* oneself from the material structure of living (Aristotle, *Metaphysics*, I 982 b). In a similar mood, we may think that a theory of circumscribed reasoning presupposes both the consideration of immediate context (first-order context) and the identification of more distant and general contexts (higher-order contexts). The intellectual strategy I am describing has long been known. Already at the time of presocratic philosophy, certain writers emphasized the cognitive value of human practical activities as a route to the discovery of general principles. For example, in the *Corpus Hippocraticum* we find an essay *Perì Diaìtes*, which argues that human beings 'know what they do, ignore what they imitate'. Rodolfo Mondolfo noted that, according to the author of *Perì Diaìtes*, natural processes as such 'are unknown [...] and invisible to human beings', whereas techniques are 'visible and known, as they are the product of their work' (Mondolfo 1956: 130). A theory of circumscribed reasoning suggests we pay close attention to *realized* patterns of effective action. These are patterns of action *productive of results* (intended or unintended). In particular, circumscribed reasoning provides a cue into realized co-ordination and its principles. A theory of circumscribed reasoning applied to realized co-ordination presupposes: (i) the ability to identify a *relevant context* (this is not obvious, as the measure of relevance may be difficult), (ii) the ability to single out a set of *1st order salient features* (features immediately salient within the relevant context), (iii) the ability to identify a set of *higher order salient features* (features salient both in the relevant context and in other contexts). Step (i) suggests the need to identify *congruence* between the realized pattern of co-ordination and certain features of the environment in which co-ordination takes place. Step (ii) calls attention to the need of detecting *framing structures* (rules governing the *joint occurrence* of predicates, and thus the activation of mental associations). Step (iii) emphasizes the importance of *abstraction devices* (rules governing the comparison between different contexts).

3 Congruence in Context

Co-ordination 'in context' presupposes the ability to see a pattern of human actions that fit one another relatively to a given environment (congruence). It is known that 'it is only in an abstract axiomatic system that congruence can be brought down to the level of identity in any simple way' (Suppes 1984: 166). In general, congruence is associated with similarity (rather than identity). Indeed, it has been argued that 'there is no final or ultimate level of congruence' and that 'there is no realistic bound to the number of levels' (ibid.). In his philosophical account of the 'imitative arts', Adam Smith outlines a theory of congruence that is especially interesting with regard to the formation of congruence in a social universe. The core distinction, in this connection, is the one between 'exact resemblance' and 'imperfect resemblance' as applied to 'objects of the same kind', or to 'separated and unconnected' objects (Smith 1980 [1795]: 176-86). Exact resemblance suggests congruence when objects of the same kind are parts 'of another whole' (ibid.: 177). In this case, each part is expected 'to bear a certain correspondence' to the other parts, and congruence follows from symmetry. Congruence among objects of the same kind is required when these objects are parts of another whole. In this case, the larger whole is expected to be 'made up of exactly similar parts facing each other or around an axis' (*Concise Oxford Dictionary* 2001: 1450). This pattern of congruence

> is frequently considered as a beauty, and the want of it as a deformity; as in the correspondent members of the human body, in the opposite wings of the same building, in the opposite trees of the same alley, in the correspondent compartments of the same piece of carpet-work, or of the same flower-garden, in the chairs or tables which stand in the correspondent parts of the same room, etc. (Smith 1980 [1795]: 176).

Imperfect resemblance substitutes exact resemblance when human attention is focused upon 'objects of the same kind, which in other respects are regarded as altogether separate and unconnected' (Smith ibid.: 176-77). In this case, congruence derives from the discovery of *some* degree of likeness, and is associated with analogy rather than symmetry. In other words, the mutual 'fitting' of separate and unconnected objects emerges from a clear view of their differences (see also Porta and Scazzieri 2003). Partial similarity suggests a pattern of congruence that would indeed be disturbed by too exact a matching of similar parts (or of relative positions around an axis). As a result, congruence would result from the discovery that matching is possible in the midst of diversity (and is thus compatible with the co-existence, or adjacency, of highly differentiated objects). In Smith's own words,

> artificial fruits and flowers sometimes imitate so exactly the natural objects which they represent, that they frequently deceive us. We soon grow weary of them, however [...] But we do not grow weary of a good flower and fruit painting (Smith 1980 [1795]: 181).

In this case, congruence is suggested by partial likeness. Indeed, it is precisely the bounded character of likeness that re-enforces emotional congruence among separate and unconnected objects (such as real and painted flowers). Smith's argument suggests a complex relationship between congruence and diversity. For the nature of congruence seems to change as one moves from the comparison of objects that are parts of 'another whole' (Smith) to the comparison of separate and unconnected objects. At one extreme, the distance between objects is minimal, and congruence is associated with symmetry. At the other extreme, the distance between objects can be very large, and yet some congruence may be detected by means of partial likeness and analogy. Symmetry and analogy emerge as polar cases of congruence. In both cases, a relationship is established between clearly identifiable and distinguishable objects. However, congruence based on symmetry (or *symmetry congruence*) presupposes the structural identity of different component parts of a whole. On the other hand, congruence based on analogy (or *analogy congruence*) is open to a diversity of relative positions in the space of attributes. The theory of resemblance suggests that social co-ordination may be open to a variety of routes, depending upon which particular pattern of congruence is relevant in each specific case. We may conjecture that symmetry congruence and analogy congruence are relevant under different social circumstances. The former (symmetry congruence) enhances the likelihood of co-ordination when relative social positions are clearly established, and symmetrical roles can be unambiguously identified. The latter (analogy congruence) is especially relevant when individuals (or social groups) can be 'ordered' along multiple scales, and the relative positions of individuals (or social groups) $A_1, A_2, \ldots A_k$ may be different on each scale. A preliminary interpretation of symmetry congruence suggests that it may be a critical co-ordinating device in a social universe associated with a single pattern of relative positions. On the other hand, analogy congruence (rather than symmetry congruence) could be essential to achieve some degree of co-ordination in a social set in which alternative patterns of relative positions exist side by side[4]. The theory of resemblance calls attention to the cognitive set-up of social co-ordination. In particular, it stresses that co-ordination often emerges from a process in which complexity is reduced by means of purpose-oriented filtering. This process presupposes the ability to discover resemblance, to generate *ad hoc* focal points, and to organize co-ordination around centers of convergent expectations (see also Scazzieri 2001a and 2001b; Porta and Scazzieri 2001). The discovery of resemblance is an essential preliminary step for social co-ordination. It may be described as the realization that diversity makes co-ordination more effective provided an appropriate core of similar attributes is identified. The argument above calls attention to the manifold structure of resemblance, and suggests a conceptual framework that is set out below: (i) Identity and difference reflect the position of any given object with respect to other objects (rather than the intrinsic features of the various objects). For example, two objects o_i and o_j

---

[4] It may be argued that symmetry congruence is most easily detected when a single structural description covers the whole array of social positions, and that analogy congruence steps in when social positions are conducive to multiple classifications and rankings.

could be seen as 'close' or 'distant' (in terms of similarity features) depending upon the collection of objects to which they belong. Partially similar objects are often considered to be identical from the point of view of a particular collection (*congruence class*). As a result, objects o_i and o_j may be identical in terms of congruence class C_a, but different in terms of congruence class C_b. For example, in a classified library, economics books appropriately shelved are considered to be identical from the point of view of the library's classification system, but they might appear as entirely different books in a non-classified library. In formal terms, identity and difference may be defined as binary relations on a set of objects Ω. The two relations are mutually exclusive: if the identity relation ($o_i \, I \, o_j$) holds, then the difference relation ($o_i \, D \, o_j$) does not hold (and vice versa). The above argument entails that the same objects o_i and o_j could be seen as identical or different objects according to the congruence class to which they belong. (ii) Different congruence classes have a different impact upon the resemblance structure of any given collection of objects. For example, there are collections (such as books in a classified library, or the 'set of coach-horses' mentioned by Smith[5]) in which any given element belongs to a particular collection by virtue of its *lack* of distinctive characteristics relative to the other elements in the same collection. On the other hand, there are cases in which membership of a collection leaves the distinctive features of its elements unaltered. A relevant example could be a set of paintings in a museum, or a set of medals in a collector's drawer. It may be conjectured that resemblance is related to congruence in two different ways according to whether symmetry congruence or analogy congruence is considered. (see above). Symmetry congruence presupposes the structural equivalence of any given element in the collection (identity makes any element a perfect substitute for any other element of the same collection). Analogy congruence does not require structural equivalence and leaves room for diversity within a set of heterogeneous elements. (iii) The influence of imperfect resemblance on congruence is different according to whether symmetry congruence or analogy congruence is sought. This has far reaching implications as to the pattern of realized co-ordination that may be observed. In the former case (symmetry congruence) 'distant' individuals (or social groups) find co-ordination increasingly difficult as the number of non-common characteristics is increased. A logical basis for this proposition is that it would be *increasingly difficult* to unambiguously 'locate' individuals (or groups) with respect to any given axis of symmetry. This is because a large number of non-common features may require that individuals (or groups) be 'measured' against one another along

---

[5] See Smith 1980 [1795]: 177.

multiple scales. In the latter case (analogy congruence) the situation is entirely different. For the likelihood of co-ordination would generally increase as a more diverse social universe is considered. A logical basis for this proposition could be that individuals (or groups) are no longer looking for a single axis of symmetry. Indeed, any given individual (or group) would not generally expect, in a diverse social universe, a significant degree of symmetry congruence relative to other individuals or groups. With reference to this case, we may conjecture that most individuals (or groups) would be able to relate with each other in multiple ways. In this case, the multiplicity of social scales turns diversity into an advantage from the co-ordination point of view. In other words, imperfect resemblance makes individuals (or groups) *more likely* to recognize partial similarity, as any set of agents cannot be expected to share more than a few common characteristics. In short, co-ordination thrives on cognitive abilities that imperfect resemblance breeds. And this would ultimately mean the ability to make effective use of imagination from scanty evidence. Individuals (groups) used to detect partial similarity in the midst of diversity are more likely to identify patterns of possible congruence even if only a small set of characteristics is common to all. The role of imagination in suggesting economic and social linkages that explicit resemblance would exclude is akin to its role in suggesting conceptual (and linguistic) associations that explicit verbal description may conceal. On this point, the penetrating remarks by Cesare Beccaria in the Chapter 'Delle idee espresse e delle idee semplicemente suggerite' (On expressed ideas and on simply suggested ideas) of his *Ricerche intorno alla natura dello stile* are worth recalling: 'accessory ideas (have entirely different effects) when they are expressed with exactly correspondent terms, and when (on the contrary) they are simply suggested or aroused in the reader's or listener's soul' (Beccaria 1971 [1770], vol. 1: 223). Beccaria then goes on to argue that

> ideas that are simply suggested do not enter into the syntax of a proposition, which is independent of them: they do not last in the human mind as long as the ideas directly recalled by words; even if they may be awakened, just like them (when the occasion arises). This means that a greater effect is obtained by lesser time and effort (ibid.: 225).

Imagination is also central to Adam Smith's account of mirroring and social knowledge. In particular, Smith calls attention to the role of imagination in the deliberate construction of the counterfactual scenarios in which the impartial spectator provides a standard of judgment (see Smith 1976 [1759]; see also Scazzieri 2006). It is worth noting that Beccaria's reasoning leads to a type of social congruence in which ideas 'that are simply suggested' play a central role. On the other hand, Smith highlights the formation of social congruence as a process unfolding through a hierarchy of stages, of which the deliberate fiction of the impartial spectator is the most elaborate one.

4 Framing and Analogy

Framing is associated with the identification of features and of *one or more* congruence relationship(s) among features. As a matter of fact, features appear to have certain embedded 'fitting properties', and this introduces a number of implicit or 'natural' associations among features belonging to particular subsets (or classes of *conforming features*). This suggests that frames are built upon 'bundles of concepts and predicates', which tend to be activated at the same time (Bacharach 2001: 5)[6]. Daniel Dennett, who main-

---

[6] This conception of a frame is directly associated with the idea of simultaneous activation of predicates, while the structural conditions for simultaneous activation are not directly considered. In particular, a Bacharach frame is prima facie independent of the relation among predicates that one would wish to examine. In this way, Bacharach frames are distinct from the Kripke frames considered in modal logic (see Kripke 1959). For, in the latter case, the very definition of a frame (as a pair <W,R>, in which W is a set of possible worlds and R a relation holding between these worlds) includes the structural feature(s) associated with R. On the other hand, Bacharach's conception of a frame appears to be quite close to the one adopted in frame semantics. In this connection, Charles Fillmore maintains that one would not normally 'expect to find father, mother, son, daughter, brother, and sister separated from each other, or buy, sell, pay, spend, and cost, or day, night, noon, midnight, morning, afternoon, and evening. These words form groups that learners would do well to learn together, because in each case they are lexical representatives of some single coherent schematization of experience or knowledge. In each case, to understand what any one member of such a group is about is, in a sense, to understand what they are all about [...] What holds such word groups together is the fact of their being motivated by, founded on, and co-structured with, specific unified frameworks of knowledge, or coherent schematizations of experience, for which the general word frame can be used' (Fillmore 1985: 223). Fillmore also calls attention to John Stuart Mill's view that 'when we call one man a father, another his son, what we mean to affirm is a set of facts, which are exactly the same in both cases. To predicate of A that he is the father of B, and of B that he is the son of A, is to assert one and the same fact in different worlds' (Mill 1846: 29, as quoted in Fillmore, 1985, p. 224). Fillmore comments that '[t]he idea of a presupposed structure of relationships (the fundamentum relationis) against which words like son and father are understood, is very much like the notion of a semantic frame: we can know the meanings of the individual words only by first understanding the factual basis for the relationship which they identify' (Fillmore, 1985, p. 224). Cognate uses of the concept of 'frame' may be found in artificial intelligence and cognitive psychology. For example, Marvin Minsky introduced the concept of frame to describe a context-specific data-structure, that is, 'a data-structure representing a stereotyped situation, like being in a certain kind of living room, or going to a child's birthday party' (Minsky 1975: 212). A related use may be found in the conception of frame as a set of 'structures of expectations' (Tannen 1979: 144). More specifically, the frame problem in artificial intelligence may be described as 'the problem of determining what facts about the world stay the same when an action is performed' (Morgenstern 1991: 134). In this connection, frames have been associated with histories, that is, with '[pieces] of spacetime with natural boundaries, both temporal and spatial' (Hayes 1985, as quoted in Sandewall 1991: 203). Histories (in this sense) may be classified into types, and lead to taxonomies ('listing of all the possible kinds of history of a certain type') (ibid.). The analysis of frames in cognitive psychology

tains that it may be useful to think of frames without presupposing any prior scheme of semantic categories, has proposed a more radical conception of frame. In his view, 'knowledge of situations and events in the world' could be represented 'by what might be called sequences of verbal snapshots. State S, constitutively described by a list of sentences true at time t asserting various n-adic predicates true of various particulars, gives way to state S', a similar list of sentences true at t' '(Dennett 1990:167). He then asks whether it would not be better 'to reconceive of the world of planning [that is, the world of human intentions and actions] in terms of histories and processes' (ibid.). In this case,

> instead of trying to model the capacity to *keep track of things* in terms of principles for pressing through temporal cross-sections of knowledge expressed in terms of terms (*names* for *things*, in essence) and predicates, perhaps we could model keeping track of things more directly, and let all the cross-sectional information about what is deemed true moment by moment be merely implicit [...] from the format (ibid.: 167-68).

In either case, any given frame is associated with a particular 'collection of classifiers', which may be activated under specific (and context-dependent) circumstances (see Bacharach 2001; see also Mehta, Starmer and Sugden 1994; Bacharach and Bernasconi 1997; Janssen 2001 and 2003)[7]. In general, *more than one* frame is consistent with any given set of features[8]. However, not all possible frames are equally salient under given circumstances. It is reasonable to think that framing would primarily be associated with the cognitive and linguistic ability to grasp specific problem situations

---

has moved from the consideration that 'basic human mental operations operate over cultural and personal assemblies of knowledge. Some of these assemblies will be widely shared in a culture, and expressions in the culture's language will evoke them [...] Cognitive scientists call such assemblies of knowledge "frames". Frames are conventional packets of knowledge that usually include roles [...] and various interactions between elements' (Turner 2001: 12-13).

[7] The so-called 'commercial transaction frame' provides a vivid illustration of the simultaneous activation of predicates under specific circumstances. Verbs such as buy, sell, pay, spend, cost, and charge are all referring to 'different aspects of the frame' (Petruck 2003: 1). As a result, 'knowing the meaning of any one of these verbs requires knowing what takes place in a commercial transaction and knowing the meaning of any one verb means, in some sense, knowing the meaning of all of them' (ibid.).

[8] This property is at the root of the framing problem in artificial intelligence, in which '[t]he Frame Problem is the problem of too much knowledge. In its simplest terms: [t]here is too much information about change to consider at any given time. How do we limit what to look at, and still get reasonable results with adequate error recovery?' (Nutter 1991: 176). In Nutter's view, this embarrassment of riches may be sorted out 'by a mechanism for context selection and limitation via relevance and salience' (ibid.: 177). This leads him to argue that 'progress on this one issue of salience promises tremendous paybacks across the board, both for Artificial Intelligence research and for cognitive science in general' (ibid.: 186). The relationship between inferential ability and inductive effectiveness is also examined in Arlo-Costa 2001.

through the activation of a particular set of 'naturally connected' features. It is reasonable to assume that frames would often be associated with relations among attributes, and that such relations will often be of the causal type[9]. In short, framing would generally rely upon pre-existing cognitive structures (the different subsets of naturally connected features), but only specific (contingent) circumstances could turn a virtual frame into an effective one.

The above argument suggests that the switch from one frame to another could result from two distinct sets of causes: (i) one frame could be substituted for another because the 'natural associations' among features have changed; (i) one frame could be substituted for another because the activation criterion is changed[10]. In the former case, we have moved to a different structural principle of fitting. In the latter case, circumstances have brought about a different concentration of attention, so that different sets of naturally connected features come to light.

The dynamics of framing shows the interplay between structural principles and evolutionary (historical) principles. In particular, the process by which agents (or groups) switch from one frame to another may be understood in terms of a hierarchy of changes, in which both long- and short-term factors play a role. Any given change of structure (the collection of classifiers) may or may not be associated with an actual change of frame. At the same time, a change of *activated* frame (a collection of structurally related *and* salient features) may take place even if the set of available frames has not changed. In the short-run, the collections of classifiers are given, and agents (or groups) switch from one frame to another primarily as a result of a different concentration of attention. In the long run, classifiers themselves may change. In this case, framing dynamics could be associated with the following set of causes (taken independently or in some combination): (i) a new collection of classifiers is introduced; (ii) a different activation criterion is adopted. We may also conjecture that certain features of any given

---

[9] Robert Axelrod has called attention to the role of cognitive mapping in decision-making by proposing a conceptual system derived from the notion of causation: '[t]he concepts a person uses are represented as points, and the causal links between these concepts are represented as arrows between these points. This gives a pictorial representation of the causal assertions of a person as a graph of points and arrows. This kind of representation of assertions as a graph will be called a cognitive map' (Axelrod 1976: 5; see also Axelrod 1972). A frame may also be considered as a cognitive map (as defined above) if the corresponding attribute set has a sufficient causal structure.

[10] In either case, it may be argued that any solution to the framing problem is highly context-dependent, as framing is often associated with specific intentions and specific available information (see Etherington, Kraus and Perlis 1991). It has also been argued that successful framing presupposes 'the ability to reach conclusions that, while not strictly entailed by what is known, are highly plausible' (Etherington, Kraus and Perlis 1991: 43; see also McCarthy and Hayes 1969; McCarthy 1980).

frame are relatively more persistent than others. For example, classifiers shared by all available frames in a given situation are more persistent than less common classifiers. This is because classifiers of the former type would necessarily be present in all frames derived from the same structural principle. We may also conjecture that the likelihood of any given classifier is likely to increase as that particular classifier enters an increasing number of virtually available frames.

Framing dynamics combines features of continuity (within any given set of available frames) and discrete jumps (from one 'virtual set' to another). This means that a frame that is salient at any given time could change gradually or abruptly as a result of the following causes: (i) a change in the composition and extension of the set of available structures; (ii) a change in the concentration of attention (change of salience). In general, any increase in the number of common classifiers across different frame structures increases the likelihood of continuous (or 'feature-preserving') shifts from one frame to another within the set of available structures. This follows directly from the definition of continuity within the space of available frames. Let the set of frames $\mathbf{F}$ include sets $\mathbf{F}i$'s $(i = 1, ..., k)$, such that any given frame $\mathbf{F}i$ is identified by a particular collection of classifiers $\{\Phi i\}$. If we define continuity within $\mathbf{F}$ as a property of the (non-empty) intersection among all collections of classifiers Φi's, we may expect that continuity would be maximal if that intersection includes all classifiers in Φi's (this is clearly the extreme case in which all classifiers are common). It follows that any increase in the number of common classifiers across sets $\mathbf{F}i$'s increases the density of $\mathbf{F}$ and thus also the likelihood that a frame switch (within $\mathbf{F}$) would preserve a greater number of common classifiers.

A different concentration of attention, in general, makes individuals (or groups) to shift from one set of classifiers to another. The shift may be more (or less) feature-preserving depending on the number of common features across frames. We may conjecture that, in general, a shift within set $\mathbf{F}$ would be more feature-preserving than a shift from $\mathbf{F}$ to $\mathbf{F}'$. The reason of this would be that a shift to a different set of virtual frames would often entail the shift to a completely different collection of classifiers, or at any rate a reduction in the number of classifiers that are common.

5 Abstraction and Prototypes

Frames give salience to contexts. They are thus of primary importance for realized co-ordination[11]. A *salient context* may be defined as the set of be-

---

[11] There is thus a close relationship between framing, determination of identity and social congruence through group identification (see, in particular, Bacharach 2006: 69-94).

havioral beliefs associated with a particular frame. Let S_i be the set of behavioral beliefs ($i = i, ..., k$) that are salient in a particular context. This context may be either homogeneous or internally differentiated. We may conjecture that, in the former case (homogeneous beliefs), individuals (or social groups) are structurally equivalent with respect to each other. This means that any given individual derives her (his) specific attributes from his (her) position in the social universe. In other words, individual attributes derive from the social structure, rather than the other way round. In particular, co-ordination is often associated with symmetry congruence (as defined above). The case of heterogeneous beliefs may be sharply different. Here, individuals (or groups) are *not* structurally equivalent with respect to one another. This means that any given individual (or group) is associated with a cluster of attributes that cannot fit a fixed social structure. In this case, individuals (or groups) may be arranged along *multiple scales*, and co-ordination is often associated with *congruence by analogy*. In other words, individuals (social groups) $A_1, A_2, ..., A_k$ may be associated with a variety of possible social structures. Congruence may be detected through social exploration, which we may describe as thorough search of local likeness among individuals (or groups). This argument calls attention to the critical role of contexts in social co-ordination. Contexts determine whether co-ordination is primarily associated with symmetry congruence or analogy congruence. They also determine the specific route followed by co-ordination in the case of heterogeneous beliefs and social diversity. In the latter circumstance, a diverse social universe could generate a multiplicity of ties due to the working of imperfect resemblance. In particular, individuals (or social groups) $A_1, A_2, ..., A_k$ could be associated with a variety of characteristics, and adjacent characteristics could provide 'likeness ties' along a number of different paths. Let us consider, as an example, the following distribution of characteristics across individuals (or social groups) A_1, A_2, A_3:

$A_1 = \{a_1, a_2, ..., a_k\}$,
$A_2 = \{a_k, a_{k+1}, ..., a_{k+p}\}$,
$A_3 = \{a_{k+p}, a_{k+p+1}, ..., a_{k+p+s}\}$

Case 1. 'Single bridge' resemblance

The above likeness structure is an extreme case of what we may call *deterministic resemblance*. Each pair of individuals $\{A_1, A_2\}$, $\{A_2, A_3\}$, $\{A_1, A_3\}$ shares either a single characteristic or none at all. This leads to a simple (and predictable) pattern of social congruence, such that A_1 relates to A_2 via the common characteristic a_k, and A_2 relates to A_3 via the common characteristic a_{k+p}. There is no tie between A_1 and A_3. The above pattern of congruence follows the resemblance structure $\{a_k, a_{k+p}\}$. This means that social co-ordination is derived from a simple and 'compulsive' structure of ties. We are dealing with a diverse social universe in which individuals are sharply different from one another, and social co-ordination reflects the existence of single 'bridges' between individuals or social groups. To give an example, a set of agents in which multi-characteristics subjects have nothing in common except citizenship (for a first pair of individuals), or natural language (for a second pair of individuals), would be an instance of the deterministic resemblance described above.

A different distribution of characteristics may generate a completely different resemblance structure. Let us consider the following situation:

$A_1 = \{a_1, a_2, ..., a_k, a_{k+p}\}$,
$A_2 = \{a_1, a_k, a_{k+1}, ..., a_{k+p}\}$,
$A_3 = \{a_2, a_{k+p}, a_{k+p+1}, ..., a_{k+p+s}\}$

Case 2. 'Multiple bridge' resemblance

In this case, we are removed from deterministic resemblance, and we get to a situation in which individuals (or social groups) A_1, A_2, A_3 may be 'tied up' with one another in a number of alternative ways. For example, A_1 may get connected with A_2 by means of similarity feature a_1 or similarity feature a_{k+p}. A_2 may connect with A_3 by means of the single similarity feature a_{k+p}. A_1 may connect with A_3 by means of similarity feature a_2 or similarity feature a_{k+p}. In this case, social co-ordination could take a variety of routes. For example, the co-ordination regime of agents A_1 and A_2 would generally be different according to whether the similarity bridge is feature a_1 or feature a_{k+p}. Similarly, the co-ordination regime of agents A_1 and A_3 is likely to be different according to whether the corresponding similarity bridge is feature a_2 or feature a_{k+p}. A variety of possible ties suggests *stochastic resemblance*. In other words, multiple virtual ties generate a space of events in which actual resemblance (that is, resemblance as associated with a specific co-ordination pattern) becomes a random variable. Stochastic resemblance calls attention to what may be called the *co-ordination freedom* of individuals (or social groups). This may be defined as the freedom of individuals (or groups) to pick up one or more features of similarity from among a larger set of alternatives, and to derive social co-ordination from these selected feature(s). In this case, effective co-ordination would reflect a blend of 'local' skills and serendipity. Local skills enable individuals (or social groups) to explore an immediate relational neighborhood and to identify a resemblance structure within a diverse social universe. Serendipity enables individuals (or groups) to meet unexpected features of similarity in a larger social sphere. We may conjecture that effective co-ordination derives its strength from the ability to combine local concentration of attention with extensive influence outside the immediate neighborhood. In this case, co-ordination is initially rooted in local abilities to recognize relevant features of similarity. The subsequent evolution of co-ordination could result from unexpected encounters, which are to a large extent associated with the characteristics of the initial concentration on attention (the initial focus adopted by a core set of co-ordinating agents). Considering the previous distribution of characteristics may highlight this point. If A_1 and A_2 connect with each other by means of similarity feature a_2, a co-ordination pattern is generated that would exclude A_3. On the other hand, if A_1 and A_2 derive co-ordination from similarity feature a_{k+p}, the same co-ordination regime is likely to include, in due course, individual A_3 as well. To sum up, probabilistic resemblance calls attention to the fact that social co-ordination is open to a multiplicity of routes, and emphasizes that co-ordination is often a 'mixed outcome' of structural opportunities and chance. Structural opportunities reflect the space of events as recognized by co-ordinating agents. Chance is often 'solicited' by individual abilities in exploring a particular problem space and searching for satisfactory solutions. Probabilistic resemblance is the breeding ground of co-ordination between heterogeneous agents under conditions of structural uncertainty[12]. This means that, if agents were allowed to interact in a diverse social universe where multiple ties would be possible, and co-ordination would be influenced by the way in which similarity features are recognized in specific cases of social interaction. Imperfect resemblance would be at the root of co-ordination. The reason is that, under conditions of social diversity, any given individual (or social group) is a highly differentiated bundle of characteristics, so that no individual (or group) can be assigned a fixed position in the existing social set-up. This means we may seldom anticipate which specific resemblance structure turns out to be relevant under any given set of circumstances. And we may seldom anticipate which pattern of social co-ordination would be established accordingly. Probabilistic resemblance suggests that social co-ordination is generally associated with analogy congruence rather than symmetry congruence. This is because the relative positions of individuals (or social groups) with respect to each other would not be unambiguously determined.

---

[12] Following a recent formulation by I. Gilboa and D. Schmeidler, we may distinguish between 'risk' (associated with situations in which probabilities are known), 'uncertainly' (associated with situations in which states of the world are known but probabilities are not) and 'structural ignorance' (associated with situations in which neither states of the world nor probabilities are known) (see Gilboa and Schmeidler 2001: 45). Structural uncertainty may be defined as the cognitive situation in which individuals do nor know *ex ante* what the problem space is, and which probability distributions should be considered.

For example, individuals A_i and A_j could be assigned ranking positions 1 and 2 respectively if similarity feature a_k is considered, and ranking positions 2 and 1 if the relevant similarity feature is a_{k+p}. In other words, a situation in which the focus of co-ordination may shift from one similarity feature to another, is one in which co-ordination cannot be based upon symmetry (see above). In general terms, no individual (or social group) can be sure about her (his) position relative to other individuals (or social groups), as long as 'bridges' (between individuals or groups) derive from a *sufficient variety* of similarity features. In short, multiple virtual 'bridges' suggest that individuals (or groups) may be located around multiple axes of symmetry (see also above). We may conjecture that symmetry congruence may not be a feasible option if the number of possible axes of symmetry is too large. A social universe characterized by a high degree of diversity is one in which individual elements (subjects or social groups) may be arranged according to a large number of alternative patterns of symmetry. This suggests that social co-ordination may be exceedingly difficult if agents try to follow a *single* criterion of symmetry. For any given axis of symmetry is associated with a particular way in which individuals (or groups) relate with one another in terms of some type of 'perfect correspondence' (which often entails a definite constellation of commitments and rights). But individuals (or groups) characterized by a variety of possible similarity features are unlikely to adopt a narrow pattern of co-ordination as long as other options are available to them. This makes symmetry congruence of little use as a means to achieve social co-ordination. Imperfect resemblance suggests a different view of congruence (analogy congruence). This view emphasizes that congruence may derive from the ability to discover similarity features in the midst of variety, and to conceive patterns of co-ordination that, contrary to 'simple' symmetry congruence, allow individuals to interact along a multiplicity of relative positions and social dimensions. In the latter case, individuals (and social groups) may be able to discover that local co-ordination is feasible on the basis of partial similarity, and that co-ordination derived from partial similarity may reach a wider social context than co-ordination based upon any simple symmetry criterion. In case 2 above (multiple-bridge resemblance) A_1 may connect with A_2 by means of tie a_k or tie a_{k+p} and it may connect with A_3 by means of a_2 or a_{k+p}. A_2 may connect with A_3 by means of a_{k+p} only. This means that co-ordination may follow either the pattern of *universal congruence* associated with similarity feature a_{k+p}, or patterns of *local congruence* such as those associated with similarity features a_k, a_2 and a_{k+p}. It is reasonable to conjecture that universal congruence will generally be associated with co-ordination around a single axis of symmetry. This would make co-ordination relatively predictable but will constrain it within the domain of a single similarity feature. On the other hand, local congruence may be associated with co-ordination around multiple axes of symmetry. In the latter case, co-ordination is associated with structural uncertainty, for individuals (or social groups) would be unable to identify *ex ante* which similarity features are relevant in each particular case. However, local congruence may also be compatible with a diverse set of overlapping connections, and could introduce co-ordination in a wider social sphere.

As argued above, framing gives salience to contexts.[13] However, framing itself derives its potential from a deeper cognitive structure. This is because effective frames must suggest connections (resemblances and associations) beyond their original domain. Effective frames should be at the same time expansible and contractible. These properties are associated with a *framing matrix*, that is, with a prototype suggestive of more (or less) extensive connections. Lotfi A. Zadeh has recently discussed a conceptual structure that may be useful in this context (see Zadeh 2003 a and b). In particular, Zadeh introduces the concept of *protoform*, which is defined as 'an abstracted summary' for any given collection of objects (Zadeh 2003a: 1). More specifically, 'a protoform A, of an object, B, written as $A = PF(B)$, is defined as a deep semantic structure of B' (ibid.). Zadeh gives the following example as 'a very simple illustration' (ibid.): 'The protoform of proposition "Eva is young" is $A(B)$ is C, where A is abstraction of "age", B is abstraction of "Eva" and C is abstraction of "young".' (ibid.).

Two propositions p and q may have identical protoforms. In this case, they are considered to be 'protoform-equivalent' (or *PF-equivalent*: *PFE (p,q)* (ibid.). A central concept in protoform theory is that of 'idealized protoform' (or *i.protoform*). An idealized protoform (like a Platonic idea) may be *conceived* independently of concrete forms, and may be used to group concrete objects into categories (see also Rosch 1973). In Zadeh's words,

> examples of i.protoforms are geometrical objects such as line, circle, square and ellipse. As an illustration, the concept of oval objects may be defined by employing an ellipse as an i.protoform (ibid.: 4).

At this stage, the distance between an oval object and its i.protoform (the ellipse) may be used to determine 'the grade of membership of A in the fuzzy set of oval objects' (ibid.). The relationship between prototypes and real objects (or, more abstractly, between protoforms and concrete forms) may be represented in Figure 1.

---

[13] This complex nature of contexts has its counterpart in the 'maieutic' nature of much of economic analysis. For in its case the ability to identify latent characteristics and dispositions is at least as important as parameter controllability and manipulability (see Scazzieri 2003: 90-95).

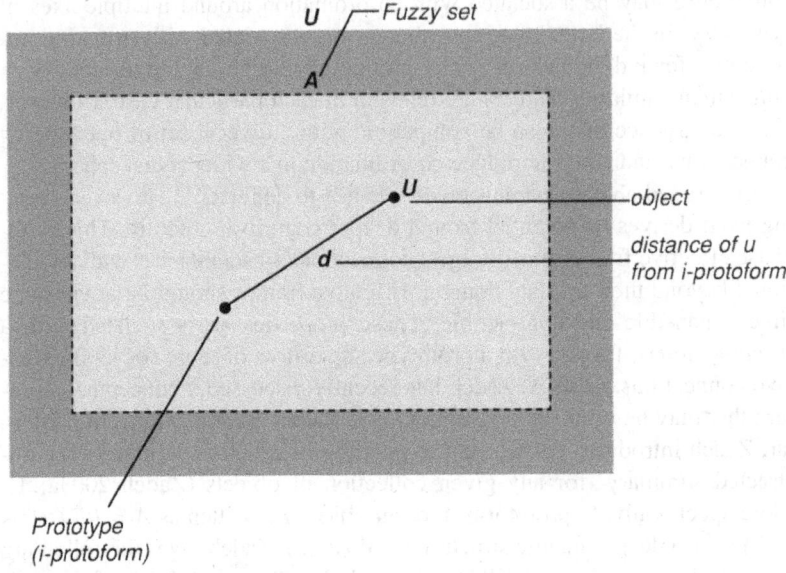

Figure 1. Prototypes and real objects (from Zadeh 2003b: slide 73)

6 Co-ordination and Reasoning

It is time to sum up the gist of this paper. I have argued that the recent shift of attention away from virtual co-ordination has made *context* a central point of attention. This is associated with greater emphasis upon the pragmatic structure of action and choice. I have also argued that a context-bound reconstruction of co-ordination cannot claim to be a theory. This is especially so as *identification of context* is not a trivial matter. I have also argued that context relevance presupposes a notion of congruence and a focusing device (framing). Finally, I have maintained that framing derives its effectiveness from a deeper structure. This is the perceptual and cognitive structure at which prototypes are generated and their relationship to concrete objects is determined. The emphasis upon co-ordination and context suggests a theoretical shift, in which perceptions are seen as complex objects. Much of co-ordination is determined at the level of perceptual structures (categories), but this level is itself internally differentiated and exceedingly complex. This is an exciting area of interdisciplinary research that is worth exploring.

References

Aristotle. ms 4th cent. BC. *Metaphysics*. Loeb edn., translated by H. Tredennik. Cambridge, MA: Harvard University Press.

Arlo-Costa, H. 2001. Trade-Offs between Inductive Power and Logical Omniscience in Modeling Context. *Context 2001*, eds. V. Akman et al., 1-14. Berlin, Heidelberg: Springer Verlag.

Axelrod, R. 1972. *Framework for a General Theory of Cognition and Choice*. Berkeley: University of California.

Axelrod, R. ed. 1976. *Structure of Decision. The Cognitive Maps of Political Elites*. Princeton, NJ: Princeton University Press.

Bacharach, M. 2001. Framing and Cognition in Economics: The Bad News and the Good. *International School of Economic Research, XIV Workshop: Cognitive Processes and Rationality in Economics*, 1-13. University of Siena: mimeo.

Bacharach, M. 2006. *Beyond Individual Choice. Teams and Frames in Game Theory*, eds. N. Gold and R. Sugden. Princeton and Oxford: Princeton University Press.

Bacharach, M. and Bernasconi, M. 1997. An Experimental Study of the Variable Frame Theory of Focal Points. *Games and Economic Behavior* 19(1): 1-45.

Beccaria, C. 1971 [1770]. Ricerche sulla natura dello stile. *Opere*, vol. 1, ed. S. Romagnoli, 197-336. Firenze: Sansoni.

Crimmins, M. 1991. Context in the Attitudes. *Linguistics and Philosophy* 15(2): 185-98.

Dennett, D. 1990. Cognitive Wheels: the Frame Problem of AI. *The Philosophy of Artificial Intelligence*, ed. M. Boden, 147-70. Oxford: Oxford University Press. (Originally published in C. Hookway (ed.) 1984. *Mind, Machines, and Evolution: Philosophical Studies*, 129-51. Cambridge: Cambridge University Press.)

Etherington, D.W., Kraus, S. and Perlis, D. 1991. Limited Scope and Circumscriptive Reasoning. *Reasoning Agents in a Dynamic World: The Frame Problem*, eds. K.M. Ford, and P.J. Hayes, 43-54. Greenwich: JAI Press.

Fillmore, C.J. 1985. Frames and the Semantics of Understanding. *Quaderni di semantica* 6(2): 222-54.

Gilboa, I and Schmeidler, D. 2001. *A Theory of Case-Based Decisions*. Cambridge: Cambridge University Press.

Giunchiglia, F. 1993. Contextual Reasoning. *Epistemologia* 16: 345-64.

Hayes, P. 1985. The Second Naïve Physics Manifesto. *Formal Theories of the Commonsense World*, eds. J.R. Hobbs and R.C. Moore, 1-36. Norwood, NJ: Ablex.

Janssen, M.C.W. 2001. Rationalizing Focal Points. *Theory and Decision* 50: 119-48.

Janssen, M.C.W. 2003. Cooperation and Coordination. *Brain and Behavioral Sciences* 26: 165-66.

Kripke, S. 1959. A Completeness Theorem in Modal Logic. *Journal of Symbolic Logic* 24: 1-14.

McCarthy, J. 1980. Circumscription – A Form of Non-Monotonic Reasoning. *Artificial Intelligence*, 13: 27-39.

McCarthy, J. 1993. Notes on Formalizing Context. *Proceedings of the 13th International Joint Conference on Artificial Intelligence (IJCAI), Chambéry, France.* http://dli.iiit.ac.in/ijcai/IJCAI-93-VOL2/CONTENT/content.htm (on line version accessed 7.1.2007).

McCarthy, J. and Hayes, P.J. 1969. Some Philosophical Problems from the Standpoint of Artificial Intelligence. *Machine Intelligence 4*, eds. B. Meltzer and D. Michie, 463-502. Edinburgh: Edinburgh University Press.

Mehta, J., Starmer, C., Sugden, R. 1994. The Nature of Salience: an Experimental Investigation of Pure Coordination Games. *The American Economic Review* 84(3): 658-73.

Mill, J.S. 1846. *A System of Logic.* New York: Harper and Brothers.

Minsky, M. 1975. A Framework for Representing Knowledge. *The Psychology of Computer Vision*, ed P.H. Winston, 211-77. New York: McGraw-Hill.

Mondolfo, R. 1956. *Alle origini della filosofia della cultura.* Bologna: Il Mulino.

Morgenstern, L. 1991. Knowledge and the Frame Problem. *Reasoning Agents in a Dynamic World: The Frame Problem*, eds. K.M. Ford and P.J. Hayes, 133-70. Greenwich: JAI Press.

Nutter, J.T. 1991. Focus of Attention, Context, and the Frame Problem. *Reasoning Agents in a Dynamic World: The Frame Problem*, eds. K.M. Ford and P.J. Hayes, 171-88. Greenwich: JAI Press.

Petruck, M.R. 2003. Frame Semantics. *Handbook of Pragmatics*, eds. J. Verschueren, J.-O. Östman, J. Blommaert and C. Bulcaen. Amsterdam and Philadelphia: John Benjamins http://frament.icsi.berkeley.edu/papers/miriamp.FS2.pdf (on line version accessed 7.1.2007).

Porta, P.L. and Scazzieri, R. 2001. Coordination, Connecting Principles and Social Knowledge: An Introductory Essay. *Knowledge, Social Institutions and the Division of Labour*, eds. P.L. Porta, R. Scazzieri and A. Skinner, 1-32. Cheltenham, UK and Northampton, MA: Edward Elgar.

Porta, P.L. and Scazzieri, R. 2003. Accounting for Social Knowledge: The Relevance of Adam Smith's Framework. *Cognitive Developments in Economics*, 107-32. London: Routledge.

Richards, D. and Simoff, S.J. 2001. Design Ontology in Context – A Situated Cognition Approach to Conceptual Modelling. *Artificial Intelligence in Engineering* 15(2): 121-36.

Rosch, E. 1973. Natural Categories. *Cognitive Psychology* 4(3): 328-50.

Sandewall, E. 1991. Towards a Logic of Dynamic Frames. *Reasoning Agents in a Dynamic World: The Frame Problem*, eds. K.M. Ford and P.J. Hayes, 201-17. Greenwich: JAI Press.

Scazzieri, R. 2001a. Patterns of Rationality and the Varieties of Inference. *Journal of Economic Methodology* 8(1): 105-10.

Scazzieri, R. 2001b. Analogy, Causal Patterns and Economic Choice. *Stochastic Causality*, eds. M.C. Galavotti, P. Suppes and D. Costantini, 123-39. Stanford, California: CSLI Publications.

Scazzieri, R. 2003. Experiments, Heuristics and Social Diversity: A Comment on Reinhard Selten. *Observation and Experiment in the Natural and Social Sciences*, ed. M.C. Galavotti. *Boston Studies in the Philosophy of Science* 232: 85-98. Dordrecht, Boston, London: Kluwer Academic Publishers.

Scazzieri, R. 2006. A Smithian Theory of Choice. *Adam Smith Review* 2: 21-47.

Schelling, T.C. 1960. *The Strategy of Conflict*. Cambridge, MA and London, England: Harvard University Press.

Simon, H.A. 1983. *Reason in Human Affairs*. Oxford: Basil Blackwell.

Smith, A. 1980 [1795]. *Essays on Philosophical Subjects*, eds. W.P.D. Wightman and J.C. Bryce. Oxford: Oxford University Press.

Smith, A. 1976 [1759]. *The Theory of Moral Sentiments*, eds. D.D. Raphael and A.L. Macfie. Oxford: Oxford University Press.

Suppes, P. 1984. *Probabilistic Metaphysics*. Oxford and New York: Basil Blackwell.

Tannen, D. 1979. What's in a Frame? Surface Evidence for Underlying Expectations. *New Directions in Discourse Processing*, ed. R.O. Freedie, 137-81. Norwood: Ablex.

The Concise Oxford Dictionary. 2001. Tenth Edition, revised, ed. J. Pearsall. Oxford: Oxford University Press.

Turner, M. 2001. *Cognitive Dimensions of Social Science*. Oxford: Oxford University Press.

Zadeh, L.A. 2003a. Protoform Theory and Its Basic Role in Human Intelligence, Deduction, Definition and Search. *Performance Metrics for Intelligent Systems* Amsterdam and Philadelphia: John Benjamin. http://www.isd.mel.nist.gov/research_areas/research_engineering/Performance_Metrics/PerMIS_2003/Proceedings/Zadeh.pdf (on line version accessed 7.1.2007)

Zadeh, L.A. 2003b. Computing with Words and Perceptions (CWP) – A Paradigm Shift in Computing and Decision Analysis. Computer Science Division, Department EECS, University of California at Berkeley (30 June 2003), http://www-bisc.cs.Berkeley.edu (on line version accessed 7.1.2007).

III Situations and Reasoning

10

Rationality and its Bounds: Re-Framing Social Framing

MATTHIAS KLAES

1 Introduction[1]

Social scientific thought is riddled by a basic dichotomy. Analysis of individual behavior has found itself caught between an individualist perspective driven by rational choice theory, and a perspective that lends more weight to cultural and institutional forces shaping the behavior of individuals. This second perspective accords collective entities such as class, status, norms and values explanatory and at times also ontological primacy. In disciplinary terms, this basic dichotomy of social theorizing has given rise to a stereotypic division of labor between the disciplines of economics and sociology (Holmwood and Stewart 1991, 1994). According the stereotype, economics proceeds from the rational decisions of atomistic individuals, while sociology is preoccupied with social collectives and a holistic view of social structure.

Recent work in behavioral economics and related fields has made important steps towards broadening the economic approach by turning attention away from classical notions of rationality toward the concept of bounded rationality. In particular, bounded rationality conceptually forms part of attempts that demand descriptive accountability of the rational choice paradigm in economics. In contrast with the rationality concept at the heart of *homo oeconomicus* traditionally conceived which runs together

---

[1] Without implicating them in any way I am indebted to discussions with David Bloor, John Davis, Mihaela Kelemen, Martin Kusch, Rolland Munro, Roberto Scazzieri, and Patrick Suppes, who have helped sharpening my thoughts on the issues explored in this chapter.

normative and descriptive aspects of human behavior, theories of boundedly rational behavior strive for empirical adequacy.

In the main, the strategy has been to realize this empiricist program by broadening the rational choice paradigm in the direction of psychology, to the neglect of a similar broadening in the direction of sociology. This bias results from the persistence of the stereotypic division of labor between individualist and collectivist approaches in the social sciences. Behavioral and experimental economists pay little more than lip service to social framing effects. While a small but increasing number of studies consider the influence of social framing on economic decision-making, these studies proceed on an impoverished understanding of the social, treating social framing as inessential in a sense that will be spelled out below.

This chapter will argue for an essential notion of social framing effects. The argument will proceed as follows. Section 2 revisits what is arguably one of the clearest expressions of the divide between economics and sociology, by turning to the distinction between logical and non-logical action introduced by the economist-sociologist Vilfredo Pareto. Section 3 explores how the concept of bounded rationality has been employed to broaden the logical action paradigm in economics towards its counterpart of non-logical action. Section 4 illustrates the role of social framing effects by means of an example drawn from economics, that of successfully performed transactions in anonymous non-repetitive encounters. Section 5 argues that in conceptual terms, social framing needs to be understood in the more general context of human intentionality, where rational behavior can be addressed as a particular kind of intentional response to environmental factors. Finally, section 6, which draws from Pettit's (1993) dual distinction between atomism versus holism on the one hand, and individualism versus collectivism on the other hand, introduces the distinction between essential as opposed to inessential social framing effects in a systematic way and concludes that departures from psychological notions of bounded rationality require a theory of essential social framing, in the sense that the social frames intentional behavior in a constitutive way.

2 Rationality and its Residual

In his *Trattato di Sociologia Generale*, Pareto (1966) contrasts the category of 'logical action' – which he regards as one of the central categories of economic analysis – with the category of 'non-logical action'. Logical action is that action to which economic analysis applies. It refers to a framework which derives its conclusions from the premise that atomistic individuals act instrumentally rational to fulfill their exogenously given wants. Pareto suggests that this type of action can only account for a subset of the world of social phenomena. Those phenomena that cannot be subsumed under the category of logical action he addresses residually as belonging to the realm of 'non-logical' action (see Klaes 2003; Parsons 1937).

As a result of confining logical action to the realm of economic theory (Pareto 1964 [1896-97]), the *Trattato* concentrates upon non-logical action. In the rationalist terms of the means-end framework, non-logical action appears to be based on ignorance and error. Actors simply fail to employ the means best suited, given local circumstances, to achieve their ends. Pareto comes to the conclusion that in the majority of cases where individual behavior does not seem to be individually rational, actors tend to justify their behavior in terms of higher-order ends such as 'justice' which are difficult to reconcile with the individualist outlook of the atomistic individual as posited in the logical action framework of economics. Non-logical action is an aggregate phenomenon which only becomes recognizable as the shared conduct of a group of individuals, according to custom and internalized norms of behavior.

With the central explanatory role accorded in economics to Pareto's logical action, non-logical action has traditionally been relegated to residual categories such as economic friction:

> The disturbing effects of causes that are not economic, on the action of the causes that are strictly so called, may be regarded as an 'economic friction'. [...] Not only the customs, but the vices, follies, and mistakes of men are accountable for economic friction (Davidson 1896: 160).

In modern economics, these frictions are largely addressed in terms of various notions of transaction cost (Klaes 2000). Ultimately, they are left unexplored, in the sense that they take the place of exogenous factors that are relegated to the territory of sociology and renegade traditions in economics such as institutional economics. But if both types of action address a common domain of investigation, that of institutionally situated individual behavior, then it may, in terms of an attempt at explanatory unification, pay off turning aspects of the residual into a 'positive' explanatory category, to use a terminology first proposed by Parsons (1937). In other words, quite apart from the separate question of the success or not of the rational actor paradigm, there may be some merit in qualifying the rationality postulate that underlies underlying logical action so that it would take account of aspects of our decision-making hitherto confined to the realms of non-logical action.

It is motives of this kind that have led to bounded notions of rationality (cf. Klaes and Sent 2005). As a matter of fact, the concept of bounded rationality is at the forefront of a rigorous expansion of the concept of rationality into the domain of its residual, that of Pareto's non-logical action.

Mounting empirical and experimental counterevidence to the strong rationality assumptions of the logical action paradigm in economics and allied fields has led to the emergence of a new behavioral economics that seeks formalizing these departures and to test psychological predictions of bounded rationality models (e.g. Kahneman and Tversky 1974, 1979). Adopting the perspective of utility-maximization and Bayesian probability judgments, this literature evaluates the cognitive character of conformity or deviation from the benchmarks of strict rationality. One of its main achievements has been a clear separation between strict rationality as a normative yardstick against which actual decision-making may be assessed, and models of boundedly rational decision-making that seek to account for human decisions as empirical phenomena in need of causal explanation, whether they adhere to classical rationality postulates or not.

3 Bounded Rationality and Framing Effects

Bounded rationality is commonly defined on the basis of the cognitive limitations of decision-makers, both in terms of their limited knowledge, and of their limited 'computational capacity' (Simon 1987: 266). It has both an internal and an external dimension. A decision-maker with unlimited cognitive processing capacity may still struggle to measure up to strict rationality standards if living in an uncertain world. This uncertainty could be due to the stochastic or, as some would have it, non-ergodic nature of the environment in which decision-making takes place. There may also be competing theories of rational decision-making under such conditions. Conversely, a being of sufficiently limited cognitive capacity will, even if living in a completely deterministic environment, fail to display rational behavior.

Traditional approaches to decision-making under uncertainty have concentrated on external bounds to rational decision-making. Their main focus has been on how to conceptualize uncertainty in probabilistic terms to allow a rational evaluation of uncertain prospects. Expected utility theory has been the dominant approach here, following Bernoulli's (1954 [1738]) seminal work. In short, knowing the payoff matrix of possible random outcomes, the assumption is that an individual will choose according to the expected utility of particular courses of action (rather than the expected payoff). This would of course depend on knowledge of the relevant probabilities.

One-off events that are not amenable to a frequentist interpretation of such probabilities initially seemed to fall outside such a framework of analysis. In economics, this prompted Knight (1921) to suggest a distinction between quantifiable risk, and unquantifiable uncertainty. Savage (1954) demonstrated however that as long as the preferences of a decision-maker obey certain axioms, the behavior of this decision-maker can be analyzed as if expected utility was maximized on the basis of subjectively assigned probabilities.

As it turned out, there are important decision problems that violate one or several Savage axioms. Take for example Ellsberg's (1961) paradoxes. Ellsberg identified a number of scenarios where adherence to the Savage axioms did not seem to be plausible. Here is one: Consider random draws from an urn of 90 balls. Each ball is colored red, black, or yellow. All you know is that there are 30 red balls in the urn. You are now faced with two sets of alternative bets, each time receiving the same given sum of money if you win. In set I, you either win if drawing a red ball (a), or if drawing a black ball (b). In set II, you either win if the ball you draw is red or yellow (c), or alternatively if it is black or yellow (d).

Most individuals Ellsberg consulted preferred bet (a) over bet (b), and bet (d) over bet (c). This choice behavior is inconsistent with expected utility theory. A preference of (a) over (b) indicates that the individual attaches a higher probability to drawing red than to drawing black. But this implies that the individual should also attach a higher probability to drawing red or yellow (c), compared to drawing black or yellow (d).

An individual preferring (a) over (b) while preferring (d) over (c) seems to have been guided more by the particular formulation of the decision problem than by strictly rational considerations. As stated above, the choice problem allows attaching a known probability to only some of the alternative outcomes. Given that the number of red balls (a) and black and yellow balls (d) in the urn is known with certainty, individuals appeared to have selected against (b) and (c). In other words, if subjectively attached probabilities played a role at all, they did so in a weighted form, taking into account non-probabilistic aspects of the decision problem at hand.

Kahneman and Tversky (1974, 1979)[2] have taken this and similar observations that point to the moderation of probability assessments by context-specific weightings as the basis of what they call 'prospect theory'. Prospect theory purports to be an alternative theory of decision-making under uncertainty where bounded rationality is operationalized by postulating various framing effects that influence the weightings moderating subjective probability assessment. In prospect theory, choice is conceptualized as a two-stage process. In the first stage, the choice problem is 'edited' or 'framed'. This occurs by taking the context and contingencies of how the choice problem presents itself into account. In the second stage, the framed alternatives are then evaluated. Contrary to traditional rational choice the-

---

[2] See also Kahneman, Slovic and Tversky 1982; Tversky and Kahneman 1981, 1986.

ory, Kahneman and Tversky's theory has no normative ambitions. Hence, explaining observed choice behavior takes precedent over adherence to the classical rationality postulates.

One should note that prospect theory does not aspire to a fully formulated theory of framing. Framing effects remain defined rather loosely: 'Framing is controlled by the manner in which the choice problem is presented as well as by norms, habits, and expectancies of the decision maker.' (Tversky and Kahneman 1986: S257). This apparent lacuna is openly admitted but not regarded as a weakness (ibid.: S273). For the most part, Kahneman and Tversky restrict their analysis to relatively simple cases of framing, which remain associated with the linguistic presentation of a choice problem. They admit the further relevance of psychological framing effects that reach beyond the linguistic level. Rarely if at all do they engage with framing effects situated at the social level, such as the norms to which they refer above.

Kahneman and Tversky's attempts to broaden traditional conceptions of rationality are therefore biased towards the atomistic individualism of the logical action framework. Within the traditional dichotomy between logical and non-logical action, they rest content with incorporating merely non-social aspects of non-logical action into qualified notions of rationality. Hence Kahneman and Tversky's focus on presentational context and the individual's habits and psychological makeup, coupled with a reluctance of engaging with the possibility of a sociology rather than or in addition to a psychology of choice under uncertainty.

It is only recently that social framing has received more than passing attention in economic psychology and experimental economics. Carpenter, Burks and Verhoogen (2005) for example acknowledge that to establish the external validity of laboratory experiments, it is necessary to analyze the social context of individuals, even if they are placed in artificial laboratory scenarios. On the one hand, individuals are prone associating the laboratory context with a particular social context they prominently encounter in their daily lives. On the other hand, their behavior will be affected both by the social relationships between them and the other individuals they encounter in the laboratory context, and the relationships between them and the experimenter. Claims to any general validity of laboratory results must thus withstand variation in the social context of the experiment, or else be formulated as social frame specific.

There is a small but growing literature now exploring culturally specific framing effects (e.g. Henrich, Boyd, Bowles, Camerer, Fehr, Gintis and McElreath 2001; Carpenter 2002). Nevertheless, behind this interest in social framing alongside framing effects associated with properties of the individual (such as habits, individual histories that shape subjective probabilities, etc) there still looms the traditional divide between logical and non-logical action.

Empirical studies may explain choice behavior in various proportions of individual and social framing effects. This by itself will do little however to advance a conceptual understanding of bounded rationality. A convincing theory of bounded rationality will have to confront the issue head on. Methodologically, this requires engagement with the thorny issue of human intentionality. If social norms are supposed to affect individual behavior directly, and not merely via the range of available courses of action open to individual choice, such intentionality seems compromised. Put differently, if the concept of bounded rationality, through incorporation of social framing effects, seeks to expand into the realm of non-logical action by reducing individual decision rules to social norms, it will become questionable whether that concept still constitutes a species of rationality, after all.

4 Economics and Transactional Framing

Let us consider how social framing effects may affect economic behavior by turning to an economic puzzle. The puzzle is centered on transactional contexts that, if seen from an individualist rational choice perspective, do not seem to require costly expenditure on the part of individuals while, in practice, they will typically decide to incur such expenditure. The issue turns on apparently irrational behavior in non-repeated anonymous encounters (see Klaes 2002). While ad-hoc rationalizations of observed behavior abound, they stretch the traditional rational actor paradigm to its explanatory limits.

Imagine you are sitting in a café, in a city you are unlikely to visit again. Neither food nor service were particularly impressive. Nevertheless, when it comes to moving on, you feel a peculiar compulsion: somehow, it still seems proper and called for to leave a tip on the table. Your rational self simply wants to walk out. Yet, your inner voice begs to differ. Might not the wage of staff be set in expectation of your tip, at exceedingly low levels? What would the individual that served you think of you if you just walked off? Is the sum in question really worth the time pondering about all these issues? In the end you leave a modest token amount, not because you found a good reason for doing so but because it simply struck you as what you should do. You have no rational explanation for it, and clearly, you could have acted differently. Neither did you act blindly, nor unintentionally. Still, your own standards of rationality had suggested a different course of action. In fact, your rational self still maintains that you should not have left that tip on the table. Maybe you followed a habit, but on reflection, and comparing it to what you would properly regard as habits of yours, you did not recognize it as such.

If the above example seems excessively contrived consider a variation. You flag down a taxi. Upon completion of the journey the driver points to the meter, and before getting off the car you settle the outstanding amount. But why? What would have prevented you from simply leaving the taxi without paying? Conversely, assume that you have just handed over the sum indicated by the meter. What prevents the taxi driver from pretending that payment is still due?

The only way out consists of allowing for some mechanism of contract enforcement. The problem with this solution to the *ex post* bilateral bargaining problem resides in the dilemma that conceding either party any means of enforcement that will render the other compliant will offer this same party the opportunity to defect on its part. If the passenger pays under the impression of the driver's biceps and pecs[3] instead of leaving the car right away, the driver should use the physical advantage to extort a second payment. Similarly, if the driver's fear of the passenger's angry response or threat of legal action prevents a second demand for payment, this same response or threat could be used by the passenger in the first place to claim that payment had been made already.

There is no straightforward solution to the bilateral bargaining problem in this and similar scenarios. More generally, the rationalist mechanism stipulated by Coase (1960, 1981) to yield a solution to the problem cannot be relied upon if there is a danger of opportunistic exploitation (cf. Schlicht 1996). Nevertheless, we witness countless successfully completed 'taxi ride' transactions of the type described above in our daily lives. So how credible is the physical threat of the taxi driver's biceps in the first instance? And are there any deterrents to keep taxi drivers themselves in check?

While there certainly are reported cases of passengers simply leaving the car without paying after having arrived at the desired destination, typically, the driver – instead of resorting to physical means of enforcing payment – would alert colleagues and the police of the incident, with good chances for the perpetrator being apprehended shortly afterwards.[4] The existing institutional context seems to provide a sufficient deterrent for the passenger to honor the initial contract. Similarly, the legal system could plausibly be expected to enforce compliance on the part of the driver. If a

---

[3] On the way to the airport, I once took the opportunity to politely discuss the enforcement problem with a female taxi driver in downtown New Orleans. She calmly drew my attention to a hand gun underneath her seat. She also stressed that she would only pick up passengers from major inner-city hotels.

[4] I learned this from a judge involved in such cases.

'double payment' case went to court, and both parties issued conflicting statements, the judge would decide on the basis of internal consistency and plausibility of the statements. If there turned out to be an accumulation of similar cases on the driver's record, their credibility would be seriously undermined. In addition, any conviction would endanger continuation of the taxi license and thus the driver's livelihood. Again, the institutional context of the taxi ride transaction seems to provide a sufficient deterrent against *ex post* opportunism on the part of the driver.

Institutional context, and thus social norms and the social framing of economic action, is crucial for the successful bilateral completion of 'taxi ride' type transactions. This is of course no novel insight (cf. Polanyi 1944; Granovetter 1985). But again, taking instances of non-logical action of this kind seriously in economics tends to be hampered by the fact that it is always possible *ex post* to construct an individual cost-benefit calculus that explains compliant behavior. The limits of such an approach in the context of social framing are obvious. Boundedly rational agents are simply not able to generally engage in the purported assessments and calculations that ensure compliance. Does this mean that we should conceptualize them as social drones who blindly enact social rules? Yet again, if they are to be preserved as intentional agents, their intentionality requires more deeply probing foundations than those offered by Pareto's dichotomy.

5 Rationality and Intentionality

The rational actor paradigm at the core of modern economics is not usually discussed in the context of human intentionality. If it is ever put into a broader perspective at all, then this is done as part of the recent literature on economic psychology that emerged from the bounded rationality literature. Yet, given that rational choice theory traditionally conceived does not necessarily purport to be a psychological theory, it seems more than apt to pursue the bounded rationality theme into philosophical debates on practical reasoning. Intentionality as a technical term addresses the 'aboutness' of mental states such as beliefs, hopes, desires, fears, love and hatred. To the extent that a mental state is directed at anything beyond itself, it has an intentional aspect. Often, the content of an intentional state can be expressed as a full proposition. For example, I may believe (hope, desire, fear, etc) that P, with P standing for a particular proposition like 'It will rain tomorrow'.[5]

---

[5] Intentional states of this kind are also known as 'propositional attitudes'. Note that intentions themselves are only one particular kind of intentional state.

Beliefs and desires are intimately connected to accounts of rational action. Consider my desire that it should not rain tomorrow, coupled with my belief that it will in fact rain tomorrow if I am going to leave the house in the morning without my umbrella. Given my belief and desire, it would be subjectively rational for me to take my umbrella with me when I go out that day. In fact, I would, if challenged as to why I had taken my umbrella with me, cite both as reasons for my behavior. Intentional states are candidate reasons for action. They 'rationalize' a particular behavior.

One could carry this example one step further (e.g. Searle 1983: 160-79), by approaching meaning itself as an intentional phenomenon. In the umbrella example, there is a difference between me just uttering the words 'It will be raining today' when I leave the house without my umbrella, and my uttering these words *and meaning them*. What I will have done in the case of the latter is intentionally impose the conditions of satisfaction of an intentional state, i.e. my belief that it will rain under these circumstances, on a particular act (of utterance), to use Searle's terminology. Meaning in this context has an indexical aspect, which adds an intentional dimension to the physical act of mere utterance.

Questions regarding rationality and meaning are therefore closely related. Searle (2001: 22-24, 109; see also Searle 1983) for example argues that any account of rationality should address rationality as a faculty of human beings based on their ability to reason about their actions. And this reasoning activity is tied to language and communication. Once I give a good reason for a particular intentional phenomenon, I may be said to have provided an explanation for it. Whether this explanation is convincing or acceptable is another matter, of course. If you ask me in our umbrella example 'Why do you believe that it will rain if you leave your umbrella at home?' I will be hard pressed to provide you with a rational justification for my belief. Nevertheless, I can give you a convincing reason, by referring to a particular superstitious compulsion of mine when it comes to umbrellas and rain.

For Searle, rationality is not a separate human faculty. It is implicit in human intentionality as such, since intentional states give us reasons for our actions. Why did I take the umbrella? Because I believed that if I did not take it, it would rain with certainty. As soon as we seek for reasons however, we subject our intentional states to the constraints of rationality. These constraints can be very real, otherwise I should have no trouble convincing you that my umbrella superstition is rationally justified. Holding a belief means being open to the challenge by others to justify that belief, and a prominent way of justification consists of appealing to commonly accepted standards of rationality.

Here however lies the crux of the matter, and the weakness of Searle's account of rationality. He himself refers to a striking example of how prone we are to assume shared standards of rationality where in fact, no such common standards prevail. Searle (2001: 6) recounts visiting a high ranking US defense official during the Vietnam War. Searle tried to convince him that the strategy of bombing North Vietnam was irrational. As a response, the friend drew a diagram comparing the marginal utility of resistance to the marginal (dis)utility of being bombed. At the point where the two curves intersected, the enemy was bound to give up according to the defense official's analysis: 'All we are assuming is that they are rational'. Bombing would therefore be a winning strategy. The irony that shows up in Searle discussion is that whenever one seeks to make the alleged constraints of rationality explicit, they become subject to debate, the same debate in fact that, in his account, makes rationality an intentional faculty. If anything, drawing attention to the intentional nature of rationality only serves to underline the social framing of rationality.

6 Essential versus Non-essential Social Framing

In effect, Searle's argument, carried to its conclusion, amounts to the assertion that rationality, as a set of standards of human behavior, is a social institution (Searle 1995: 59-78). This brings us back to the same threat to intentionality that we have already identified in our discussion of boundedly rational agents, whereby intentionality risks being compromised by social structure. If the very capacity of rational decision-making is intrinsically social, would this not risk falling victim to precisely that social drone so rightly criticized (Wrong 1961)? One helpful starting point for answering this question is Pettit's (1993) distinction between individualism versus collectivism on the one hand, and holism versus atomism on the other hand (see also Tuomela 1994). Pettit rightly points out that we are not faced with a simply dyadic opposition between individuals and social structure, but with two separate issues that need to be disentangled.

One the one hand, the interrelation of individual intentionality and social structure is of a 'vertical' nature. If one grants social entities existence in their own right one needs to confront the question of whether these entities in fact compromise or override individual intentionality. For Pettit, this turns on whether one takes an individualist or a collectivist perspective. On the other hand, social entities relate individuals to each other in a 'horizontal' way. The question here is to what extent individuals depend on other individuals for some distinct capacities, that is, whether essential capacities of any given individual can be properly understood without considering individuals in separation from one another. Adopting Pettit's terminology, atomists will deny that any such capacities exist, while holists will argue in their favor.

We arrive thus at four different positions that one may hold regarding the nature of social entities in their relation to individual intentionality. Atomist individualism will deny any ontological status to social entities, regarding them as mere epiphenomena of individuals and their interaction with each other. Atomist collectivists, in contrast, will accept the existence of social regularities in their own right in that they have the potential of overriding individual intentionality. Holist collectivists will add to the atomist collectivist position that some characteristics essential to individual intentionality are inherently social in nature, while individualist holists will deny that social regularities compromise individual intentionality in this way.

Pettit himself defends an individualist holist position, but his classification has broader application. Like Searle, he regards human intentionality as invariably tied to rationality criteria. Without such criteria, we would have no way of systematically linking certain of our intentional states, notably intentions, to desirable outcomes. But to the extent that one allows departures from the atomist individualist position, one accepts that rationality is socially framed.

Pettit's terminology enables us to distinguish between non-essential and essential social framing in boundedly rational conceptions of individual decision-making. The claim that social institutions influence the choice context for rational decision-making, and that social entities, like natural entities, enter such decision-making, is largely uncontroversial. To allow for such influence is fully compatible with atomist individualism. Let us therefore define social framing to be essential if it amounts to a position different from atomist individualism within Pettit's fourfold differentiation. To arrive at such a position, we have to either relax atomism, or individualism

6.1 Essential Framing: Atomism Relaxed

The question of atomism – Pettit's horizontal issue – turned on whether or not individuals relied, for at least some of their core characteristics, on others. To clarify what is at stake with this question, consider a Hobbesian account of a social contract entered into by autonomous individuals. Such an account relies on the possibility of essentially a-social, atomistic individuals. A social holist will deny this possibility, by calling into question a purely individualist capacity of individuals to meaningfully follow even simple rules.

Rules can be understood in two different ways. Meaning determinists (Bloor 1997: 3) hold that what we do when we follow a rule is to 'grasp' its meaning. Once we have grasped a rule, we would, so the suggestion goes, know how to apply it to future instances. Take the example of the sequence of even numbers. This sequence is a result of following the rule 'add 2'. A meaning determinist would hold that once the meanings of 'add' and '2' are fixed, possibly together with auxiliary concepts such as 'sequence', it seems fully clear what we must do to follow the original rule. However, this confronts us with an infinite regress, because all we have done is to shift attention to the meaning of these newly brought in concepts. Eventually, meaning will have to be fixed by different means (cf. Klaes 2006; Kripke 1982). A meaning determinist would solve this problem by pointing out that once we have grasped a concept there is a specific mental content which guides us through new cases. The ability to follow rules, in this account, amounts to a purely individualist capacity since rules are reduced to specific mental content.

Bloor, following Wittgensteinian 'private language' arguments (cf. Kripke 1982), is highly skeptical of giving mental content such a prominent role in concept application, due to cognitive limitations. Instead he suggests an alternative account which he calls 'meaning finitism'.[6] In the meaning finitist account of rule following and concept application, the move to the next instance is not intuitive or interpretive but 'blind' (Bloor 1997: 19). This blindness is a logical blindness. There is noting in a given rule that logically or semantically compels us to a particular next step. Instead, the factors at work have a causal psychological or instinctive origin: 'When we are confronted with a finite set of examples we do not extract from them any general idea, rather, we instinctively pass on to what strikes us as the next step or the next case.' (ibid.: 14). Our response is due to an 'innate but socially educated' tendency to perceive similarities (see also Schlicht 1998, Klaes 2002).

Up to now, meaning finitism departs from meaning determinism only to the extent that the individual's ability to apply a particular rule is explained differently. The next instance of rule application is arrived at instinctively, not because we have grasped a particular content. So far, atomism would remain intact. But the finitist account of concept application allows for factors other than just instincts and habits to influence how we extend past conceptual usage to new instances. Contrary to meaning determinism, meaning finitism demands that each new application is determined afresh by the factors and contingencies operative at that time. But these factors need not be limited to the psycho-biological make-up of the individual. Bloor suggests a second set of influences that we should assume to be op-

---

[6] This terminology is inspired by Mary Hesse's (1974) account of classification within her network model of scientific theories.

erative, which are inherently social in character. Correct concept application should be understood as agreement in action: 'To make a "wrong" move is ultimately to make a move that leads the individual along a divergent path. To be wrong is to be deviant ...' (Bloor 1997: 16).

Following a rule therefore does not reduce to mental content but to being aligned in certain ways with the members of a given community. Contrary to the meaning determinist account however, this implicit consensus is open ended, since it only ever stretches across a subset of past concept applications that finds its boundary in the status quo, whereas in meaning determinism, mental content also fixes future instances.

While Pettit himself follows a slightly different line of argument, he arrives, like Bloor along Wittgenstein's private language argument at essentially the same conclusion (see also Wittgenstein, 1953; Kripke 1982). In order to be able to follow rules, individuals rely on social interaction in a constitutive sense. In Pettit's terminology, both he himself and Bloor assume a social holist position, which extends to rationality, too: they both hold that the normativity of the rules of rational conduct can only be grounded in interaction.

We therefore end up with a social holist argument for regarding social framing as essential for the constitution of human intentionality, and rational decision-making in particular. Rules of what counts as rational conduct need to be understood in a finitist way. This makes their application to the next instance open-ended. Whether or not behavior is rational only ever emerges in the normativity conferred by the continuous interaction of fellow individuals.

6.2 Essential Framing: Individualism Relaxed

Let us now turn to the second possibility of moving from non-essential to essential social framing of intentional behavior, by exploring whether a commitment to social holism prejudges in any way Pettit's vertical issue, that between individualism and collectivism. Pettit (1993: 172-75) himself is adamant that it does not. In fact, his chief motivation of having distinguished the horizontal from the vertical issue consists in establishing the compatibility between social holism and an individualist perspective which leaves individual intentionality intact in respect to any overriding or transforming influences of social entities.

What then is the case against collectivism? To begin with, acknowledging that social properties such as an individual's status within a given group impact on the intentional responses of other individuals does not commit oneself to a collectivist position. After all, social entities are not the only entities to influence our intentional responses in this way: they do so alongside non-social entities such as natural objects or human artifacts. All that we require of social entities, for them to be able to exert such an influence, is that they exist mind-independently in quite the same way as non-social entities do. Brute facts, such as the concrete wall that stands in our way, affect our intentional responses to our environment because they exist independent of that intentionality. We cannot wish them away. Social facts share this inertness vis-à-vis individual intentionality. True, social facts are contingent in certain ways on mental entities. They presuppose human intentionality. But social institutions such as the status of an individual within a group are not dependent on a particular intentional response of any one group member. It is only in their collectivity that group members sustain the institution of status.

This feature of social entities such as status has given rise to a theory of social institutions which regards them as communal performatives (see Barnes 1995, Bloor 1997, Searle 1995, Kusch 2002; cf. Austin 1956). They are constituted of utterances that are self-realizing: If group members, in their collective practices, ascribe a status to a particular individual, this individual will through those actions have acquired the status in question. The performatives are also self-referring. A particular member of the group is its leader because she is taken to be the leader.

The question now is whether these performatives that constitute social entities pose a threat to the position of the individualist. Take for example the opinion of a high-status individual within a group. The opinion of this individual tends to exert a significant influence on which opinions other group members hold. The individual's status is a social entity, and what we have just described is a regularity on the social level, or social regularity in short. And this social regularity impacts on the intentional regularities as we find them for example in the responses of other group members. Does it thus undermine their primacy?

As long as we can identify some form of continuity between the intentional level and the level of social regularities, the answer is negative. The regularity in the above example is causally continuous with the intentional level since we can express this influence on the basis of causal regularities of group behavior. At worst, the opinions of some individuals will be swayed in ways that these individuals would resist under certain favorable conditions, conditions which would ensure rational responses. High status individuals do therefore not undermine the possibility of an autonomously intentional response as such.

Likewise, there are regularities which, while not causally continuous with individual intentional regularities, are nevertheless logically continuous with them. Logical continuity is a common relationship between micro-

and macrophenomena. Consider Schelling's (1969) neighborhood segregation models. In these models, individuals have a preference for not being in a local minority: they will move elsewhere if this condition is no longer fulfilled. This regularity at the micro level results in complete segregation at the macro level, even for the case that each and every individual is opposed to macro-level segregation as an outcome. We do not therefore have strict causal continuity between individual intentional regularities and the obtaining macro regularity. But the macro regularity will obtain in all possible worlds in which the intentional regularity obtains. It is therefore logically continuous with it.

Let us, with Pettit, refer to the social regularities considered so far as social-intentional regularities. This is to distinguish them from Pettit's social-structural regularities. Social-structural regularities are causally discontinuous with the intentional level, as in the two preceding examples. But they are also logically discontinuous with intentional regularities. In other words, given a particular intentional make-up, we can imagine a world in which the social regularity obtains just as well as one in which the regularity does not obtain. In other words, the intentional level fails to fix social-structural regularities. Imagine for example a world in which certain gate-keeping arrangements ensure that only certain types of behavior are tolerated in a given group (Pettit 1993: 124). The obtaining social regularities as they relate to this group will, given a particular intentional make-up, obtain in all possible worlds in which the gate-keeping arrangement holds. They are thus contingent on this boundary condition. Without it, the intentional level will not fix the social regularity: it may obtain in some worlds, but not in others.

Now consider the case of a particular candidate for a social-structural regularity: that of the 'folk psychology' at the root of our intentional responses. What if this folk psychology may actually be best understood as a social-structural regularity? This possibility would amount to standing Pettit's overall framework on its head, which seeks to ground social regularities in intentional regularities. But as Paprzycka (1998) has pointed out, Pettit's arguments in favor of an individualist perspective on folk psychology and thereby individual intentionality is at best ad hoc. Once a collectivist interpretation of folk psychology is acknowledged in Pettit's analysis, one gets invariably drawn towards either atomistic or holist collectivism overall.

Among the various proposals of a collectivist interpretation of folk psychology, that of Kusch (1997) is particularly relevant for our discussion since it draws on Bloor's social ontology. Kusch argues that 'I-talk' and thereby 'the self' as it is conventionally understood, is a social institution in the sense of the collective performatives that we have introduced above. The only way we make sense of our own intentionality and mental experience is through this 'I-talk'. The key step in Kusch's argument is the realization that 'I', our first-person expression, is a self-referring expression. He argues that it is self-referential in two ways: First, as a concept, along the lines considered above when we discussed meaning in terms of rule following. Second, 'I-talk' is not only self-referential on the level of the collective, it is so on the individual level, too. If an individual engages in 'I-talk', what they refer to is not a mysterious 'self' but other 'I-talk' that they engage in.

By being self-referential in these two ways, our 'I-talk' assumes a self-realizing and self-sustaining nature. In other words, it stabilizes the 'I' as a social institution. In a similar vein, Kusch regards mental states such as beliefs or desires as social artifacts which, while grounded in biological universals, are shaped and sustained collectively. If this is indeed the case we should expect to find cultural and historical variability of this institution. Kusch accepts this implication of cultural and historical contingency of folk psychology. He points to anthropological studies of societies whose folk psychology appears to lack concepts we regard central, including 'belief' or the self (Needham 1972, Lienhardt 1961, Howell 1981), or to the conceptual histories of *Annales* historians such as Bloch (1962 [1936]) or Febvre (1982 [1942]).

The upshot of Kusch's position is the possibility of a collectivist holist position within Pettit's typology. If folk psychology is a social institution, then human intentionality is in fact constituted as a social-structural regularity. This provides the strongest possible case for essential social framing of boundedly rational behavior. In such behavior, seeking to incorporate the potential influence of shifting social context must, for the collectivist, amount to the pursuit of a red herring, since rationality itself is a cultural entity that it will be difficult to consider in separation from what, for the individualist, would merely appear its social context.

7 Conclusion

We started out with a discussion of the rational choice paradigm in the social sciences, as brought to the point by Pareto's distinction between logical and non-logical action. Traditional rational choice theory suffers from an intrinsic tension between descriptive and normative ambitions when it comes to account for human decision-making. Recent developments in behavioral and experimental economics have sought to differentiate these two dimensions by working towards a descriptively accurate theory of decision-making, reserving normative claims to the traditional model.

One of the key conceptual developments in these new approaches to the study of individual choice has been the emergence of a range of bounded rationality notions both in economics and allied social sciences. This chapter has been concerned with the nature of these bounds. One finds in the bounded rationality literature ready acknowledgement of the crucial influence of social factors on individual decision-making. In particular, the external validity of some findings from experimental economics is difficult to establish without reference to social framing effects.

But once it is acknowledged that social structure, as captured in the concept of social frames, genuinely impacts on individual choice, one finds oneself confronted precisely with Pareto's divide between logical and non-logical action, and between the primacy of individual rationality versus the primacy of social entities such as institutions. Behavioral economists have to date largely restricted themselves to psychological models of human decision-making. Given that the disciplines of economics and psychology share a common methodologically individualist outlook, this comes as little surprise. Nevertheless, once social framing effects are allowed to play an essential role in bounded conceptions of rationality, the implied theory of the social requires careful spelling out.

Pettit's distinction between the horizontal and the vertical issue in social ontology allows to address the implicit philosophical commitment of current attempts to operationalize bounded rationality in behavioral economics. Due to its individualist foundations, the rational actor paradigm in economics lacks a theory of the social that would reach beyond the acknowledgement of inter-individual exchange of signals. In Pettit's terms, it amounts to the atomist individualist stance in social ontology. Conceptualizing social framing effects along these lines amounts to acknowledgement of inessential social framing in the terms of the present chapter.

By contrast, we defined as essential social framing any allowance for departures from the atomist individualist stance, either by relaxing the atomist presumption towards a holist position, or by relaxing the individualist presumption towards a collectivist position. As a matter of fact, once one accepts arguments for a holist stance towards social objects such as institutions, assuming an individualist or collectivist holist position turns precisely on whether folk psychology is construed in individualist or collectivist terms. For collectivist holists such as Bloor or Kusch, both Pettit's individualist holism, and atomist collectivism as the other 'mixed' position in Pettit's classification, must appear as inconsistent intermediate positions. While they acknowledge the essentially social nature of institutions in some respects, they fail to grasp the full import of this social dimension.

For our discussion of the framing of rationality, this means that while the arguments in favor of both holism and collectivism independently establish the essentially social nature of such framing, they should be seen in conjunction. Embracing such holist collectivism amounts to the recognition of the fundamentally social nature of human intentionality and thus to a sociological and institutional reconstruction of folk psychology.

References

Austin, J.L. 1961 [1956]. Performative Utterances. *Philosophical Papers*, eds. J.O. Urmson and G.J. Warnock, 220-30. Oxford: Clarendon.

Barnes, B. 1995. *The Elements of Social Theory*. London: UCL Press.

Bernoulli, D. 1954 [1738]. Exposition of a New Theory on the Measurement of Risk. *Econometrica* 22: 23-36.

Bloch, M. 1962 [1936]. *Feudal Society*. London: Routledge and Kegan.

Bloor, D. 1997. *Wittgenstein: Rules and Institutions*. London: Routledge.

Carpenter, J. 2002. Measuring Social Capital: Adding Field Experimental Methods to the Analytical Toolbox. *Social capital and economic development: Wellbeing in developing countries*, eds. J. Isham, T. Kelly and S. Ramaswamy, 119-37. Northampton: Elgar.

Carpenter, J., Burks, S. and Verhoogen, E. 2005. Comparing Students to Workers: The Effects of Social Framing on Behavior in Distribution Games. *Field Experiments in Economics*, eds. J. Carpenter, J.A. List and G. Harrison, 261-90. Greenwich, CT: JAI Press.

Coase, R.H. 1960. The Problem of Social Cost. *Journal of Law and Economics* 3: 1-44.

Coase, R.H. 1981. The Coase Theorem and the Empty Core: A Comment. *Journal of Law and Economics* 24: 183-87.

Davidson, M.G. 1896. Friction in Economics. *Dictionary of Political Economy*, vol. 2, ed. R.H. Inglis Palgrave, 160-61. London: Macmillan.

Ellsberg, D. 1961. Risk, Ambiguity, and the Savage Axioms. *Quarterly Journal of Economics* 75: 643-69.

Febvre, L. 1982 [1942]. *The problem of Unbelief in the Sixteenth Century: The Religion of Rabelais*. Cambridge, MA: Harvard University Press.

Granovetter, M. 1985. Economic Action and Social Structure: The Problem of Embeddedness. *American Journal of Sociology* 91: 481-510.

Henrich, J., Boyd, R., Bowles, S., Camerer, C., Fehr, E., Gintis, H. and McElreath, R. 2001. In Search of Homo Economicus: Behavioral Experiments in 15 Small-Scale Societies. *American Economic Review* 91: 73-78.

Hesse, M.B. 1974. *The Structure of Scientific Inference*. London: Macmillan.

Holmwood, J. and Stewart, A. 1991. *Explanation and Social Theory*. Basingstoke: Macmillan.

Holmwood, J. and Stewart, A. 1994. Synthesis and Fragmentation in Social Theory: A Progressive Solution. *Sociological Theory* 12: 83-100.

Howell, S. 1981. Rules Not Words. *Indigenous Psychologies: The Anthropology of the Self*, eds. P. Heelas and A. Lock, 133-43. London: Academic Press.

Kahneman, D., Slovic, P. and Tversky, A. 1982. *Judgement under Uncertainty: Heuristics and Biases.* Cambridge: Cambridge University Press.

Kahneman, D. and Tversky, A. 1974. Judgment under Uncertainty: Heuristics and Biases. *Science* 185: 1124-31.

Kahneman, D. and Tversky, A. 1979. Prospect Theory: An Analysis of Decision under Risk. *Econometrica* 47: 263-91.

Klaes, M. 2000. The History of the Concept of Transaction Costs: Neglected Aspects. *Journal of the History of Economic Thought* 22: 191-216.

Klaes, M. 2002. Some Remarks on the Place of Psychological and Social Elements in a Theory of Custom. *American Journal of Economics and Sociology* 61: 519-30.

Klaes, M. 2003. Residual Categories and the Evolution of Economic Knowledge. *The Evolution of Scientific Knowledge*, eds. H.S. Jensen, L.M. Richter and M.T. Vendelø, 37-56. Cheltenham: Elgar.

Klaes, M. 2006. Founding Economic Concepts. *Storia del Pensiero Economico* 3(1): 21-37.

Klaes, M. and Sent, E.-M. 2005. A Conceptual History of Bounded Rationality. *History of Political Economy* 37: 27-60.

Knight, F.H. 1921. *Risk, Uncertainty and Profit.* Boston: Mifflin.

Kripke, S. 1982. *Wittgenstein on Rules and Private Language.* Oxford: Blackwell.

Kusch, M. 1997. The Sociophilosophy of Folk Psychology. *Studies in the History and Philosophy of Science* 28: 1-25.

Kusch, M. 2002. *Knowledge by Agreement.* Oxford: Clarendon.

Lienhardt, R.G. 1961. *Divinity and Experience.* London: Oxford University Press.

Needham, R. 1972. *Belief, Language, and Experience.* Oxford: Blackwell.

Paprzycka, K. 1998. Collectivism on the Horizon: A Challenge to Pettit's Critique of Collectivism. *Australasian Journal of Philosophy* 76: 165-81.

Pareto, V. 1964 [1896-97]. *Cours d'Économie Politique*, ed. G.H. Bousquet and G. Busino. Genève: Droz.

Pareto, V. 1966. *Sociological Writings*, ed. S.E. Finer, transl. D. Mirfin. London: Pall Mall.

Parsons, T. 1937. *The Structure of Social Action*, 2 vols. [2nd ed. 1949]. New York and London: Free Press and Collier-Macmillan.

Pettit, P. 1993. *The Common Mind.* Oxford: Oxford University Press.

Polanyi, K. 1944. *The Great Transformation.* New York: Rinehart.

Savage, L.J. 1954. *The Foundations of Statistics.* New York: Wiley.

Schelling, T. 1969. Models of Segregation. *American Economic Review* 59: 488-93.

Schlicht, E. 1996. Exploiting the Coase Mechanism: The Extortion Problem. *Kyklos* 49: 319-30.

Schlicht, E. 1998. *On Custom in the Economy.* Oxford: Clarendon.

Searle, J. 1983. *Intentionality.* Cambridge: Cambridge University Press.

Searle, J. 1995. *The Construction of Social Reality*. London: Penguin.

Searle, J. 2001. *Rationality in Action*. Cambridge, MA: The MIT Press.

Simon, H.A. 1987. Bounded Rationality. *The New Palgrave Dictionary of Economics*, vol. 1, eds. J. Eatwell, M. Milgate and P. Newman, 266-68. London: Macmillan.

Tuomela, R. 1994. In search for the common mind. *International Journal of Philosophical Studies* 2: 306-21.

Tversky, A. and Kahneman, D. 1981. The Framing of Decisions and the Psychology of Choice. *Science* 211: 453-58.

Tversky, A. and Kahneman, D. 1986. Rational Choice and the Framing of Decisions. *Journal of Business* 59: S251-78.

Wittgenstein, L. 1953. *Philosophical Investigations*, transl. G. Anscombe 1967. Oxford: Blackwell.

Wrong, D.H. The Oversocialized Conception of Man in Modern Sociology. *American Sociological Review* 26: 183-93.

11

Causal Pluralism and Context[*]

MARIA CARLA GALAVOTTI

The paper heralds a pluralistic approach that combines the mechanical and manipulative theories of causality, aware of the intrinsic context dependence of causal attributions. It is argued that the assumptions underpinning causal attributions and the restrictions imposed upon them within various contexts should be taken into account, and the same holds for the nature of the information available. Similarly, the aims to which causal discourse is put within a given context should be considered, especially in connection with explanation, prediction and manipulation. Instead of giving a univocal definition of causality, one should start from a careful consideration of the context surrounding causal analysis, and proceed from there to a characterization of causal relations within a given context.

1 How Many Pluralisms?

The debate on causality recently opened towards pluralism. So much so that Christopher Hitchcock, in his 'How to be a causal pluralist'[1] gives a taxonomy of the different kinds of pluralism advanced in the literature on causality. Hitchcock distinguishes the following versions of pluralism:

1. 'Pluralism about causes', namely the thesis that every event has many causes and depending on the context one focuses on one or other of them.

---

[*] In memory of Federico Stella, unforgettable friend and master of criminal law, epistemology, and compassion, who drew my attention to the context dependence of causality but died too early to comment on this paper.

[1] Hitchcock's paper was presented at the 7th Pittsburgh-Konstanz Colloquium on 'Causation: Historical and Contemporary Perspectives' (Konstanz, May 26-29, 2005) as a comment on my talk 'Plurality in Causality'. Both papers will be published in the volume of the proceedings of that conference. See Campaner and Galavotti Forthcoming and Hitchcock Forthcoming a.

This represents a weak form of pluralism; so weak that, according to Hitchcock, it can be agreed upon by everyone.

2. 'Methodological pluralism', of which Hitchcock distinguishes two versions. According to its 'scientific version' there are many different ways in which one can investigate causal claims and detect causal relationships. For instance, this can be done through observation or controlled experiments, or adopting different modes of investigation.

3. The 'philosophical version' of methodological pluralism claims that causality can be studied from a variety of different theoretical approaches, such as 'regularities, probability, counterfactuals, manipulability relations, processes or mechanisms, and others'.

4. 'Intramural pluralism' is the thesis that a variety of causal concepts can be defined within a single theoretical framework. For instance, Hitchcock mentions 'direct and indirect causes' and 'net and component effects'.[2]

5. 'Hybrid pluralism' results from a combination of methodological and intramural pluralism, holding that there are basic patterns of causal dependence which can be used to define an array of further causal concepts. For example, Pearl's models describe mechanisms (taken in the functional sense) that generate certain patterns of causal dependence, which can give way to manipulations, counterfactuals and probabilistic dependencies.

6. 'Extramural pluralism' is the view that there are various distinct causal notions, like type and token causation, or Salmon's two types of causal accounts based respectively on statistical relevance and causal mechanisms defined in terms of processes. In this connection, Hitchcock claims that the distinction between type and token causation 'conflates a number of other distinctions (including the distinction between net and component effects), and ... once these distinctions are disentangled, one is left with a version of intramural pluralism'.

7. 'Disciplinary pluralism'. According to this version of pluralism different disciplines employ different notions of causality. Hitchcock is convinced that the differences between the uses of causality made within the various branches of science can be accounted for in terms of other kinds of pluralism (methodological or extramural).

8. 'Wittgenstein pluralism'. Hitchcock identifies this with the kind of pluralism embraced by Nancy Cartwright, who claims that there are myriad ways in which causal concepts are used, and the notion of cause is nothing but an abstraction from them. Therefore, various approaches to causation

---

[2] This distinction has been highlighted by Hitchcock in a number of papers, including Hitchcock 2001.

are equally useful, because they only capture part of what is meant by the notion of cause.[3]

9. 'Radical pragmatism'. This is the label attached to van Fraassen's view, according to which causality is radically context dependent, and expresses a relevance relation linking an answer to a why-question. Hitchcock does not regard this as a genuine form of causal pluralism and claims that it can be conflated with extramural pluralism.

Hitchcock's classification is no doubt an elegant and useful philosophical exercise, throwing light on the different causal notions advanced in the literature. As an immediate reaction to Hitchcock's taxonomy, it could be observed that all versions of pluralism he describes share a common trait: they appeal to context in some way or other. In spite of the fact that causal pluralism leads directly to the idea that causality is context dependent, the notion of context itself receives little attention and few authors feel the need to clarify it and to specify in what sense causality is context dependent. An effort in this direction will be made in the following pages, but before embarking on the task let us revisit some of the main theories of causality on the market to see how they relate to context. This will also allow for some further considerations on causal pluralism.

2 Two intuitions

The kind of pluralism heralded here is not easy to locate within Hitchcock's classification. It revolves around the conviction that there are two fundamental intuitions underlying causal attributions, namely the mechanical notion of causation and the manipulative view. In the philosophical literature, such intuitions have inspired a number of approaches, including Wesley Salmon's probabilistic mechanicism and Huw Price's agency theory, which can be taken as the two poles of the debate on causality.

Incidentally, such a dual character of the notion of causality seems to find support from research in cognitive psychology done by Henrik Walter and his team, pointing to two different concepts of causation, one mechanical, referring to some external mechanism that we recognize through observation, and one 'actionist', relating to action intended to accomplish a certain task. In order to corroborate this idea, Walter runs various experiments aimed to show that different areas of the brain are excited when one or other of the two concepts of causation are recognized by the subject, confronted with situations representing either of them[4].

---

[3] See especially Cartwright Forthcoming.
[4] See Walter Forthcoming.

Let us consider Salmon's probabilistic mechanicism and Price's agency theory of causation, and point out how they stand opposed to each other in various respects. Salmon's theory of causality serves to revive the mechanical ideal of explanation coached in probabilistic terms and is inseparable from his theory of explanation. This is divided into two distinct levels. First we have the 'statistical relevance' model of explanation, according to which events are explained by locating them in a network of statistical relations holding between the properties relevant to their occurrence. This is obtained by restricting the reference class to which the explanandum event belongs by progressive inclusion of relevant properties and exclusion ('screening off') of irrelevant ones, to the point where all and only relevant properties are taken into account. The canon yielding the proper (homogeneous) reference class is statistical relevance.[5] At the second level, explanatory power rests on causal processes, defined as spatio-temporal continuous entities able to transmit 'marks' – subsequently substituted by 'conserved quantities'. Causal processes are the building blocks of causal mechanisms, which in turn are the components of the causal structure of the world. Explaining means locating events within the causal structure of the world[6].

The two levels of explanation devised by Salmon correspond to two kinds of causality, namely 'statistical causality', which is defined in terms of statistical relationships and corresponds to what is usually called in the literature 'type causality' (or causality referring to kinds of events), and 'aleatory causality', which is defined in terms of processes, and corresponds to what is usually called 'token causality' (or causality referred to single events)[7]. In Salmon's view statistical causality, which employs notions like relevance and screening off, can be defined in purely statistical terms making use of probability values alone. The same does not hold for aleatory causality, which rests on the notion of causal process. This is not statistical in kind, being rather a theoretical notion (spatio-temporal causal processes are unobservable) making reference to physical properties. For this reason, Salmon characterizes aleatory causality as 'ontic'. Salmon's distinction falls into what Hitchcock labels as 'extramural pluralism', but as a matter of fact pluralism is alien to Salmon's position, which identifies genuine causality with aleatory causality, the sole that can sustain explanation and understanding of phenomena by locating them in the causal structure of the world. Only in the late 90s did Salmon revise his position to cope with various objections raised among others by Hitchcock and James Woodward. He came to regard statistical and aleatory causality as complementary, thereby

---

[5] See Salmon 1971 for details.
[6] Salmon 1984 is where this idea is developed at length.
[7] See Salmon 1990 and other papers included in Salmon 1998.

admitting that the geometrical network provided by processes has to be implemented with information on statistical relevance relations to allow recognition of the properties carrying explanatory power[8].

As a further result of such a revision, Salmon conceded that pragmatic considerations are not alien to the analysis of causation, first of all because this can be done at different levels of abstraction depending on the context, and moreover because they guide the identification of what is to be taken as explanatorily relevant. The following passage, taken from Salmon's last paper on causation, documents this turn:

> The major obstacle to the creation of a fully objective and realistic theory of cause-effect relations is the fact that the instances we tend to select are highly context dependent. ... It seems obvious that the selection of the causal field is guided by pragmatic considerations, and is, therefore, context dependent. ... I conclude that cause-effect statements are almost always – if not always – context dependent (Salmon 2002: 125).

These claims remind us of the first kind of pluralism in Hitchcock's taxonomy, but it should be kept in mind that Salmon never abandoned that ideal of an objective notion of causality and explanation, which inspired his whole production. So much so, that in the same paper he put forward the notion, absent from his earlier production, of *complete causal structure*, standing for the entire causal network in 'any convex chunk of space-time – that is, of the universe' (ibid.: 125). The complete causal structure is deemed objective, for it is 'a fact of nature that exists quite independently of our knowledge or interests' (ibid.: 126); it will never be known in full detail, but it can be approached by approximation, following a 'research strategy' which suggests 'to look at phenomena on a smaller scale when the larger scale view is unsuccessful' (ibid.: 129).

The above passage suggests that Salmon entertained the conviction that one could move in a relatively unproblematic way from a type level analysis to a token level analysis. But it should be added that he had in mind physics as a privileged field of application of his theory; in fact his last contribution to causation ends as follows:

> It seems that my account should hold in the natural sciences – including biology, but not quantum mechanics. I am not confident that it is suitable for psychology and the social sciences. ... My aim has been to examine causality at what might be characterized as the 'deepest metaphysical level'.
> The account that has emerged removes this concept from the field of metaphysics and transports it to physics (ibid.: 131).

---

[8] See Salmon 1997.

Salmon's attempt at developing a theory of causality designed to combine property and token causality within a unified theory of explanation results in a very restricted applicability. This is the price he pays for making the asymmetry of causation depend ultimately on spatio-temporal continuous processes, a notion that is inapplicable in fields like economics, psychology, medicine, and the social sciences in general, which happen to offer the most extensive ground of application of causal concepts. Equally problematic is the notion of homogeneous reference class at the core of his statistical-relevance model.

While Salmon takes an ontic approach to causality and conjugates causality with explanation, Huw Price embraces a pragmatical viewpoint that relates causation to our perspective as agents and does not establish a strong connection between causation and explanation. Price's 'agency' account of causality, which he developed partly in collaboration with Peter Menzies, regards causality as related to the agent's perspective, in the sense that to think of A as a cause of B is to regard A as a potential means for achieving the end B. Causal asymmetry originates in our experience as agents – an idea that Price borrows from the philosophy of Frank Plumpton Ramsey. Causes are seen as potential means, and effects as potential ends.

The problem of spurious causation is deemed to find a natural solution in this approach because the means-end relation, also rooted in the agent's experience, is apt to drive judgment towards asymmetrical correlations rather than to mere statistical correlations, which are usually symmetrical. Price and Menzies' agency theory of causation is formulated in probabilistic terms – the deterministic case being a limiting case of the indeterministic one. Accordingly, the means-end relation on which the theory is grounded is characterized in terms of 'agent probabilities', to be thought of as conditional probabilities,

> assessed from an agent's perspective under the supposition that the antecedent condition is realized *ab initio*, as a free act of the agent concerned. Thus the agent probability that one should ascribe to B conditional on A ... is the probability that B would hold were one to choose to realize A (Menzies and Price 1993: 190)[9].

Price's manipulative view of causality is openly anthropocentric, because causality is taken as 'a manifestation of the fact that causal concepts originate in our experience as agents' (Price 1992a: 501). In order to accept the agency theory one has to regard human beings as actors rather than pure observers. This inspires the label 'perspectivalism' attached by Price to his own viewpoint, which extends beyond causation, to laws, theories and probability. Strictly speaking, Price's approach is not Humean, but instead

---

[9] See also Price 1992b and 1996.

of appealing to non-Humean concepts which are modal or metaphysical in character, it embraces a pragmatist perspective which makes causality depend on the agent's knowledge and beliefs. As observed by Price, looking at causality as perspectival in character does not put it beyond the reach of science, nor does it rule out a realist account of causation. A realist, who wanted to interpret observed correlations as expressions of objective causal relations existing in the world, might still be ready to admit that 'as agents in the world, we are capable of exploiting these relations to further our ends' (Price 1991: 172).

The theory of causation developed by Price provides a general epistemological framework apt to accommodate more specific accounts developed within particular contexts. Therefore, this perspective makes causality intrinsically context dependent. Price's theory obviously has a strong pragmatic flavor, radically different from Salmon's viewpoint, which attaches an ontic import to causation. A further difference lies in the fact that, unlike Salmon, Price does not tie causation to explanation. This brings Price's theory close to a long-standing tradition in econometrics, according to which causation merits consideration independently of explanation, as it allows for manipulation and robust prediction. Price's theory concerns type causation; however, he claims to be confident that the perspectival account can help clarify some aspects of the relationship between type and token causation[10].

Salmon's and Price's theories give flesh and blood to the two basic intuitions about causation, namely the mechanical view, according to which there are causal mechanisms 'out there', which are responsible for the phenomena we experience, on the one hand, and the idea that causation is a feature of our nature of human beings acting in the world, on the other. These theories stand opposed in various respects: the first is ontic, the second anthropocentric; the first conjugates causality with explanation, the second does not; the first relies on an objective notion of probability, namely the frequency interpretation, the second is not explicit on this point, but its reliance on Ramsey's ideas calls for the subjective notion of probability. Furthermore, Salmon's account of causality is specific and meant to cover token causation, but has very restricted applicability; instead Price's view is very general and therefore widely applicable, but it has to be supplemented with more detailed accounts in order to be applied to a specific context.

With respect to the mechanical and manipulative concepts of causation, notions like 'regularity' and 'counterfactual' – the ingredients of David Hume's definition of the 'causal connection' – can be regarded as transversal, in the sense that they find room within both mechanical and manipulat-

---

[10] The problem is discussed in Price 1992b.

ive theories. Equally transversal is the distinction between type and token causation.

Incidentally, it could be added that, after various attempts to banish counterfactuals from his theory of causation and explanation in response to objections raised by Hitchcock and Woodward, Salmon admitted that counterfactual considerations have a role to play within explanation, by virtue of the strong connection between statistical relevance and counterfactual information. However, he turned to what he took as 'relatively unproblematic' counterfactuals supported by well-established statements of statistical correlations, based on observed frequencies[11], rather than to Lewis style counterfactuals in terms of possible worlds. Insofar as Price is concerned, he regards agency theory as a good substitute for the counterfactual theory and argues that the agency theory not only conveys the same sort of counterfactual information conveyed by Lewis' theory, but it does so in a less controversial way, because it does not need any postulate on similarity among possible worlds[12].

3 Other Approaches

The literature offers a number of alternative views of causation, which stand so to speak in between the two we have just considered. Somewhere in the middle could be located the theory developed by Judea Pearl, which has become very influential. Building on the techniques of representing statistical associations by means of graphs, Pearl suggests that causal relationships be represented by means of 'directed acyclic graphs' (DAG), also called Bayesian networks 'to emphasize three aspects: (1) the subjective nature of the input information; (2) the reliance on Bayes' conditioning as the basis of updating information; (3) the distinction between causal and evidential models of reasoning, a distinction that underscores Thomas Bayes' paper of 1763' (Pearl 2000: 14). The causal interpretation attached to such networks results from a combination of the functionalist notion of mechanism and manipulability. Put briefly, causal Bayesian networks are taken to represent ordered structures of variables exhibiting certain stability conditions, which can lead to manipulations. Such a 'mechanism-based conception of interventions' (ibid.: 24) is the cornerstone of a theory of causality that regards the latter as a useful instrument for prediction and intervention. A clear-cut distinction between 'seeing' and 'doing' underlies Pearl's treatment of causation, where the quantities determined through observation are systematically distinguished from those obtained through experiment. This distinc-

---

[11] See Salmon 1997.
[12] See Price 1991 on this point.

tion plays a crucial role in connection with prediction of the results of controlled experiments from observed probabilities, which is a main task of causality.

Pearl also considers the explanatory use of causal models 'to provide an "explanation" or "understanding" of how data are generated' (ibid.: 25), or to convey information on 'how things work' (ibid.: 26). A crucial role is assigned to the stability of causal structures, which should be durable over time and invariant across a variety of situations. Models characterized by such features of robustness allow for predictions and manipulations that are bound to hold for wide ranges of circumstances. So conceived, 'the explanatory account of causation is merely a variant of the manipulative account, albeit one where interventions are dormant' (ibid.). Pearl has recently refined his theory, putting more emphasis on 'actual causes' and explanation. His work in this connection, whose technicalities cannot be recollected here[13], regards causality as intrinsically context dependent, for he makes the whole edifice of causation rest on modeling, which in turn requires various assumptions so strictly linked with context as to justify the claim that 'the choice of model is a subjective one' and 'depends to some extent on what the model is being used for' (Halpern and Pearl 2005: 878). Furthermore, explanation is defined 'relative to the agent's epistemic state' (ibid.: 897).

A manipulative theory of causation intended to avoid the anthropocentric character of Price's has been developed by James Woodward, who defines causation in terms of invariance under a set of interventions. Such a relativized notion of invariance, which he borrows from the literature on econometrics[14], involves an appeal to context. This makes Woodward's notion of causation intrinsically context dependent. A similar character pertains to Woodward's conception of laws, taken as generalizations that are invariant, or stable 'across some sufficiently large and otherwise "suitable" range of changes in conditions and circumstances ("initial conditions")' (Woodward 2002a: 383).

Woodward establishes a strong link between causation and explanation. Based on the above mentioned notion of laws he develops a notion of explanation revolving around the idea that

> to explain an explanandum is to show how changes in it counterfactually depend on changes in the factors cited in the explanans ... The relevant notion of counterfactual dependence (or of answering a what-if-things-had-been-different question) is captured by counterfactuals the antecedents of

---

[13] Recent developments of Pearl's theory are to be found in Halpern and Pearl 2005. Lindley 2002 nicely summarizes Pearl's viewpoint as expressed in Pearl 2000; Lindley's article is followed by a comment on Pearl by N.D. Singpurwalla, and by Pearl's replies.

[14] The econometric approach is discussed in Galavotti and Gambetta 1990 and 1999.

> which have to do with interventions. ... When a generalization relating X and Y is invariant in this way, we may think of it as telling us how to manipulate Y if (perhaps contrary to actual fact) it *were* possible to intervene to change X. In this sense the theory ... embodies a 'manipulationist' conception of explanation (Woodward 2001: 5)[15].

Manipulation is not taken relative to experiments that are actually performed, but rather to hypothetical experiments, that is to potential 'appropriately designed experimental manipulation' (Woodward 2003b: 90). The transposition of causation from agency to manipulability in terms of hypothetical experiments answers the need, deeply felt by Woodward, to contrast the halo of subjectivism surrounding Price's agency theory of causation, judged 'not just wrong but crazy' (ibid.: 109), to embrace a form of 'instrumental realism', taken to imply objectivism, but no ontological commitment.

In the mechanical camp, various theories have been put forward after Salmon's, including that of Peter Machamer, Lindley Darden and Carl Craver, conceived for application in neurobiology and related fields. These authors define mechanisms in terms of both the entities that compose them and the activities they perform. Mechanisms are complex systems organised into a multi-level hierarchical structure, whose distinctive feature is the 'productive continuity' between the various stages characterizing their activity. The components of mechanisms exhibit specific spatio-temporal features, and their productive stages are characterized by certain phases, a given duration, and so on. Explanation of phenomena is obtained by describing by which mechanism they are produced and how[16]. According to Machamer, Darden and Craver, explanation can also be given by means of 'mechanism schemata', namely mechanisms that receive an incomplete description, to be formulated at different levels of abstraction. This introduces a context dependent element into their theory, which is more flexible than Salmon's and looks therefore capable of a wider applicability.

In addition to those outlined above, the literature offers a whole array of theories of causality. For instance, other mechanical theories have been put forward by Phil Dowe, Stuart Glennan and Jim Bogen, while the approach combining functionalism and manipulability has been advocated among others by Clark Glymour, Peter Spirtes and Richard Scheines, and has a long tradition in econometrics. Although some of these accounts are meant for application within some specified field, most of them are advanced with some pretence of generality. They may qualify as pluralistic in one sense or

---

[15] This theory is developed in detail in Woodward 2003a and Hitchcock and Woodward 2003.
[16] See Machamer, Darden and Craver 2000.

the other of Hitchcock's classification, but they are intended to capture the meaning of causality in general.

An exception to this tendency is represented by the work of one of the pioneers of probabilistic causality, namely Patrick Suppes, whose theory is intended to make it applicable to the various contexts where causal speech occurs[17]. Suppes' notion of causality can be formulated both in terms of events and of random variables, and is compatible with different interpretations of probability. Remarkably, no 'ultimate genuine causes' are contemplated within this theory. On the contrary, the notion of cause is strictly linked to the specification of the set of concepts on which a cause is to be defined within a given context. This point, repeatedly stressed by Suppes in his writings, is nicely expressed in the following statement: 'I do think that the insistence on relativizing the analysis of cause to a particular conceptual framework is a point on which to make a stand' (Suppes 1979: 24). This I take to be a genuinely pluralistic attitude, inspired by the conviction that any attempt at working out a notion of causality applicable to every situation in which causal speech occurs is deemed to failure, because different contexts call for a different characterization of it. Suppes' theory of causality, whose pluralistic flavor has made it somewhat unpopular, was conceived as a starting point, from which to move to more detailed accounts to be given within specific contexts. This brings us back to context and to the need, already stressed at the outset, for a deeper analysis of the notion of context itself.

4 The Context Dependence of Causality

Suppes does not analyze this notion in great detail but gives us a hint, by calling attention to a distinction between contexts characterized by extensive experimentation and contexts that are not. He brings out this distinction in the course of a discussion of the problem of passing from type to token causation in the probabilistic case. In spite of the fact that this passage is unwarranted, predictions of individual events based on type kind relations are made every day, for instance by meteorologists. According to Suppes, such inferential procedures depend ultimately on 'judgment as to how the knowledge one has is used and assessed' (Suppes 1993 [1984]: 130). If such knowledge includes widely accepted laws backed by extensive scientific experimentation, the shift from type to tokens will be more warranted, but there will always be additional elements to be evaluated case by case. If the information available does not stand on a strong experimental basis, addi-

---

[17] See Suppes 1970.

tional care will be required. Other elements, such as the qualitative complexity and diversity of cases under investigation, also matter.

A few more words on the distinction between type and token causation seem to be in place. Its importance is widely recognized by statisticians, starting with Irving John Good:[18] another pioneer of probabilistic causality like Suppes. On the contrary, the impact of this distinction is by and large underestimated by philosophers. The distinction intertwines with the dichotomy between explanation and prediction, because explanation has to do with token causation, while prediction has often to do with type causation. As a matter of fact, predictions can also be made on the basis of (symmetrical) statistical correlations. Again, whether predictions need to be based on correlations or on more robust relations, such as causal relations, can only depend on the context, and on the use to which predictions are put in a given context. Predictions involving manipulation, such as political intervention in the case of economics, or various treatments in the case of medicine, are usually based on causal relations.

As we saw, Salmon regards the shift between type and token as unproblematic, provided that causal processes and mechanisms can be identified. However, as admitted by Salmon himself, this does not seem possible except in some restricted areas of physics, if at all. The idea that knowledge of mechanisms allows for prediction as well as explanation of phenomena is rooted in Laplacean determinism, and is greatly intuitive. Though fascinating, Salmon's extension of this idea to the probabilistic case is highly problematic, because in most fields one lacks widely accepted nomological knowledge that would allow identification of indeterministic mechanisms.

The alternative approach suggested by Hitchcock and Woodward, which defines explanation in terms of stability and links it to manipulability, is much more flexible, but it is not completely clear how it can deal with token causality. Whether an explanation conforming to the requirements imposed by Hitchcock and Woodward is judged satisfactory or not depends crucially on the context in which it is produced. To take an example discussed by Woodward, it seems doubtful that everyone would be satisfied with saying that a certain patient P recovered from breast cancer because she was given chemotherapy, and it is known that 'for *some* individuals, recovery counterfactually depends on some possible intervention that realizes A' (Woodward 2002b: 317) where 'A' stands for the administration of chemotherapy. Maybe the patient will be satisfied with this explanation, but a medical team carrying out research on cancer will want to know more about the recovery of P, to see what other factors were present and contributed to the success of her treatment. Let us take the case of a worker who,

---

[18] See Good 1961-62 and 1983.

after being exposed to a certain substance, say asbestos, for a long period of time developed lung cancer. Would it be enough to establish a causal relation between these two facts to say that lung cancer in *some* cases depends counterfactually on exposure to asbestos? There is no doubt that an explanatory account that does not hold for tokens would be considered unsatisfactory in a criminal trial[19]. One might add that knowing that certain relationships are stable and can lead to successful (or safe) interventions does not automatically involve explanation (and understanding) of what happened in a particular case, unless some additional knowledge on the mechanism at work is available.

Undeniably, one is often faced with statistical relations that are not backed by widely accepted theoretical knowledge. Under certain conditions of robustness (like stability) such relations can be given a causal interpretation and support manipulations and predictions, supported by higher or lower degrees of probability. But explanation is quite another matter: to explain a particular event on the basis of probabilistic relations one would have to rely on knowledge of (probabilistic) mechanisms, but these are mostly unknown. This calls attention to another feature that can be taken to characterize context. As suggested by Elliott Sober[20], contexts where causal relations are derived from theories should be distinguished from those where such knowledge is not available, and causal relations are obtained by adopting techniques of various kinds. The nature of such techniques is a further element entering in the specification of causal relations, and so is the nature of the data to which they are applied. Especially relevant is whether such data are obtained by observation or experimentation, which brings us back to Suppes' hint.

The notion of context is at the core of Bas van Fraassen's pragmatics of explanation, according to which an explanation is an answer to a why-question, and is a three-term relation between the person who poses the question, the person who answers, and the context[21]. Van Fraassen's position is no doubt a form of pluralism, and is in fact contemplated by Hitchcock's taxonomy. However, it does not have much to do with causality, which is certainly not van Fraassen's primary interest, which is confined to explanation. It has the merit of providing a conceptual framework apt to support the claim that the same explanatory account can be satisfactory within a certain context and unsatisfactory within another. From the point of view of van Fraassen's pragmatics one can also make sense of the claim that causal analysis can be conducted at different levels of abstraction, de-

---

[19] In Italy this kind of risk crimes fall under criminal law.
[20] See Sober 1985 and 1988.
[21] See van Fraassen 1980.

pending on the context, albeit no strict link between explanation and causality is established in his viewpoint, as we already remarked.

Peter Menzies recently addressed the context dependence of causality, by developing a general conceptual framework for a context sensitive notion of causal dependence. Menzies focusses on 'systems', conceived as sets of objects that are internally organized in a distinctive way, and defines a 'kind of system' as 'a set of particular systems sharing the same intrinsic properties and relations (state variables) whose evolution over time conforms to certain laws' (Menzies 2004: 156). Context is then defined in terms of kinds of systems, and causality is accounted for in terms of 'difference making', by means of a notion of counterfactual that is itself context sensitive, because the similarity condition is not defined in terms of possible worlds, but in terms of alternative courses of development of systems. Menzies highlights important aspects of the context dependence of causality. However, the notion of law, which plays a crucial role in his account, is beset with difficulties and there is a tendency to take it too as context dependent.[22]

The same applies to the theory of explanation of Halpern and Pearl, which involves 'reference to the physical laws underlying the connection between the cause and the effect' (Halpern and Pearl 2005: 897). Such a theory, by the way, has a distinctive pluralistic flavor.

5 More Pluralism

My leaning towards pluralism in causality dates back a long time, and has been bolstered by the growing literature on causation, despite the more or less explicitly 'monistic' character of most theories on the market.[23] The kind of pluralism I favor is a combination of the mechanical and manipulative theories, aware of the intrinsic context dependence of causal attributions.

In a recent paper, Hitchcock rightly observed that the notion of causality is more useful in the social sciences than in highly theoretical sciences like physics.[24] To be sure, it is precisely the use made of causality within the so-called special sciences that strongly suggests a pluralistic attitude. Medicine, for instance, is a field where causal talk frequently arises. As a case study, Raffaella Campaner and I have considered DBS (deep brain stimulation), a treatment of Parkinson's disease,[25] coming to the conclusion that

---

[22] See, for instance, the debate on *ceteris paribus* laws in Earman, Glymour and Mitchell, eds. 2002.
[23] See Galavotti 1990, 1991, 1999, 2001 and Campaner and Galavotti Forthcoming.
[24] See Hitchcock Forthcoming b.
[25] See Campaner and Galavotti Forthcoming.

causal analysis conducted in this case makes use of manipulative as well as mechanical causation, and moreover both Salmon's notion of causal process and the notion of mechanism developed by Machamer, Darden and Craver have a role to play. Furthermore, causal attributions of the type kind intertwine with causal attributions of the token kind. Similarly, data are sometimes referred to individuals and at other times to the population.

Another discipline making extensive use of causal notions is econometrics, where causality is usually defined with reference to manipulability, but a functionalist notion of mechanism is also crucial. The problem of aggregation arising within econometrics shows how type and token causation, or the analysis conducted at the macroeconomic and microeconomic levels, should not be conflated, but seen as complementary.[26]

Criminal trial offers a peculiar context for the application of causality. In a criminal trial what matters are singular causal attributions *ex post*. Information on probabilistic correlations detected at the population level (*ex ante*) is of little use, because of the impossibility, in most cases, of passing from information regarding the population to the single case. To circumvent this difficulty and comply with the standard of proof of 'beyond any reasonable doubt', the requirement that the probability is close to 1 is generally adopted. Lower values of probability might be judged satisfactory and in accordance with this principle, provided that detailed information on the mechanism (causal process, causal chain) leading to the crime under trial could be provided, but this is hardly ever the case. One should notice that in the context of criminal trial it is crucial that a complete description of the event (crime) under consideration *ex post* is produced.

Things are different with apportioning moral responsibility. In this case, a description of the event *ex post* does not suffice. Take the well known example of the man traveling in the desert with a bottle that somebody filled with poisoned water, who dies of thirst because someone else made a hole in the bottle. There seems to be little doubt that both men, the one who poisoned the water and the one who made the hole in the bottle, are morally responsible for attempting to kill the victim, but only the one who made the hole is criminally responsible, given that the victim died of thirst.

The case of civil trial is still different. In this case, information of the type kind, for instance information related to risk assessment, matters, and is usually taken into account, depending on the probability attached to a given event (greater or less than 50%). It is remarkable that in legal contexts the representation of causal relations by means of Bayesian nets plays a

---

[26] See Galavotti and Gambetta 1999.

prominent role, especially in connection with the evaluation of the relationships between various pieces of evidence.

To be sure, I am not embracing the kind of pluralism Hitchcock labeled 'disciplinary pluralism'. I am rather holding that the assumptions underlying causal attributions and the restrictions imposed upon them within various fields should be taken into account. Similarly, the aims to which causal discourse is put within a given context should be considered, especially in connection with explanation, prediction, and manipulation. The nature of the information available is also relevant: in particular, one should distinguish between data obtained through direct or indirect observation and data obtained through experimentation.

An openly pluralistic standpoint was recently taken by Stathis Psillos, with the end in view of combining the mechanical notion of causation with the counterfactual account. Through a detailed examination of some theories of causation, including those of Woodward and of Machamer, Darden and Craver, Psillos is led to conclude that the counterfactual account of causation is more fundamental than the mechanical one, because the latter needs the former. In fact 'establishing the causal status of each part of a mechanism would require finding out (or estimating) its causal effect. The best way to do this is by non-mechanistic means, and in particular by means of the counterfactual approach' (Psillos 2004: 315). The counterfactual approach favored by Psillos is that developed by Donald Rubin, Paul Holland and other statisticians, also known as the Potential-Response model of causal inference.

The combination of mechanicism and manipulability that I have been advocating resembles Psillos' pluralism, but unlike Psillos I do not regard counterfactuals as the most fundamental ingredient of causality. An interesting and original feature of Psillos' account lies with the fact that he adopts a notion of counterfactual rooted in statistical practice. However, the approach developed by Rubin and others is not the only theory of causal inference on the market, as Psillos is fully aware. According to the alternative theory developed by Philip Dawid, causal inference can be performed without making use of counterfactuals.[27] Incidentally, Dawid points out that counterfactuals have to do with token causality, not so much with type causality, a point overlooked by philosophical theories of causality – as remarked earlier. Furthermore, he argues that counterfactuals should not be taken as primitive with respect to modeling; quite on the contrary 'it is counterfactuals that are grounded in, and take their meaning from, the model' (Dawid 2001: 66). Dawid also insists on the context dependence of causality and calls attention to the necessity to make explicit mention of the

---

[27] See Dawid 2001 and Forthcoming.

assumptions underlying the choice of whatever model and method is adopted for performing causal analysis.

6 Conclusion

In view of the preceding remarks, I find it difficult to disagree with Suppes' claim that the notion of causality, especially if taken in a probabilistic sense, is deeply context dependent. It seems that instead of giving a univocal definition of causality, one should start from a careful consideration of the context surrounding causal analysis, and proceed from there to a characterization of causal relations within a given context.

It is undeniable that both manipulability and mechanisms have to do with causality, and play a role within causal discourse. Rephrasing Psillos' claim that '*both* mechanisms and counterfactuals are helpful', I would say that '*both* mechanisms and manipulability are helpful'. As I argued elsewhere,[28] the mechanical notion of causation can play a useful heuristic role for causal analysis. In a similar vein, Psillos gives some hints about the usefulness of mechanisms, claiming that they can 'help deal with the endogeneity problem' (Psillos 2004: 316), and can guide the search for common causes. Manipulability, on the other hand, is an essential ingredient of statistical analysis aimed to establish causal relations, based on robustness properties like stability.

Let me conclude with one suggestion and one parallel. The suggestion is that causal pluralism can find a natural framework in the agency theory advocated by Price; the parallel is with the subjective notion of probability. While regarding probability as an ingredient of our knowledge, the subjective theory of probability draws a line between its definition and its evaluation, in which connection various methods are admitted, insofar as they satisfy the requirement of coherence. Similarly, the idea that causality is rooted in our perspective as agents is compatible with a variety of ways of characterizing causal relations, depending on the context.

References

Campaner, R. and Galavotti, M. C. Forthcoming. Plurality in Causality. *Causation: Historical and Contemporary Perspectives*, eds. P. Machamer and G. Wolters. Pittsburgh: University of Pittsburgh Press.

Cartwright, N. Forthcoming. *Hunting Causes and Using Them: Approaches in Philosophy and Economics*. Cambridge: Cambridge University Press.

---

[28] See Galavotti 1999 and 2001.

Dawid, P. 2001. Causal Inference without Counterfactuals. *Foundations of Bayesianism*, eds. D. Corfield and J. Williamson, 37-74. Dordrecht: Kluwer.

Dawid, P. Forthcoming. Counterfactuals, Hypotheticals and Potential Responses: A Philosophical Examination of Statistical Causality. *Causality and Probability in the Sciences*, eds. F. Russo and J. Williamson. London: College Publications.

Earman, J., Glymour, C. and Mitchell, S. (eds.) 2002. *Ceteris Paribus Laws. Erkenntnis* 57 (3).

Galavotti, M.C. 1990. Explanation and Causality: Some Suggestions from Econometrics. *Topoi* 9: 161-69.

Galavotti, M.C. 1991. Probability and Causality. *Atti del Congresso 'Nuovi problemi della logica e della filosofia della scienza'* (Viareggio, 8-13/1/1990), vol. I: *Filosofia della scienza e fondamenti della probabilità e della statistica*, eds. M.C. Galavotti and D. Costantini, 69-82. Bologna: CLUEB. Also in Galavotti, M.C. 2002. *Probabilità, induzione, metodo statistico*, 149-62. Bologna: CLUEB.

Galavotti, M.C. 1999. Wesley Salmon on Explanation, Probability and Rationality. *Experience, Reality and Scientific Explanation*, eds. M.C. Galavotti and A. Pagnini, 39-54. Dordrecht-Boston: Kluwer.

Galavotti, M.C. 2001. Causality, Mechanisms and Manipulation. *Stochastic Causality*, eds. M.C. Galavotti, P. Suppes and D. Costantini, 1-13. Stanford: CSLI Publications.

Galavotti, M.C. and Gambetta, G. 1990. Causality and Exogeneity in Econometric Models. *Statistics in Science. The Foundations of Statistical Methods in Biology, Physics and Economics*, eds. R. Cooke and D. Costantini, 27-40. Dordrecht-Boston: Kluwer.

Galavotti, M.C. and Gambetta, G. 1999. Theory and Observation in Econometric Models: a Constructivist Approach. *Incommensurability and Translation*, eds. R. Rossini Favretti, G. Sandri and R. Scazzieri, 339-49. Cheltenham/Northampton: Edward Elgar.

Good, I.J. 1961-62. A Causal Calculus, Part I and II. *British Journal for the Philosophy of Science* 11: 305-18; 12: 43-51; *Errata and Corrigenda* 13: 88.

Good, I.J. 1983. *Good Thinking: The Foundations of Probability and its Applications*. Minneapolis: University of Minnesota Press.

Halpern, J. and Pearl, J. 2005. Causes and Explanations: A Structural-Model Approach. Part I: Causes. Part II: Explanations. *British Journal for the Philosophy of Science* 56: 843-87; 889-911.

Hitchcock, C. 2001. A Tale of Two Effects. *The Philosophical Review* 110: 361-96.

Hitchcock, C. Forthcoming a. How to be a Causal Pluralist, *Causation: Historical and Contemporary Perspectives*, eds. P. Machamer and G. Wolters. Pittsburgh: University of Pittsburgh Press.

Hitchcock, C. Forthcoming b. What Russell Got Right. *Causation, Physics and the Constitution of Reality. Russell's Republic Revisited*, eds. H. Price and R. Corry. Oxford: Oxford University Press.

Hitchcock, C. and Woodward J. 2003. Explanatory Generalizations: Part I: A Counterfactual Account; Part II: Plumbing Explanatory Depth. *Nous* 37(1): 1-24, (2): 181-99.

Lindley, D. 2002. Seeing and Doing: the Concept of Causation. *International Statistical Review* 70: 191-97.

Machamer, P., Darden, L. and Craver, C. 2000. Thinking about Mechanisms. *Philosophy of Science* 67: 1-25.

Menzies, P. 2004. Difference-making in Context. *Causation and Counterfactuals*, eds. J. Collins, N. Hall and L.A. Paul, 139-80. Cambridge, MA: MIT Press.

Menzies, P. and Price, H. 1993. Causation as a Secondary Quality. *British Journal for the Philosophy of Science* 44: 187-203.

Pearl, J. 2000. *Causality. Models, Reasoning, and Inference*. Cambridge: Cambridge University Press.

Price, H. 1991. Agency and Probabilistic Causality. *British Journal for the Philosophy of Science* 42: 157-76.

Price, H. 1992a. Agency and Causal Asymmetry. *Mind* 101: 501-20.

Price, H. 1992b. The Direction of Causation: Ramsey's Ultimate Contingency. *PSA 1992*, vol. 2, eds. D. Hull, M. Forbes and K. Okruhlik, 253-67. East Lansing: Philosophy of Science Association.

Price, H. 1996. *Time's Arrow and Archimedes' Point*. New York/Oxford: Oxford University Press.

Psillos, S. 2004. A Glimpse of the *Secret Connexion*: Harmonizing Mechanisms with Counterfactuals. *Perspectives on Science* 12: 288-319.

Salmon W.C. 1971. Statistical Explanation. *Statistical Explanation and Statistical Relevance*, eds. W.C. Salmon, R. Jeffrey and J.G. Greeno, 29-87. Pittsburgh: University of Pittsburgh Press.

Salmon, W.C. 1984. *Scientific Explanation and the Causal Structure of the World*. Princeton: Princeton University Press.

Salmon, W.C. 1990. Causal Propensities: Statistical Causality vs. Aleatory Causality. *Topoi* 9: 95-100. Also in Salmon 1998, 200-7.

Salmon, W.C. 1997. A Reply to Two Critiques. *Philosophy of Science* 64: 461-77.

Salmon, W.C. 1998. *Causality and Explanation*. New York, Oxford: Oxford University Press.

Salmon, W.C. 2002. A Realistic Account of Causation. *The Problem of Realism*, ed. M. Marsonet, 106-34. Ashgate: Aldershot.

Sober, E. 1985. Two Concepts of Cause. *PSA 1984*, vol. 2, eds. P. Asquith and P. Kitcher, 405-24. East Lansing: Philosophy of Science Association.

Sober, E. 1988. Apportioning Causal Responsibility. *The Journal of Philosophy* 85: 303-18.

Suppes, P. 1970. *A Probabilistic Theory of Causality*. Amsterdam: North Holland.

Suppes, P. 1979. Self-profile. *Patrick Suppes,* ed. R. Bogdan, 3-56. Dordrecht: Reidel.

Suppes, P. 1984. Conflicting Intuitions about Causality. *Causation and Causal Theories.* eds. P. French, T. Yuehling, and H. Wettstein, *Midwestern Studies in Philosophy* IX: 158-68. Also in Suppes, P. 2003. *Models and Methods in the Philosophy of Science: Selected Essays*, 121-140. Dordrecht-Boston: Kluwer.

van Fraassen, B. 1980. *The Scientific Image.* Oxford: Oxford University Press.

Walter, H. Forthcoming. Mental Causation in Cognitive Neuroscience. *Causation: Historical and Contemporary Perspectives,* eds. P. Machamer and G. Wolters. Pittsburgh: University of Pittsburgh Press.

Woodward, J. 2001. Law and Explanation in Biology: Invariance is the Kind of Stability that Matters. *Philosophy of Science* 68: 1-20.

Woodward, J. 2002a. Review of Ronald Giere's *Science without Laws. Philosophy of Science* 69: 379-84.

Woodward, J. 2002b. There is No Such Thing as a *Ceteris Paribus* Law. *Erkenntnis* 57: 303-28.

Woodward, J. 2003a. *Making Things Happen.* New York/Oxford: Oxford University Press.

Woodward, J. 2003b. Experimentation, Causal Inference, and Instrumental Realism. *The Philosophy of Scientific Experimentation,* ed. H. Radder, 87-118. Pittsburgh: The University of Pittsburgh Press.

12

Causal Medical Reasoning: Therapies and Pre-emption

RAFFAELLA CAMPANER

This paper tackles some very specific aspects of the debate on causation, no doubt one of the most fertile and diversified discussions in contemporary philosophy of science. After sketchily recalling the main features of the counterfactual approach, I focus on the notion of pre-emption and its implications. The paper aims to show how such a notion can help us grasp some aspects of causal medical reasoning as implemented in certain therapeutic situations.

1 Counterfactual Causation and Pre-emption

An increasingly broad range of philosophical theories try to capture our multi-faceted 'conflicting'[1] intuitions about causality, and/or scientific use of the notion of cause. Our interest in causation often has a practical, or 'manipulative',[2] slant: we want to know what causes an event in order to bring about, or prevent, a similar event at other times. As Tim Maudlin states, 'causal claims are therefore deeply implicated with the sorts of future subjunctives used in practical deliberation: if we should do X (which we might or might not, for all we now know) then the result would be Y', and 'the future subjunctive is a close cousin to the counterfactual conditional' (Maudlin 2004: 419).[3]

---

[1] See Suppes 1984.

[2] See, for example, Price 1991 and 1992; Menzies and Price 1993; Woodward 2003; Gillies 2005.

[3] Maudlin is, in any case, strongly against any counterfactual approach to causation. He thinks that 'causation is not to be analyzed in terms of counterfactual dependency at all, no matter how many equants and epicycles are appended to the original rough draft' (ibid.: 420), and that

A largely successful approach to causation sees counterfactual dependence as the key to causation. According to Lewis' original counterfactual analysis – by large the most famous version of this kind of approach –, C causes E if and only if C and E are distinct events, they both occur, and if C had not occurred, E would not have occurred either.[4] If we consider the possible chain of intermediate events, we can more precisely claim that: C causes E if and only if

> 'C and E are distinct, they both occur and there is a (possibly empty) set of events $[D_1, D_2, ..., D_n]$ such that if C had not occurred, D_1 would have not occurred, and if D_1 had not occurred, D_2 would have not occurred, ..., and if D_n had not occurred, E would have not occurred' (Collins, Hall and Paul 2004: 16).

The core intuition is simple, the analysis attractive, and it has given rise to a profusion of ideas, especially in the last decade.

However, a number of examples have proved resistant to counterfactual analysis, and have led to the introduction of further notions aimed at revising the original approach. The notion of *pre-emption*, in particular, has been introduced to indicate cases in which C causes E, but E would have occurred even if C had not, because it would have been brought about by some alternative cause, C_1. One of the most frequent examples in the literature in this respect is that of Billy and Suzy both throwing a rock at a window. Each throw would be enough, by itself, to break the window, but Suzy's rock gets there first, and it is therefore *her* throw, and not Billy's, that shatters the window. Nevertheless, had not Suzy's throw shattered the window, Billy's would have done so: it is not the case that, had Suzy not thrown the rock, the window would have not broken. In other words, pre-emption highlights the existence of a sort of 'backup process', or several 'backup processes', that may take the place of the causal production that actually occurs. The pre-empted cause is still on its way when the pre-empting one brings about its effect, and runs into completion only after the latter has been produced. As Jonathan Schaffer puts it, pre-emption reveals that

> simple counterfactual dependence is *not necessary* for causation, because in evaluating the counterfactual's implications of C's not occurring, we hold the presence of the backup fixed, and so still get E (Schaffer 2000: 176).

'the counterfactual approach has had a good long run, and it has not provided simple and convincing responses to the problem cases it has faced' (ibid.: 442).

[4] I do not introduce here any specific theory of eventhood or characterization of the identity conditions of events, but simply take the notion of event in its intuitive and ordinary sense, as something which occurs. For a critical survey of some positions in the complex debate on such a notion, see for example Paul 2004.

Another special kind of redundant causation is given by cases of *trumping*, in which the alternative, excluded or 'trumped' cause, 'could have brought about the effect at the *very same time*, and with the very same properties as [the trumping cause] did' (Paul 2004: 215). To mention here too an example from the literature, let us take a sergeant and a major shouting an order to their platoon at the same time, and the soldiers obeying. Since soldiers have to obey the highest in rank, in this case they do so because they are responding to the major's order, not to the sergeant's: the former *trumps* the latter. Nevertheless, had the major kept silent and only the sergeant had shouted his order, the soldiers would have obeyed it. Unlike standard pre-empted processes, trumped processes do run their full course: both orders reach the soldiers at the same time.[5] Whereas the effects of the pre-empted cause would usually have been slightly different from the actual effect of the pre-empting one (e.g., they would have occurred a little later), in cases of trumping, had the trumped cause occurred, the effect would have been brought about in the same time and manner.

Problems pointed out by recent analyses of pre-emption and trumping have highlighted the need for a more sophisticated treatment of causation. Amongst the various attempts to refine the relation of counterfactual dependence on behalf of the defenders of the counterfactual approach, Lewis introduced the notion of *influence*.[6] Seeing that confining dependence to *whether* an effect occurs *if* the cause occurs is too restrictive, Lewis suggests that causation should be defined in terms of *a pattern of dependencies* between events. Relevant events to be considered in assessing a causal relation are

> alterations of the events for which the causal relation is being evaluated. ... The alterations are used to help us represent different ways C and E could have occurred. ... Under Lewis's account, an event C influences an event E if and only if there is a substantial range $C_1, C_2, C_3, \ldots$ and $E_1, E_2, E_3, \ldots$ of not-too-distant alterations of C and E such that if C_1 had occurred, then E_1 would have occurred, and if C_2 had occurred E_2 would have occurred, and so on. In this way we check to see if whether, when and how E occurs depends on whether, when and how C occurs. If there is a sufficiently large range of direct dependencies between alterations of E and C, then C influences E, and so C causes E (Paul 2004: 215-216).[7]

---

[5] On this, see Schaffer 2000 and Ramachandran 1997.

[6] See Lewis 2000.

[7] Let us take an alteration of an event to be 'an actualized or unactualized event that occurs at a slightly different time or in a slightly different manner from the given event' (Menzies 2004: 146). For a discussion on the notion of alteration of an event, see Lewis 2000. Amongst other attempts to solve problems raised by pre-emption, let us just mention here Peter Menzies' con-

This approach embraces a number of ways in which the effect can depend on its cause: instead of adopting a notion of just whether-whether dependence, the idea is that we conceive of causal influence as being a matter of *whether*, *when* and *how* something happens depends on *whether*, *when* and *how* something else does. According to this new theory of causal influence, had the cause been different *in some respect*, the effect would also have been different *in some respect*: we can count C as a cause of E if 'there is a suitable pattern of counterfactual dependence between various different ways C or something like it might have occurred and correspondingly ways in which E or something like it might have occurred' (Hall 2004: 237).

I will not go further into recent refinements of the counterfactual view, but will rather show in the following sections how considerations on preemption can apply to situations considered in the sciences. To such a purpose, two examples from clinical medicine are presented.

2 Two Medical Cases
2.1 HIV and Anti-AIDS Therapies

'... The anatomy of a clinical decision is a complicated interplay of several different modes of reasoning and inquiry' (Pellegrino 1983: 164), therefore my aim is not to reconstruct a complete model of standard clinical reasoning, but just to indicate how some of the concepts emerging in the latest literature on causation can be analyzed in the context of some medical therapies. Albert, Munson and Resnik claim that

> the ways in which the good clinician acquires, evaluates, and employs information to reach conclusions about diagnoses and treatments seem almost inexplicable, but in fact the processes involve intellectual methods that can be explicitly stated. ... Processes of actual clinical reasoning begin with the evaluation of the patient, move to establishing a diagnosis, and end with decisions about managing the patient's illness (Albert, Munson and Resnik 1988: 3).

Clinical reasoning and decision-making take place within a dense conceptual matrix. Study-cases are at the centre of the web, and they can help us understand how clinicians reason when they reason well and successfully. Nowadays two of the major topics in the headlines are studies on AIDS and cancer, and these are the cases I shall address. After a sketchy account of the bio-chemical processes involved in these diseases, I will outline some fundamental features of the therapies most commonly used to combat them.

As we all know, AIDS is one of the largest pandemics in the history of modern medicine. It was in 1981 that clinical reports described a new ma-

---

tinuous processes (1989); Michael McDermott's minimal counterfactual sufficiency (1995); Mural Ramachandran's minimal-dependence sets (1997).

lignant syndrome which could not be traced back to any known disease and which appeared to affect the immune system. It was clear that its pathogenic agent was present in blood, plasma and seminal fluid and that it was transmitted by means of sexual contact or contamination with infected blood. It was initially labelled 'GRID', namely 'gay-related immune deficiency', and in 1982 it was officially defined 'Syndrome of Acquired Immune Deficiency'. During the Eighties the mechanism by which HIV destroys the immune system was gradually elucidated, and although the viral theory is not the only one devised to account for AIDS it is still the most widely accepted.[8] The morphological structure of HIV particles comprises a nucleus, enveloped by a lipoprotein capsid, containing two identical strands of RNA. The viral particle also contains all the enzymes necessary for its replication: reverse transcriptase (RT), integrase (p32) and protease (p11). The virus's favored target is the T4 lymphocyte, damage to which in the immune system is responsible for the destruction of immune defenses encountered in patients with AIDS. In extremely simplified terms, HIV function is outlined in Figure 1 and the numeration present therein. HIV specifically recognizes protein CD4, present on about the 60% of T lymphocytes, which interacts with the viral protein gp120 to allow another viral protein (gp41) to penetrate the double lipid layer of the cell under attack (so-called 'host-cell'). That is how the free virus (1) and the host-cell bind together (2). The binding occurs because of the virus's nature: being a parasitic organism, it needs to bind to a host-cell in order to replicate. In the 'binding and fusion' phase, the virus binds to the cell at the level of external receptors, by virtue of a specific link between the proteins situated on the virus surface and the proteins which play the role of receptors on the surface of T-cells.[9]

---

[8] In 1984 a new retrovirus, HIV-1, was isolated and recognized as the cause of AIDS; in 1986 a second kind of HIV, called HIV-2, was isolated. HIV-1 is a retrovirus and belongs to the family of lentiviruses. Infections with lentiviruses typically show a chronic course of disease, a long period of asymptomatic latency, persistent viral replication and involvement of the central nervous system. The actual immune deficiency may be less severe in individuals infected by HIV-2.

[9] Proteins in the virus' membrane (gp120 and gp41) are strongly attracted by receptors CD4, CCR5 and CXR4, which are situated on the external surface of immune T cells and normally allow the communication between cells and stimulate specific responses of the body to many common infections.

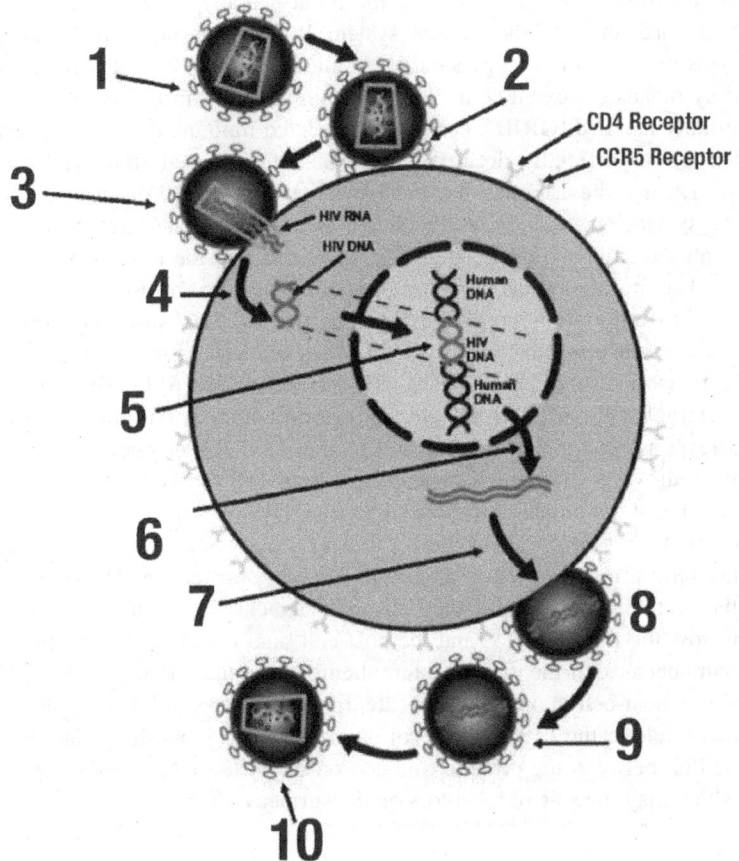

Figure 1
1: Free Virus – 2: **Binding and Fusion**: Virus binds to cell at two receptor sites – 3: **Infection**: Virus penetrates cell. Contents emptied into cell – 4: **Reverse transcription**: Single strands of viral RNA are converted into double-stranded DNA by the reverse transcriptase enzyme – 5: **Integration**: Viral DNA is combined with the cell's own DNA by the integrase enzyme – 6: **Transcription**: When the infected cell divides, the viral DNA is 'read' and long chains of proteins are made – 7: **Assembly**: Sets of viral protein chains come together – 8: **Budding**: Immature virus pushes out of the cell, taking some cell membrane with it – 9: Immature virus breaks free of the infected cell – 10: **Maturation**: Protein chains in the new viral particle are cut by the protease enzyme into individual proteins that combine to make a working virus.

Once bound to the host-cell, HIV injects its genetic material, penetrates the host-cell and infects it (3). This step allows the virus to replicate. Genetic information is contained in the RNA strands protected by the nucleocapsid. The nucleocapsid is partially dissolved and the single strands of viral RNA are converted into DNA strands by the 'reverse transcriptase' enzyme (4). This process is called 'reverse transcription': the reverse transcription enzyme exploits the nucleotides in the host-cell cytoplasm (i.e., a constitutive element of its DNA) to transform RNA into a copy of DNA. In phase (5), viral DNA completely integrates with the genetic material of the human cell: viral DNA moves towards the host-cell nucleus, and then penetrates the cell's DNA thanks to another viral enzyme, called 'integrase'. By this mechanism, the HIV genetic material now contained in the host-cell nucleus will make the host-cell build up new viral molecules whenever it tries to build up new proteins. When the infected cell divides to replicate, DNA separates into two complementary strands of messenger-RNA (mRNA), which at this point also contain the instructions for the constitution of new viral material (namely, protease, reverse transcription, integrase, structural proteins, etc.). Thus, when the host-cell replicates, long chains of proteins are formed (6), and then combine (7). The new viral material moves toward the cell wall and pushes against it to get out (8). Once it is independent from the cell which it has exploited to replicate (9), HIV matures (10): the long protein chains of the new viral particle are cut by the enzyme 'protease' into shorter sequences, thus forming the material necessary for the virus' activity (i.e. enzymes). During this cycle, a huge number (up to some millions) of new viral cells originate, whereas host-cells are destroyed. Hence, the immune system is severely damaged and various infections follow. Clinicians usually speak of AIDS when CD4 cells number fewer than 200 per mm^3 of blood, while a normal, healthy person has an average 1000 CD4 per mm^3 of blood. The most common consequences of HIV include serious weight loss and severe infections of the intestines, brain and eyes.

Therapies aim to exploit the way in which the virus replicates to reduce its effects on the immune system. No resolutive treatment has been developed so far. At the moment, the main purpose of the most commonly used antiviral therapies is to prolong patients' lives, reducing side-effects as much as possible. The aspect which interests us most here is that different therapeutic interventions are normally adopted at the same time and targeted at different stages of the viral life-cycle. In principle, each step of viral replication could be the target of some medical substance. The main therapeutic techniques discovered so far can act:
– at the level of cell-receptors (2): there is an attempt to prevent the virus from binding with the host-cell by giving it a 'fake target'. The pharmaceutical substances which work in this way, called 'entrance inhibitors', are still largely under experimentation and function in two ways:

• they intervene on the host-cell receptors, mainly by means of some synthetic receptor-decoys, which bind with the cell receptors and modify them;

• they can intervene on the virus capsid. Some drugs, for example, use a substance known as T-20, which binds to a portion of gp41 and prevents HIV from binding to the potential host-cell.

– at level (3): the activity of the viral RNA is stopped at the point in which it is leaving the virus and entering the human cell. This is pursued by making the viral RNA combine with a complementary synthetic sequence ('chimera').

– at level (4): reverse transcriptase is inhibited. In different ways, a number of drugs prevent RNA from transforming into a double helix of DNA.

– at level (5): HIV-integrase is inhibited, so that viral DNA does not enter the host-cell nucleus and hence does not integrate with its DNA.

– at levels (6) and (7): some substances still under experimentation aim at blocking transcription.

– at level (8): the virus is prevented from leaving the host-cell.

– at levels (9) and (10): HIV-protease, responsible for transforming the virus from its inactive to its mature and active form, is inhibited. Various drugs bind to HIV protease and block its catalytic activity.

All the therapeutic steps listed only halt disease development temporarily: the virus action is significantly slowed down and controlled, but its presence is not completely eliminated. Treatment is particularly difficult for various reasons: replication must be avoided in an extremely high number of viruses; an extremely large number of variables are at play in the organism; viruses modify very quickly in time, and hence therapies constantly need to hit slightly different targets, and drug resistance is developed on behalf of the virus; clinical treatment is often compromised by poor compliance of the patient, who does not respect the strict schedule for the drug intake. For these reasons, the standard procedure promotes various therapeutic interventions *at the same time*. Drugs are prescribed in the form of a cocktail, so that several (usually three or four) concomitant pharmacological strategies are implemented.[10] The key-idea is that an intervention at level (2), for example, may fail, but then one at level (4) or (5) may succeed, and again, if not, the virus could be killed at level (7) or (8).[11]

---

[10] For example, the 'World AIDS conference' which took place in Vancouver in 1996 labeled HAART (highly active antiviral therapy) the therapeutic protocol consisting in a treatment with a combination of different inhibitors.

[11] Here the whole description is very simplified. It considers only the relationship between the virus, the host-cell and the therapeutic techniques. The situation is much more complex: when a certain substance is assumed, it inevitably interacts with a series of other substances in the

2.2 Cancer and Chemotherapy

A clinical treatment that presents analogies with anti-AIDS strategies is chemotherapy in cancer management. In many respects anti-tumor therapies were the precursors of anti-HIV drugs and, like the latter, have not yet triumphed over the disease. In general terms, tumor development results from an excessive proliferation of cells belonging to various organs and apparatuses. Whereas normal healthy cells are born and die at a standard controlled rate, cancer cells replicate rapidly, according to a mechanism that is only partly known.

Cancer treatments include surgical operations, radiotherapy and chemotherapy. These can be adopted separately or in various combinations. Chemotherapy – the focus here – is based on the idea that various chemical substances interfering with cellular replication can be exploited to block the replication process: chemical substances classified as 'antitumoral' or 'antineoplastic' are devised to destroy cancer cells by stopping their replication or growth. As is the case for AIDS treatment, chemotherapy involves a number of concomitant therapeutic interventions by means of different chemical substances, the cocktail aiming at 'hitting' cancer cells at different phases of their replication. This is sketchily outlined in Figure 2, which illustrates the replication phases of the cancer cells as the main 'trunk' of the 'tree', and the kinds and sites of some chemical treatments as the lateral 'branches'. Intervening substances can be approximately classified as:
– Antimetabolites: they intervene at the level of precursors, or 'metabolites', inhibiting a process essential for cellular life and reproduction.
– Alkylating agents: they bind to DNA strands, twisting the symmetry of the double helix. They reduce the mass of the tumor, but have serious side effects due to their lack of specificity and consequent toxicity.
– Intercalating agents: they penetrate the double helix of the DNA, perpendicular to its axis.
– Antimitotic agents: they block the normal occurrence of mitosis in various ways.

These four groups of substances intervene at different stages of cell replication and their prescription is related to the kind of cancer to be treated since each kind of tumor is sensitive only to certain classes of chemical substances. The choice of the substances to employ and their doses also depend on which apparatus is affected by the cancer, the patient's general conditions, his/her initial reactions to the treatment, and so forth.

---

body, and partly loses its efficacy. Furthermore, treatments so far devised are not very selective and damage different cells of the organism, producing side-effects.

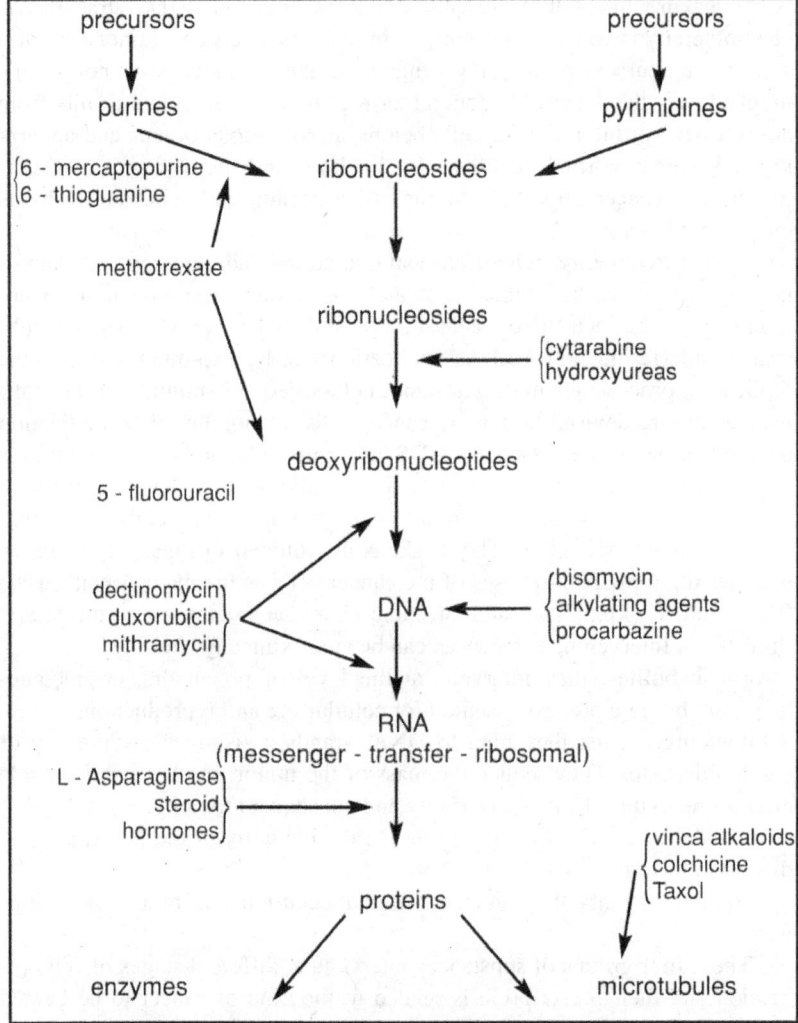

Figure 2: Summary of Anticancer Drug Mechanisms and Sites

Chemical substances in chemotherapy are prescribed in some combination to attack the disease at a number of levels and to optimize the efficacy of the treatment. This is particularly necessary because, like HIV cells, cancer cells tend to modify their deepest structure quickly and develop some resistance to treatment, especially after repeated cycles of application. Many drugs are thus prescribed at the same time, to overcome cancer cell variations and resistance to treatment: so-called 'combination chemotherapy' increases the chances of success.

3 Medical Reasoning and Pre-emption

The definition of clinical practice is by no means unequivocal. Broadly speaking, a therapy can be defined as 'a technical *intervention* or *interaction* predicated on rational, scientific understanding' (Agich 1983: 239, italics added). This pair of examples displays a symmetry: all the therapeutic interventions described can count as manipulative causes, by means of which we interfere with the process in order to stop it. Knowledge about chemical substances is thus exploited to understand pathological situations.

These manipulative relations are preventive rather than productive: instead of having a cause bringing about an effect, here the cause is required to prevent the effect from occurring. The crucial considerations are of the 'what-if-things-had-been-different' sort, the manipulative, preventive cause being something which makes a difference to the occurrence/non-occurrence of the effect. Such causal relations can be expressed in counterfactual terms: a given therapy prevents the disease from further developing just in case it is performed, the disease's development is blocked – or, rather, slowed down – and, had the therapy not been performed, the disease would have progressed. In sum, in the absence of the therapeutic intervention, the death of at least some viruses/cancer cells would not have occurred either. Given that the therapies' final results are far from certain, a probabilistic reading of manipulative causation is more properly required: had the pharmacological manipulation of HIV/cancer cells not occurred, the chance of their death would have been much smaller than it in fact was.[12]

These clinical examples seem to constitute a scenario where the notions of manipulation and pre-emption blend, in the development of practical therapeutic strategies for balancing risks and benefits. In the kind of causal reasoning underlying anti-HIV therapy and chemotherapy, attention is paid to the backup relations between various possible manipulative causes. In both cases clinical problems are solved by formulating a small number of previously tested alternative solutions. These alternative solutions directly translate into treatment alternatives, which are applied *concomitantly*. The ideas of pre-empting and pre-empted cause emerge from the analysis of the *clinical decision to prescribe* a defined and combined therapy. Like Susan and Billy throwing the rock simultaneously, different drugs are taken at the same time. Unlike the bottle, in both examples the drugs' target tends to

---

[12] See Lewis 1986b.

move on with its life-cycle, and drugs try to interfere at different, subsequent phases of the replication process. Any drug being effective can make drugs acting at earlier stages of the process redundant. The intervention which successfully stops a given virus'/cancer cell's replication process can be considered a case of pre-empting causation, or better of *pre-empting prevention*: intervening causes are aimed at stopping HIV/cancer cell replications and hence at preventing AIDS/cancer from progressing. In both cases, the pattern of the therapeutic strategy more specifically mirrors cases of *late pre-emption*, namely cases in which – in Laurie Paul's words – 'the pre-empted cause B would have caused the very same effect E, but *slightly later* than the pre-empting cause C caused it. In these cases, the pre-empted causal chain is prevented by the occurrence of the event itself, before the pre-empted cause can cause it' (Paul 2004: 214). Had not an intervention obtained its effect, another might have done so slightly later: if a given pharmacological substance succeeds, we can claim that, had it not succeeded, the intervention at the next level would have done so, or, rather, might have done so.[13] Instead of a single causal chain linking a single therapy to the patient's recovery, there is a range of possible alternative causal chains that can lead from the administration of some therapy to the slowing down of the disease. The alternative chains are 'cut' once the pre-emptive one, i.e. the first really effective therapy, successfully hits its target.

Since some viruses/cancer cells manage to survive, it is once again *probabilistic pre-emption* that underlies therapeutic reasoning. Whereas in Suzy and Billy's case we know that, had the window not been shattered by Suzy's throw, it would no doubt have been shuttered by Billy's, the anti-AIDS therapy and chemotherapy represent two pre-emption-like situations *precisely by virtue of* their probabilistic character. The prescription of a cocktail of substances is aimed at increasing the overall probability of stopping the destruction of the immune system/of a certain apparatus, because the clinician cannot but predict that a given substance has a given chance to kill the virus.

Pre-emption is not regarded here as a challenge for a counterfactual account of the phenomena under examination, but is rather thought of as representing the deepest structure of therapeutic reasoning. On the other hand, the situations analyzed do not mirror one of trumping. I have mentioned how viruses and cancer cells are continuously changing. Because of this, some cells often escape *all* alternative manipulative causes. Hence not all processes connecting the assumption of a given cocktail of drugs and its hitting a specific stage of the HIV/cancer cell replication run to completion:

---

[13] We can make such a claim for all stages at which some drug intervenes, up to the one before the last.

our medical cases do not resemble trumping cases in that not all the alternative causes are actually linked to their effects.

Some further interesting considerations on causal reasoning in medicine are suggested by reflections on the notion of causation as influence as introduced in Section 1. In both examples considered, a cocktail treatment is employed to reach a single target, namely the slowing down and, hopefully in cases of tumors, the end of the disease. However, the various preempting and pre-empted causes obtain the very same effect only in a loose sense. Strictly speaking, HIV/cancer is attacked at different stages of the replication process, which is hence interrupted at different points. In other words, if the clinically relevant overall effect is basically the same, i.e. stopping disease progression, the single alternative causes which the therapy is composed of and the single effects each of them reaches are different: not only do the times, but also the *ways* in which single viruses/cancer cells die vary according to which drug successfully attacks them. This clearly recalls the notion of influence, and the need to specify what is meant by 'being different' in assessing 'what if things had been different' relations.

Such specification turns out to be crucial also for distinguishing between genuine causes and mere background conditions. An example somewhat related to medicine made by Lewis himself can illustrate issues arising in this respect.[14] Let us suppose that a particular poison kills its victims more painfully and slowly if it is taken on a full stomach; let us also imagine that a certain victim takes it just after eating pudding. Eating pudding has a causal influence on his death, since it affects the time and manner in which death occurs, yet the eating cannot be properly conceived of as a cause of the victim's death. Lewis' theory of influence has been criticized for not accounting adequately for such cases: 'certainly an event can have a causal influence on another without being among its causes. ... As it stands, the new theory lacks the resources to identify an event's causes from among those things that merely had some causal influence on it' (Collins 2004: 114). This remains a central and controversial problem for medicine too, and for clinical medicine in particular: it is extremely important to detect which features of the patient, which portions of his/her personal and clinical history are causally relevant to the onset of his/her disease and to recovery. Identifying what count as genuine pathogenetic factors is essential for the development of general therapies to be adopted by all patients with the same disease.

Once accidental conditions and causes are distinguished, the time comes to discover why a particular cause was the pre-empting one. Once a specific

---

[14] See Lewis 1986b: 198-99.

cocktail treatment has been adopted, the clinician will leave the conditional theoretical level, and try to reach a – more or less precise – understanding of what has actually happened, of which cause or causes have been preempted, which one has eventually succeeded, and why. Although it is possible to reformulate the problem as one moves along, and to collect some data routinely, we are unlikely to ever get to know *all* the details about the success of a specific intervention. Yet only a continuous refinement of our understanding of its causal features can lead to the refinement of therapeutic strategies. Improving therapeutic techniques involves not only the *identification* of the actual cause among a range of potential ones, but also a comprehension of *why that very cause* was the successful one, and was not preempted: 'the pre-empted cause is causally irrelevant to the effect (and thus is not a cause of it)' (Kvart 2004: 359), and one of the targets of clinical medicine is an in-depth understanding of the reasons behind causal irrelevance.

In trying to distinguish events that count as more or less remote causes from others that are not, 'one thing we might have is a practical concern for prediction and/or control. We might like to know how we could have prevented a certain event, or whether a similar event is likely to occur in future situations that are, in some specified respects, similar' (Maudlin 2004: 440). Theoretical and practical aspects of medicine here appear to go hand in hand. An enormous wealth of information has been accumulated on the mechanisms of AIDS and cancer, and it accounts for the choice of treatments. Although causal manipulations can be and often are used in a heuristic sense, when determining which therapeutic interventions to perform we *already* have to bring in causal judgments. In other words, it is by virtue of our knowing that HIV and cancer cells develop in a such-and-such way that we work out a pattern of alternative manipulative, preventive causes. It is in evaluating their efficacy that some sort of counterfactual reasoning comes into play. Counterfactuals crucially refer to possible events which do not take place. When applying the therapies in the kind of cases described, the clinician is taking into account not only what happens, but also what would happen if a particular intervention did not hit its target. Although here I do not want to enter the debate on a possible world semantics for counterfactuals, evaluating larger or smaller possible departures from actuality and why they occur is crucially important for the development of clinical medicine. 'When doing science, we identify the potential causes eligible to bring about an effect ..., and then alter the potential causes and observe the effect for changes' (Paul 2004: 221). If a given therapy does not succeed, we are interesting in finding out precisely in which other clinical and pathological situation it would have done so. Important consequences could be drawn from a detailed identification of the possible circumstances in which therapies would work and patients would recover, and from a complete discovery of the differences between such circumstances and the actual ones.

4 Concluding Remarks

Clinical reasoning processes and combines information. Any physician has two fundamental tasks: making a diagnosis and deciding on the best form of treatment for the patient's problem.

> Each phase of the process of clinical reasoning involves aspects that are peculiar to medicine, but each phase also involves more general principles.
> ... These principles are often ones shared with other disciplines, disciplines that specifically seem distant from clinical medicine. Thus, we find ourselves encountering topics in statistics, formal logic, the philosophy of science and decision analysis (Albert, Munson and Resnik 1988: 4).

Objections against the original counterfactual analysis and various attempts to refine it have been made with the purpose of reaching a closer match with commonsense intuitions about causation. Such attempts can have interesting implications with respect to the meaning and use of causation in the sciences too.

The somewhat limited scope of the preceding sections has been to present notions emerging from the debate on the counterfactual approach as a conceptual resource for fields other than philosophy, and more specifically for medical practice. I believe the notion of pre-emption is one of the – so far underestimated – contributions that philosophy of science can make to the understanding of causal clinical thinking. At the same time, I have tried to show how further clarification is required to make a significant step forward in mapping clinical reasoning. It is important to realize what features of the various pre-empting and pre-empted causes are responsible for the process occurring the way it does, and hence to uncover which features are essential to the therapeutic intervention and which, instead, are merely accidental. This in turn calls for more reflections. In reconstructing causal medical reasoning, context-sensitivity must also be taken into account. In assessing causal relations, the context should be carefully considered, since the complete physical situation is not normally known in every single detail. As suggested, for example, by Hart and Honoré (1985) and recalled more recently by Peter Menzies (2004), the context plays an essential role in the assessment of causal relations.[15] In analyzing pre-emption like situations for therapeutic purposes, the clinical mind will surely select portions of the

---

[15] Menzies claims it is a mistake to believe that 'causation is an absolute relation, specifiable independently of any contextual factor' and suggests that the concept of cause should be analyzed 'as a difference-maker that integrates a certain contextual parameter into the relevant truth conditions' (Menzies 2004: 139).

causal history under examination and choose what level of fine, or coarse, graininess its analysis should have according to the circumstances.[16] All these aspects are crucial for *any* attempt to evaluate the conditionals that form the heart of any counterfactual analysis, and are particularly important for any causal reasoning aimed at a pragmatic intervention. A therapeutic situation is a typical situation which depends in a number of ways on the context in which it takes place,[17] and on its possible variations.

Given the many facets of medical reasoning, weaving the diverse threads of concepts and research methods used in clinical medicine into a single fabric is an extremely difficult task, largely shirked by the contemporary philosophical debate on causation thus far. Nevertheless, this debate can provide very interesting and successful tools to clarify the nature and scope of therapeutic relationships and reasoning on a conceptual level. The discussion on causation ongoing in philosophy of science can help shed much light on the cognitive aspects of clinical medicine; it might delve into the clinical mind and lay bare the processes of reasoning involved in arriving at and justifying clinical decisions. In turn, instead of testing any proposed analysis of notions such as those of prevention, pre-emption and trumping against imaginary cases that will probably never occur, cases of actual experience should be considered. Recent counterfactual accounts have not reached a consensus, and their views have often driven the debate towards totally artificial examples. It has been commented, for example, that 'Lewis and his followers have made ingenious and lengthy efforts to render the counterfactual theory foolproof. ... All this is at the price of making the original, intuitively very plausible, account of causation very complicated and counter-intuitive' (Psillos 2000: 100), and it has been claimed that 'attempts to fix the counterfactual analysis have become ever more subtle, and complicated, and convoluted' (Maudlin 2004: 421). If some folk conception of causation we all hold is too simplistic, many philosophical accounts, and their convolutions, turn out to be alien to reality. Actual scientific practice, and clinical real situations in particular, offer an alternative to test many of the promises and problems with extant counterfactual analyses of causation. 'In the last three decades or so, causation seems to have become something of a philosophical workhorse: philosophers have offered causal accounts of knowledge, perception, mental content, action, explana-

---

[16] On this, see for example Ned Hall: 'I think that causal judgments are tacitly relative to the level of description we adopt when giving an account of the relevant chain of events (and that this choice of level of description will be a feature of the context in which we are making our causal judgments). ... Obviously, another major piece of unfinished business is to spell out the relevant notion of 'levels of description', and to explain exactly how such levels find their way into the contexts in which we make our causal judgments' (Hall 2004: 274).

[17] On this, see for example Agich 1983: 233-234, and Szawarski 2004: 61.

tion, persistence through time, and decision-making, to name a few' (Hall 2004: 267). Clinical reasoning too could prove a terrain of fruitful confrontation in evaluating the health and prospects of different philosophical accounts, and help avoiding the development of baroque constructions.

Acknowledgments

I am grateful to Peter Menzies for his comments on an early draft of this paper.

References

Agich, G.J. 1983. Scope of the Therapeutic Relationship. *The Clinical Encounter. The Moral Fabric of the Patient-Physician Relationship*, ed. E.E. Shelp, 233-50. Reidel: Dordrecht.

Albert, D.A., Munson, R., Resnik, M.D. (eds.) 1988. *Reasoning in Medicine. An Introduction to Clinical Inference*. Baltimore and London: The Johns Hopkins University Press.

Collins, J. 2004. Preemptive Prevention. *Counterfactuals and Causation*, eds. J. Collins, N. Hall and L.A. Paul, 107.118. Cambridge MA: The MIT Press.

Collins, J., Hall, N., Paul, L.A. 2004. Counterfactuals and Causation: History, Problems, and Prospects. *Counterfactuals and Causation*, eds. J. Collins, N. Hall and L.A. Paul, 1-58. Cambridge, MA: The MIT Press.

Gillies, D. 2005. An Action-Related Theory of Causation. *British Journal for the Philosophy of Science* 56: 823-42.

Hall, N. 2004. Two Concepts of Causation. *Counterfactuals and Causation*, eds. J. Collins, N. Hall and L.A. Paul, 225-76. Cambridge, MA: The MIT Press.

Hart, H.L., Honoré, A. 1985 [1965]. *Causation in the Law*. Oxford: Clarendon Press.

Kvart, I. 2004. Causation: Probabilistic and Counterfactual Analyses. *Counterfactuals and Causation*, eds. J. Collins, N. Hall and L.A. Paul, 359-86. Cambridge, MA: The MIT Press.

Lewis, D. 1986a. *Philosophical Papers*. New York: Oxford University Press.

Lewis, D. 1986b. Postscript to 'Causation', *Philosophical Papers*, vol. II, 172-213. New York: Oxford University Press.

Lewis, D. 2000. Causation as Influence. *Journal of Philosophy* 97: 182-97.

Maudlin, T. 2004. Causation, Counterfactuals, and the Third Factor. *Counterfactuals and Causation*, eds. J. Collins, N. Hall and L.A. Paul, 419-43. Cambridge, MA: The MIT Press.

McDermott, M. 1995. Redundant Causation. *The British Journal for the Philosophy of Science* 40: 523-44.

Menzies, P. 1989. Probabilistic Causation and Causal Processes: A Critique of Lewis. *Philosophy of Science* 56: 642-63.

Menzies, P. 2004. Difference-Making in Context. *Counterfactuals and Causation*, eds. J. Collins, N. Hall and L.A. Paul, 139-80. Cambridge, MA: The MIT Press.

Menzies, P. and Price, H. 1993. Causation as a Secondary Quality. *British Journal for the Philosophy of Science* 44: 187-203.

Paul, L.A. 2004. Aspect Causation. *Counterfactuals and Causation*, eds. J. Collins, N. Hall and L.A. Paul, 205-24. Cambridge, MA: The MIT Press.

Pellegrino, E. 1983. The Healing Relationship: The Architectonics of Clinical Medicine. *The Clinical Encounter. The Moral Fabric of the Patient-Physician Relationship*, ed. E.E. Shelp, 153-72. Reidel: Dordrecht.

Price, H. 1991. Agency and Probabilistic Causality. *British Journal for the Philosophy of Science* 42: 157-76.

Psillos, S. 2000. *Causation and Explanation*, ch. 3, 81-106. Chesham: Acumen.

Ramachandran, M. 1997. A Counterfactual Analysis of Causation, *Mind* 106: 263-77.

Schaffer, J. 2000. Trumping Pre-emption. *Journal of Philosophy* 97: 165-81.

Suppes, P. 1984. Conflicting Intuitions about Causality. *Midwest Studies in Philosophy* IX, eds. P.A. French, T.E. Uehling and H.K. Wettstein, 150-68. Dordrecht-Boston: Kluwer. Reprinted in Suppes, P. 1993. *Models and Methods in the Philosophy of Science: Selected Essays*, 121-40.

Szawarski, Z. 2004. The Concept of Placebo. *Science and Engineering Ethics* 10: 57-64.

Woodward, J. 2003. *Making Things Happen*. New York-Oxford: Oxford University Press.

13

Abduction in the Context of a Reasoning Process: the SCIFF Framework

MARCO ALBERTI, FEDERICO CHESANI, MARCO GAVANELLI,
EVELINA LAMMA AND PAOLA MELLO

The aim of this work is to show that the Peircean notion of abduction, even if in a limited way, can be expressed declaratively by using logic programming (suitably extended). To this extent, the concepts of surprising fact, explanation and confirmation and the dynamic view of the entire process of reasoning, are mapped in logic, and a sound and complete abductive proof procedure (called $SCIFF$) has been defined and implemented in order to automatically perform such a reasoning. This allows us to better understand the fundamental concepts of abductive reasoning, and to support operationally, by using $SCIFF$, some forms of reasoning such diagnosis, planning, specification of open artificial societies, and deontic reasoning.

1 Introduction

Research on abductive reasoning in Artificial Intelligence dates back to 1973 (Pople 1973), but it is only fairly recently that it has attracted great interest.

By following Peirce's formulation (Hartshorne and Weiss 1965) the cognitive process of abductive reasoning may be described as follows: a novel or anomalous experience causes a *surprising fact* generating a state of doubt. Therefore, abductive reasoning is triggered: it consists of explaining the surprising fact in response to the state of doubt. The doubt, however, is not destroyed since an abductive explanation is just a suggestion to be tested before it becomes a belief (Aliseda 2000).

Peirce's formulation has been the starting point of recent studies and implementation of abductive reasoning, such as abductive logic programming (Kakas, Kowalski and Toni 1998).

However, if we consider these works related with abduction and its mapping in computational logic (and logic programming in particular), we can see that the focus is mainly on the abductive inference, while the global process of reasoning is not yet considered.

The notions of logical inference and abduction that Peirce proposes go beyond logical formulation. These notions are linked to his epistemology, a dynamic view of thought, and respond to a deep philosophical concern, that of studying the nature of synthetic reasoning (Aliseda 2000).

As pointed out by Shanahan and Randell (2004) in the context of active visual perception, in essence, perception, cognition and action must act in concert to carry out what philosophers of science call hypothetical-deductive reasoning. This comprises three steps. First, data and facts are perceived or observed. Second, the most promising hypotheses are formulated. Third, hypotheses lead to expectations on the external world, which are tested by carrying out experiments in order to be possibly confirmed.

The aim of this work is to show that this notion of abduction, even if in a limited way, can be expressed declaratively by using abductive logic programming (suitably extended).

To this extent, the concepts of surprising fact, explanation and confirmation and the dynamic view of the entire process of reasoning, have been mapped in an abductive logic framework, and a sound and complete abductive proof procedure, *S*CIFF (Alberti, Gavanelli, Lamma, Mello and Torroni 2005b) has been defined and implemented in order to automatically perform such a reasoning.

This allows us to better understand the fundamental concepts of abductive reasoning.

More in detail, the fundamental conceptsthat are taken into account in the *S*CIFF abductive framework are:

(i) the notions of surprising facts or observations, which dynamically trigger or influence the reasoning process;

(ii) the notions of explanation/prediction;

(iii) the notion of confirmation and, in particular, what it means for an observation to confirm an hypothesis, and what kind of hypothesis need or can be confirmed.

Operationally, our framework follows the human hypothetical-deductive reasoning in that the steps of observation, hypothesis generation and fulfillment do not need to be sequentially executed, but can be suitably interleaved in order to discard unpromising hypotheses as soon as possible.

The work is structured as follows. In Section 2 the *SCIFF* abductive framework is presented informally, under the perspective of hypothetical-deductive reasoning, using diagnosis as a running example. In Section 3, examples related to specification of open artificial societies, deontic reasoning, and abductive event calculus are given. Related work and conclusions follow.

2 The *SCIFF* Framework

In this section, we informally introduce the *SCIFF* framework, and we show how it supports the features of hypothetical reasoning by using medical *diagnosis* (one of the best known applications) as a running example.

For a formal introduction to the framework, the reader can refer to previously published papers (Alberti, Gavanelli, Lamma, Mello and Torroni 2005b).

The *SCIFF* abstract framework is strongly related to classical abductive frameworks, but it takes the happening of events into account, thus supporting a more dynamic style of hypothetical reasoning. We first recall the classical definition of Abductive Logic Program (ALP), then we extend it for the dynamic case.

An ALP (Kakas, Kowalski and Toni 1998) is a tuple $\langle KB, IC, A \rangle$ where *KB* is a logic program, (i.e., a set of clauses), *A* is a set of predicates that are not defined in *KB* (called *abducibles*), and *IC* is a set of formulae called *Integrity Constraints*. An abductive explanation for a goal G is a set Δ of ground literals whose predicate symbols are in *A*, such that $KB \cup \Delta \models G$ and $KB \cup \Delta \models IC$, for some notion of entailment $\models$.

In order to cope with hypotheses which need confirmation, in the *SCIFF* framework we extend the concept of ALP. We represent the new knowledge acquired during the reasoning process by means of *events*. New events may dynamically arrive and are encoded into atoms of the form $\mathbf{H}(D,T)$, where D is a ground term representing the event and T is an integer representing the time at which the event happened. An example of event is

$\mathbf{H}(temperature(36.5), 19)$

which could represent the fact that a patient's temperature at 7p.m. was 36.5 Celsius degrees. Such events are recorded in a history **HAP** (a set containing atoms with functor **H**), which defines a predicate **H**. The history dynamically grows during the computation, as new events take place. We do not model the source of events, but that can be thought as a queue of events received in the same temporal order in which they happen.

Differently from classical ALP frameworks, the *SCIFF* framework provides two kinds of abducibles.

(i) *hypotheses*, as classically understood in ALP frameworks. For instance, *disease(flu,T)* could represent a hypothesis that a patient has flu at time *T*.

(ii) *expectations*, which represent hypotheses on past or future events (*predictions*). Expectations represent events that are expected to (but might not) happen (*positive* expectations, of the form $\mathbf{E}(D,T)$), and events that are expected *not* to (but might) happen (*negative* expectations, of the form $\mathbf{EN}(D,T)$). For instance, $\mathbf{E}(\textit{temperature}(T_1);T);T_1 < 37$ could mean that a patient is expected to exhibit a temperature lesser than 37 Celsius degrees, as specified by the CLP[1] constraint on the *T* variable.

Semantically, expectations differ from hypotheses in that they are required to be *confirmed* (or *fulfilled*) by events; otherwise, expectations are *violated* and must be rejected.

An expectation is fulfilled if the history contains a matching event. For example, in case of an event $\mathbf{H}(\textit{temperature}(36.5),19)$ the expectation above would be fulfilled. Conversely, a negative expectation is fulfilled if the history does not contain a matching event.

Violation is defined as the negation of fulfillment: a positive expectation is violated if the history does not contain a matching event, a negative expectation is violated if the history does contain a matching event.

Similarly to other abductive frameworks, SCIFF performs abduction starting from a *surprising fact* (represented by a *goal*), according to the clauses in a *knowledge base*.

For example, a headache could be explained by a flu, but in this case the temperature cannot be lesser than 37 Celsius degrees:

symptom(headache,T) ← *disease(flu,T)*,
$\mathbf{EN}(\textit{temperature}(T_1),T),T_1 < 37$

The headache might also be explained by the Rocky Mountain Spotted Fever, and in this case one can foresee the appearance of pink spots on the patient's skin within two days:

symptom(headache,T_1) ← *disease(rocky mountain spot fever,T_1)*,
$\mathbf{E}(\textit{pinkspots}T_2),T_1 < T_2 < T_1 + 48$

See how easily the development of the illness can be described, together with its temporal landmarks and deadlines.

Moreover, expectations can indicate the expected outcome of exams, implicitly asking for new information or suggesting to the doctor possible tests that would support the diagnosis. In the example, another cause of

---

[1] Constraint Logic Programming: see Jaffar and Maher 1994.

headache might be meningitis, and in this case the diagnosis would be supported by a spinal tap giving evidence of a cryptococcus infection:

$$symptom(headache,T) \leftarrow disease(meningitis,T),$$
$$E(exam(spinal\ tap,\ Cryptococcus),\ T_1),\ T_1 > T$$

However, in the *SCIFF* framework, the surprising fact, represented by the goal, is not the only source of abduction. The happened events and the generated hypotheses and expectations can be specified to generate further hypotheses and expectations (the *deductive* phase of hypothetical-deductive reasoning). This is done by means of *integrity constraints*, which in our framework are forward rules such as the following:

$$disease(rocky\ mountn\ spot\ fever,T) \rightarrow E(cure(tetracycline),\ T_1)$$
$$\vee\quad E(coma,\ T_2),\ T_2 < T_1 + 7$$

which expresses that a rocky mountain spot fever should be cured by means of tetracycline, or coma is expected by seven days.

Given such a (obviously simplified, but realistic) knowledge base, in case of headache (represented by a *symptom(headache*,10) goal), the *SCIFF* would propose a *flu* as possible explanation. The diagnosis comes together with the expectation **EN**$(temperature(T_1);T)$, $T_1 < 37$, so if temperature happens to be 36 Celsius degrees, the diagnosis correctness will be in doubt, and another explanation must be found, coherent with the new information. The alternative diagnosis *Rocky Mountain Spotted Fever* can be formulated, and it is conjoined with the expectation of appearance of *pink spots* within two days. The non occurrence of pink spots on the third day will be a surprising fact, in that the expected evolution of the disease is not corroborated. Again, the third hypothesis will be formulated: *meningitis*. This assumption suggests the *spinal tap*, which might be performed by the doctor or not. If the exam has the expected result, then the diagnosis is confirmed.

The *SCIFF* language, here informally introduced by means of examples, has an operational counterpart, the sound and complete *SCIFF* abductive proof procedure (Alberti, Gavanelli, Lamma, Mello and Torroni 2005b).

SCIFF, inspired by the IFF proof procedure (Fung and Kowalski 1997), each status of the reasoning is represented by a data structure (node), to which one or more transitions can be applied, to generate child nodes. Possible transitions are, for example, the generation of an expectation, or the insertion of an event into the history. Starting from an initial node, which represents the starting point of the reasoning process, *SCIFF* builds a reasoning tree, and terminates when either a fulfillment node is found (i.e., one where the necessary hypotheses and expectations have been generated, and the expectations are fulfilled), or each leaf node is of violation. *SCIFF* has been implemented in SICStus Prolog (SICStus 2003), which exploits, in particular, the *CHR* library (Frühwirth 1998) and the underlying constraint solvers, in order to deal with CLP constraints.

3 Applications

In this section, we show how, beside diagnosis, further different application fields (namely planning, open society modeling, and deontic reasoning) can be viewed as forms of hypothetical-deductive reasoning, and how they are supported by the *SCIFF* framework.

3.1 Planning with Abductive Event Calculus

A classical application of abductive proof-procedures is the *Abductive Event Calculus* (Eshaghi 1988). The Event Calculus (EC) (Kowalski and Sergot 1986; Shanahan 1999) introduces a set of properties, called *fluents*, that may hold in a system in some time intervals. The EC consists of four ingredients.

(*i*) A set of causal relations are known, stating which events initiate or terminate the validity of a fluent. For example, a description of a robot in the block world could enclose the fluents *ontable*(X) (block X is on the table) and *holding*(X) (the robot holds in its hand the block X). Rules could state that putting a block on the table initiates the fluent 'lock is on the table' provided that the robot was holding the block

initiates(*putdown*(X),*ontable*(X),T), ← *holdsat*(*holding*(X),T).

Picking up a block X terminates the validity of 'X is on the table'

terminate(*pickup*(X),*ontable*(X)).

(*ii*) The initial situation is provided by means of the *initially* predicate. For example, the robot is initially holding block number 1:

initially(*holding*(1)).

(*iii*) A narrative of happened events is given; for example

happens(*putdown*(1),(3).
happens(*pickup*(1),(5)

(*iv*) The general theory of the EC (independent of the world): rules 1.1 state that a fluent holds at a given time either if it was initially true or it has become true after some happened events, and it has not been *clipped*, i.e., its truth has not been terminated in the meanwhile.

$$
\begin{aligned}
&holdsat(F,T) &&\leftarrow\ initially(F),\ not\ clipped(0,F,T).\\
&holdsat(F,T) &&\leftarrow\ happens(E,T_1),\ initiates(E,F)\\
& && \quad not\ clipped(T_1,F,T) \hspace{2cm} (1)\\
&clipped(T_1,F,T_2) &&\leftarrow\ happens(E,T),\ T_1 < T < T_2,\\
& && \quad terminates(E,F)
\end{aligned}
$$

Given the four ingredients, deduction can infer that the fluent *ontable*(1) is true at time 4 and it is false at 2 and 10.

Eshaghi (1988) noted that by interpreting the event calculus in abduction he could solve planning problems. The user states the initial situation (through the *initially* predicate) and a goal, requiring typically the validity of some fluents in the final situation. The narrative of events is no longer given, but is considered as a set of actions that should be performed in order to obtain the goal; i.e., *happens* atoms are abducible. In the example, if the goal was

$$holdsat(ontable(1), 10). \hspace{5cm} (2)$$

the Abductive Event Calculus (AEC) would reply that in order to obtain the goal, the *putdown* action should be performed before time 10.

Many works address planning through abduction. In some works the precedence relationship between events is abducible (Shanahan 2000a). Others use a discrete representation of time and can enjoy the power of a constraint solver (Kakas, van Nuffelen and Denecker 2001; Endriss, Mancarella, Sadri, Terreni and Toni 2004a).

In the *SCIFF* framework, the AEC can be easily cast. The notions of happened event and expectation are not confused: what is planned or supposed to happen might not coincide with the actual happening. An agent could plan to perform an action, but the action might fail. In the block world example, a block could slip, making a *pickup* action unsuccessful. The robot expected to pickup the block, but the actual action did not match. This surprising event generates the need for another explanation that might be that a retrial is necessary to accomplish the task, or that a totally different plan must be taken.

We refine previous work in which plans are defined through *happens* predicates, and propose to design plans by means of *expected events*. If the agent wants to get to a goal state, it should perform the planned actions, so it is *expected* to execute them in order to get the desired objective. By no means, the actions in the plan are already *happened* at planning time.

Positive expectations (**E**) state actions that should be taken in order for the plan to be effective. **EN** expectations (that do not exist in previous abductive event calculus proposals) inform about those actions that should not be executed in order for the plan to be successful.

The AEC theory in SCIFF can be given with the following rules:

$holdsat(F,T)$ ← $initially(F), unclipped(0,F,T)$
$holdsat(F,T)$ ← $E(A,T_1), 0 < T_1 < T$ (3)
                  $initiates(A,F,T_1), unclipped(T1,F,T)$.

$unclipped(T_1,F, T_2), terminates(A,F,T_3) \rightarrow \mathbf{EN}(A,T), T_1 < T < T_2$ (4)

The rules in Eq. (3) are direct translation of the first two in Eq. (1).

We introduce a new abducible predicate, *unclipped*, to represent the *not(clipped)* literals found in the classical event calculus. In order for the plan to be successful, the fluent should not be clipped in the given time interval. This is ensured by the application of the integrity constraint (4), which imposes that every event that would terminate the validity of the fluent is expected not to happen (in the given time interval). This mechanism lets us exploit better the underlying constraint solver, which is tailored to reason about positive and negative expectations. Moreover, the planner will provide explicitly which actions should be carefully avoided not to threaten the executability of the plan by means of negative (**EN**) expectations.

In the block world example SCIFF provides

$\exists_{T_1} \forall_{T_2: T_1 < T_2 < 10} \mathbf{E}(putdown(1),T_1 \mathbf{EN}(pickup(1),T_2)$,

i.e., in order to achieve the goal (2) the robot should putdown block 1, and it should avoid picking it up before time 10.

3.2 Open Society Modeling

In this section, we show how the SCIFF framework has been used for the specification and verification of particular multiagent systems,[2] called *open agent societies*, in the context of the EU project SOCS (IST-2001-32530, http://lia.deis.unibo.it/Research/Projects/SOCS/).

In the MAS literature, the term *openness* has been used with several meanings. In the following, we summarize two of the most widely accepted definitions.

Two commonly accepted definitions have been given by Davidsson (2001) (a society is open if there are no restrictions for agents to join and leave it) and by Artikis, Pitt and Sergot (2002) (in an open society, the internal architecture of the members is not observable, and their behavior is not predictable and may not be cooperative).

---

[2] Also MAS, for short, in the following; for an introduction to MAS, the reader can refer to Wooldridge 2002.

While these two concepts of openness are in principle independent, it is reasonable for a society that is open in one sense to be open in the other sense, too.

The openness of a society impacts on what can be specified of it, and on what needs to be specified. Since the internal architecture, internal state or policies of the members are not, in general, accessible, it is not possible to give the specification of an open society by constraining the internal state of the members, but it is only possible to verify their externally observable behavior, i.e. their actions.

The *SCIFF* framework has been applied to the specification of open agent societies as follows:
 – events (**H**) represent the agent observable behavior
 – expectations (**E, EN**) represent the agent *desirable* behavior
 – integrity constraints represent agent interaction protocols (Alberti, Chesani, Gavanelli, Lamma, Mello and Torroni 2005a), or the social semantics of agent communication languages (Alberti, Ciampolini, Gavanelli, Lamma, Mello and Torroni 2003)
 – the knowledge base represents declarative knowledge about the society
 – a goal may represent a social aim, to be achieved by the agents.

Given the openness of the societies, it cannot be assumed that the agents will behave as is expected. In this perspective, expectations play the role of *hypotheses* on the agent behavior.

If the agents are compliant to the protocols, the hypotheses will be confirmed (fulfilled); otherwise, they will be disconfirmed (violated), as reflected in the *SCIFF* notion of fulfillment.

Given the specification of an open society and a history of events, the compliance of the history to the specification is checked by the *SCIFF* proof procedure.

The *SCIFF* proof procedure has been integrated into a software component (SOCS-SI) (Alberti, Chesani, Gavanelli, Lamma, Mello and Torroni 2006a) which has been interfaced to various multiagent system platforms.

The FIPA *query_ref* protocol

As a simple example of a social specification, let us consider the *query_ref* protocol (FIPA Query Interaction Protocol 2001), proposed by the FIPA consortium (http://www.fipa.org).

The protocol works as follows: an agent *A* requests a piece of information from an agent *B*. *B* may either provide the information or refuse it, by a given time interval; the two replies are mutually exclusive.

Specification 3.1 shows the integrity constraints for the *query_ref* social specification.

$$\begin{aligned}
&\mathbf{H}(tell(A, B, query\_ref(Info), D), T) \wedge \\
&qr\_deadline(TD) \\
\rightarrow \quad &\mathbf{E}(tell(B, A, inform(Info, Answer), D), T1) \wedge \\
&T1 < T + TD \\
\vee \quad &\mathbf{E}(tell(B, A, refuse(Info), D), T1) \wedge \\
&T1 < T + TD
\end{aligned}$$

$$\begin{aligned}
&\mathbf{H}(tell(A, B, inform(Info, Answer), D), Ti) \\
\rightarrow \quad &\mathbf{EN}(tell(A, B, refuse(Info), D), Tr)
\end{aligned}$$

Specification 3.1: Integrity Constraints for the *query_ref* social specification

Intuitively, the first integrity constraint means that if agent A sends to agent B a *query_ref* message, then B is expected to reply with either an *inform* or a *refuse* message within *TD* time units, where *TD* is defined in the Knowledge Base by the *qr_deadline* predicate (with the example in Specification 3.2, the value of *TD* would be 10).

The second integrity constraint means that, if an agent sends an *inform* message, then it is expected not to send a *refuse* message at any time.

$qr\_deadline(10).$

Specification 3.2: Social Knowledge Base for the *query_ref* social specification

3.3 Deontic reasoning

In this section, we show how the SCIFF framework can be used to express concepts usually handled by means of Deontic Logic.

Deontic Statuses of Actions

The birth of modern Deontic Logic can be traced back to the '50s (Wright 1951).

Deontic Logic enables to address the issue of explicitly and formally defining norms and dealing with their possible violation. It represents norms, obligations, prohibitions and permissions.

Being obligatory, being forbidden and being permitted are indeed the three fundamental *deontic statuses* of an action, upon which one can build more articulate normative conceptions. Following Sartor (2004), we summarize the intuitive meaning of the deontic statuses of an action.

Obligations. To say that an action is *obligatory* is to say that the action is due, has to be held, must be performed, is mandatory or compulsory. Obligations are usually represented by formulas as **Obl** A, where A is any (positive or negative) action description, and **Obl** is the deontic operator for obligation to be read as 'it is obligatory that'.

Prohibitions. The idea of obligation is paralleled with the idea of *prohibition*. Being forbidden or prohibited is the status of an action that should not be performed. Prohibitions are usually represented by formulas as: **Forb** A where A is any (positive or negative) action description, and **Forb** is the deontic operator for prohibition to be read as 'it is forbidden that'.

Permissions. The third basic deontic status, besides obligations and prohibitions, is *permission*. Permissions are usually represented by formulas as: **Perm** A where A is any (positive or negative) action description, and **Perm** is the deontic operator for permission to be read as 'it is permitted that'.

Deontic statuses of actions are not independent from each other, but they are logically connected. For example, **Obl** A entails **Perm** A, and both are incompatible with **Forb** A.

Deontic statuses of actions can be viewed as hypotheses on the behavior of subject who will act accordingly to a specification. For example, if an action is obligatory and it is assumed that the subject from whom the action is expected is willing to respect the obligation, then it can be hypothesized that the action will be performed.

Mapping Deontic Statuses to Expectations

We propose the mapping shown in Table 1. In this paper we motivate the mapping only intuitively; in Alberti, Gavanelli, Lamma, Mello, Sartor and Torroni (2006b) we provide a formal support to the mapping, based on a similarity between our abductive semantics and the Kripke semantics of deontic operators.

Operator	Abducible
Forb A	$EN(A)$
Obl A	$E(A)$
Perm A	$\neg EN(A)$
Perm *NON* A	$\neg E(A)$

Table 1: Deontic notions as SCIFF expectations

The first line of the table proposes a correspondence between the notion of prohibition (which requires an action not to be performed) and ours of negative expectation (which requires an event not to belong to the history).

In fact, the correspondence is more apparent looking at our concept of *fulfillment* (see Section 2), which requires, for a set of expectation to be fulfilled, the absence, in the history of events, of any event matching a negative expectation. This definition resembles closely the reduction of the prohibition operator proposed by Meyer (1988), where 'it is forbidden to perform (an action) α in (a state) σ if one performs α in σ one gets into trouble' (in that paper, 'trouble' means an 'undesirable state of affairs'; which is a good description of our state of violation).

Reasoning in a similar way, it is possible to notice a correspondence between the notion of obligation (which requires an action to be performed) and ours of positive expectation (which requires an event to belong to the history), as shown in the second line in Table 1.

Moreover, since a negative expectation **EN**(A) has to be read as *it is expected not A* (i.e., it is a shorthand for **E**(*not A*)), its (explicit) negation, ¬ **EN**(A), corresponds to permission of A. Finally, exploiting the logical relations among obligation, prohibition and permission, the fourth line of Table 1 shows how to map permission of a negative action.

Example: from a Software License Agreement

As an example, we show how two clauses of a software license agreement can be expressed by means of *SCIFF* integrity constraints, interpreting expectations as deontic operators, according to Table 1.

$$\mathbf{H}(tell(Owner, User, licence(Sw, Operations, Beginning, End), Context, T_{licence})$$
$$\land price(Sw, Price) \qquad (5)$$
$$\rightarrow$$
$$\mathbf{E}(tell(User, Owner, pay(Sw, Price), Context, T_{pay})$$

The meaning the integrity constraint in Equation 5 is that if the owner (possibly a software house) grants the user a license to use the software for certain operations in a certain time interval, then the user is obliged to pay the price of the software to the owner.

$$\mathbf{H}(use(User, Sw, use(Operation1, Machine1), Context, Tuse1) \land$$
$$\rightarrow \qquad (6)$$
$$\mathbf{EN}(use(User, Sw, use(Operation2, Machine2), Context, Tuse2) \land$$
$$Machine1 \neq Machine2$$

The meaning of the integrity constraint in Equation 6 is that the user is only allowed to use the software on one machine.

4 Related Work

Many abductive proof procedures have been proposed in the past; the reader can refer to the exhaustive survey by Kakas, Kowalski and Toni (1998). This work is mostly related to the IFF (Fung and Kowalksi 1997), which it extends in several directions, as explained in the paper.

Other proof procedures deal with constraints; in particular ACLP (Kakas, Michael and Mourlas 2000) and the *A*-system (Kakas, van Nuffelen and Denecker 2001) deeply focus on efficiency issues. Both use integrity constraints in the form of denials, instead of forward rules, and both abduce only existentially quantified atoms.

The integration of the IFF with constraints has been explored, both theoretically (Kowalski, Toni and Wetzel 1998), and in an implementation (Endriss, Mancarella, Sadri, Terreni and Toni 2004b). These works, however, do not deal with confirmation of hypotheses and universally quantified variables in abducibles.

Sergot (1983) proposed a framework, *query-the-user*, in which some of the predicates are labeled as 'askable'; the truth of askable atoms can be asked to the user. Our **E** predicates may be seen as asking information, while **H** atoms may be considered as new information provided during search. However, differently from Sergot's query-the-user, $\mathcal{S}$CIFF is not intended to be used interactively, but rather to provide a means to generate and to reason upon generated expectations, be they positive or negative. Moreover, $\mathcal{S}$CIFF presents expectations in the context of an abductive framework (integrating them with other abducibles).

Hypotheses confirmation was studied also by Evans and Kakas (1992), where hypotheses can be corroborated or refuted by matching them with observable atoms: an explanation fails to be corroborated if some of its logical consequences are not observed. The authors suggest that their framework could be extended to take into account dynamic events, possibly queried to the user: *'this form of reasoning might benefit from the use of a query-the-user facility'*.

In a sense, our work can be considered as a merge and extension of these works: it has confirmation of hypotheses, as in corroboration, and it provides an operational semantics for dynamically incoming events, as in query-the-user.

The dynamics of incoming events can be seen as an instance of an Evolving Logic Program (Alferes, Brogi, Leite and Pereira 2002). In EvoLP, the knowledge base can change both because of external events or because of internal results. $\mathcal{S}$CIFF does not generate new events, but only expectations about external events. Our focus is more on the expressivity of the expectations than on the evolution of the knowledge base.

Speculative Computation (Satoh, Inoue, Iwanuma and Sakama 2000) is a propositional framework for a multi-agent setting with unreliable communication. When an agent asks a query, it also abduces a default answer; if the real answer arrives within a deadline, the hypothesis is (dis-)confirmed; otherwise the computation continues with the default. In our work, expectations can be confirmed by events, with a wider scope: they are not only questions, and they can have variables, possibly constrained.

Among the works on abductive event calculus, we cite Shanahan (2000b), because his work too has a concept of expectation: a robot moves in an office, and has expectations about where it is standing, based on the values obtained by sensors. While our expectations should match with actual events, in Shanahan's work events and expectations are of the same nature, and both are abduced. Our expectations are more expressive, as they can be positive and negative. We also have a different focus: while we assume that the history is known, he proposes to abduce the events.

5 Conclusions

In this paper we have shown, by means of example from several application fields, that the *SCIFF* Abductive Logic Programming framework can express the fundamental features of hypothetical-deductive reasoning. The *SCIFF* framework is equipped with a sound and complete abductive proof procedure, which is able to take into account dynamically upcoming facts, and to confirm or disconfirm the generated hypotheses according to observations and evidences.

We have shown that this allows us to better understand the fundamental concepts of abductive reasoning and to implement, by using *SCIFF*, some fundamental forms of reasoning such as scientific reasoning, diagnosis, deontic reasoning, temporal reasoning and social reasoning. Even if the emphasis of the present paper is on applications and examples, the system here described has been implemented (see http://lia.deis.unibo.it/research/sciff/) and is being tested on significant examples, especially in the field of specification and verification of open artificial societies.

Acknowledgments

We wish to thank the organizers and participants of the European Science Foundation exploratory workshop on 'Rationality and Patterns of Reasoning' (Bertinoro, Italy, Fall 2004) for their useful and insightful feedback on the *SCIFF* framework.

We also wish to thank Paolo Torroni, who contributed to the *SCIFF* framework and to many of its applications, and Giovanni Sartor, who contributed to the mapping of deontic operators to *SCIFF* expectations.

This work is partially funded by the Information Society Technologies program of the European Commission under the IST-2001-32530 SOCS Project (http://lia.deis.unibo.it/research/socs/), and by the MIUR COFIN 2003 projects *Sviluppo e verifica di sistemi multiagente basati sulla logica* (http://www.di.unito.it/massive/), and *La Gestione e la negoziazione automatica dei diritti sulle opere dell'ingegno digitali: aspetti giuridici e informatici*.

References

Alberti, M. Ciampolini, A., Gavanelli, M., Lamma, E., Mello, P. and Torroni, P. 2003. A Social ACL Semantics by Deontic Constraints. *Multi-Agent Systems and Applications III. Proceedings of the 3rd International Central and Eastern European Conference on Multi-Agent Systems, CEEMAS 2003*, Prague: June 16-18, eds. V. Marík, J. Müller and M. Pechoucek, vol. 2691 of *Lecture Notes in Artificial Intelligence*, 204-13. Berlin: Springer-Verlag.

Alberti, M., Chesani, F., Gavanelli, M., Lamma, E., Mello, P. and Torroni, P. 2005a. The SOCS Computational Logic Approach for the Specification and Verification of Agent Societies. *Global Computing: IST/FET International Workshop, GC 2004 Rovereto, Italy, March 9-12, 2004 Revised Selected Papers*, eds. C. Priami and P. Quaglia, vol. 3267 of *Lecture Notes in Artificial Intelligence*, 324-39. Berlin: Springer-Verlag.

Alberti, M. Gavanelli, M., Lamma, E., Mello, P. and Torroni, P. 2005b. The Sciff Abductive Proof-procedure. *Proceedings of the 9th National Congress on Artificial Intelligence, AI*IA 2005*, vol. 3673 of *Lecture Notes in Artificial Intelligence*, 135-47. Berlin: Springer-Verlag.

Alberti, M., Chesani, F., Gavanelli, M., Lamma, E., Mello, P. and Torroni, P. 2006a. Compliance Verification of Agent Interaction: a Logic-based Software Tool. *Applied Artificial Intelligence*, 20(4-5): 133-57.

Alberti, M., Gavanelli, M., Lamma, E., Mello, P., Sartor, G. and Torroni, P. 2006b. Mapping Deontic Operators to Abductive Expectations. *Computational and Mathematical Organization Theory*, 12(2-3): 205-25.

Alferes, J.J. Brogi, A., Leite, J.A. and Pereira L.M. 2002. Evolving Logic Programs. *Proceedings of the 8th European Conference on Logics in Artificial Intelligence (JELIA'02)*, eds. S. Flesca, S. Greco, N. Leone, and G. Ianni, vol. 2424 of *Lecture Notes in Artificial Intelligence*, 50-61. Berlin: Springer-Verlag.

Aliseda, A. 2000. Abduction as Epistemic Change: A Peircean Model in Artificial Intelligence. *Abduction and Induction: Essays on their Relation and Integration*, eds. P. Flach and A. Kakas, ch. 3, 45-58. Dordrecht: Kluwer Academic Publishers.

Artikis, A., Pitt, J. and Sergot, M. 2002. Animated Specifications of Computational Societies. *Proceedings of the First International Joint Conference on Autonomous Agents and Multiagent Systems (AAMAS-2002), Part III*, Bologna, Italy, July 15-19, eds. C. Castelfranchi and W. Lewis Johnson, 1053-61. New York: ACM Press.

Davidsson, P. 2001. Categories of Artificial Societies. *Engineering Societies in the Agents World II*, vol. 2203 of *Lecture Notes in Artificial Intelligence*, eds. A. Omicini, P. Petta, and R. Tolksdorf, 1-9. 2nd International Workshop (ESAW'01), Prague, Czech Republic, July 7, 2001, Revised Papers. London: Springer-Verlag.

Endriss, U., Mancarella, P., Sadri, F., Terreni, G. and Toni, F. 2004a. The CIFF

Proof Procedure for Abductive Logic Programming with Constraints. http://www.doc.ic.ac.uk/~ue/ciff/ciff.pdf.

Endriss, U., Mancarella, P., Sadri, F. Terreni, G. and Toni, F. 2004b. The CIFF Proof Procedure for Abductive Logic Programming with Constraints. *Logics in Artificial Intelligence, 9th European Conference, JELIA 2004, Lisbon, Portugal, September 27-30, 2004, Proceedings*, vol. 3229 of *Lecture Notes in Artificial Intelligence*, eds. J.J. Alferes and J.A. Leite, 31-43. Berlin/Heidelberg: Springer-Verlag.

Eshaghi, K. 1988. Abductive Planning with the Event Calculus. *Logic Programming, Proceedings of the Fifth International Conference and Symposium on Linear Programming*, Seattle, Washington, 562-79. Cambridge, MA: The MIT Press.

Evans, C.A. and Kakas, A.C. 1992. Hypotheticodeductive Reasoning. *Proceedings of the 5th International Conference on Fifth Generation Computer Systems*, Tokyo, 546-54. Tokyo: IOS Press.

FIPA Query Interaction Protocol, August 2001. Published on August 10th, 2001, available for download from the FIPA website, http://www.fipa.org.

Fung, T.H. and Kowalski, R.A. 1997. The IFF Proof Procedure for Abductive Logic Programming. *Journal of Logic Programming* 33(2): 151-65.

Frühwirth, T. 1998. Theory and Practice of Constraint Handling Rules. *Journal of Logic Programming* 37(1-3): 95-138.

Hartshorne, C. and Weiss, P. (eds.) 1965. *Collected Papers of Charles Sanders Peirce, 1931-1958*, vol. 2. Harvard: Harvard University Press.

Jaffar, J. and Maher, M.J. 1994. Constraint Logic Programming: a Survey. *Journal of Logic Programming* 19-20: 503-82.

Kakas, A.C., Kowalski, R.A. and Toni, F. 1998. The Role of Abduction in Logic Programming. *Handbook of Logic in Artificial Intelligence and Logic Programming*, eds. D.M. Gabbay, C.J. Hogger and J.A. Robinson, vol. 5, 235-324. Oxford: Oxford University Press.

Kakas, A.C., Michael, A. and Mourlas, C. 2000. ACLP: Abductive Constraint Logic Programming. *Journal of Logic Programming* 44(1-3): 129-77.

Kakas, A.C., van Nuffelen, B. and Denecker. M. 2001. A-System: Problem solving through abduction. *Proceedings of the Seventeenth International Joint Conference on Artificial Intelligence, Seattle, Washington, USA (IJCAI-01)*, August 2001, ed. B. Nebel, 591-96. Seattle: Morgan Kaufmann Publishers.

Kowalski, R.A. and Sergot, M. 1986. A Logic-based Calculus of Events. *New Generation Computing* 4(1): 67-95.

Kowalski, R.A., Toni, F. and Wetzel, G. 1998. Executing Suspended Logic Programs. *Fundamenta Informaticae* 34: 203-24.

Meyer, J.J. Ch. 1988. A Different Approach to Deontic Logic: Deontic Logic Viewed as a Variant of Dynamic Logic. *Notre Dame J. of Formal Logic* 29(1): 109-36.

Pople, H.E. 1973. On the Mechanization of Abductive Logic. *Proceedings of the 3rd International Joint Conference on Artificial Intelligence*, 147-52. Stanford, CA.

Sartor, G. 2004. Legal Reasoning: A Cognitive Approach to the Law. *A Treatise of Legal Philosophy and General Jurisprudence* 5, 1-385. Berlin: Springer Verlag.

Satoh, K. Inoue, K., Iwanuma, K. and Sakama, C. 2000. Speculative Computation by Abduction under Incomplete Communication Environments. *Proceedings of the Fourth International Conference on Multi-Agent Systems* 263-70. Boston, MA: IEEE Press.

Sergot, M.J. 1983. A Query-the-user Facility of Logic Programming. *Integrated Interactive Computer Systems*, eds. P. Degano and E. Sandwell, 27-41. Amsterdam: North Holland.

Shanahan, M. 1999. The Event Calculus Explained. *Artificial Intelligence Today: Recent Trends and Developments*, vol. 1600 of *Lecture Notes in Computer Science*, eds. M. Wooldridge and M.M. Veloso, 409-30. Berlin: Springer Verlag.

Shanahan, M. 2000a. An Abductive Event Calculus Planner. *Journal of Logic Programming* 44(1-3): 207-40.

Shanahan, M.P. 2000b. Reinventing Shakey. *Logic-based Artificial Intelligence*, 233-53. Boston: Kluwer Academic Publishers.

Shanahan, M. and Randell, D. 2004. A Logic-based Formulation of Active Visual Perception. *KR*, eds. D. Dubois, C.A. Welty and M.-A. Williams, 64-72. AAAI Press.

SICStus prolog user manual, release 3.11.0, October 2003. http://www.sics.se/isl/sicstus/.

Wooldridge, M. 2002. *Introduction to Multi-Agent Systems*. London: John Wiley & Sons, Ltd.

Name Index

Abbott, D. 3, 77, 78, 86
Agich, G.J. 263, 268, 269
Akman, V. 205
Albert, D.A. 256, 267, 269
Alberti, M. 8, 271-73, 275, 279, 281, 285
Alferes, J.J. 283, 285, 286
Aliseda, A. 271, 272, 285
Allais, M. 46, 47, 55, 57
Almeida, M.J. 162
Anscombe, F.J. 41, 57
Anscombe, G. 231
Aoki, M. 97-99, 116
Aquinas, Saint Thomas 16, 34
Archimede, 251
Aristotle, 1, 2, 6, 14-16, 19, 30-32, 34, 35, 42, 44, 52, 55, 173, 190, 205
Arlo-Costa, H. 196, 205
Arrighi, C. 13
Artikis, A. 278, 285
Ascher, W. 179, 184
Asquith, P. 251
Atkinson, D. 3, 77
Atwood, M.E., 167, 169, 184
Aumann, R. 41, 57, 153, 162
Austin, J.L. 225, 229
Axelrod, R. 197, 205

Bacharach, M.O.L. 162, 195, 196, 198, 205
Bachelier, L. 89, 91, 92, 97
Barnes, B. 225, 229
Basili, M. 35
Batens, D. 58
Bayes, T. 91, 240
Beccaria, C. 194, 205
Becker, G. 174, 184
Behrens, W.W. III 182, 185
Bell, D.E. 51-53, 57
Bermúdez, J. 138
Bernasconi, M. 196, 205
Bernoulli, D. 214, 229
Bernoulli, J. 88
Bettman, J.R. 29, 34
Beziau, J.-Y. 27, 35
Bicchieri, C. 153, 162, 178, 184
Binmore, K. 153, 162
Blackburn, P. 27, 34
Bloch, M. 227, 229
Blommaert, J. 206
Bloor, D. 211, 222-26, 228, 229
Bodapati, A. 14, 32, 35
Boden, M. 205
Bogdan, R. 252
Bogen, J. 242
Boltzmann, L. 91, 103
Bos, J. 27, 34
Bose, S.N. 103

Bouchaud, J.P. 112, 116
Bousquet, G.H. 230
Bovens, L. 3, 61, 139
Bowles, S. 216, 229
Boyd, R. 216, 229
Bratman, M. 135, 138
Brogi, A. 283, 285
Broome, J. 4, 5, 119, 124, 134, 135, 138, 139, 153, 162
Brown, M. 116
Brown, S.C. 29, 34
Bryce, J.C. 207
Buchanan, J. 168
Bulcaen, C. 206
Burks, S. 216, 229
Burns, T. 179, 184
Burnyeat, M.F. 32, 34
Busino, G. 230

Camerer, C. 216, 229
Campaner, R. 8, 233, 246, 249, 253
Carpenter, J. 216, 229
Carroll, L. 128, 138
Cartwright, N. 234, 249
Castelfranchi C. 285
Chapman, S. 102
Chesani, F. 8, 271, 279, 285
Christensen, D. 146, 162
Ciampolini, A. 279, 285
Clements, M. 185
Coase, R.H. 218, 229
Collins, J. 251, 254, 265, 269, 270
Cont, R. 112, 116
Cooke, R. 250
Corfield, D. 250
Corry, R. 250
Costantini, D. 4, 87, 100, 102, 116, 207, 250
Cournot, A.A. 178
Craik, F.I.M. 29, 34
Craver, C. 242, 247, 248, 251
Crimmins, M. 188, 205
Cross, N. 170, 184

Darden, L. 242, 247, 248, 251

Davidson, D. 149, 162
Davidson, M.G. 213, 229
Davidsson, P. 278, 285
Davis, J. 211
Dawid, P. 248, 250
de Finetti, B. 40, 41
de Marchi, N. 184
Degano, P. 287
Denecker, M. 277, 282, 286
Dennett, D. 195, 196, 205
Dimitri, N. 35
Dirac, P. 103
Doty, R.W. 18, 34
Dowe, P. 242
Drolet, A. 2, 13, 14, 32, 35
Dubois, D. 287
Durup, G. 18, 34

Earman, J. 246, 250
Eatwell, J. 231
Eells, E. 49, 58
Ehrenfest, P. 91, 92, 105, 106, 116
Ehrenfests, T. 91, 92
Einstein, ?. 91, 92, 97, 103
Ellsberg, D. 48, 54, 58, 215, 229
Endriss, U. 277, 283, 286
Ericsson, N.R. 186
Eshaghi, K. 276, 277, 286
Etherington, D.W. 197, 205
Evans, C.A. 283, 286

Febvre, L. 227, 229
Fehr, E. 216, 229
Fermi, E. 103
Fessard, A. 18, 34
Fillmore, C. 195, 205
Finer, S.E. 230
Finucane, M.L. 50, 58
Fishburn, P.C. 43, 58
Fisher, I. 95
Fisher, R. 95
Flach, P. 285
Flesca, S. 285
Forbes, M. 251
Ford, K.M. 205, 206

Freedie, R.O. 207
French, P. 252
French, P.A. 270
French, S. 51, 52, 58
Friedman, M. 168
Frisch, R. 95
Frühwirth, T. 276, 286
Fung, T.H. 275, 282, 286

Gabbay, D.M. 286
Galavotti, M.C. 1, 7, 58, 184, 207, 233, 241, 246, 247, 249, 250, 289
Gambetta, G. 241, 247, 250
Gärdenfors, P. 56, 58
Garegnani, P. 88, 116
Garibaldi, U. 4, 87, 100, 102, 116
Gauss, C.F. 95
Gavanelli, M. 8, 271-73, 275, 279, 281, 285
Gibbard, A. 119, 138
Gibrat, R. 96
Giere, R. 252
Gigerenzer, G. 185
Gilboa, I. 35, 201, 205
Gillies, D. 253, 269
Gintis, H. 216, 229
Giunchiglia, F. 188, 205
Giurgea, C. 18, 34
Glennan, S. 242
Glymour, C. 242, 246, 250
Gold, N. 205
Gonzalez, W.J 5, 165, 167, 168, 170, 172, 176, 177, 180, 181, 183-85
Good, I.J. 37, 244, 250
Graham, G. 170, 185
Granovetter, M. 219, 229
Greco, S. 285
Greeno, J.G. 251

Habermas, J. 171, 185
Hagen, O. 57
Hall, N. 251, 254, 256, 268-70
Halpern, J. 241, 246, 250
Hansson, B. 48, 58

Hardiman, T.P. 186
Harmer, G.P. 3, 77, 78, 86
Harrison, G. 229
Harsanyi, J. 67, 76
Hart, H.L. 267, 269
Hartmann, S. 3, 61
Hartshorne, C. 271, 286
Hayes, P.J. 195, 197, 205, 206
Heaviside, O. 67, 72
Heelas, P. 229
Hendry, D.F. 185, 186
Henrich, J. 216, 229
Hesse, M.B. 223, 229
Hicks, J. 168
Hieronymi, P. 125, 138
Hitchcock, C. 233-37, 240, 244-46, 248, 250, 251
Hobbes, T. 2, 14
Hobbs, J.R. 205
Hochwarter, G. 13
Hogarth, R.M. 186
Hogger, C.J. 286
Holland, P. 248
Holmwood, J. 211, 229
Honoré, A. 267, 269
Hookway, C. 205
Howell, S. 227, 229
Hull, D. 251
Hume, D. 2, 14, 28, 33, 65, 76, 134, 138, 239
Hurley, S. 162

Ianni, G. 285
Inglis Palgrave, R.H. 229
Inoue, K. 283, 287
Isham, J. 229
Iwanuma, K. 283, 287
Iyengar, R. 78, 86

Jaffar, J. 274, 286
James, W. 16, 34
Janssen, M.C.W. 196, 205
Jeffrey, R. 251
Jeffrey, R.C. 44, 58
Jensen, H.S. 230

292 / NAME INDEX

Joyce, J.M. 159, 162

Kadane, J.B. 41, 51, 58, 59
Kahneman, D. 3, 7, 30, 34, 35, 45-48, 58, 176, 215, 216, 230, 231
Kakas, A.C. 272, 273, 277, 282, 283, 285, 286
Kandel, E.R. 18, 35
Kant, I. 123, 138, 165
Kelemen, M. 211, 214
Kelly, T. 229
Keynes, J.M. 4, 89-96, 99, 116
Kirman, A. 104-108, 110-12, 116
Kitcher, P. 251
Kitcher, Ph. 170, 185
Klaes, M. 7, 211, 213, 217, 223, 230
Knight, F.H. 214, 230
Kohli, R. 78, 86
Kolmogorov, A. 102
Kowalski, R.A. 272, 273, 275, 276, 282, 283, 286, 287
Kraus, S. 197, 205
Kripke, S. 195, 206, 223, 224, 230
Kronecker, L. 102
Kuipers, T. 184
Kusch, M. 211, 225-28, 230
Kvart, I. 266, 269
Kyburg, H. 56, 58

Lamma, E. 8, 271-73, 275, 279, 281, 285
Laplace, P.-S. 88, 91, 95
Larkey, P.D. 51, 58
Latsis, S. 186
Lehman, F. 28, 35
Leibniz, G.W. von 92
Leite, J.A. 283, 285, 286
Leone, N. 285
Levi, I. 49, 56, 58, 139, 140, 147, 148, 156-63
Lévy, P.P. 96
Lewis Johnson, W. 285
Lewis, ?. 240
Lewis, D. 148, 254, 255, 263, 265, 268, 269

Lienhardt, R.G. 227, 230
Lindley, D. 241, 251
List, J.A. 229
Llewellyn, J. 179, 185
Lock, A. 229
Luce, D. 55, 56, 58
Luce, M.F. 29, 34

Macfie, A.L. 207
Machamer, P. 242, 247-52
Maher, M.J. 274, 286
Maher, P. 147, 162
Mancarella, P. 277, 283, 286
Mandelbrot, B. 97
Mantegna, R.N. 96, 116
Marík, V. 285
Markov, A.A. 91, 102, 106, 112
Marsonet, M. 251
Mason, J. 184
Mathias, P. 184
Maudlin, T. 253, 266, 268, 269
Maxwell, J.C. 103
McCain, K.W. 167, 169, 184
McCarthy, J. 188, 196, 206
McClennen, E. 151, 162
McDermott, M. 256, 269
McElreath, R. 216, 229
McGuire, C.B. 186
McKeon, R. 34
McKinsey, J.C.C. 149, 162
Meadows, D.H., 182, 185
Meadows, D.L. 182, 185
Mehta, J. 196, 206
Mello, P. 8, 271-73, 275, 279, 281, 285
Mellor, D.H. 58, 163
Meltzer, B. 206
Mendel, G. 91
Menzies, P. 238, 246, 251, 253, 255, 267, 269, 270
Meyer, J.J. Ch. 281, 287
Michael, A. 282, 286
Michie, D. 206
Milgate, M. 231
Mill, J.S. 195, 206

Millar, A. 138
Miller, N.E. 19, 35
Minsky, M. 195, 206
Mirfin, D. 230
Mirowski, P. 88, 116
Mitchell, S. 246, 250
Mondolfo, R. 190, 206
Moore, R.C. 205
Morgan, M. 167, 185
Morgenstern, L. 195, 206
Morgenstern, O. 39, 41, 59
Morrison, M. 167, 185
Mourlas, C. 282, 286
Müller, J. 285
Mulreany, M. 186
Munevar, G. 184
Munro, R. 211
Munson, R. 256, 267, 269

Naill, R.F. 182, 185
Nash, J. 177
Nebel, B. 286
Needham, R. 227, 230
Newell, A. 29, 35
Newman, P. 231
Newton, I. 91
Neyman, J. 59
Nidditch, P.H. 138
Niiniluoto, I. 166, 170, 171, 180-83, 185
Nowack, A.S. 86
Nutter, J.T. 196, 206

Ockenfels, A. 178, 179, 185
Okruhlik, K. 251
Olsaretti, S. 138
Olsson, E.J. 162, 163
Omicini, A. 285
Östman, J.-O. 206

Pagan, A.R. 179, 185
Pagnini, A. 250
Pappas, C. 37
Paprzycka, K. 226, 230

Pareto, V. 76, 96, 212, 213, 219, 227, 228, 230
Parkinson, ?. 246
Parrondo, J.M.R. 77, 78, 82, 84-86
Parsons, T. 213, 230
Paton, H.J. 138
Paul, L. 254, 255, 264, 266, 269, 270
Paul, L.A. 251
Pavlov, I. 17, 18
Payne, J.W. 29, 34
Pearl, J. 234, 240, 241, 246, 250
Pearsall, J. 207
Pechoucek, M. 285
Pegis. A.C. 34
Peijnenburg, J. 3, 77
Peirce, C. 8
Peirce, C.S. 271, 272
Pellegrino, E. 256, 270
Pereira, L.M. 283, 285
Perlis, D. 197, 205
Petruck, M.R. 196, 206
Petta, P. 285
Pettit, P. 153, 162, 212, 221, 222, 224, 226-28, 230
Pitt, J. 278, 285
Pochhammer, L.A. 103
Polanyi, K. 219, 230
Polya, G. 108, 114
Pople, H.E. 271, 287
Porta, P.L. 191, 192, 206
Potter, S. 179, 185
Priami, C. 285
Price, H. 235, 236, 238-42, 249-51, 253, 270
Psillos, S. 248, 249, 251, 268, 270

Quaglia, P. 285
Quételet, A. 88, 95, 97

Rabelais, F. 229
Rabinowicz, W. 5, 139, 151-53, 155, 156, 159-63
Radder, H. 252
Radner, R. 186
Raiffa, H. 149, 163

294 / NAME INDEX

Raiffa, H. 51-53, 57
Rainey, H.J. 19, 35
Ramachandran, M. 255, 256, 270
Ramaswamy, S. 229
Ramsey, F.P. 5, 37-43, 45, 49, 58, 59, 139, 144, 163, 238, 239
Randell, D. 272, 287
Randers, J. 182, 185
Raphael, D.D. 207
Rawls, J. 53, 67, 76
Reder, M.W. 186
Reny, P. 153, 163
Rescher, N. 165, 176, 177, 185
Resnik, M.D. 256, 267, 269
Richards, D. 188, 206
Richter, L.M. 230
Rios Insua, D. 51, 52, 58
Robertson, J. 179, 185
Robertson, S. 138
Robinson, J.A. 286
Roby, T.B. 17, 35
Romagnoli, S. 205
Rosch, E. 203, 206
Rossini Favretti, R. 250
Rubin, D. 248
Russell, B. 250
Russo, F. 250

Sadri, F. 277, 283, 286
Sahlin, N.-E. 2, 37, 43, 53, 55, 56, 58, 59
Sakama, C. 283, 287
Salmon, W. 234-40, 244, 247, 251
Salmon, W.C. 180, 185
Samuelson, L. 179, 185
Sandewall, E. 195, 206
Sandri, G. 250
Sandwell, E. 287
Sartor, G. 280, 281, 284, 285, 287
Sato, K. 116
Satoh, K. 283, 287
Sattath, S. 30, 35
Satterfield, T. 50, 58
Savage, L.J. 37, 40-43, 45, 48, 51, 55, 59, 214, 215, 229, 230

Scazzieri, R. 1, 6, 187, 191, 192, 194, 203, 206, 207, 211, 250, 289
Schaffer, J. 254, 255, 270
Scheines, R. 242
Schelling, T. 226, 230
Schelling, T.C. 187, 207
Schervish, M. 41, 59
Schick, F. 144, 163
Schlicht, E. 218, 223, 230
Schmeidler, D. 201, 205
Schram, A. 176, 185
Schumpeter, J.A. 95
Schwartz, J.H. 35
Schwartz, T. 150, 163
Searle, J. 7, 220-22, 225, 230, 231
Seidenfeld, T. 41, 56, 59
Selby-Bigge, L.A. 138
Selten, R. 177-79, 184, 185, 207
Sent, E.-M. 213, 230
Sergot, M. 276, 278, 285, 286
Sergot, M.J. 283, 287
Shanahan, M. 272, 276, 277, 287
Shanahan, M.P. 284, 287
Sheffield, F.D. 17, 35
Shelp, E.E. 269, 270
Sherman, N. 32, 34, 35
Sichel, W. 186
Simoff, S.J. 188, 206
Simon, H.A. 6, 29, 30, 33, 35, 77, 86, 166, 168, 169, 171-79, 182, 184, 186, 187, 207, 214, 231
Simonson, I. 30, 35
Singpurwalla, N.D. 241
Skinner, A. 206
Skorupski, J. 138
Skyrms, B. 144, 147, 148, 153, 155, 157, 158, 163
Slater, P.J.B. 19, 35
Slovic, P. 30, 35, P. 45, 59, 215, 230
Smith, A. 190, 191, 193, 194, 206, 207
Smith, V. 176
Sobel, J.H. 153, 163
Sober, E. 245, 251

Spirtes, P. 242
Stanley, H.E. 96, 116
Starmer, C. 196, 206
Stella, F. 233
Stenwall, R. 37
Stewart, A. 211, 229
Stiglitz, J.E. 183, 186
Sugden, R. 153, 162, 196, 205, 206
Suppes, P. 1, 2, 13, 14, 27-29, 32, 35, 43, 59, 149, 162, 187, 190, 206, 207, 211, 243-45, 249-52, 253, 270, 289
Szajowki, K. 86
Szawarski, Z. 268, 270

Tannen, D. 195, 207
Teller, P. 148, 163
Terreni, G. 277, 283, 286
Timmerman, J. 138
Tolksdorf, R. 285
Toni, F. 272, 273, 277, 282, 283, 286, 287
Torroni, P. 272, 273, 275, 279, 281, 284, 285
Tulving, E. 34
Tuomela, R. 221, 231
Turner, M. 196, 207
Turner, P. 167, 186
Tversky, A. 3, 7, 29, 34, 35, 45-48, 51-53, 55, 57-59, 214-16, 230, 231

Uehling, T.E. 270
Urmson, J.O. 229

van Bendegem, J.P. 58
van Fraassen, B. 145, 148, 163, 235, 245, 252
van Nuffelen, B. 277, 282, 286

Vareman, N. 2, 37
Veloso, M.M. 287
Vendelø, M.T. 230
Verhoogen, E. 216, 229
Verschueren, J. 206
von Neumann, J. 39, 41, 59
von Winterfeldt, D. 55, 56, 58

Wallace, J. 134, 138
Walter, H. 235, 252
Warnock, G.J. 229
Weirich, P. 49, 53, 54, 59
Weiss, P. 271, 286
Welty, C.A. 287
Westcott, J.H. 184
Wettstein, H. 252
Wettstein, H.K. 270
Wetzel, G. 283, 287
Wiener, N. 97
Wightman, W.P.D. 207
Williams, J.C. 167, 169, 184
Williams, M. 37
Williams, M.-A. 287
Williamson, J. 250
Winston, P.H. 206
Wittgenstein, L. 167, 224, 231
Wolters, G. 249, 250, 252
Woodward, J. 236, 240-42, 244, 248, 251-53, 270
Wooldridge, M. 278, 287
Wrong, D.H. 221, 231

Yuehling, T. 252

Zadeh, L.A. 203, 204, 207
Zahn, E.K.O. 182, 185
Zarembka, P. 116
Zuberbühler, K. 19, 35

Subject Index

Abductive
    event 8, 273, 276, 277, 284, 287
    explanation 271, 273
    expectation 285
    framework 272-74, 283
    inference 272
    logic (programming) 8, 272, 273, 284, 286, 287
    proof procedure 8, 271, 272, 275, 276, 282, 284, 285
    reasoning 271, 272, 284
    semantics 281
Analogy 29, 57, 88, 95, 159, 191-95, 199, 201, 202, 207, 261
Argument vi, 1, 3, 5, 27, 44, 45, 55, 90, 106, 108, 125, 135, 139-41, 143, 145, 147, 148, 150, 151, 156-61, 163, 187, 191-93, 221, 223, 224, 226-28
Aristotelian notion of rationality 31
Artificial v, xi, 5-8, 34, 35, 77, 78, 165-73, 175-77, 179, 181, 183-86, 191, 205, 206, 216, 268, 271, 273, 284-87, 289
Association 2, 13, 14, 26, 28, 31, 33-35, 187, 189, 190, 194, 195, 197, 203, 240

Backward induction 147, 148, 150-55, 162, 163

Bayesian approach
    and F.P. Ramsey's contribution 40
    and utility maximization 214
    and causal relationships 240, 247
    and Bayesian networks 240, 247
Beliefs 2, 3, 5, 7, 14, 37, 38, 40, 44, 45, 47, 50, 51, 54, 120, 121, 123-30, 132, 133, 139, 140, 142, 160, 162, 178, 199, 219, 220, 227, 239
Behavioral 16, 17, 35, 37, 43, 44, 52, 54, 98, 198, 199, 211, 212, 214, 227-29
Behaviorism 16, 29
Bounded rationality: see 'Rationality, bounded'

Calculus 8, 71, 92, 95, 219, 250, 273, 276-78, 284, 286, 287
Causal
    accounts 234, 268
    analysis 7, 8, 233, 245, 247, 249
    asymmetry 238, 251
    attribution 7, 233, 235, 246, 247, 248
    chain 247, 264
    concept 234, 238
    connection 133, 239

298 / SUBJECT INDEX

  dependence 234, 243, 246
  discourse 7, 233, 248, 249
Causal (continued)
  explanation 214
  inference 248, 250, 252
  influence 256, 265
  interpretation 240, 245
  mechanism 234, 236, 239
  medical reasoning vi, 8, 253, 267
  model 240, 241
  pluralism vi, 7, 233, 235, 249
  process 119, 126, 236, 244, 247, 269
  reasoning 8, 263, 265, 268
  relation 7, 233, 239, 244, 245, 247, 249, 255, 263, 267, 276
  structure 8, 236, 237, 241, 251
Causality
  aleatory 236, 251
  probabilistic 7, 243, 244, 247, 251, 270
  token 7, 236, 238, 244, 248
  type 7, 236, 248
Causation (mechanical, theory of) 235, 236, 238-42, 247, 248
Cause 8, 15, 28, 197, 198, 213, 233-35, 237, 238, 241, 243, 246, 249-51, 253-56, 263-67, 274
Choice 1-7, 13, 14, 29, 30, 32-35, 42, 43, 46, 47, 52, 53, 59, 61, 66, 86, 98, 105, 109-11, 113, 137, 140, 144, 150-59, 161-63, 173, 174, 177, 178, 181, 186-89, 204, 205, 207, 211, 212, 215-17, 219, 222, 227, 228, 231, 241, 249, 261, 266
Cognition 29, 205, 206, 272
Cognitive psychology 29, 235
Condition 2-5, 30, 38, 40-42, 51, 75, 78, 87, 99, 101, 103, 113, 123, 128, 135, 136, 139, 141, 144, 146, 148, 150, 161, 172, 173, 180, 182, 188, 201, 214, 220,
      225, 226, 238, 240, 241, 245, 246, 261, 265
Conditioning 17-19, 26, 28, 70, 240
Confirmation 8, 58, 271-73, 283
Context 30, 61, 65, 66, 70, 74, 76, 104, 183, 188, 189, 190, 198, 199, 202, 203, 204, 212, 216, 216, 217, 218, 222, 227, 233, 235, 239, 241, 243
  and causal analysis 7, 233, 235, 239, 241,245, 246, 248, 249, 267, 272, 283
  and cognitive procedures 1
  and conceptual tools 9
  and co-ordination 188, 190, 199, 202, 204
  and reasoning 7, 8
  and utility function 49
  genetic 86
  hierarchical structure of 6
  identification of 190, 204
  institutional 7, 218, 219
  relevant 190
  salient 189, 190, 198, 203
  social 188, 216, 227
  transactional 217
  of evaluation 61, 62, 65, 66, 70, 74, 76
Decision
  behavior 45
  clinical d. 256, 263, 268
  frame 30
  model 50, 51
  rational d. 1, 42, 45, 51, 53, 58, 211
  theory v, 1-3, 5, 37, 40, 42, 44, 45, 50-54, 57-59, 162, 182
Decision-making 5, 40, 42, 44, 45, 49-53, 57, 59, 63, 77, 82, 140, 141, 144, 145, 149, 155, 159, 161, 172, 177, 186, 212-15, 221, 222, 224, 227, 228, 256, 269
Deduction 27, 42, 207, 277
Deductive reasoning: see 'Reasoning, deductive'

Degressive
proportionality 3, 61, 62, 64, 68, 70, 75, 76
representation (model of)
Deontic
constraints 285
logic 8, 280, 287
operator 280-82, 284, 285
reasoning: see Reasoning, deontic
Descriptive
decision model 50
economics 177
knowledge 180
model 45
rationality 177
science 169, 179-81, 183
theory 2, 3, 45, 49-52, 57
Design vi, 5, 6, 75, 165-71, 175, 176, 179-84, 206
Diagnosis 8, 157, 256, 267, 271, 273-76, 284
Disunification, in decision-making 140, 141, 145, 149, 159-61
Dutch book
diachronic 139, 143, 145, 148, 157, 162, 163
synchronic 139, 141, 143, 144, 157, 161
theorem 37, 39

Econometric model 95
Economic rationality 175, 178
Economics vi, xi, 1, 5-7, 87-89, 91, 92, 95-97, 99, 103, 111, 124, 165-69, 172-81, 183-86, 189, 193, 205, 211-14, 216, 217, 219, 227-29, 231, 238, 244, 249, 250, 289
Econophysics 4, 87, 96, 116
End-means rationality 122, 123, 131-35
End-means reasoning 5
Epistemic probability 90
Epistemic
rationality 178
utility 171, 180
Ethics 34, 35, 76, 174, 270
Evaluation 48, 57, 61, 62, 65, 66, 70, 74, 76, 109, 136, 165, 176-78, 214, 248, 249, 256
Evaluative rationality 175-78
Expectation 3, 4, 50, 70, 81, 89, 90, 92, 93, 111, 145, 160, 155, 192, 207, 217, 272, 274, 275, 277-79, 281, 282-85
Expected utility 1, 3, 13, 32, 33, 38, 39, 41, 42, 44-47, 49-51, 57, 58, 64, 67, 70-72, 77, 162, 173, 214, 215
Explanation
abductive 271, 273
causal 214, 237-41, 246, 250, 251, 270
theory of 236, 238, 246
Exploitation 5, 139, 140, 145, 147, 148, 150, 155, 157-60, 218
Ex-probability 4, 87, 90-92, 94, 95

First-order model 123, 125, 128
Focal point 192, 205
Frame
cognitive 1
decision 30
mental 4
rational 5
social 212, 216, 228
virtual 197, 198
Framework
abductive f. 272-74, 283, 284
epistemological f. 239
of economics 177, 179, 213
means-end f. 213
on rationality 172, 177
rationality f. 187, 189
stochastic f. 87
theoretical f. 55, 58, 116, 234
Framing
effect 7, 214-17
dynamics of 197, 198

300 / SUBJECT INDEX

of rationality 228

Framing (continued)
    social f. vi, 7, 211, 212, 216, 217, 219, 221, 222, 224, 227-29
    theory of 7, 216
    transactional f. 7, 217

Game 4, 43, 47, 58, 78, 86, 88, 95, 162, 163, 178, 185, 206, 229
Game theory 59, 163, 173, 176, 177, 182, 205
Habit 2, 4, 13-16, 19-26, 30-35, 216-18, 223
Holism 212, 221, 224, 228
Hypothesis 57, 90, 92, 145, 158, 179, 272-75, 279, 281, 283, 284

Indeterministic mechanism 244
Induction 148, 150, 152-55, 162, 163, 285
Induction backward reasoning 147, 148, 150-53
Information 7, 8, 29, 30, 34, 41, 49, 55, 78, 79, 105, 131, 163, 178, 188, 196, 233, 237, 240, 241, 243, 247, 248, 256, 258, 266, 267, 274, 275, 279, 283, 284
In-probability 4, 87, 90-93, 95, 96, 103
Instrumental
    rationality 135, 176, 178, 179, 212
    reasoning 5, 131, 134-38, 161
Interpolative method 109
Intention 5-7, 119, 121, 125, 130-38, 196, 222
Intentionality 7, 212, 217, 219-22, 224-27, 229, 230
Invariance 7, 99, 241, 252
Irrationality 55, 157, 160, 174
Irrational strategy v, 3, 77, 78

Judgment 2, 13, 21, 35, 48, 194, 214, 230, 238, 243, 266

Krasia 5, 122, 125, 136, 137
Kratic reasoning 120, 121, 125, 136-38

Limited rationality 42, 187-89 (see also Rationality, bounded)

Majority 15, 46, 67, 71, 75, 76, 112-14, 213
Manipulability 234, 240, 242, 247-49
Manipulation 7, 183, 233, 234, 239-42, 244, 245, 248, 250, 263, 266
Mechanical view 7, 247
Mechanism 7, 28, 33-35, 40, 49, 77, 78, 99, 218, 230, 234, 235, 236, 239, 240, 242, 244, 245, 247-51, 257, 259, 261, 262, 266, 278
Medical reasoning vi, 8, 253, 263, 267, 268
Method 3, 19, 33, 34, 37-39, 41, 50, 51, 95, 96, 109, 115, 182, 186, 229, 249, 250, 252, 256, 268, 270
Model
    of boundedly rational decision-making 214
    of degressive human decision behavior 45,
    of degressive proportionality 62, 69, 70, 76
    of descriptive science 183
    of equal representation 61, 66
    of limited rationality 187
    of proportional representation 3, 61, 66, 68
    of psychological phenomena 2, 13, 14
    of rational decision-making 45
    of reasoning 123, 125, 127, 240
    of regressive proportionality 0,
    of representation 3, 61-64, 66-68

of standard clinical reasoning 256
of the design sciences 166
Modeling 66, 87, 162, 186, 205, 206, 241, 248, 276, 278
Modus ponens 122-24, 126, 128-30, 132
Modus tollens 130, 132-34

Narrative method 3, 50, 51
Neighborhood segregation model 226
Neuroscience 2, 14, 17, 252
Norm 42, 57, 70, 211, 213, 216, 217, 219, 280
Normative
   belief 119, 121, 136, 137
   decision theory 2, 3, 42, 44, 50, 52, 54
   economics 177

Open society modeling 8, 276, 278
Operational method 38

Paradox 3, 55, 57, 84, 162, 163, 215
Parrondo Paradox 3, 77, 78, 82, 84-86
Practical
   rationality 1, 2, 147, 150, 177-79
   reasoning 4, 5, 121-23, 130-35, 138, 219
Pragmatic
   argument vi, 5, 139-41, 143, 147, 150, 157, 159-61
   reason 5
Prediction vi, 5-7, 50, 90, 151, 159, 162, 165-70, 172, 179-86, 214, 233, 239-41, 243-45, 248, 266, 272, 274
Predictive model 50
Predictive science 180
Pre-emption vi, 8, 253-55, 263, 264, 267, 268, 270
Preference 2, 3, 13, 14, 29, 30, 32, 38, 39, 41-47, 54, 55, 59, 138-41, 149-52, 155-57, 214, 215, 226
Probabilistic causality 7, 243, 244, 247, 251, 270
Probability
   axioms of 40
   conditional p. 44, 92, 95, 111, 145, 146, 238
   diachronous p. 84
   distribution 47, 93, 94, 96, 99, 102, 103, 106, 108, 114
   epistemic p. 90
   equilibrium p. 94, 103, 106, 108, 114
   function 38, 43, 44, 47, 100
   high-order p. 37
   law of 5, 37-39, 139, 141, 144
   measure 3, 39-41, 44, 49
   objective p. 91
   ontological p. 90
   perception of 48
   philosophy of 89, 94, 95
   standard p. axiom 139, 141, 159
   standard p. law 143
   subjective p. 14, 29, 37, 40, 41, 46, 48, 57, 217, 218
   synchronous p. 84
   theory 37, 39, 40, 110, 249
   transition 87, 92, 99, 102, 103, 106-109, 111, 112
   weight of 48
Procedural rationality 174, 175, 186
Procedure 1, 8, 51, 153, 167, 243, 260, 271, 272, 275, 276, 279, 282, 284-86
Protoform 203, 207
Prototype 4, 6, 198, 203, 204
Psychology xi, 2, 14, 16, 29, 31, 35, 57, 166, 172, 174, 175, 179, 180, 186, 206, 212, 216, 219, 226-31, 237, 238
Psychological
   measurement 2, 14
   mechanism of human decision-making 49, 228

Rational
  agent 1, 2, 5, 6, 38, 51, 178, 219, 221
  behavior 37, 45, 77, 174, 175, 212, 214, 227
  choice 1, 14, 30, 33, 35, 155, 156, 177, 178, 186, 189, 211, 212, 215, 217, 219, 227, 231
  decision 1, 42, 45, 51, 53, 57, 58
  decision-making 42, 44, 45, 49, 53, 82, 186, 214, 221, 222, 224
  strategy 4, 178
Rationality
  Aristotelian notion of 31
  axioms 13, 49, 53
  bounded r. 7, 30, 33, 173, 178, 185, 186, 211-15, 217, 219, 227, 228, 230, 231
  canons of 157
  cognitive r. 177, 178
  constraints vi, 5-7, 139, 141, 161, 220, 221
  descriptive r. 177
  dynamic r. 49
  economic r. 172, 175, 178
  epistemic r. 178
  evaluative r. 175-78
  instrumental r. 135, 176, 178, 179
  means of 165
  normative r. 177
  patterns of v, 207
  perfect r. 3, 187, 188
  practical r. 1, 2, 147, 150, 177-79
  procedural r. 174, 175, 186
  requirements of 120-24, 126, 129-31, 141
  standards of 7, 217, 220, 221
  substantive r. 174, 175
  technological r. 168, 170, 171

theory of 29, 138

Reasoning
  abductive r. 271, 272, 284
  backward-induction r. 147, 148, 150-53
  causal r. 8, 263, 265, 268
  clinical r. 8, 256, 267, 269
  conscious r. 121, 124, 125
  deductive r. 272, 273, 275, 276, 284, 286
  deontic r. 271, 273, 276, 280, 284
  dominance r. 148, 155
  hypothetical-deductive r. 272, 273, 275, 276, 284
  instrumental r. 5, 131, 134-38
  kratic r. 120, 121, 125, 136-38
  medical r. vi, 8, 253, 263, 267, 268
  model of 123, 125, 127, 128, 240
  mode of 256
  pattern of xi, 2, 8, 9, 284
  practical r. 4, 5, 121-23, 130-35, 138, 219
  process vi, 8, 120, 128, 129, 136, 138, 189, 268, 271-73, 275
  tree 275
  theoretical r. 5, 121, 123-25, 127, 129-37
  theory of 189
  therapeutic r. 8, 264
  unconscious r. 121
Research
  applied 180, 181, 183, 185
  basic 180, 181
  descriptive 45
  empirical 45, 50, 183
  experimental 50

Salience 6, 198, 203, 206
Second-order belief 124, 128

Second-order model 123-25, 127, 128
Social frame 212, 216, 228
Strategy v, 3, 4, 30, 38, 50, 51, 77-80, 83-86, 92, 98-100, 103-105, 107, 109-114, 190, 207, 212, 221, 237, 260, 261, 263, 264, 266
   irrational s. v, 3, 77, 78
   rational s. 4, 178

Technique 27, 50, 166, 170, 181, 190, 240, 245, 259, 266
Therapy 8, 253, 256, 259, 260, 261, 263-67
   anti-HIV 263, 264
   chemotherapy 8, 244, 261-64
   radiotherapy 261
Treatment 8, 45, 91, 240, 244, 246, 255, 256, 259-63, 265-67

Unconditional 38, 137
Unification, in decision-making 161
   (see also disunification, in decision-making)
Utilitarian method 33

Voting v, 3, 61, 62, 64, 69, 70, 71, 75